Collective Structures of Imagination in Jungian Interpretation

Contemporary Psychoanalytic Studies

Editor

Jon Mills
Adelphi University

Associate Editors

Gerald J. Gargiulo
Ronald C. Naso

Editorial Advisory Board

VOLUME 30

The titles published in this series are listed at *brill.com/cps*

Collective Structures of Imagination in Jungian Interpretation

Edited by

Robert A. Segal, Ilona Błocian and Andrew Kuzmicki

TUTA SUB AEGIDE PALLAS · 1683 ·

BRILL

LEIDEN | BOSTON

Cover illustration: The photo shows a Japanese *bunraku* scene. Image made available under the Pixabay License.

Library of Congress Cataloging-in-Publication Data

Names: Segal, Robert Alan, editor. | Błocian, Ilona, editor. | Kuzmicki, Andrew, editor.
Title: Collective structures of imagination in Jungian interpretation / edited by Robert A. Segal, Ilona Błocian and Andrew Kuzmicki.
Description: Leiden ; Boston : Brill, [2022] | Series: Contemporary psychoanalytic studies, 1571-4977 ; volume 30 | Includes bibliographical references and index.
Identifiers: LCCN 2022029845 (print) | LCCN 2022029846 (ebook) | ISBN 9789004468740 (hardback ; alk. paper) | ISBN 9789004468757 (ebook)
Subjects: LCSH: Jungian psychology. | Imagination.
Classification: LCC BF173.J85 C586 2022 (print) | LCC BF173.J85 (ebook) | DDC 150.19/54--dc23/eng/20220825
LC record available at https://lccn.loc.gov/2022029845
LC ebook record available at https://lccn.loc.gov/2022029846

Typeface for the Latin, Greek, and Cyrillic scripts: "Brill". See and download: brill.com/brill-typeface.

ISSN 1571-4977
ISBN 978-90-04-46874-0 (hardback)
ISBN 978-90-04-46875-7 (e-book)

This book is printed on acid-free paper and produced in a sustainable manner.

Contents

Figures

Contributors

Robert A. Segal
Sixth Century Chair in Religious Studies, University of Aberdeen, UK

Ilona Błocian
Institute of Philosophy, Center for Interdisciplinary Research and Philosophy of Culture, Bachelardian Society "Mythopoeia", University of Wrocław, Poland.

Andrew Kuzmicki
Polish Online Journal of Analytical Psychology, JungPoland.org, UK

Hannah Armbrust
Center for Studies of the Person-CSP, Jung Center of Houston, TX, Private Practice Psychotherapist in Bloomington, IN, US

Josefa Bayes-King†
International Association for Analytical Psychology (IAAP), Australia

John Beebe
International Association for Analytical Psychology (IAAP), Past President of the C.G. Jung Institute of San Francisco, US

Stefano Carpani
C.G. Jung Institute Zürich-Küsnacht, Department of Psychosocial and Psychoanalytic Studies, University of Essex, UK

Johann Graaff
Southern African Association of Jungian Analysts, Cape Town, RPA.

Norifumi Kishimoto
Shizuoka General Hospital, Japan

Maria Kostyszak
Institute of Philosophy, Center for Interdisciplinary Research, Bachelardian Society "Mythopoeia", University of Wrocław, Poland.

Ewa Kwiatkowska
Institute of Sociology, Center for Interdisciplinary Research and Philosophy of Culture, Bachelardian Society "Mythopoeia", University of Wrocław, Poland.

Monica Luci
Italian Association of Analytical Psychology (IAAP), Center for Trauma, Asylium and Refugees, University of Essex, UK.

Kamila Morawska
Center for Interdisciplinary Research, Bachelardian Society "Mythopoeia", University of Wrocław, Poland.

Patrycja Neumann
Institute of Philosophy, Center for Interdisciplinary Research, University of Wrocław, Poland.

Gustavo Orlandeli Marques
Sociedad Brasiliera de Psychologia Analitica (Brazilian Society for Analytical Psychology; SPrPA); International Association for Analytical Psychology (IAAP), Brazil.

Kathrin Schaeppi
International School of Analytical Psychology Zürich (ISAPZURICH), International Association for Analytical Psychology (IAAP), AGAP, ASP, Switzerland

Lidar Shany
Pacifica Graduate Institute CA, US, C.G. Jung Institute Zürich-Küsnacht

Bojana Stamenkovic Rudić
International Association for Analytical Psychology (IAAP), Serbia

Vicky Jo Varner
C. G. Jung Institute of Los Angeles, US.

Helge Michael Osterhold
California Institute of Integral Studies, US

Michał Wróblewski
Institute of Sociology, Mikołaj Kopernik University in Toruń, Poland

Introduction: Archetypes and Imagination

Ilona Błocian and Andrew Kuzmicki

Jung's conception is often understood as a psychological one; research indicates sometimes its philosophical foundations and context, and seldom its social dimension. However, this dimension does exist and it is to some extent related to the general interest of all psychoanalysis in social issues.

Psychoanalysis introduced the social dimension to its theoretical horizon early; most often it dates to 1921 due to the publication of Freud's text on the psychological conditions of social processes, crowd behavior, institution structure, and leadership itself. This dimension, however, seems to have been noticed by him much earlier because it is embedded in the concept of the situation of the individual and the research on the psychological aspects of trauma; neuroses themselves refer to it indirectly. Putting the structure of an individual's situation in psychoanalysis is a collision of drive and a cultural inhibition. The inhibition conditions the adaptability of the individual, adaptations, traumas, and neuroses. Freud has already dealt with a wide spectrum of social phenomena: war and its causes, leadership the emergence of social institutions in traditional cultures (family structure, taboos, totemism, marriage rules, magical thinking, and hypothetical beginnings of religion, animism); he explained them by referring to psychological processes related to incestuous tendencies, projection, repression, identification, and the formation of ideals of the "I." In the whole current, the reference to the social dimension is also a significant area—this is the leading theme for Adler, Fromm, and American neo-psychoanalysis. The environmental and social conditions are becoming as important as those of an evolutionary-anthropological nature. In research on psychoanalysis, interpretations, and comments, the significance of socio-cultural dimension was noticed early and understood differently as, for example, artificially and quite late incorporated into it, the result of its "expansion into related fields" (C. Thompson)[1] and inefficient in the study of cultural phenomena (L. Kołakowski),[2] sometimes valid and present from the beginning (I. Kästner, Ch. Schröder),[3] creating the

1 C. Thompson, *Psychoanalysis: Revolution and Development*, (New York: Thomas Nelson, 1967).

2 L. Kołakowski, *Psychoanalityczna koncepcja kultury*, [in:] idem, *Czy diabeł może zostać zbawiony i 27 innych kazań*, (London: Aneks 1984).

3 I. Kästner, Ch. Schröder, *Zygmunt Freud (1856–1939). Badacz umysłu. Neurolog. Psychoterapeuta*, (Wrocław: Arboretum 1997).

 | DOI:10.1163/9789004468757_002

foundations for a kind of hermeneutics of the unconscious,] "hermeneutic pillar" (P. Kutter;[4] criticism of such approaches – A. Grünbaum[5]).

1 Philosophical, Anthropological, and Social Aspects of the Main Notions in Jung's Conception

Against this background are also the positionings of social issues in Jung's conception. They take place right at the core of his concept, although Jung uses the term *collective* rather than *social*; the first notion applies to each of its basic categories, such as the unconscious and the archetype. The concept of self also has some connection with it. There are research devoted to this aspect of Jung's work. The approach to the unconscious as a psychological basis of social phenomena is emphasized in them, and sometimes it is noticed that the concept of unconsciousness "is specifically sociological" (I. Progoff).[6] It is seen as the source of "archetypal sociology" (R. Gray)[7] and highlights the connection with the ideas of Lewis Mumford, Paul Tillich, Arnold Toynbee, Max Weber, Émile Durkheim, and Erich Neumann. Jung himself often refers to the work and conceptions of Lucien Lévy-Bruhl, Marcel Mauss, and Henri Hubert. There are also approaches to his concept in the perspective of political thought and the "political development of a person" (A. Samuels).[8]

The main elements in Jung's psychology—the unconscious, archetype, and self—have a common source in philosophical language and give his psychology philosophical, anthropological, and sociological character rather than a psychological or psychiatric one. He expresses this awareness for example, in relation to the notion of archetype. He discovers this philosophical heritage it in Philo's *De opificio mundi* ("the original image in one and special mind directing the universe"), *Corpus Hermeticum* (God as "archetypal light") and in Dionysius the Areopagite.[9] Many Jung's attempts to define the main concepts refer to philosophy, sociology, and anthropology to a much greater extent

4 P. Kutter, *Współczesna psychoanaliza. Psychologia procesów nieświadomych*, (Gdańsk: Gdańskie Wydawnictwo Psychologiczne, 2000).

5 A. Grünbaum, *The Foundation of Psychoanalysis: A Philosophical Critique*, (Berkeley: University of California Press, 1984).

6 I. Progoff, *Jung's Psychology and Its Social Meaning*, (New York: Grove Press, 1955), 37–38.

7 R. Gray, *Archetypal Explorations: An Integrative Approach to Human Behavior*, (Hove-New York: Routledge, 1996).

8 A. Samuels, *The Political Psyche*, (London: Routledge, 1993).

9 C. G. Jung, *Correspondence, (1941–1949)*, v. II, trans. F. Périgant, C. Maillard, (Paris: Albin Michel, 1993), 269; letter to V. White; 4.09.1948. [Further: C II].

than to psychology.[10] This is demonstrated, for example, by the description of the archetype in one of Jung's letters: "This is why I define archetypes both as forms which elude all sensual representation and which, from experience to experience, change into a variety of material."[11] This statement, like many others, shows the philosophical nature of the concept: a hidden structure that remains outside the direct, literal connection with the historical and cultural forms of its manifestation, a kind of *noumenon*, thing-in-itself, beyond direct manifestation. In Jung's view, these structures have an impersonal and collective character: "This particular psyche behaves as if it were one and not divided into a multitude of individual souls. It is not personal. It's everywhere and always the same."[12]

The unconscious, the basis of these forms, is psychic, which for Jung means that it must show "the lightest trace of the will opposing the functioning of instincts according to the laws of automatism."[13] Mental reality is peculiar, has its own laws, is a *sui generis* sphere.[14] It means that one need to search for its laws and that is the aim of psychology.

2 Empirical Aspects of the Unconscious Conception

Kazimierz Pajor emphasizes the change that took place in the characterization of the unconscious in the main stages of the development of Jung's conception: from the history of the idea of unconscious which was associated with the speculative method, Jung seeks to capture the empirical foundations of unconscious processes.[15] This movement of transferring the concept into the framework of another discipline has its justification in the medical type of education of Freud and Jung, although in the case of Jung there is an attempt to link the speculative origin of the concept with the psychological reference framework.[16]

10 More on this topic– cf. I. Błocian, "Archetype of the Trickster in the Writings of C. G. Jung" *Studia Religiologica* 53 (3) 2020, s. 227–238.

11 Ibidem, 28.

12 Ibidem, 136; letter to J. B. Rhine; October 1945.

13 Ibidem, 212; letter to V. White; 23.04.1947.

14 Ibidem, 224–225; letter to E. Neumann; 1.07.1947.

15 K. Pajor, *Rola archetypu w analitycznej psychologii C. G. Junga*, (Poznań: Papieski Wydział Teologiczny, 1992), 42. Jung himself wrote that Freud "empirically proved the existence of the unconscious psyche" - C. G. Jung, *Wspomnienia, sny, myśli. Przy współpracy z Anielą Jaffé*, (Warszawa: Wrota, 1993), 203. [Further – WSM].

16 Jung was sometimes very critical to his own profession, not so much psychological one as psychiatric - psychiatrists play with their tools often without the slightest knowledge

Pajor considers Edgar Bérillon, Alfred Binet, Pierre Janet, Louis Maury, Charles Richet, and Hippolyte Taine as precursors of this second, much more contemporary perspective, and finally psychoanalytical approaches. Freud himself, contrary to interpretations of Jacques Lacan, strongly emphasized the evolutionary nature of the unconscious as a collective heritage of species. He did so in many of his major works. For example, in the *Introduction to Psychoanalysis* he wrote that ontogenesis is a repetition of phylogenesis[17] and that unconsciousness is determined by the experience (experiences) of the ancestors[18] ("strain heritage")[19] also forming their phantasies,[20] which he understands—similar to Jung—as a kind of "mental reality,"[21] and even a "hidden mental state."[22] Sometimes, he himself refers to P. Janet (*idées inconscientes*).[23] Although the unconscious, like *contradictio in adiecto*, "does not know that it knows", the justifications of its functioning hypothesis are, among others, studies on the hypnosis of Ambroise-Auguste Liébault and Ernst Bernheim in Nancy.[24]

With the notion of archetype in Jung's conception, Pajor also defines the origins of the concept in two ways. The first way is philosophical: through Plato, Philo of Alexandria, Saint Irenaeus of Lyon, Duns Scotus, Dionysius Areopagite, Saint Augustine, Scholasticists, Nicolas Malebranche, Immanuel Kant, and Artur Schopenhauer.[25] The second way is anthropological or sociological: through Adolf Bastian, Jacob Burkhardt, Lucien Lévy-Bruhl, Henri Hubert, and Marcel Mauss.[26] Combining these ways of thinking gives very peculiar effects: the distinction into the sphere "in itself," empirically "empty" but

---

and responsibility – C. G. Jung, *Correspondance (1950–1954)*, v. III, trans. C. Maillard, Ch. Phligier-Maillard, (Paris: Albin Michel, 1994), 242–243. [Further – C III].

17 S. Freud, *Wstęp do psychoanalizy*, trans. S. Kempnerówna, F. Zaniewicki, (Warszawa: PWN, 1984), 323.

18 Ibid, 329. Freud believed that this permanent structure made dreams images similar, both today and 3,000 years ago – Ibid., 105. Even the language itself contains the "ancient sediments" of past stages in the history of mental life – Ibid., 116–17. In the context of the coexistence of two mental systems; conscious and unconscious, and the clash of their activities and dynamics, it is possibleaccording to Freud to distinguish to the highest degree the "unconscious intentions" causing an individual mental processes – Ibidem, 89.

19 Ibidem, 369.

20 Ibidem, 337.

21 Ibidem, 335.

22 Ibidem, 209.

23 Ibidem, 245.

24 Ibidem, 120.

25 Jung himself often mentions conceptions of Kant, E. von Hartmann, J. Burckhardt, and F. Nietzsche (*Wspomnienia...*, 129–31). He also frequently refers to his readings of A. Schopenhauer's texts ("the great discovery" of Schopenhauer –) (see Ibid., 89).

26 K. Pajor, *Rola...*, 58–61.

evolutionary ("engram," "mneme of the species")[27] shaped and active *facultas praeformandi* ruling the sphere of collective imagination and giving expression (actualizing themselves) in socially, emotive, and memory-active ideas that govern collective life. Hence the dilemma of their *a priori* (the "a priori structural forms of the instinctive foundation of consciousness,"[28] "a priori of the personal psyche"),[29] but at the same time the cumulative, *a posteriori* nature of accumulating experience. Jung himself, in *Memoirs, Dreams, Reflections,* writes that "timeless man," the self—like the "archetype of orientation and meaning"[30]—penetrates the life of man "as if in a scuba diver's costume,"[31] and "realizing yourself is the only goal of human life."[32] Jung's conclusion is that it is a "provisional" nature of human existence in the phenomenal world.[33]

Therefore, the unconscious, in both Freud's and Jung's terms, is seen as an intrapsychic, internal sphere (beyond space-time conditionings)[34] and a kind of direct connection autonomous reality on the one hand evolutionary and inertial, and on the other—slowly responding to the processes of historical and social change. It has a character of an original process (Freud), or it is a process itself (Jung).[35] Jung notes the dilemma of the inertia of the archetypal ground and its dynamic and variable nature: "Despite their conservative nature, archetypes are not static, but on the contrary, they are in constant flow of the dramatic process of becoming."[36] This flow still forms the potential for shaping order and giving sense, however, leaving the chaotic initial state. This is well illustrated by R. Brooke's interpretation of archetype: It highlights a center of meanings and potentialities of typical adaptations; "archetype is the condition the 'being-in-the-world' of corporality in a hermeneutic relation to meanings."[37]

Despite such solutions, this "dramatic process of becoming" means, after all, the diversity of socio-historical cultures and orders. It is difficult to understand them only as historical variables of the "robes" of manifestation of a certain ahistorical module of evolutionary, genre potency of the unconscious. This

---

27 Ibidem, 70.
28 Ibidem, 407.
29 Ibidem, 195.
30 C. G. Jung, *Wspomnienia*, 237.
31 Ibidem, 379.
32 Ibidem, 397.
33 C III, 189; letter to A. Jaffé; 16.09.1953.
34 WSM, 357.
35 Ibidem, 249.
36 C III, p. 235; letter to V. White; 10.04.1954.
37 R. Brooke, *Jung and Phenomenology,* (New York – London : Routledge, 1991), 13.

dilemma is very deep in the theoretical horizon of Jung's concept; and in many accusations and critics he was expressed, including considering his "dialogue with the Orient."[38] On the one hand, it was noticed that he "was building a hermeneutic bridge with the East," that he was a "natural hermeneut," and that the methodological framework of the concept of unconsciousness was conducive to formulating conclusions about the common ground of religious experience; but on the other, many accusations of this hermeneutic work of Jung: eclecticism, lack of consideration of the cultural context and individual diversity of experiences, consideration of the historical situation of the recipient but not the text itself, the change of dialogue (with "Orient") into a monologue, lack of understanding of the nature of meditation, reduction of the spiritual to the psychic, and many others.[39] It seems that some of them are justified: for example, the historical and cultural context of the creation of philosophical or religious texts with their symbolism is not actually taken into account by Jung, but other interpretations are structurally associated with the range of its basic concepts, unconsciousness, archetype, and psyche, and they are devoted precisely to extracting the structures of human experience. Considering the process of expanding the meaning of the conception of the unconscious, paving its way in the development of its ideas to the widest philosophical meaning, that is, the hidden matrix for forms of reality (similar to the unconscious will in the view of Schopenhauer or the unconsciousness of Eduard von Hartmann), it is difficult to charge here reductionism, and even material forms are conceived here as proto-psychic, psychoid, and they tend to psychic, archetypal, and spiritual levels.

3 The Situation of a Modern Individual

The position of the individual, even in the perspective of Jung's social writings, and especially maybe in them, is central. A human being is a "social micro cosm"[40] and the only real carrier of life.[41] The situation of a modern individual is special in the archetypal context, because "our myth is dumb founded."[42] Modern individual is lonely and moves away from the life of the unconscious;

38 J. J. Clarke, *Jung and Eastern Thought: A Dialogue with the Orient*, (London: Routledge, 1994), 143.

39 Ibidem, 145, 164, 167, 171, 175.

40 C. G. Jung, *The Undiscovered World*, CW v. 10; idem, *Teraźniejszość i przyszłość*, [in:] idem, *Przełom cywilizacji, Dzieła*, t.10, trans. R. Reszke, (Warszawa: KR 2009), 298.

41 Ibidem, 266–267.

42 WSM, 388–389.

he is alienated from this common matrix and from the mass that other people are. So he confesses to us his "proud misery,"[43] in the background of which totalitarianism and concentration camps can be seen. In Jung's letters one can often find this tone, similar in pronunciation to that also expressed, for example, in *Answer to Job*,[44] our times are times of darkness (letter from 1953);[45] the process of confrontation with the shadow has not even begun yet. Our age is disturbed, he writes earlier; it is the result of chaos, worldview shock; it is the time of the "historical storm" in which the voices of demagogues and the tone of propaganda can be heard.[46] However, this situation has changed rapidly since the 1950s. Jung followed it, being a frequent participant in socio-historical events for many decades before World War I and II; it was a time of the greatest war conflicts in the modern world, the emergence of authoritarian and totalitarian orders, changes in the organization of international relations, mass processes, the formation of mass societies, and the impact of their culture.[47] Considering the fact that Jung gave unconscious conditions, the very concept of terms much deeper and broader than in other psychoanalytical approaches, the gap between archaic, evolutionary conditions of man and his rapidly changing socio-historical situation, had to be understood in his conception as very deep. This gap is a measure of the degree of necessary forms of adaptation and its deficiencies, and consequently also of disorders, diseases, and suffering. There is also a quantum of suffering behind cultural and social development. In a mass society, in a mass state its development opportunities should be protected because they are at the highest risk. Culture, social institutions, and power structures are unable to provide it and moreover, are not interested in it. Adaptation will therefore increasingly mean succumbing to conventions and the superficial, inauthentic functioning of social masks. According to Jung, only such a mass man can form in such a socio-political reality. Jung presents this figure like Herbert Marcuse's "one-dimensional" man, Hannah Arendt's *homo consumens* and Erich Fromm's mercantile personality; but his image has some peculiarities. He is critical, like others during this period, he defines the same main features of inauthenticity, reduction, deformation of development, and blurring of the significance of the individual in the "social machine" of mass, which is governed by the "logic of large numbers." Specific features

43 C. G. Jung, *Problem psychiki człowieka współczesnego (1928/69), Dzieła,* t.10, 86.

44 C. G. Jung, *Odpowiedź Hiobowi*, trans. J. Prokopiuk, (Warszawa: Ethos, 1995).

45 C III, 200–201; letter to V. White; 24.11.1953.

46 C. G. Jung, *Przedmowa do:* Aufsätzezur Zeitgeschichte (1946), *Dzieła,* t. 10, 187–188.

47 More on this topic – I. Błocian, *C. G. Jung – myśl i krytyka społeczna*, (Wrocław: Wydawnictwo Uniwersytetu Wrocławskiego, 2018).

of Jung's criticism are the depth of the gap between contemporary ways of living in mass society and the depth of the soul's needs of primary experiences expressed in the launch of creative processes in art, the depth of religious experiences, and especially those conditioning their individual character.

•••

Our volume contains texts whose authors extract aspects of social thought inherent in Jung's concept, examining its sources, indicating what sources he drew from, where its conditions are constituted, and defining its horizon, consequences, explanatory elements In modern science, social psychology, sociology, or social philosophy. **Part 1 of the volume (*Collective Structures of the Unconscious*)** consists of texts that identify fundamental questions and categories that enable the creation of a relationship between mental reality, collective imagination, and social phenomena. J. Beebe considers the status of basic approaches, categories, and their matrixes in the history of thought. Other authors (I. Błocian, E. Kwiatkowska) discuss the relationship of Jung's social thought to psychological, anthropological conceptions (E. Kwiatkowska, I. Błocian) and sociological ones (J. Graaf).

John Beebe poses a question about the ontological status of psychic reality. The posed question is very central for Jung's conception: it is an attempt to understand mental reality, how it is possible, how it affects human experience, and in what ways it is related to the process of forming dreams. By following the motives of dream and patients's associations, Beebe ventures to present the impact of a formal and purposeful cause in the process of human psychic development. He analyzes the profound influence of the self-archetype in challenging the ego's blockade of empathy and involvement in the fate of other people. The importance of common life and responding to social and historical processes for self-understanding is strongly noted. The author conceives of the psyche as a certain autonomous reality, indirectly tangible, but exerting a very strong influence on all mental processes.

Ilona Błocian's text presents this social dimension of Jung's thought and the main problems associated with it. There are many questions about the relationship that can occur between a differentiation of collective and social levels. A lot of Jung's writings refer directly to the issues of social thought and his comments to current situations or events of a socio-political nature, such as totalitarianism, political leadership, or contemporary forms of religiosity. They present a special relationship between the individual and society, the archetype and the historical, social dimensions, between mass processes and collective imagination. The author compares various concepts of collective imagination and approaches to their anthropological background (C. G. Jung, G. Durand, Ch. Taylor). The juxtaposition of these forms of reflection opens the way to understanding a particular power of collective imagination.

Ewa Kwiatkowska's chapter is written from the perspective of cultural sciences, the iconic turn in contemporary humanities and the question whether the psychoanalytical, Jungian, or Lacanian traditions have to propose a special way of thinking about the image or—to a lesser extent—a way of directing attention to the specificity or importance of the social and individual visual sphere. The author emphasizes the Jungian (Gilbert Durand) and Lacanian (Claude Lévi-Strauss) kinds of recognition, and she proposes the division between linguistic and iconic unconscious approaches. The conclusion is the indication that although Jungian psychology is completely unsustainable in cultural sciences because of its unscientific, metaphysical assumptions, it opens the research perspective of the autonomous validity of the visual sphere. Lacan eliminates it, understanding the imaginary as the sphere of individual escape from social reality.

Part 2 of the present volume (*Social Imaginarium*) is devoted to the analysis of specific sets and structures organizing images with a social impact, social imaginaries reflected in architectural forms (V. J. Varner, M. Luci), literature (K. Morawska), films and psychotherapeutic practices (B. Rudić, M. Kostyszak), myths (H. Hennebert, P. Neumann), images themselves (K. Schaeppi, N. Kishimoto), or even forms of dance (J. Bayes-King).

Vicky Jo Varner's text is an interpretation of the figures of gargoyles, demons, and bestiaries on portals, architectural and furniture elements. The author refers to iconoclasm and iconophilia in Christian traditions and against this background showing the special position of image and imaging. In this imaging, personification refers to the spectrum of fragmentary personalities that become visible and accessible to consciousness. This is valuable from the point of view of both psychotherapy and self-knowledge processes because one relates to the other. The author also refers to her own experience as a Guided Imagery practitioner.

Monica Luci's text signals the perspective of the creating ego and self-processes taking place through relationships with the environment (sense of touch—"wall," "walls"). The author enables in-depth insight in the sources and psychological effects of political events (building and dysfunctions in the meaning of security, identity, conflicts, discrimination, stereotyping). It is an attempt to analyze psychological, anthropological, and socio-political levels and their archetypal character reflected in mythological sets connected with the god Hermes. The analysis arises in dialogue with many authors: Donald Woods Winnicot, Didier Anzieu, Pierre Janet, Lucien Lévy-Bruhl, and Murray Stein.

Kamila Morawska's chapter concerns a connection between bachelardism and psychoanalytic conceptions (Sigmund Freud, Carl Gustav Jung). Gaston Bachelard read Jung, referred to him, to the notion of unconsciousness, archetype, and image. He conceived man as an "imaginative being"; imaging is the very essence of human psychology. Thus Bachelard referred to the notion of archetype, and Jungian influence is most clearly seen in his conception of human being and mental activity. The author also comments on Bachelard's relation to Freud's psychoanalysis and his use of the term "psychoanalysis" in various, specific contexts ("psychoanalysis of objective knowledge").

Bojana Rudić refers to the post-war and post-conflict situation in the Balkans. The author evokes a fragment of a film depicting normal, everyday behavior in groups in the background of helicopters of the war conflict. She diagnoses the situation of relations between the communities of the Balkan peoples as taking place on an archetypal set and heavily influenced by the archetype of the Trickster and the god Hermes. This is a situation of the suspension and dissolution of mental structures and a sense of boundaries in some correspondence to the social collective life of the inhabitants of the Peninsula as life precisely on limits. The analysis also points to a significant migration of people to a degree greater than in any part of Europe. The author presents possible positive solutions (consciousness of fragmentary particles and trends of unconscious processes, maturity achieved by awareness of contradictions in which the process of dissolving structures will cause a kind of suspension in the lives of individuals and collectivities).

Maria Kostyszak tries to present film and literature in their support of "shadow therapy." The author examines several examples of movies and novels (Olga Tokarczuk, Swietłana Aleksiejewicz, Agnieszka Holland et al.) She also presents multi-faceted understandings of evil, as in the specific Jungian conception of evil, the confusion of values and counter-values. The author points to the political and social, collective forms of shadow, characteristic of the Euro-Atlantic circle, raised on the basis of colonialism, war conflicts, and the erosion of the values of life and nature, forms of evil specific to to it. Action for profit, not paying attention to the threat posed to the health and life of other people, lack of empathy, exploitative attitude to nature and "full animal life," lack of moral principles "covered with hypocrisy" and leading to indifference, impatience, one-sidedness, and lack of responsibility – the core of an "excess of negativity." The film can influence the processes of specific therapy by awakening consciousness and by training the imagination.

Hannah Hennebert's chapter presents the Amazonian myth about Yusha Kuru (Yushan Kuru) and its role in the collective imagination of the Kaxinawa people. The author reconstructs the myth itself. The meaning of the figure of the goddess and the interpretation of her figure is brought out through the work of Jung, Neumann, Joseph Campbell, and Mircea Eliade; decisive here seems to be the archetype of the Great Mother with its healing and destructive aspects.

Patrycja Neumann's text confronts common elements and different approaches to the myth of the hero of Carl Gustav Jung, James Hillman, and Joseph Campbell. This is a confrontation in which differences are strongly emphasized, among others identifying the main axis of the formation of the heroic myth in the interaction of the ego archetype. The author underlines Hillman's critical attitude to the increase in the ego importance in our culture and presents a discussion between different approaches to myth in contemporary research inspired by Jungian statements.

The text by Kathrin Schaeppi is focused on comparison elements of Jung's and H. af Klint's images. It is inspired by the "archetypal number," and it is treated as a key to understanding the meaning of images. The stages of individual development are matched up, as in Jung's case, with the engravings of *Rosarium Philosophorum*. The author seeks not only figurative and symbolic forms of analogy between Jung and af Klint but also their common interests in spiritism and paranormal phenomena.

Norifumi Kishimoto writes about the test with a tree drawing as one kind of projection test. The image can serve as a tool for understanding psychic processes in patients. This test might work as a trigger of communication, as a hook of projection, and might open a way to express oneself. It might function as a kind of "mirror" that encourages the subject to reflect himself. Kishimoto also interprets various kinds of tree drawings, for example, in the form of the Moebius Tree. The visions of a patient suffering from leukemia are described in detail and are juxtaposed with Jungian interpretations of *Rosarium Philosophorum*. The projection itself can be a therapeutic factor because it has become "a mirror where the patients look back on themselves."

Josefa Bayes-King writes about dance as a pre-verbal method of communication that transfers the cognitive element from generation to generation. Dance expresses emotional nuances, traumas, traditions. It started in Australia as a form of treatment, especially among Aborigenal peoples. They believe that they are communing with the tradition from which they are cut off by "White Australia."

Lidar Shany analyzes the element of femininity as the core of Erich Neumann's interests. She believes that his conception can be viewed from an ecopsychological perspective. Ecopsychological approaches draw attention to the human relationship to the natural environment and its psychological consequences. They show how the loss of the bond with the earth and the female element leads to depression, to the "cold core" in the individual's relations to outer world. The author presents conception of psychic development in both collective and individual aspects of Neumann's grasp. She relates it also to the Jung's and André Green's idea of an emotionally inactive "dead mother complex." In the negative scenario of that complex the child cannot establish a positive bond with the world and with himself. The author shows the connections among Jung, Neumann, and Green on negative forms of mental development.

Johann Graaff presents some connections in the symbolic interpretation of social phenomena among Jung, Clifford Geertz, and Robert Darnton. He maintains that Jung himself mixes social, individual, and psychological orders. He notes critically that one cannot properly speak of sociology in Jung's research, and even his hermeneutics is the hermeneutics of faith. The claims here relate to huge time horizons and archetypal psycho-history. Overwhelmed by the figure of Wotan and with great sympathy for the "folk" movement, Jung builds his statements on his own insights rather than on an empirical basis.

Part 3 of the volume (*Psychological Significance in Social Processes*) consists of texts on the analysis of contemporary social processes, their possible explanations, ways of understanding Jung's social thought ("archetypal sociology") and the critique of contemporary (twentieth-century) phenomena. The pillars of these aspects of Jung's concept should be seen in the sharp clash of the evolution of the unconscious and the rapid pace of changes in mass, industrial, and post-industrial society.

Andrew Kuzmicki searches for instinctive patterns in the social hierarchy. He presents data from ethology, observation of animal behavior, and the distribution of images of hierarchical structures in many cultures. The author points to the V. Pareto conception and to the so-called Gini factor illustrating contemporary social inequalities. The influence of the education factor and the choice of a more democratic way of social organization and distribution of foods are possibilities that could solve some of the unjust regulations. Hierarchical order seems to have an instinctive and archetypal foundation, but this does not mean that in the social dimension it cannot be corrected, changed, or better adapted to the conditions of life in our rapidly changing digital society.

Helge M. Osterhold reconstructs the relationships between individual and collective levels and compares the social and psychological dimensions in Jung with those in contemporary social psychology. The author refers to Joseph Henderson's category of the "cultural unconscious." He also presents Jung's conception reading through the prism of Terror Management Theory and the fear of death as first, archetype of experience, and second, as a factor that strongly influences the social behavior of groups towards each other. In the light of Jung's conception, the meaning of "quiet, humble ego" related to the maturity of individuation may seems very important from the point of view of lowering social anxiety and accepting otherness related to group diversity. The chapter is a confrontation of Jung's psychology with contemporary social psychology in the wake of current challenges, ecological and terrorist threats, and the collapse of traditional values.

Gustavo Orlandeli Marques writes about a long-lasting effect—beginning in the sixteenth century—of the myth of the good king, who is the savior of his people. He sees Sebastianism as a political and religious movement influencing both political wings in many centuries of Brazilian history. The author sees the people's expectation of a messiah who will lead the people to a new, better beginning as a desire of a mythological nature, present in large number of myths and by myths influencing collective imagination. It has a character of a factor dynamizing the political scene, strengthening the tendency to resist corruption of the ruling groups, but at the same time the tendency to remain helpless and wait for external action.

Stefano Carpani analyzes in a critical way the possible problems and contradictions among the conceptions of the Frankfurters, Freud, Jung, and Fromm. He confronts critical views of the Frankfurt School with an approach to mental health as a recognition of who someone is, the process of potencies realized in Jung's and Fromm's conceptions, and the problems of modern digital society. The author emphasizes the anti-consumer values present both in Jung's social thought, neo-psychoanalysis and the Frankfurt School thought—he also discusses problems and experiences in psychotherapeutic processes.

Michał Wróblewski's chapter is an indication of the social consequences of the views of Zenon Dudek, Tomasz Olchanowski, and Wojciech Burszta on *imagopathy* and *logereia*, the so-called *percepto-culture* of contemporaneity. This psychological and anthropological approach to mental processes is taking place in the era of virtual-visual contemporary communication. Societies resemble collectives of "hungry ghosts," in which the process of separation of the real from the virtual does not occur. In this *technopolis* environment, man becomes an egoistic predator seeking to satisfy the "principle of efficiency" (the Frankfurt School's) replacing the "principle of reality." These processes have the psychological consequences to which individuals are subjected. The author claims that Jung's cultural psychology refers to a certain "art of life" in ancient forms of wisdom, which seems to be necessary for the trails to create some contemporary principles of an organization of life in our societies.

References

Błocian I., *C. G. Jung – myśl i krytyka społeczna*, Wrocław: Wydawnictwo Uniwersytetu Wrocławskiego, 2018.

Błocian I., "Archetype of the Trickster in the Writings of C. G. Jung", *Studia Religiologica* 53, no. (3/2020): 233–244.

Brooke R., *Jung and Phenomenology,* New York – London: Routledge, 1991.

Clarke J. J., *Jung and Eastern Thought: A Dialogue with the Orient*, London: Routledge, 1994.

Freud S., *Wstęp do psychoanalizy*, trans. S. Kempnerówna, W. Zaniewicki, Warszawa: PWN, 1984.

Gray R., *Archetypal Explorations: An Integrative Approach to Human Behavior*, Hove-New York: Routledge, 1996.

Grünbaum A., *The Foundation of Psychoanalysis. A Philosophical Critique*, Berkeley: University of California Press, 1984.

Jung C. G., *Correspondance (1941–1949)*, v. II, trans. F. Périgant, C. Maillard, Paris: Albin Michel, 1993.

Jung C. G., *Correspondance (1950–1954)*, v. III, trans. C. Maillard, Ch. Phligier-Maillard, Paris: Albin Michel, 1994.

Jung C. G., *Wspomnienia, sny, myśli. Przy współpracy z Anielą Jaffé,* Warszawa: Wrota, 1993.

Jung C. G., *Problem psychiki człowieka współczesnego (1928/69),* [in:} idem, *Przełom cywilizacji, Dzieła,* t.10, trans. R. Reszke, Warszawa: KR, 2009.

Jung C. G., *Odpowiedź Hiobowi*, Warszawa: Ethos, 1995.

Jung C. G., *Przedmowa do:* Aufsätze zur Zeitgeschichte (1946), [in:] idem, *Przełom cywilizacji, Dzieła,* t.10, trans. R. Reszke, Warszawa: KR, 2009.

Jung C. G., v. 10; idem, *Teraźniejszość i przyszłość,* [in:] idem, *Przełom cywilizacji, Dzieła,* t.10, trans. R. Reszke, Warszawa: KR, 2009.

Kästner I., Schröeder Ch., *Zygmunt Freud (1856–1939). Badacz umysłu. Neurolog. Psychoterapeuta*, Wrocław: Arboretum, 1997.

Kołakowski L., *Psychoanalityczna koncepcja kultury,* [in:] idem, *Czy diabeł może zostać zbawiony i 27 innych kazań*, London: Aneks, 1984.

Kutter P., *Współczesna psychoanaliza. Psychologia procesów nieświadomych,* Gdańsk: Gdańskie Wydawnictwa Psychologiczne, 2000.

Pajor K., *Rola archetypu w analitycznej psychologii C. G. Junga*, Poznań: Papieski Wydział Teologiczny, 1992.

Progoff I., *Jung's Psychology and its Social Meaning*, New York: Grove Press, 1955.

Samuels A., *The Political Psyche*, London: Routledge, 1993.

Thompson C., *Psychoanalysis: Revolution and Development*, New York: Thomas Nelsons and Sons, 1967.

PART 1

Collective Structures of the Unconscious

CHAPTER 1

Why Is This Real?

John Beebe

Abstract

Jung's phrase "die Wirklichkeit der Seele," usually translated as "the reality of the psyche," literally means "the reality of the soul." Caring for the soul was central to Jung's work. The reality of the soul is not equivalent to what Freud called "psychic reality," which refers to whatever the psyche is grappling with in a given time. We may think of dreams as messages from the soul, but in what sense are these messages "real"? Working with a patient's dream in which men kill and butcher an elephant, this paper explores how a dream can move us to engage more fully with reality—in the case of this dream, helping us to see, among other things, how racism has disabled the feeling function. Aristotle's doctrine of the Four Causes is applied to try to answer the questions, "Why has the dream come? In what way is it illuminating reality?" According to Aristotle, the four causes—Material Cause, Efficient Cause, Formal Cause, and Final Cause—are needed to provide a full explanation for how reality is transformed. In an exchange with audience members, we find the Stoic idea of "the hidden sympathy of all things" is linked to *unus mundus* to show how messages from the soul connect us to a reality that is much larger than the individual.

Keywords

reality of the psyche, dreams, Aristotle's Four Causes, *unus mundus*

The idea of collective structures of imagination is a very good one. I live in a collective structure of imagination. The practice of analysis *is* a practice of imagination, including (on the part of those who participate in it, the patient and the analyst) that we know what we're talking about. Even if I, as the analyst, talk back with the patient, there's still the question a patient asked me once a long time ago: What are you thinking? I've never forgotten that question; it's haunted me. At that time, I was a great believer in self-disclosure, and I said, I was wondering when you were going to pay me. That was an interesting interaction, in which the shadow was quite evident; and that's great. The

 | DOI:10.1163/9789004468757_003

trouble is, surely that wasn't all I was thinking, even though it was what I was thinking at that moment.

So here is another chance for me to share, this time with you, what I'm thinking when I do my work. As I work, I'm constantly haunted by the ideas of my forefathers, and so whether they're right or wrong, they're in the room; they're the working background. One idea that has both haunted me and informed my work, even though the more I try to probe into it, the less philosophical ground I can find for it, is Jung's idea of the "reality of the psyche." Now, that's an English translation that I think we ought to dispense with because it collides and competes with Freud's perfectly reasonable concept of psychic reality.[1] It also introduces a word, *psyche*, which is fraught with ambiguity. Two of the worst words in psychology are *psyche* and *psychosis*. Try to find an exact meaning of either word! At least the English translation of the Freudian "psychic apparatus" is more honest, but still, this question of what psyche is remains. And in fact, "the reality of the psyche" isn't a good translation of the title of the compilation of his own and followers' articles that Jung published in 1934—"*Wirklichkeit der Seele*"[2]—because it means "the reality of the soul," not "the reality of the psyche." We should say "reality of the soul," which is also a very different thing from simply saying psychic reality. When we make the soul the reality a Jungian analyst is trying to address, we're getting closer to what Jung wanted us to do, what in his darkest and final moment in 1960, he confessed very plainly that he had failed to get others to do in his lifetime. A letter he wrote to Eugene Rolfe, just seven months before he died, said it all.

> I have failed in my foremost task, to open people's eyes to the fact that man has a soul and there is a buried treasure in the field and that our religion and philosophy are in a lamentable state. Why indeed should I continue to exist?[3]

Since I take seriously Jung's idea of what we owe the dead,[4] I see effort today as continuing in the project of persuasion that Jung left unfinished. I want to see

---

1 Psychic Reality. https://www.encyclopedia.com/psychology/dictionaries-thesauruses-pictures-and-press-releases/psychic-reality Consulted October 30, 2019.

2 C. G. Jung, *Wirklichkeit der Seele. Anwendungen und Fortschritte der neueren Psychologie.* (Zurich: Rascher, 1934).

3 E. Rolfe, *Encounter with Jung* (Boston: Sigo Press, 1989), 158.

4 C. G. Jung, *Liber Novus = The Red Book* (New York & London: W. W. Norton, 2009), 295–297; S. L. Stephens, *Jung and the Dead: Visions, Active Imagination and the Unconscious Terrain* (London & New York: Routledge, 2020), 44–45; J. Hillman & S. Shamdasani, *Lament of the Dead: Psychology after Jung's* Red Book (New York: W. W. Norton, 2009), 84–85.

how I can move it along by saying how the questionable idea of the reality of the soul has managed to haunt me. I actually enact that idea every day in a ritual that is a collective structure of imagination. In one sense, what you're going to hear is fantasy as I enact it in a dialogue with myself when I listen to my patients, and that communicates itself to them when I talk to them, the fantasy that the soul is speaking through the dream and that it does have a reality.

The question that haunts me as I work with patients is this: Why is this real? This person is telling me this, and I can certainly reduce it or confine it to that person's psychic reality and the way life experience has taught him or her to see things this way. Or I can say, no, the soul is really speaking through what the person is saying to me and what the soul is saying *is* real in some way. If so, I have to ask myself, why is this real?

Psychic reality, the term of Freud, is defined at Encyclopedia.com as "a concept developed by Freud to denote the level of reality specific to unconscious processes, psychic reality from an epistemological standpoint refers to the object, as psychoanalysis attempts to characterize, understand and explore." In other words, it's just what, if you're a working analyst, you're talking about all day long.

Now, Freud fully accepts the ambiguity of anything produced by the psychic apparatus, and that is a tremendous strength because he recognizes that the ground is always shifting underneath us and that what we think is real psychically at one time, we're going to just dispense with as a fiction that we shouldn't have gotten into at another time in the course of the analysis. That its reality is elusive is one of the normal behaviors of the psyche under the process of psychoanalysis. Freud simply accepts the ambiguity and deals with it as a part of what he terms psychic reality.

Jung moves this idea of the analytic process toward an epiphany by making it serve what he called the soul's *wirklichkeit*. The psychoanalytic historian Ernst Falzeder, who has a good sense of how Jung used and played with German, has told me (2019) that *wirklichkeit* involved, for Jung, a play on two different words, *wirk*, which is reality and *wirk*, which means work. I see there the influence of William James' pragmatism, which Jung was saying around 1915 was too "business-like" for him,[5] but Jung was nothing if not a pragmatist when he was talking about what he experienced as an analyst about the reality of the soul. He was speaking about that in his patients and in himself that worked to effect change. He was very interested in how the soul impinges in a way that

5 J. Beebe & E. Falzeder (eds.), *The Question of Psychological Types: Correspondence of C.G. Jung and Hans Schmid-Guisan. 1915–1916* (Princeton: Princeton University Press, 2012), 41.

cannot be denied and works therapeutically on the person. That is a very different idea of reality than many people have.

Yet it is one that can be demonstrated when we take the trouble to remember and engage with a dream, as I must do regularly in my practice as an analyst. When I start to regard the dream, splitting the difference between Freud and Jung, as an expression either of psychic reality or of the reality of the soul, I often remind myself that I'd do better to start with Homer. In a famous sequence in *The Odyssey*, Book 19, lines 560 to 569, Penelope has a dream that Odysseus is about to return. She immediately says (as I will paraphrase) "Well yeah, I had that dream, but two are the gates of shadowy dreams. One is fashioned of horn, polished horn whereas the other is fashioned of ivory, sawn ivory, and the dreams that pass through the gates of polished horn bring true issues to pass, but the dreams that pass through the gates of sawn ivory deceive man." This involves a play on words between horn, which is *karos* in Greek, and *kryno*, which is to fulfill. It has to do with the notion that the horn, a pure animal product that is polished, has a tendency to complete or fulfill itself and can be relied on to be real and come true. By contrast, the word for ivory, *elephas*, which obviously gets us to elephant, has a play on words with *elephairoma*, which means "to deceive." Think today of the much trafficked-in ivory that is so prized and used in all kinds of ways. When the dream goes through gates made of ivory, you can count on it to deceive. Penelope said (and again I paraphrase), "I'm pretty sure that my dream of Odysseus returning is of the latter sort; it went through the gates of ivory, and it's not likely to come true."

Here is Homer's wonderful irony, because Penelope's dream did come true; Odysseus had returned, and thus it did reflect a real thing and is an example of part of what Jung means by the reality of the psyche. I've had many such dreams that I was not willing to believe and that turned out to be astonishingly true and specific. Many people have. I can't wait for science to catch up with this, but try to make that a theory of dreams, and then all of the dreams that don't come true would immediately be counterexamples, so it's a very interesting conundrum that hasn't moved much since the time of Homer.

Let me tell you about a dream that has an elephant. This was dreamed by a patient of mine. First, I just want to say the littlest bit about the patient. He's an American professional man like me and he had this dream on October 8 of 2014. What follows is his account of it, as said to me in analysis.

> There is a verbal statement in the dream: Life goes on until the tree stops. In the visual aspect of the dream, which is in two parts, the tree is getting an elephant. In the first part, there were white men, white guys, and they somehow butchered this elephant and hung it up in a tree. The elephant was really butchered. It had been hacked; its body cut in two. The second part

> of the dream is the elephant, which is now hung up in the tree like "Strange Fruit," like a lynching.

Now I'm going to talk about my process in working with the dream with the patient. The first thing that passed through my mind was already building towards something I was going to share with the patient, but before I dared share it, I had to check something out because I was temporarily confused. As I thought about "elephant," I actually had to say to the patient, "Are elephants indigenous to Africa?" We think of them so often in relation to India, that I found myself wondering, but no sooner had I said that than I could see in my mind Hannibal's elephants crossing the Alps, and I realized that they had come from Carthage. Of course elephants had to be endemic to Africa. That's how my mind is working, and I'm remembering how amazing that invasion was: the greatest general in the world coming by elephant from Africa and crossing the Alps to invade Rome. It really still rocks me. And as soon as I said that, and my patient was nodding, "Yeah, they're endemic to Africa," I immediately responded to the elephant image and said the thought that I was afraid to share; but it was my immediate thought, and I said to my patient, "This is the strength of Africa." My train of associations (in my notes) were Hannibal and that invasion and Carthage itself, "Carthage must be destroyed." Carthage was totally destroyed by Rome.

The patient's own association reporting the lynching of the elephant, as he put it, was to the song, "Strange Fruit." Immediately I mentioned Billie Holiday. My patient doesn't know that from the time I was fifteen, when I started my collection of jazz records, one of three records that I got from my favorite teacher selling 78 rpm records was Billie Holiday. I was absolutely hooked from that point on, until I actually saw her around my twentieth birthday, the year she died. I mean, she was everything to me. There wasn't a day in my life when I didn't listen to Billie Holiday. I don't listen to her as much now because it's actually too powerful.

Jung says, we always dream what's between ourselves and the other. The patient couldn't have done better in that respect than with that association to "Strange Fruit." There I was with Billie Holiday again. She sang to protest the racist lynchings that had killed the man she thought was her father. It turns out that Clarence Holiday might not have been her actual father. He was at least one of her mother's lovers, but she was led to believe he was her father and thus took his name, and he was lynched. "Strange Fruit" has such long legs, by the way, in terms of the politics of America. It was written in 1937 by a man named Abel Meeropol, who used the pen name Lewis Allan. He was an amazing person, a Jewish man who raised the children left by Ethel and Julius Rosenberg—sons who were six and ten when their parents were executed during the McCarthy era. He very much concerned himself with justice.[6] My patient, by the way, is a Jewish man; that's a piece of the history, the association and the transference and countertransference. From there, we talked about "the strength of Africa" being up in that tree, having first been carved by the hunters. As I see the dream now and think of the elephant being carved, I think of colonialism and all of those countries carved out of Africa. I also think of Africa as this very large continent, and I want to come back to that because there's a reason, I think, for Africa and its strength being symbolized in this particular patient's dream by the elephant and also being told to me. But right now, we were busy associating it to an immediate reality facing us in America.

You have to recall that between 2014 and 2016, there was an Ebola outbreak in West Africa and that on August 8 of 2014, the World Health Organization had declared the deteriorating situation in West Africa a public health emergency of international concern. That's a category designated only for events with a risk of potential international spread or that requires a coordinated international response. As soon as I mentioned the Ebola crisis, my patient and I were both shocked to consider that, having listened to all the news that was mounting on a daily basis in the American press, nobody here seemed to care about the coordinated international response for the sake of Africa. What they were interested in was keeping *it* out of *our* country. That has become a theme of nationalism around the world, as you know, and it's a big, big issue today. But in 2014, as we sat there, both of us were beginning to feel the horror and the selfishness of seeing that elephant in the tree that represented for us at that moment in the therapy, thanks to what I had said, the strength of Africa being attacked, being basically lynched, while people like us were busy trying to protect themselves. There was something obscene about the way that the view of the World Health Organization, the need for a coordinated international response, had been discounted in the American discourse.

On September 30, 2014, our American Center for Disease Control had confirmed the first travel-associated case of Ebola diagnosed in the United States in a man who had traveled from West Africa to Dallas, Texas. I think we both had probably heard that because it was on the news. I only learned, much later, as I was preparing for the 2019 Wrocław conference that the patient in Dallas, Texas, died on October 8, 2014, the same day that my patient had this dream.

I have noticed this again and again, where there are very significant dreams, the unconscious has a remarkable ability to know things before we know them consciously. For instance, on the night of the 1972 Watergate break-in,

6 D. Margolick, *Strange Fruit: The Biography of a Song* (Philadelphia: Running Press, 1977).

I dreamed I was talking to Nixon. Shortly after, I had a dream about an ex-candidate for vice president. I thought, what is an ex-candidate for vice president? Six weeks later, Thomas Eagleton had to step down as McGovern's vice-presidential running mate. It's like Jung dreaming about the assassination of a crown prince months before an assassination of a crown prince started World War I.

Gregory Bateson, whom I heard lecture in 1970 at Stanford, said, if you think that what passes along a nerve axon is an impulse, you're never going to understand how the mind is connected to nature, but if you will understand that what passes along a nerve axon is "news of a difference," then you'll get it. His final book, *Mind and Nature,* lays all this out. I prefer, however, his *Steps to an Ecology of Mind,* where everything is, as I think it should be, a series of tentative probings. That idea of "a news of a difference" has informed me ever since when I work with dreams. I want to see what news of a difference there is in the dream.

I hope this makes clearer how I came to ask the question that was driving me while I was talking about this dream with the patient: Why is this dream real? Why is this real? Also, how is it working? What is it working toward? As my patient and I were talking, we both had to confess that there's this tremendous, I don't know whether to call it an *aporia*—a conundrum—or a *lacuna* —a gap—but it's this: both of us, rightly or wrongly, pride ourselves in our empathy, we make feeling for others a project, we live for it, we care about it, we go to a great effort to hold ourselves responsible for that, and yet both of us had to admit, as we confronted this dream, that we just don't think about Africa. I've sometimes played the subject-guessing game Twenty Questions with people, and it rarely crosses my mind when trying to locate something geographically to think of the African continent. I've been to Africa twice. I loved Doris Lessing's *African Stories*. I loved all her *Children of Violence* series. I wanted to go to Africa at one point when I was an undergraduate: I was planning to be in Brazzaville on the day that independence got declared. I got up at 4 in the morning to see on TV Nelson Mandela get out of prison. I mean, it isn't that I haven't thought about Africa, but left to my own devices on a daily basis, it's amazing how I just turn the page on African suffering, and when I was realizing what was happening with Ebola, I said, there it is; these really are the white hunters stringing Africa up in a tree. We were both looking at that; and for my patient, who had had quite a number of dreams that placed him in certain places around the time something was about to happen in that place, the fact that he didn't feel about Africa turned out to be very meaningful to him because he could see it was a place where his feeling wasn't working. Why wasn't it working? The structure-limiting moral imagination that we were working with was simply racism. It's easy to see the suffering of people of another color in a way that is different from the suffering that you really embrace and care about and take seriously. That was a tough one for both of us to sit with, but it was one of the things the dream moved us to consider.

Trying to honor Jung's idea that there is a reality of the soul and that when we listen to a dream, we should be engaging with that reality, I realize that not only Penelope, but also I have, despite my Jungian background, despite my love of the dream, despite the degree that dreams have helped me, a certain aversion to taking them seriously. When I was in analysis in San Francisco with Joe Henderson, who long before had been analyzed in Switzerland by Jung, I would bring my dreams all typed out and hand them over to him. I remember him saying to me, one week, you know, there was a baby born in one of those dreams you handed to me last week. I didn't remember it at all. Thanks to him saying that, I read the dream over, and it became one of the two or three pivotal dreams of my analysis. But it wouldn't have been, if not for Joe. I would have dismissed and forgotten the dream as one that had "passed through the gates of ivory." "Oh, I know why I had that dream. That's not going to happen. It's not real." But the dream cared enough to dream itself into being, so I should ask, in what sense is it the reality of the soul? Why is it real? How is it real?

As I began to look into that, I stumbled upon something that is famous in philosophy but not in psychology: Aristotle's Four Causes. I love Aristotle. I find him more interesting than Plato. But that is certainly not C.G. Jung's opinion. Where Jung and Aristotle would come together is that the dream is a *natural* product. That's a big thing for Aristotle. A natural product is something that has, embodied within it, principles of motion and rest. This reminds me of Chinese philosophy in the Book of Changes, the *I Ching*. Joe Henderson liked to call it the book of "constancy and change," and I can see why. Living things have a tendency to remain like something at rest, even though they also have an intrinsic motion that is also characteristic of them, which means they move in certain directions that allow them to change.

The Four Causes are: the Material cause, the Efficient cause, the Formal cause, and the Final cause. Cause is an overly general translation into English of an untranslatable Greek word, *aition*, which in the plural is *aitia*. It was used a lot by Plato; and when Aristotle used it, he assumed everybody knew what it meant, so he never defined it. There's a vast literature now on what *aitia* might mean.[7] But for Plato, *aitia* was essentially the cause of something blameworthy.

---

7 C. Natali, "*Aitia* in Plato and Aristotle. From Everyday Language to Technical Vocabulary." In C. Viano, C. Natali, and M. Zangano (Eds.) *Aitia I. Les quatres causes: origines et interprétation* (Leuven: Peeters, 2013), 39–73.

It could be either to blame or to give credit, but it had to do with who or what is responsible.

In the *Material cause,* you're trying to get at what's the matter; and of course, in this dream, what's the matter, what's not right, is that that elephant has been hacked to death and now is being hung out to dry on a tree that, according to the patient, looked like the dead tree in Dali's *The Persistence of Memory.* One could amplify the image of the dead tree by connecting it to the archetype of the Dead Mother, an internal object most thoroughly explored by the French psychoanalyst André Green.[8]

The dead mother, when encountered within or projected onto the analyst, is guilty of an enormous lack of empathy for the child. The dead spot in my empathy and in my patient's empathy that could let us forget about Africa and need this dream to compensate us both was speaking to the dead mother in both of us. Another piece of the tree is the overinsistence on the *family tree* that's at the heart of nationalism. Nationalism was once described by a Jungian analyst colleague, Lois Khan, as the narcissism of nations.[9] I think that's a lovely way of putting it. This overemphasis on kinship—we will pay for welfare as long as it goes to people who could be in our family tree, is part of the deadness of the tree on which this elephant is hung. All of that seems to be what's the matter. There was once a paper called, "What Is the Matter with Mother?"[10] Now we have to ask, what is the matter with the mother in us? I work with people all over the world now by Skype and other telemedia, and it's amazing how often patients present dreams in which the Mother is in trouble. Empathy, the maternal principle, is under attack or suffering unhealth.

I think the *Efficient cause* was awareness that the critical moment had come when someone had died of Ebola in an American hospital and there was going to be a real clamping down on keeping anything from Africa out of America. It's understandable as containment of a contagion, but movies like *Contagion*[11] help us see how that rationale can quickly devolve into loss of integrity and of empathy.

The *Formal cause* of this dream involves its substance, our sense of shock over what has happened to alter the natural shape, appearance, or arrangement—this is Aristotle's nod to Plato—of the elephant. The Formal expectation that has been violated is that the elephant should exist in its natural

8 A. Green, "The dead mother." In *On Private Madness* (London: Hogarth Press, 1986), 142–173.

9 L. Khan, personal communication, 1993.

10 P. Berry. "What Is the Matter with Mother?" Lecture #190, September 2, 1976. (Kings Lynn, UK: The Guild of Pastoral Psychology, 1978).

11 *Contagion,* motion picture, directed by S. Soderbergh, 2011.

form. Haunting the dream, therefore, at the Formal level of what brought it into being, is what's been done to the elephant. You can also say, however, that there's a Platonic Form for the good, pure, and beautiful thing being injured: in our culture, one might find that Form in the crucifixion of Jesus. There are many examples in myth and story in which the form of something is abused and disrespected. I'm thinking here that the substantial presence as it ideally should be, the elephant in its natural form, takes us into the idea of the big heart of a living elephant. I do think that if you listen to every dream, you will find that Freud is right; somewhere there is a wish. There is a wish in the dream to have a heart that's big and beating and healthy in ourselves that remembers and that is alive and capable of the empathy needed to take care of each other. Let's just say, is it asking too much that we be empathic? Sometimes it feels like it is, but the dream didn't think so; the dreamer didn't think so. The dream wished us to be better, to be more whole in our empathy, to have the big heart of the Self which creates an *unus mundus*.

That moves us to the *Final cause*. If we get away from the Final cause as being limited to teleology and the sense of a divine purpose, I'd like to take from Confucian philosophy the all-important idea of *completion*.[12] If you set it as your task to use your extraverted feeling function as my patient did, then to complete it is not only to care about what's happening in your own country or in certain countries you've visited. It also matters in the places you don't think about. To complete it is to make your empathy apply to everything. It's when we arrive at the final cause of a dream that we complete our understanding of why an image that appears in it, even if perfectly acceptable as a portrait of someone's inner truth, can also claim to be speaking accurately to an outer reality as well. The picture of reality that a dream provides does not just emerge when the dream is amplified skillfully in the light of outer events. It has to be strong and arresting yet simple enough to convince us that its purpose is to disclose reality to us. The dream is perched in the transcendent middle ground between subjective and objective ways of perceiving. Diotima, describing to Socrates that place that Love occupies (for her it was between mortal and divine, making Eros a daimon in the Greek hierarchy of consciousnesses) referred to that middle ground as a *metaxy*, which seems to have meant betweenness.[13] As such, it is where the axes of orientation to reality that Jung named space/time

12 See for instance, *The I Ching*, translated by Richard Wilhelm & Cary Baynes, 3rd edition, p. 14 (line text for Hexagram 2, "Six in the third place"). Princeton: Princeton University Press, 1967.

13 James M. Rhodes, "What is the Metaxy?" https://voegelinview.com/what-is-the-metaxy-diotima-and-voegelin/.

and causality/synchronicity[14] intersect. That meeting place, for Diotima, is the ground occupied in the soul by Love, which can scarcely be framed to belong to self alone, but brings self into relationship, however ambivalent, with what is going on in other minds, including in some traditions the mind of God. It is in that liminal place, belonging neither to self nor other, that our minds, led by dreams, stumble upon reality. The access to reality that I am claiming for psyche, at least when in Love, is grounded in the capacity it has to get us to appreciate truth when it is persuasively shown to us, and to make me long for that glimpse when I haven't gotten it. Getting within shouting distance of the truth, which is where dreams like the one I have reported take us, makes us feel complete even when they are not strictly "ours."

As far as I can see, the best philosophical analysis of Aristotle's Four Causes is by an analytic philosopher named Boris Hennig.[15] He says that to understand the Formal cause, you have to understand that for everything, there's a typical change process. That pleases me because I've worked out a trajectory for each of the eight function attitudes that Jung named for us, and the trajectory I have for extraverted feeling—the function-attitude that my patient was mainly engaging—is that it starts at the persona level, with a wonderful capacity for *validating*, which can be a cheerleading that doesn't really have very much substance to it, but can move at the ego level to something a little more fundamental, which is a real *affirming*. My patient has a tremendous capacity, which he's developed over time, to affirm. But there's kind of a *jouissance* to the function that only comes at the level of what Jung calls the self, which is a genuine *relating* to the *unus mundus*, and it seems to me that that would have been the completion that both of us, prating about the lack of caring in the world and in our government in our time, really needed this dream to help us connect with the real suffering then going on in West Africa, which was being neglected because America and probably many other countries were so busy keeping it out of their territories. That was a very obscene moment in the history of international empathy that my patient and I both recognized.

So with homage to Aristotle and to Hennig's beautiful discussion of the Four Causes, I'm saying that what I do as a Jungian analyst working with a dream is to ask what is responsible *for* the dream and what is responsible *in* the dream? I ask, Because of what did this dream occur? I look for what makes it matter and what makes it formally accurate in encoding the core situation. I am curious about what causes it to be set in motion and what makes it be capable of

14 C. G. Jung, "Synchronicity: An Acausal Connecting Principle" in The Collected Works of C. G. Jung, vol. 8 (Princeton: Princeton University Press, 1952/1960), para. 981.

15 B. Hennig, *Aristotle's Four Causes* (Berlin: Peter Lang Inc., 2018).

taking the dreamer somewhere he or she needs to go. Framed in that way, the dream is *wirklichkeit* in the sense that it works, and I try to notice how it's doing that against my resistance to seeing it as real enough to worry about. Following Aristotle, as I read him, I think we can do the work of analysis if we keep asking ourselves to find the dream's causes, its *aitia.* Then we get closer to answering "Why is this real?"

[Applause]

Questioner #1: I was fascinated about your immediate response to that dream because we're all schooled to think an elephant is a symbol of the self.

Beebe: Yes, that's right.

Questioner #1: That's where I would have immediately leapt. So what was it that made you realize it was bigger than both of you and not a run-of-the mill dream?

Beebe: Jung gave back the Formal and Final causes to a culture too busy with the Material and the Efficient causes. Following that broadening out of lines of inquiry, I think, why elephant? Where is an elephant from? Even butchered elephants don't end up in trees. Why is this elephant there? That shouldn't be like that. It was resonance to *the failure of the form,* or the attack on the form that hit me. When I first talked about this dream, an analyst colleague said the elephant's the symbol of the Self. But you see, where does that get us? I mean, that's one way of not talking about the reality of the elephant. If we accept too quickly that it's a symbol of the Self, we may miss the particularity of this dream situation. It evokes a stage of the Self that my patient's heart and his wholeness would ripen into. It was moving him toward that, but isn't it still more interesting to engage with the real elephant? I think it is. That's what I'm trying to get at. Why is this real? The Self could mean a lot of things, including, why in the world, if it means all these things, would you ever call it the Self?

Questioner #2: I admire your earlier reference to Aristotle's conception, but I wonder what is your interpretation of *unus mundus*? I think this is very connected with your trial to find what is real, if we should understand the mind as a capsule that is not connected with the world.

Beebe: *Unus mundus* is the mystery of the greater conjunction. In *Mysterium Coniunctionis*,[16] Jung talks about the stages of the conjunction. The first is a *unio mentalis*, and that's something I see in people at certain stages of therapy when they can think about their psychological experiences and interpret them. That's good as far as it goes, but usually there's a failure to *embody* that insight and enact it in an intrinsic way in their lives. The addition of the *body* is needed to make the conjunction complete. Spirit, soul, and body, you eventually need those three things to come together. That's still a very good formulation. When that occurs, the philosopher's stone is being constructed. Then, the mystery is that the thing which has brought itself together joins in the hidden sympathy of all things: a Stoic idea. That's the *unus mundus*, and I feel that my patient and I were at that point in talking about this dream. We were mutually trying to connect with the *unus mundus* and, in the face of that effort, the *aporia* for us of Africa, a vast continent, was itself the elephant in the consulting room. My patient and I both had to realize that our *unus mundus* had big holes in it. I think that's true of so many of us. Certainly it was true of Jung. He talked about the *unus mundus*; but obviously, when he was dealing with others too far from his own European experience, his horizon didn't stretch that far. Some of the things that he said about the indigenous people, for instance, that he encountered in Africa were horribly Kiplingesque and certainly poorly examined.

I take from this that it isn't that easy, even with a theory of the collective unconscious, to make the connections that constellate the *unus mundus*. It remains difficult for relatively integrated people who have done a lot of inner work and believe in wholeness. On the other hand, when we can establish a true connection between what brings one's self together and what unites the world,

16 C. G. Jung, *Mysterium Coniunctionis*, The Collected Works of C. G. Jung, vol. 14, (Princeton: Princeton University Press, 1977), pp. 469–477.

it is astonishingly gratifying. Making such connections is what I'm trying to practice every day now. Some days I get there, and some days I don't, but I'm grateful for a chance to visit other countries and do analysis in person and at a distance with people in different cultures. My patient, too, is vitally interested in the world, as so many people are today. Lots of people are trying to take their personal integration to the next step, but I would have to say, speaking as one of them, that this is a work in progress, not an achieved opus like the Philosopher's Stone. We're trying to complete it, and if we don't, surely, we'll hang separately up our different trees. I think that is where we are right now and what my patient's dream was really telling us.

References

Bateson, G. *Mind and Nature: A Necessary Unity.* New York: Bantam, 1988.

Bateson, G. *Steps to an Ecology of Mind.* Chicago: University of Chicago Press, 1972.

Beebe, J. & Falzeder, E. *The Question of Psychological Types: Correspondence of C.G. Jung and Hans Schmid-Guisan, 1915–1916*. Princeton: Princeton, N.J., 2012.

Berry, P. "What Is the Matter with Mother?" Lecture #190, September 2, 1976. Kings Lynn, UK: The Guild of Pastoral Psychology, 1978.

Contagion. Motion picture, directed by S. Soderbergh, 2011.

Falzeder, E. Personal Communication, 2019.

Green, A. "The dead mother." In *On Private Madness*. Translated by Katherine Aubertin. London: Hogarth Press, 1986.

Hennig, B. *Aristotle's Four Causes.* Berlin: Peter Lang Inc, 2018.

Hillman, J. & Shamdasani, S. *Lament of the Dead: Psychology after Jung's* Red Book. New York: W. W. Norton, 2013.

The I Ching, translated by Richard Wilhelm & Cary Baynes, 3rd edition, p. 14 (line text for Hexagram 2, "Six in the third place"). Princeton: Princeton University Press, 1967

Jung, C. G. *Wirklichkeit der Seele. Anwendungen und Fortschritte der neueren Psychologie.* Zurich: Rascher, 1934.

Jung, C. G. "Synchronicity: An Acausal Connecting Principle" in Collected Works, vol. 8. Princeton: Princeton University Press, 1960.

Jung, C. G. *Mysterium coniunctionis.* Collected Works, vol. 14. Princeton: Princeton University Press, 1977.

Jung, C. G. *Liber Novus = The Red Book.* New York & London: W. W. Norton, 2009.

Khan, L. Personal communication, 1993.

Margolick, D. *Strange Fruit: The Biography of a Song.* Philadelphia: Running Press, 2000.

Natali, C. "*Aitia* in Plato and Aristotle. From Everyday Language to Technical Vocabulary." In *Aitia I: Les quatres causes: origines et interpretation*, edited by C. Viano, C. Natali, and M. Zingano. Leuven: Peeters, 2013.

Psychic Reality. https://www.encyclopedia.com/psychology/dictionaries-thesauruses-pictures-and-press-releases/psychic-reality Consulted October 30, 2019.

Rhodes, James M. "What is the Metaxy," https://voegelinview.com/what-is-the-metaxy-diotima-and-voegelin/, consulted July 11, 2020.

Rolfe, E. *Encounter with Jung.* Boston: Sigo Press, 1989.

Stephens, S. L. *C. G. Jung and the Dead: Visions, Active Imagination and the Unconscious Terrain.* London & New York: Routledge, 2020.

CHAPTER 2

Archetypal Patterns of Imagination: Social Imaginaries

Ilona Błocian

Abstract

Jung was not particularly strongly connected with the perspective of social thought, although the main categories of his conception undoubtedly often have the adjective "collective"; they are categories of unconscious and the archetype considered as a structure of a collective nature: for example, as "categories of collective imagination". In this term, he referred to the philosophical history of the conceptions of the unconscious as a sphere conditioning all the significant processes of reality and the sociological approaches of the French school of "collective representations," which influenced his notion of the archetype. There are many dilemmas about the relationship that can occur between a differentiation of collective and social levels. A lot of Jung's writings refer directly to the issues of social thought, especially, but not only, those concentrated in the volume *Civilization in Transition*, for example, statements from his interviews, notes from meetings with him (they present extensive material of Jung's comments to current situations and events of a socio-political nature, such as totalitarianism, authoritarianism, political leadership) or the issue of contemporary forms of religiosity. Many of these writings present a special relationship between the individual and society, the archetype and the historical, social dimensions, mass processes and collective imagination, in which archetypal images operate. Jung is not the only researcher who has demonstrated a deep understanding of the problem of collective/social imagination. Similar grasps can be found, among others, in the conceptions of Gilbert Durand or Charles Taylor. The first examines the anthropological structures of these images, the second, changes in social imaginaries and their characteristics. The juxtaposition of these forms of reflection opens the way to understanding a particular power of collective imagination.

Keywords

collective imagination, social imagination, archetype, unconscious, social imaginary, anthropological structures, Jung, Durand, Taylor

 | DOI:10.1163/9789004468757_004

1 Jung and Social Writings

Jung's conception is connected with some kind of social perspective; however, its philosophical, anthropological, and psychological character rather dominate his thinking. There are arguments[1] to reconstruct social aspects of his thinking: first, many texts clustered in *Civilization in Transition*[2] are devoted to the social dimension of human life, analyses, interpretations, commentaries on social events; and the contemporary world, including forming of mass culture, society, and human being.[3] Second, his main categories as the unconscious and archetype have collective character and are involved with a dilemma of connection between "collectivity" and "society" notions. Third, whole psycho-therapeutic efforts and practices of Jung were impossible without an understanding of the social contemporary world, as he had himself underlined.

There are a lot of Jung's texts on social issues, not only those gathered in the tenth volume. Sometimes, when interpreting a problem about other issues, for example, Joyce's prose, he makes extensive references to the situation of the modern individual and the changes of the modern social world. The perspectives in his grasps often overlap, and the process of socio-cultural change and its relation with the formation of the human psyche is one of the most important.

The dilemma of the relationship between the terms *collective* and *social* in his view is also very difficult to solve because the latter is defined in various

---

1 There are researchers admitting the important role of socio-political aspects of Jung's writings—cf. I. Progoff, *Jung's Psychology and its Social Meaning*, (New York: Grove Press, 1955); idem, *The Death and Rebirth of Psychology. An Integrate Evaluation of Freud, Adler, Jung and Rank and the Impact of Their Culminating Insight of Modern Man*, (New York: The Julian Press, 1956); R. Gray, *Archetypal Explorations: An Integrative Approach to Human Behavior*, (Hove-New York: Routledge, 1996); A. Samuels, *The Political Psyche*, (London, New York: Routledge, 1993); V. W. Odajnyk, *Jung and Politics: The Political and Social Ideas of C. G. Jung*, (New York: New York University Press, 1976); R. Noll, *The Jung Cult. Origins of Charismatic Movement*, (Princeton-New Jersey: Princeton University Press, 1994); R. Main, *In a secular age: Weber, Taylor and Jung*, [*in:*] *Contemporary Influences of C. G. Jung's Thought*, eds. I. Błocian, A. Kuźmicki, (Leiden, Boston: Brill, 2018); idem, *The Rupture of Time: Synchronicity and Jung's Critique of Modern Western Culture*, (Hove: Brunner-Routledge, 2004); J. R. Staude, *From depth psychology to depth sociology: Freud, Jung, and Lévi-Strauss*, "Theory and Society" 3, 1976, nr 3;

2 C. G. Jung, *Civilization in Transition*, trans. R. F. C. Hull, [in:] Idem, The Collected *Works* (CW), v. 10, (Princeton: Princeton University Press, 1970).

3 Cf. I. Błocian, *C. G. Jung. Myśl i krytyka społeczna* (*C. G. Jung – Social Thought and Critique*), (Wrocław: Wydawnictwo Uniwersytetu Wrocławskiego, 2018).

ways. Since I dealt with this dilemma in another work,[4] I will mention only some of the most important statements.

What is social can be defined in the context of human life with other people within the framework of "agreement, competition, cooperation, exchange."[5] If one understands "social" in these terms, the archetypal structures in Jung's conception are probably just such patterns of references to the network of interpersonal relations. What is social can, however, be understood differently, for example, in the perspective of the formation of links between elements within social structures, their changes, and their impact on the life of the individual and the community ("networks of relationships and dependencies").[6] In view of the relationship level outlined in this way, it seems that the term *collective* rather than *social* is more justified in Jung's conception. Considering this dilemma, one can specify that in Jung's conception, *collective* and *social* overlap in the first sense; in the second, they are already definitely different.

The use of the term collective was also influenced by several other factors: among others Jung's reluctance to the mass processes that he observed, the creation of mass culture, mass societies, and mass man. These were processes that aroused both resentment and in-depth criticism of which many elements harmonize with the criticism of mass culture, "cultural industry," "cybernetic" society and the one-dimensional man known from the writings of the Frankfurt School, including Erich Fromm, Theodor Adorno, and Max Horkheimer, Herbert Marcuse, but also Hanna Arendt. In the case of Jung and Fromm, this social criticism most strongly emphasizes the impact that general social processes have on the psyche of the modern individual, although it does not close only in pointing to these consequences. These are complex and multi-faceted social critics in psychoanalysis and in its branches. They include a strong emphasis on the human situation in society and mass culture.

The term *collective* of the two main categories of their own conception, that is, unconsciousness and archetype, has strong and deep consequences for Jung's analysis. These terms actually come from the language of philosophy, not psychology. Such a heritage is also very important for their functioning in his conception because there are numerous ties between them and other areas of Jung's references. These concepts are also very strongly linked to each other. Changes in the understanding of the collective unconsciousness that occur with the evolution and development of the Jung conception, affect the way the category of archetype is expressed, which is largely a necessary process

4 Ibidem.

5 Z. Bauman, *Socjologia*, trans. J. Łoziński, (Poznań: Zysk i S-ka, 1996), 14.

6 Ibidem, 21.

because the last term is most often understood as a structural carrier of significance and phenomena related to the first. The very concept of the archetype is a multidimensional category; its formation took a long time, and it takes place in many texts and research perspectives in Jung's writings (psychological, psycho-sociological evolutional, anthropological, philosophical ones).

1.1 Ideae Principlales, *Archetypal Forms, Archetypal Light, Intellectus Archetypus*

This concept also had a distant and very extensive philosophical history. Jung himself mentions many related concepts or those from which he drew inspiration. Sometimes he even compared his notion to the Platonic ideas, however, making some reservation. This comparison, however, can immediately make us aware of numerous interpretation problems related to the relation of concepts (Olejarczyk 2018; Błocian - in print).[7] Ideas and archetype combine essence, generality, and hierarchical arrangement; ideas guide the development of reality, archetypes—first, the human psyche, then the psyche of the species and only in the late Jung's shots—they concern the most important processes of reality. These notions differ in the organic-biological anchoring archetypes in instincts and negative aspects related to archetypal meanings. The next sources mentioned by Jung himself are Augustinian *ideas principales*, which transfer meaning to the ideas inherent in God's mind conditioning the acts of creation[8] ("unchanging and unshakable forms"). This level is maintained by the concepts of "Archetypal Forms" (*Corpus Hermeticum*) or "archetypal light" (Ireneus of Lyon).[9] This strongly influences the ways of understanding the concept and its semantic significance itself in the Renaissance philosophy of P. della Mirandola (archetype as a pattern according to which God creates beings; Mirandola 1966), as well as the next fate of the concept becoming increasingly binding on the level of *intellectus archetypus* forming

7 A. Olejarczyk, *Collective Memory and Common Imagination – Archetypes in the Perspective of the Theory of Sign,* [in:] I. Błocian, A. Kuźmicki (eds.), *Contemporary Influences of C. G. Jung's Thought,* (Leiden-Boston: Brill, 2018). I. Błocian, *The Archetype Notion and Philosophical Approaches to the Unconscious,* [in:] L. Artamoshkina, I. Błocian, K. Morawski, *The Unconscious, Image and Politics* – [in print].

8 St. Augustine calls ideas "certain main, unshakeable and unchanging forms or principles of things. They are not formed themselves and are therefore eternal and always alike, and divine reason contains them. And while they themselves do not rise or die, according to them—as it is said—everything that can arise and perish, as well as everything that arises and dies" - St. Augustine, *De diversis quaestionibus octoginta tribus. Księga osiemdziesięciu trzech kwestii,* trans. M. Olszewski, (Kęty: Antyk, 2012), 82–83.

9 I wrote about it in the text "The Archetype of the Trickster in C. G. Jung's Writings," *Studia Religiologica,* 53 (3) 2020, s. 227–238.

a connection between human being and creator (German: *urbildlicher Verstand*), which can be found in many representatives of modern philosophy, in the philosophy of I. Kant (Paż 2019)[10] and also influencing its contemporary twentieth-century ways of functioning, for examplein M. Scheler's conception. The philosophical fate of the concept of archetype is therefore complex and refers most often to either a priori forms involved in the creation of the world or the human ability to think through these forms and capture them in transcending the level of empirical data. This heritage goes far beyond the psychological and anthropological horizon. It refers to the structures that create and organize the whole of reality.

Borrowing this concept from the philosophical dictionary, Jung combined it with the meanings of terms from other fields of knowledge and strongly contrasting with philosophical sources. This resulted in a tension which in his concept determines the dynamics of use, understanding, and interpretation.

1.2 *Instinct, Pattern of Behavior*

He often pointed to the connection of the archetype with instinctive ground. However, the archetype is sometimes understood as located on an instinctive pattern and constituting the psychological equivalent of a biological pattern of behavior. Sometimes, however, he recognized the archetype as fulfilling the role of a tool for blocking and inhibiting the pattern of instinct in phenomena such as sacrificial process or asceticism and thus becoming a tool for the constitution of the spirit. In this view, the archetype, contrary to the philosophical lineage, has a strong biological location; it comes from instinct because, according to Jung, there is no other source of life force. This way of understanding therefore falls within the anthropological and psychological horizon ("phylogenetic relic"),[11] and at certain stages of the development of his concept Jung strongly marked this evolutionary-psychological perspective.

For example, in the *Mind and Earth*, he defines:

10 "Important elements of this genesis [transcendentalism - IB] were articulated expressis verbis by Kant himself in the second edition of the *Critique of Pure Reason* (1787) in the form of a known but interpretively constantly underestimated distinction between two types of view: absolute referred to as intuitus originarius (B 72), based in the infinite intellectus, **intellectus archetypus** (B 723) and relative/contingent view, intellectus derivativus (B 72), whose base is the finite intellect" - B. Paź, *Transcendentalia czy transcendentalizm* (*Transcendentalia or transcendentalism*), [in:] http://www.ptta.pl/km/index.php?id=symp_str_7 - Accessed: 5.08.2019; [bold mine I. B.] The genesis of transcendentalism, the author indicates, indicating the probability, already in medieval scholasticism (*Scientia Dei*).

11 C. G. Jung, *Mind and Earth* (1927), [in:] CW 10, [&59], 33.

> Archetypes are systems of readiness for action, and at the same time images and emotions. They are inherited with the brain structure—indeed, they are its psychic aspect. They represent, on the one hand, a very strong instinctive conservatism, while on the other hand they are the most effective means conceivable of instinctive adaptation. They are thus, essentially, the chthonic portion of the psyche, if we may use such an expression—that portion through which the psyche is attached to nature, or in which its link with the earth and the world appears at its most tangible;[12]

and in another fragment: "[Archetypes are-I.B.] roots which the psyche has sunk not only in the earth in the narrower sense but in the world in general."[13]

Nevertheless, the very concept of collective unconsciousness and the concept of archetype tended towards philosophical approaches, although it must be admitted that Jung attempted to combine them with the evolutionary one.

1.3 *Categories of Collective Imagination,* **Représentations Collectives, Mentalité Pre-logique,** *Elementary Ideas*

Another type of source derived from anthropological and social approaches additionally increased the complexity of Jung's concept of the archetype, and it was a factor of very high significance. He often referred to the notion of the collective representations of H. Hubert and M. Mauss, and one of the most frequently used was the French term *participation mystique* of L. Lévy-Bruhl illustrating the state of the non-functioning division of the subject and object of unconscious cognition (however, in the conception of the French anthropologist, the basis was a social rather than a psychological one). Lévy-Bruhl described mystic participation as: "Sharing and participation persons and things associated in collective representation frame."[14] It can be understood as spiritual identity of associated phenomena. The whole reality is conceived as a continuum of spiritual forces. It is a principle of *post hoc ergo propter hoc* that rules the mind operation—things are associated if they are accompanied by each other.

The French anthropologist also used the concept of collective represetations. The area of ethnopsychological interests developed around primary hopes for

---

12 Ibidem, 31.

13 Ibidem.

14 L. Lévy-Bruhl, *Czynności umysłowe w społeczeństwach pierwotnych* (*Fonctions mentales dans les sociétés inférieures*), (Warszawa: PWN, 1992), 102. Idem, *How natives think*, (New York: Washington Square Press, 1966).

finding general rules governing collective thinking and imagination. Hence, it has become (and the notion of mystical participation) for Jung one of the sources of inspiration always indicated in his own understanding of the archetype. The unconscious state is therefore often characterized as a condition in which the cognitive attitude has the character of mystical participation, and there is no division into the subject and object of cognition. For Lévy-Bruhl, this was an archaic cognitive attitude associated with pre-logical thinking [*mentalité pre-logique*] (both the notions of his conception were strongly criticized as an attempt to isolate some primeval mind ruling the inferior society [*mentalité de la société inférieure*]). It can be concluded that the main categories of Jung's conception through these anthropological and social sources obtain a strong load of information about the presumed functioning of the mentality governing the collective life and areas of culture of the traditional community. These laws set collective ideas that dynamize collective imagination. Jung's interpretation is an archetypal one. Lévy-Bruhl defined collective images as: "common for the members of a given social group, transmitted from generation to generation, impose to each individual, induce a sense of respect or fear in them and adoration to their object."[15] They are based on polysynthetic perceptions, affects, affective memory, and impulses to act. Myth forms images of collective representation, and it is based on mystic participation.

1.4 *Evolutions of Archetype Notion in Jung's Writings*

The concept has a long history and concerns the development of various fields of science. In addition, its very depiction in Jung's writings in the space of the long evolution of its history changed. Many stages of the domination of some of its forms and meanings can be distinguished. The initial terms used by Jung are: *imago, imagines*; dominants soon replaced by the term *archetype*, which for a long time will refer to the biological concept, and Jung understood it as a hereditary, psychological equivalent of pattern of behavior. When juxtaposed with the significance of the archetype as a category of collective imagination, this creates the thought of an unconscious structure having the character of an instinctive behavioral pattern, which at the collective level forms certain groups or sets that are an expression of the biological basis of the species' life on the one hand, and the basic rule on the other form of collective ideas and behaviors. They reflect the most general patterns of human experience at the level of life of the species, individual, and community. Jung introduces a fairly clear division into archetypes *per se* or *in se* because, returning to the

15 Ibidem, 31.

philosophical sources of the concept, he mentioned—more than once—Kantian *noumen* (*in se*), and its phenomenal manifestation, which is the archetypal image presenting specificity of a given cultural environment and time (archetypal image). Ranges of definitions are becoming more and more powerful because Jung defines the archetype as a process in late period writings. He already associates it with the psychoid aspect and transgression into non-mental and material processes. It happens that he calls it a certain force, and even "strength in itself." The noumena character of archetype means that its sources are outside the space-time order. They are the structures conditioning the creation of the order of reality processes, taking part in biological and psychological processes, participating at the levels of anthropological structures and finally, material reality processes. In such a comprehensive view, archetypes are some superstructures of reality, just as the unconscious eventually becomes the matrix and the foundation of reality processes, also located in the material sphere outside the space-time order and beyond direct sensual perceptibility, although affecting the observable features of the processes. The archetype itself is sometimes defined in Jung's writings as a process; it is not so much a particularly important act in which the meaning of which it is conveyed is manifested, but a process of experience resulting from the semantic pattern. Finally, it is sometimes called a force that presses to some type of action.

Archetypal patterns operate with particular efficiency and beyond critical awareness, thus forming the invisible frameworks of collective and social imagination. On the other hand, its features create the most important matrix of human self-understanding and shaping the social and political life, as well as the choices that a human being makes. Individual and collective dimensions are closely connected in this archetypal approach, which determines the effectiveness of collective imagination. The most common archetype definitions that highlight its anthropological character are strongly coupled with a theoretical background in the Jung's social writings. The archetype is thus a model of experience that maintains an evolutionary-hereditary dimension. It directs human collective behavior and social history. It is characteristic that this approach definitely dominates in social writings, unlike those on religion, religious symbolism, or philosophical issues. Social writings abound in anthropological approaches to the archetype and the unconscious. The connection between "structure of the brain" and "omnipresent spirit," between what is inherited, and the cultural development of the human spirit could be examples of "anthropological-social" relation.

> This unconscious, buried in the structure of the brain and disclosing its living presence only through the medium of creative fantasy, is the

> suprapersonal unconscious. It comes alive in the creative man, it reveals itself in the vision of the artist, in the inspiration of the thinker, in the inner experience of the mystic. The suprapersonal unconscious, being distributed throughout the brain-structure, is like an all-pervading, omnipresent, omniscient spirit. It knows man as he always was, and not as he is at this moment; it knows him as myth. For this reason, also, the connection with the suprapersonal or collective unconscious means an extension of man beyond himself [...].[16]

The weakening of the connection with the unconscious results in a sense of no rooting, which is recognized as very characteristic for the present day: "Alienation from the unconscious and from its historical conditions spells rootlessness."[17]

Clearer examples of the connection between the anthropological, evolutional dimensions and the a priori structures governing the human psyche are also provided by other social writings scattered in various volumes of Jung's collected works, for example, *Analytical Psychology and Education*, dated 1926/69 (CW 17). It seems that these connections are very characteristic and appear in most terms and attempts to define the notion of the unconscious, which also affects this coupling in the concept of archetype. Sometimes the latter is described very clearly as both an "inherited system of psychic adaptation"[18] and a tool of "becoming a spirit." It also happens that the a priori and evolutional dimension is directly combined in the archetype and the unconscious definitions.

> This impersonal layer of the psyche I have termed the COLLECTIVE UNCONSCIOUS—"collective" because it is not an individual acquisition but is rather the functioning of the inherited brain structure, which in its broad outlines is the same in all human beings, and in certain respects the same even in mammals. The inherited brain is the product of our ancestral life. It consists of the structural deposits or equivalents of psychic activities which were repeated innumerable times in the life of our ancestors. Conversely, it is at the same time the ever-existing a priori type and author of the corresponding activity.[19]

---

16 C. G. Jung, *The Role of the Unconscious (1918)*, [in:] CW 10 [&13], 10.

17 CW 10, [&103], 49.

18 CW [338}, 17, 172.

19 CW 17 [&207], 101.

In a contemporary form of a continuation of Jung's thought, in Gilbert Durand's conception, archetypes are understood in a special way, paying particular attention to their accumulating in human and species development—they are "prototypes" but also "settlements." They create a kind of pre-rationality ordering experience; they act between anthropological structures of man and the environment of his life process. Thus, they are the basis for all forms of ordering, including thought and conceptual sphere—the archetype is a kind of *ante rem* in an idea.

> We choose as a hypothesis of work that there is a simple coexistence [*concomitance* - I.B.] between body movements, nerve centers and symbolic representations.[20]

Images form types: schizomorphic (heroic), synthetic (dramatic) and mystical (anti-phrase), in some sequential orderings in its isotopic classification based on the conception of anthropological structures. The same relation (image-archetype-anthropological martix [unconscious]) is highlighted in Jung's conception. The archetypes are here the structures themselves mediating between psyche and environment.

2 Archetype and Civilization: Unconscious and Imaginary

In the works on social issues collected in the book *Civilization in Transition* and many others, it can be traced to not only certain fixed sets of meanings of symbolic and imaginal formations, but also specific aspects of archetypes in the socio-historical environment of a given culture and time, in a specific *hic et nunc*.

Archetype, although its evolutional character is not an "inherited idea,"

> It should on no account be imagined that there are such things as inherited ideas. Of that there can be no question. There are, however, innate possibilities of ideas, a priori conditions for fantasy-production, which are somewhat similar to the Kantian categories.[21]

In *The Undiscovered Self*, Jung states that no European stands above the "shadow of Europe." It is such an element of heritage that is active in shaping the minds, and more broadly, in the formation of the psyche of individuals

20 G. Durand, *Les structures anthropologiques de l'imaginaire. Introducton à l' archétypologie générale*, (*The Anthropological Structures of the Imaginary*), ed. XI, (Paris: Dunod, 1992), 51.

21 CW 10 [&14], 10.

in a given cultural perspective. In this sense, the archetype has a social dimension in the process of its updating in relation to the individual and to the collective transformation of the historical process. Earlier, in 1918 Jung described some features of specific German unconscious: "We still have a genuine barbarian in us who is not to be trifled with, and whose manifestation is no comfort for us and not a pleasant way of passing the time. Would that people could learn the lesson of this war!"[22] And he considered them as very different from Jewish ones.

For the understanding of the role of collective imagination in the social writings of Jung one can use the tools of some others' conceptions from the social philosophy areas, for example, as those of Ch. Taylor's notion of social imagery;[23] however, it cannot be traced to any anthropological structures. Some of the features of social imagery are significantly near the ideas of Jung in my opinion but not in the sense of an anthropological basis. There is a question of the closeness of these two conceptions to the relation of the "enchanted world" in the Weberian frame,[24] still excluding from this the anthropological and psychological dimension."Taylor offers no hope of an alternative to modernity or a return to what he calls an 'enchanted world' view. Instead, he explains how modernity is itself a religious expression."[25] In a certain meaning it is the merit of the collective/social imaginaries notion."The social imaginary is not a set of 'ideas'; rather it is what enables, through making sense of, the practices of a society."[26]

When one tries to use this way of thinking in a Jungian context, social imagination can be conceived as a sphere penetrating very important dimensions of understanding, choices, motivation, and action in an individual-social context. The basic forms here are the archetypal patterns and their activity in collectivity in Jungian terms, because they are the structurization of the social and natural environment, and their functioning is unconscious, more fundamental, and much quicker than conscious operation of consideration and

22 CW 10, [&19], 14.

23 On the relations between Jung's and Taylor's conceptions – cf. R. Main, *In a Secular Age...*, op. cit.

24 R. Main, *In a Secular Age....*; E. Kwiatkowska,, *Ponowne "zaczarowanie". Dwie nieświadomości, ("Enchantment" again. Two unconsciousnesses)*, [in:] eds. I. Błocian, R. Saciuk, *Nieświadomość to odrębne królestwo* (*The unconscious is a separate kingdom*), (Toruń: Wydawnictwo Adam Marszałek, 2003).

25 J. Rothfork, *Modern Social Imarinaries by Charles Taylor*, "Rocky Mountain Review of Language and Literature" 2006, DOI: 10.2307/4143907.

26 Ch. Taylor, *On Social Imaginary*, https: //www.researchgate.net /publication/ 265245575 _On_Social_Imaginary – [Accessed: - 3.05.2019], 1.

rational choice. One can assume that it can be referred to some extent to the conception of the understanding and self-understanding in social behavior of P. Winch: "However, ideas cannot be detached from their social context: the relationship between the idea and the context is an internal relation."[27] In a social context that is a system of meanings that is established and rules in our ways of associating and understanding; in Jung's anthropological grasp these are the specific logic of inner-outer patterns and structures.

In Taylor's or Winch's conceptions there is no place to idea of an evolutional basis; however, the attention is focused on imagination (Taylor) or socially absorbed, established rules of associating data (Taylor, Winch).[28]

Winch draws attention: "The ways in which people imagine their social existence, how they adapt to others, how things are going on between people; it's also expectations that usually meet; and the deeper normative concepts and images underlying them."[29]

In this context imagination plays a central role in social or collective action. Imagination as a pre-critical relation between mind and outer reality is expressed through images, symbols, and myths, which seems to be crucial also in social communication. When researching people's actions, one should understand the symbolic-mythical imagery, which means "how people 'imagine' their social environment, which they often express not in theoretical terms but through images, stories and legends."[30] They form convictions, unwritten "laws" that rule our behavior to a more extensive level than we can be conscious of.[31] In Taylor's terms these are "convictions shared by large groups, by entire societies,"[32] ways of adaptations, expectations, and "deeper normative conceptions and images."[33] For Winch it would be "the ways of thinking embodied in institutions [...] determining how members of societies behave."[34] But Taylor

27 P. Winch, *Idea nauki o społeczeństwie i jej związek z filozofią*, trans. B. Chwedeńczuk, (Warszawa: Oficyna Naukowa 1995, 109). (*The Idea of Social Science and its Relation to Philosophy*, London : Routledge 1990, II ed.),

28 Winch writes referring to Weberian conception : "The *verstehen* operation is assuming *Sinn*. And *Sinn* assumes the existence of socially established rules" – Winch, op. cit., 118.

29 Taylor, *Nowoczesne imaginaria społeczne*, trans. A. Puchejda, K. Szymaniak, (Kraków: Znak 2010), 37. (*Modern Social Imaginaries*, (Durham-London: Duke University Press, 2004)).

30 Taylor, *Nowoczesne*, 37.

31 T. J. Scheff, *Schizofrenia jako ideologia* (*Schizophrenia as Ideology*), [in:] ed. K. Jankowski, *Przełom w psychologii* (*The Breakthrough in Psychology*), trans. K. Jankowski, A. Kołyszko, P. Kołyszko, (Warszawa: Czytelnik, 1978), pp. 243–245.

32 Taylor, *Nowoczesne*, 37.

33 Ibidem.

34 Winch, op. cit., 128.

described them as a "largely unstructured and unarticulated understanding of whole our situation"[35] and as a "background knowledge,"[36] in which "particular features of our world reveal its meaning"[37] with an "unlimited, indefinite nature."[38] However, the features of indeterminacy he also defines to some extent as a structuralized "internalized map of social space."[39] The character of background, the partly indistinct, partly unseen sphere of confrontation of the human mind with external, social reality can also be called, in Jung's term, "unconscious." However it is not only an indistinct medium between the mind and reality but a basic substructure of social actions. Winch notices that even "formal systems owe their lives only to the fact that their roots are rooted in real relationships with flesh and blood."[40]

For Taylor the imaginary supports the feeling that something is legitimate, "a sense of legitimacy" in ordering rules in the social sphere."This is a common understanding of issues, enabling common practices and the emergence of a sense of legitimacy shared by broad social groups."[41]

It introduces a sense of being rooted, some forms of legitimization of acting. The social area comes to be captured as self-transparent, "true" and "evident"; background knowledge "begins to determine the contours of the world."[42] Following R. Barthes and his studies on mythologies, that is myth which makes the social and historical sphere "natural."[43]

The spheres of imaginaries are not under arbitral control of social consciousness; they also are not easily accessible for investigation because they are penetrating all participants of a given culture and constitute the starting point in shaping the process of acquiring it. From that point of view these are the primeval spheres. "People acted as part of the imaginary long before they began to theorize about themselves."[44] It assumes a collective sphere mediating among people, making communication possible. It is historically and socially developed, but still not under conscious control of any individual or

---

35 Taylor, *Nowoczesne*, 39.

36 Here Taylor refers to works of H. Dreyfus, J. Searle, M. Heidegger, L. Wittgenstein, and M. Polanyi – cf. Ibidem, n. 1, 39.

37 Ibidem.

38 Ibidem.

39 Ibidem, 40.

40 Ibidem, 126.

41 Ibidem, 37.

42 Ibidem, 46.

43 R. Barthes, *Mythologies. The Complete Edition with a New Translation*, (New York: Hill and Wang, 2012).

44 Taylor, *Nowoczesne*.

even a group. "The background that gives meaning to every action is therefore wide and deep."[45]

Taylor defines "social imaginaries" as a discourse community technique or paradigm methods for associating data to form a *Gestalt image* or pattern; "It is what enables [narrative or discourse], through making sense of, the practices of a society."[46] The examples of imaginaries are premodern and modern ideas of order, sovereign people, "natural" hierarchy, hierarchical complementary of "organism" state (family, clan, diocese, city, kingdom), moral order.

It seems evident that such a sphere of "wide and deep" imaginary penetrating the basic forms of our social behavior can be, in Jungian terms, interpreted to some extent as collective structures of the unconscious. Sometimes, even the word of the "background" appears: "The collective unconscious forms the dark background against which the adaptive function of consciousness stands out in sharp relief,"[47] or

> One is almost tempted to say that everything of value in the psyche is taken up into the adaptive function, and that everything useless goes to form that inchoate background from which, to the terror of primitive man, menacing shadows and nocturnal spectres detach themselves, demanding sacrifices and ceremonies which to our biologically oriented minds seem futile and meaningless."[48]

In this perspective, collective imagination determines social dimension, although it has an anthropological basis. However, in Jung's grasp the second half of the 20th century brought the imbalance of the unconscious.[49]

For Taylor the social processes of the whole of modernity have multiform expression:

> By modernity I mean that historically unprecedented amalgam of new practices and institutional forms (science, technology, industrial production, urbanization), of new ways of living (individualism, secularization,

45 Ibidem, 42.

46 Rothfork, *Modern Social Imaginaries by Charles Taylor*, 158.

47 Jung, *The Role of the Unconscious,* [in:] CW 10, [14], 11.

48 Ibidem.

49 Sometimes Jung had referred to earlier historical events illustrating the imbalance of the unconscious: "The fact that this whole disturbance or reactivation of the unconscious took place around the year 1800 is, in my view, connected with the French Revolution. This was less a political revolution than a revolution of minds" – CW 10, [&22], p. 16.

> instrumental rationality), and of new forms of malaise (alienation, meaninglessness, a sense of impending social dissolution).[50]

All of the above-mentioned forms of modernity were criticized by Jung in social writings; forms of criticism are also dispersed in a lot of other works too. Science, technology, industry, and instrumental rationality are considered in the frame of lost knowledge of human spiritual needs and the impoverishment of symbolic life. Comfort and well-being can be achieved, but these are only a part of human needs; the barbarization of self-treatment of the individual in mass society ends in epidemics of collective hysteria and psychosis.[51] Instrumental rationality is the most dangerous faculty of the human mind; Jung named it *Déesse Raison* and saw it, similar to the Frankfurt School,[52] as a main tool of authoritarian quasi-rational slavery (although a lot differed in his conception from the theoretical horizon of this school). Processes of mass society, with their main supports of industrialization and urbanization, created a social order of anonymous crowd insane societies (similar to E. Fromm).[53] It seems that health in psychical and socio-psychical spheres is possible in Jungian frames only as a partial opposition to these vectors of social processes development: life in the small communities, rooting in some natural landscapes, some balance between "I" (concentration on self-realization) and "Others" (meaningful social connections). For Jung alienation, meaninglessness, and a sense of impeding social dissolution are not only specific "malaises"; they have a systemic nature.

They are axes of a situation of the contemporary individual constantly moving towards a certain negative goal—the loss of value in the social horizon. Thus, the power of the "logic of large numbers" and human mass management will win.

Taylor considers these processes in a more neutral way. It is caused by the starting perspective, psychological and anthropological in Jung's case[54] and

50 Taylor, *Nowoczesne*, 91.

51 Already in the second decade of the twentieth century he wrote comparing epochs of the fall of Rome and his own epoch: "Our time is fatally reminiscent of that epoch, when again everything was not in order, and again the unconscious burst forth and brought back things immemorially buried. If anything, the chaos of minds was perhaps less pronounced then than it is today" – CW 10, [&22], 16.

52 Th. W. Adorno, M. Horkheimer, *The Dialectic of Enligtenment*, trans. E. Jephcott, (Stanford: Stanford University Press, 2002).

53 E. Fromm, *The Sane Society* (London: Routledge, 1991); idem, *To Have or To Be? The Nature of Psyche* (London: Bloomsbury Publishing PLC, 2013).

54 Jung emphasized very strongly: "The layer of culture, this pleasing patina, must therefore be quite extraordinarily thin in comparison with the powerfully developed layers of the primitive psyche. But it is these layers that form the collective unconscious, together with

socio-philosophical in Taylor's. The important process is a development of the structure of the state in modern times—a lot of social practices aimed at controlling society—these are economic, social, educational, and moral goals. "Society was to be disciplined, but the true social goal was to persuade people the self-discipline;"[55] thus, the "ethics of freedom and mutual benefit" arises.[56] The two main goals of long-term transformation are safety and well-being.

It required the self-discipline and inhibiting the aggression of earlier warrior castes by founding gradually a "society of courtesy," an "ethics of sensitiveness," a "work discipline" or the "idea of self-government" in different areas of social activities. For Taylor the most important is a transformative influence of imaginaries, for Jung—loss of individual value and imbalance of the unconscious producing epidemics and preventing the primary goal—formation of self.

Taylor considers moral laws as underlying political nets of determinations: "The underlying idea of moral order stresses the rights and obligations which we have as individuals in regard to each other, even prior to or outside of the political bond. Political obligations are seen as an extension or application of these more fundamental moral ties."[57] Jung criticizes conventionality, superficiality, and lack of real transformative power of moral conventions. A real ethical sphere is being created in actions and being-in-the world of an individual. Conventions and declaration have only trivial adaptive meanings.

Thus imaginary of mass society consists of images and ideas connected with the cult of a state and a leader ("Father State," "Father-Leader").

3 Summation

Jung was consequently very critical in his notes about the social dimension of his time. One of the examples in his statement in 1924 (published in 1926):

> One can see this clearly enough from the thoughtless expectations which the spiritually immature cherish in regard to "Father State"; and where such misguided yearnings ultimately lead is shown by those countries whose leaders, skilfully exploiting the infantile hopes of the masses by

---

the vestiges of animality that lose themselves in the nebulous abyss of time" – CW 10, [16], 12. These "powerfully developed layers" have evolutionary character: As civilized human beings, we in Western Europe have a history reaching back perhaps 2,500 years. Before that there is a prehistoric period of considerably greater duration" – ibidem.

55 Taylor, *Nowoczesne*, 68.

56 Ibidem, 34.

57 Taylor, *On the Social*, 1.

> suggestion, have actually succeeded in arrogating to themselves the power and authority of the father. Spiritual impoverishment, stultification, and moral degeneracy have taken the place of spiritual and moral fitness, and produced a mass psychosis that can only lead to disaster.[58]

He emphasizes the phenomenon of massification, urbanization, and industrialization, points to many phenomena connected with them, such as the threat of individual value, sense of eradication, increasing susceptibility to quasi-rational surrender. "The tyrannical ideas" question the significance of freedom and the development of the individual at the same time. They induce a necessity to submit to the goals of a state. The characteristic traits of psychological inflation processes are some kind of "old gods" rebellion considered by Jung with big attention as an activation of deep layers of the unconscious sphere ("rustling in the primeval forest of the unconscious").[59] He interpreted it in mythological perspective as a renovation of "paganism"[60] as the cluster of processes connected with two world wars. But even after the second of them Jung observed massively "acts of political retardation": totalitarian claims of states, persecution of some groups:

> Everywhere fantastic revolutions, violent alterations of the map, reversions in politics to medieval or even antique prototypes, totalitarian states that engulf their neighbours and outdo all previous theocracies in their absolutist claims, persecutions of Christians and Jews, wholesale political murder, and finally we have witnessed a light-hearted piratical raid on a peaceful, half-civilized people.[61]

Conflicts, wars, psychic and social imbalance—it "acts on the high pressure of civilization like a cyclone and blows it away."[62] It seems that new structures ordering imagination have to appear. In Jung's view, the most important phenomenon is the mass, processes of massification, its causes and effects.

> Nevertheless, it should be clear to everyone that such a state of degradation can come about only under certain conditions. The most important

58 CW 17, [&159], 70–71.

59 C. G. Jung, *Wotan (1936/46–47)*, [in:] CW 10, [&375], 181.

60 In *Wotan* Jung even quoted Nostradamus: "In Germany shall divers sects arise, Coming very near to happy paganism" – motto, 179.

61 Ibidem [&371].

62 Ibidem, [&389], 186.

> of these is the accumulation of urban, industrialized masses—of people torn from the soil, engaged in one-sided employment, and lacking every healthy instinct, even that of self-preservation. Loss of the instinct of self-preservation can be measured in terms of dependence on the State, which is a bad symptom.[63]

Thus characteristic for the first half of the 20th century are imaginaries of authoritarian leadership (dictatorship; psychology of dictator;[64] types of leadership), cult of a state in totalitarian states, imaginaries of a mass (mass culture; recurrence, standardization) and in the most valuable insight in art—imageries of a kind of ataractic, emotionless eye registrants a flow of events (Joyce).

References

Jung C. G., *Civilization in Transition,* [in:] idem, *The Collected Works,* v. 10, trans. R. F. C. Hull, Princeton University Press, Princeton, 1970 [CW 10].

Jung C. G., *The Role of the Unconscious (1918),* [in:] CW 10.

Jung C. G., *Mind and Earth (1927),* [in:] CW 10.

Jung C. G., *Wotan (1936/46–47),* [in:] CW 10.

Jung C. G., *After the Catastrophe (1945),* [in:] CW 10.

Jung C. G., *The Development of Personality,* [in:] The Collected Works, v. 17, trans. R. F. C. Hull, Princeton University Press, Princeton 1981 [CW 17].

Jung C. G., *Analytical Psychology and Education (1926/69),* [in:] CW 17.

Jung C. G., *O rozwoju osobowości,* trans. R. Reszke, Warszawa: KR, 2015.

Jung C. G., *Psychology of Dictatorship (1938),* [in:] idem, *C. G. Jung Speaking. Interview and Encounters,* eds. W. McGuire, R. F. C. Hull, Princeton: Princeton University Press, 1977.

Jung C. G., *Diagnosing the Dictators (1939),* [in:] idem, *C. G. Jung Speaking,* op. cit.

Adorno Th. W., Horkheimer M., *The Dialectic of Enlightenment,* trans. E. Jephcott. Stanford: Stanford University Press, 2002.

Augustine St., *De diversis quaestionibus octoginta tribus. Księga osiemdziesięciu trzech kwestii,* trans. M. Olszewski, Kęty: Antyk, 2012.

Błocian I., *Pojęcie archetypu na tle filozoficznych ujęć nieświadomości,* [in:] L. Artamoshkina, I. Błocian, K. Morawski, *The Unconscious, Image and Politics* – [in print].

63 Jung, *After the Catastrophe (1945),* [in:] CW 10 [& 413], 200–201.

64 Jung, *Psychology of Dictatorship (1938),* [in:] idem, *C. G. Jung Speaking. Interview and Encounters,* eds. W. McGuire, R. F. C. Hull, (Princeton: Princeton Univerity Press, 1977; idem, *Diagnosing the Dictators (1939),* [in:] idem, *C. G. Jung Speaking,* op. cit.

Błocian I., "The Archetype of the Trickster in C. G. Jung's Writ*ings*", *Studia Religiologica* 53, no. 3 (2020): 233–244.

Błocian I., *C. G. Jung. Myśl i krytyka społeczna* (*C. G. Jung – Social Thought and Critique*), Wrocław: Wydawnictwo Uniwersytetu Wrocławskiego, 2018.

Durand G., *Les structures anthropologiques de l'imaginaire. Introducton à l'archétypologie générale,* ed. XI, Paris: Dunod, 1992.

Fromm E., *The Sane Society,* London: Routledge, 1991.

Fromm E., *To Have or To Be? The Nature of Psyche,* London: Bloomsbury Publishing PLC, 2013.

Gray R., *Archetypal Explorations: An Integrative Approach to Human Behavior,* Hove-New York: Routledge, 1996.

Kwiatkowska E., *Ponowne "zaczarowanie". Dwie nieświadomości,* (*"Enchantment" again. Two unconsciousnesses*), [in:] eds. I. Błocian, R. Saciuk, *Nieświadomość to odrębne królestwo* (*The unconscious is a separate kingdom*), Toruń: Wydawnictwo Adam Marszałek, 2003.

Lévy-Bruhl L., *Czynności umysłowe w społeczeństwach pierwotnych* (*Fonctions mentales dans les sociétés inférieures*), Warszawa: PWN, 1992.

Lévy-Bruhl L., *How natives think,* New York: Washington Square Press, 1966.

Main R., *In a secular age: Weber, Taylor and Jung,* [in:] *Contemporary Influences of C.G. Jung's Thought,* eds. I. Błocian, A. Kuźmicki, Leiden, Boston: Brill, 2018.

Main R., *The Rupture of Time: Synchronicity and Jung's Critique of Modern Western Culture,*. Hove-New York: Brunner-Routledge, 2004.

Mirandola P. della, *Godność człowieka* (*Human Dignity*), [in:] *Filozofia włoskiego odrodzenia* (*The Philosophy of the Italian Renaissance*), ed. A. Nowicki, Warszawa: PWN, 1966.

Noll R., *The Jung Cult. Origins of Charismatic Movement,* Princeton-New Jersey: Princeton University Press, 1994.

Odajnyk V. W., *Jung and Politics: The Political and Social Ideas of C.G. Jung,* New York: New York University Press, 1976.

Olejarczyk A., *Collective Memory and Common Imagination – Archetypes in the Perspective of the Theory of Sign,* [in:] I. Błocian, A. Kuźmicki (eds.), *Contemporary Influences of C.G. Jung's Thought,* Leiden-Boston: Brill, 2018.

Paź B. *Transcendentalia czy transcendentalizm,* - http://www.ptta.pl/km/index.php?id=symp_str_7 – [Accessed: 5.08.2019].

Progoff I., *Jung's Psychology and its Social Meaning,* New York: Grove Press, 1955.

Progoff I., *The Death and Rebirth of Psychology. An Integrate Evaluation of Freud, Adler, Jung and Rank and the Impact of Their Culminating Insight of Modern Man,* New York: The Julian Press, 1956.

Rothfork J., *Modern Social Imaginaries by Charles Taylor,* [in:] "Rocky Mountain Review of Language and Literature" 2006. DOI: 10.2307/4143907.

Samuels A., *The Political Psyche*, London-New York: Routledge, 1993.

Scheff T. J., *Schizofrenia jako ideologia (Schizophrenia as Ideology)*, [in:] ed. K. Jankowski, *Przełom w psychologii (The Breakthrough in Psychology)*, trans. K. Jankowski, A. Kołyszko, P. Kołyszko, Warszawa: Czytelnik, 1978.

Staude J. R., *From depth psychology to depth sociology: Freud, Jung, and Lévi-Strauss*, "Theory and Society" 3, 1976, nr 3;

Taylor Ch., *On the Social Imaginary*, https: //www.researchgate.net/publication /265245575_On_Social_Imaginary – [Accessed: 3.05.2019].

Taylor Ch., *Nowoczesne imaginaria społeczne*, trans. A. Puchejda, K. Szymaniak, Kraków: Znak 2010; [*Modern Social Imaginaries*, Durham-London: Duke University Press, 2004].

Winch P., *Idea nauki o społeczeństwie i jej związek z filozofią*, trans. B. Chwedeńczuk, Warszawa: Oficyna Naukowa 1995; [*The Idea of Social Science and its Relation to Philosophy*, London: Routledge, 1990].

CHAPTER 3

Interpretation Dilemmas Relating to Carl Gustav Jung's Concept in the Context of the Sociological-Anthropological Tradition

Ewa Kwiatkowska

Abstract

Owing to its multidimensional nature, C.G. Jung's concept can be interpreted in a variety of ways, occasionally contradicting each other. The Jungian categories are sometimes used inconsistently and eclectically in disciplines far removed from analytical psychology. This applies in particular to the attractive category of archetype, which is often used without much reflection, without taking into account its unique theoretical background. Attempts to adapt the Jungian categories to social sciences and cultural studies are not justified. Pointing to, on the one hand, naturalistic and on the other, metaphysical consequences of Jung's concept is an effective way of repudiating these attempts.

Placing Jungism in the context of the French School of Sociology and referring to the criticism of Jung's concept by Claude Lévi-Strauss highlight the reasons which make it impossible to consistently use such Jungian categories as "archetype" or "collective unconscious" in social sciences and anthropology. Despite the apparent links between the concept of the collective unconscious and, for example, Émile Durkheim's concept of collective representations or Lucien Lévy-Bruhl's concept of mystical participation (*participation mystique*), the perspectives of Jungism and social sciences are by and large contradictory, and Jungism can be not so much a rival of social sciences in explaining collective phenomena but a unique subject in these sciences.

An analysis of the notion of archetype reveals a connection to features of the *numinosum* category as understood by Rudolf Otto; the process of individuation has features of self-salvation, while the concept of synchronicity has metaphysical qualities. In view of the above, Jung's concept with the accompanying therapeutic practices can be viewed as one of the manifestations of the social process of the shift of religion from primary to secondary institutions and its privatization, a process understood as described by Thomas Luckmann.

At present the Jungian concept and the themes presented in it are also subject to naturalist interpretations (of evolutionary psychology, cognitive science, and

 | DOI:10.1163/9789004468757_005

potentially epigenetics), which, from the point of view of cultural and social sciences, has reductionist consequences.

Therefore, can the Jungian concept be in any way a point of reference for cultural studies today? Can the categories of the collective unconscious and archetype be used as, for example, heuristic tools in these studies?

It seems that an interesting perspective is provided by the distinction between the iconic and the linguistic interpretation of the unconscious as well as by the comparison of Jung's concepts and Lacan's concepts as their paradigmatic examples. Inspired in his concept by the assumptions of Lévi-Strauss' structural anthropology, Lacan implicitly continues Lévi-Strauss's criticism of the assumptions of Jungism.

In Jung's concept the collective unconscious is manifested primarily through symbolic archetypal (matrical) images with a mythopoeic potential. From the point of view of the juxtaposition between the iconic turn and the linguistic turn, this reveals the heuristic significance of the Jungian tradition to culture studies. It is among those that, by raising the value of the symbolic image, have contributed to the development of research into the cultural imaginarium. This significance of the iconic interpretation of the unconscious is recognizable only today, in the context of the iconic turn.

Keywords

Jung, collective unconscious, French School of Sociology, collective representations (*les représentations collectives*), semio-structuralism, Lévi-Strauss, Lacan, iconic versus linguistic interpretation of the unconscious

1 C.G. Jung's Concept in the Light of the Tradition of the French School of Sociology, Lévi-Strauss' Criticism, and Sociology of Religion

The multidimensional nature and long-time development of Jung's concept poses many interpretation dilemmas to contemporary scholars. Depending on their objectives, the scholars stress various aspects of Jungism (from naturalistic through psychological, phenomenological, hermeneutic to metaphysical). From the point of view of social sciences and anthropology of culture, the categories of the collective unconscious, archetype, and archetypal image are a source of many interpretative difficulties. This applies especially to the concept of archetype, which has become part of the colloquial language and is often used in a meaning far removed from the meaning originally attributed to it by Jung. The concept developed within the sphere of Jungian reflection over several decades, moving from "primordial images accumulating experiences of the ancestors" to an "introspectively recognisable form of a priori psychic orderedness."[1]

The way of understanding of the category of archetype depends on the interpretation of the very concept of the unconscious (*das Unbewusste*), and the dimensions which the category combines can be arranged as follows:

- biological dimension (evolutionary dimension);
- psychological dimension (encompassing the concept of the origin of creative processes, dreams, questions of mental disorders), which absorbs other dimensions;
- anthropological dimension (encompassing the question of the collective nature of symbolic and mythical motifs rooted in the unconscious); and
- metaphysical dimension (indicated by the transgressive nature of archetypes), explicated in the concept of synchronicity.[2]

That last dimension makes Jungian psychoanalysis different from other psychoanalytical traditions; it is its distinguishing feature, *differentia specifica*, indicating its non-scholarly nature.

The a priori, formal, and metaphysical nature of the concept of archetype, stressed especially in Jung's late writings, practically excludes its application with all its philosophical connotations in social sciences and humanities. Jung placed his reflections close to the subject matter of these disciplines. Exploring the sphere of the collective unconscious and transformative effectiveness of the symbol, he tackled topics researched in cultural anthropology and other cultural studies, posing questions in a different manner and in this, changing the meaning of some descriptive categories.

The difference between the scientific status of the notion of the collective conscious and the non-scientific notion of the collective unconscious is a starting point for a confrontation between the understanding of the unconscious

---

1 C. G. Jung, *Typy psychologiczne*, trans. R. Reszke, (Warsaw: KR 1997), 463–464 (originally published as *Psychologische Typen*, C. G. Jung, *Gesammelte Werke*, Walter Verlag, 1994); idem, *Wspomnienia, sny, myśli spisane i podane do drukiu przez Anielę Jaffé*, trans. L. Kolankiewicz (Warsaw: Wrota 1993), 40 (originally published as *Erinnerungen, Träume, Gedanken von C.G. Jung*, Zürich - Düsseldorf: Walter Verlag 1993); *idem, Rebis czyli kamień filozofów*, trans. J. Prokopiuk, (Warsaw: PWN, 1989), 523 (originally published as *Synchronizität:Einführung, Schlussfolgerung*, in *Naturerklärung und Psyche*, Zürich: Rascher Verlag, 1952).

2 The dimensions are defined differently by I. Błocian, "Jung and Social Thought: The Undiscovered Self", in *Contemporary Influences of C. G. Jung's Thought*, eds. I. Błocian, A. Kuzmicki (Leiden, Boston: Brill, 2018), 154.

in the sociological-anthropological tradition and in analytical psychology. It has been pointed out that in his concept Jung mixes German idealism and the French sociological theory.[3] This situation is one of the causes of misinterpretations of the Jungian reflection and use of the notion of archetype (often understood colloquially in any case) as a notion explaining cultural phenomena. The difference between the scientific status of the notion of collective representations (*les représentations collectives*) and the non-scientific notion of the collective unconscious is a starting point for a discussion about how Jung's concept is situated with regard to the sociological-anthropological tradition. The very term of the collective unconscious coined by Jung is somewhat misleading because of the use of the word "collective," which seemingly draws on the term collective representations (les représentations collectives). Yet the meanings of the Jungian "collective" and "unconscious" are contrary to the meanings of these terms in the French sociological-anthropological tradition.

The notion of the unconscious (Unbewusste) was one of the most important intellectual products of German idealism. The late 18th-century tendency adopting "reason", "Self," and "spirit" as principles of philosophy was transformed into different principles: "non-Self," "nature," "will," and the "unconscious." In the German tradition we can distinguish the following line of development: classical idealism—Romantic philosophy of nature—philosophy of life—psychoanalysis. In the mid-19th century, before the psychotherapeutic turn, the concept of the unconscious acquired a theoretical grounding from Arthur Schopenhauer, Eduard von Hartmann, and Carl Gustav Carus.[4] In Jung's concept a special role was played by Kant's reflections, Fichte's concept of the self, and when it came to the concept of the unconscious, Schopenhauer's philosophy of will and von Hartmann's philosophy of the unconscious.[5] By placing Jung's analytical psychology in the context of the tradition of German philosophy, especially in the context of the metaphysical concepts of the unconscious, we can explain its basic tenets.

However, the very concept of the collective unconscious did not appear as separate from the sociological tradition. It has been pointed out that the link between Durkheim's sociological concept and Jung's psychological concept

3 See, for example, J. R. Staude, "From Depth Psychology to Depth Sociology: Freud, Jung and Lévi-Strauss", *Theory and Society* 3, no. 3 (1976), 354.

4 L. Miodoński, "Nieświadome w idealizmie niemieckim", in: *Nieświadomość to odrębne królestwo..*, eds. I. Błocian, R. Saciuk (Toruń, Wydawnictwo Adam Marszałek, 2003), 53.

5 J. Prokopiuk, "Wstęp", in: C.G. Jung, *Rebis czyli kamień filozofów* (Warsaw, PWN, 1989), XIV.

emerged through Lévy-Bruhl's reflection,[6] on which Jung often drew.[7] The key to a comparison between the tradition of the French School of Sociology and the Jungian concept lies in the notion of "collective." We may wonder whether Jung formulated the notion of the collective unconscious as contrary to the notion of collective representations[8]—the authorship of which he mistakenly attributed to Lévy-Bruhl[9]—but there is no doubt that he assigned to the notion of "collective" a meaning contrary to the meaning attributed to it in sociological theories.

Durkheim's concept of collective representations (les représentations collectives) discovered culture as an element analytically distinct from the social system.[10] According to the concepts developed by the French School of Sociology, collective representations are generated socially and as such are common to all members of a society or group, differing from the states of individual consciousness.[11] The original source of logic is society, and the very categories of thinking reconstruct the social structure. In this sense these categories are social in nature.[12]

The counter-thesis to the concept of the French School of Sociology formulated by Jung does not come down to only a different placement of the collective aspect (Durkheim's concept of collective representations concerned social consciousness, while Jung combined the collective dimension with the unconscious), but also to its different understanding.

In the context of the Jungian reflection, "collective" does not mean "social" or "cultural" in the sense accepted in social sciences and comes closer to the meaning of "non-individual," "inherited," "generic," "universal."[13] Society

6 S. Shamdasani, *Jung and the Making of Modern Psychology*, (Cambridge, Cambridge University Press 2003), s. 288–293, 295–297 after R. A. Segal, "Jung and Lévy-Bruhl", *Journal of Analytical Psychology* 52 (2007), 642.

7 See C.G. Jung, *Psychologia i religia*, trans. J. Prokopiuk (Warsaw: KR, 1995) (originally published in C.G. Jung, *Gesammelte Werke*, vol. XI, 17–125) 67–68, idem, *Podstawy psychologii analitycznej. Wykłady tavistockie*, trans. R. Reszke (Warsaw: 1995), 57 (originally published *Über Grundlagen der analytischen Psychologie. Die Tavistock Lectures 1935*, Walter Verlag, 1971).

8 See S.F. Greenwood, "Émile Durkheim and C.G. Jung: Structuring a Transpersonal Sociology of Religion", *Journal for the Scientific Study of Religion* 29, no. 4 (1990), 482–495.

9 S. Shamdasani, 288–293, 295–297 after R. A. Segal, 642.

10 R.N. Bellah, "Durkheim and History", *American Sociological Review*, t.24, nr 4 (1959), 457–458.

11 See É. Durkheim, M. Mauss, "De quelques formes primitives de classification: contribution à l'étude des représentations collectives", *L'Année Sociologique*, vol. VI, 1–72.

12 É. Durkheim, M. Mauss, "De quelques formes ..", passim.

13 See C.G. Jung, *Stucture and Dymanics of The Psyche,* Collected Works, vol. 8, New York 1954, pp. 133–143; E. Kwiatkowska, *„Poszukiwanie* kultury. O jungizmie od strony

hardly appears in Jung's concept, and if it does, it emerges as an abstract idea.[14] According to Jung, society, a social group, corresponds to an artificial convention, which is contrasted with authentic development.[15]

This attitude to the idea of society is evident in, for example, Jung's misinterpretation of Lucien Lévy-Bruhl's concept of pre-logical thinking and mystical participation (participation mystique).

Robert A. Segal indicates three points in which Jung altered this concept:

- Lévy-Bruhl explains the thinking of primitive peoples sociologically, Jung psychologically (primitive people live in a state of unconsciousness);
- Jung universalizes the primitive mentality, regarding it as the original mental state of all people, and not, like Lévy-Bruhl, as a sociallydetermined state of collective mentality;
- Unlike Lévy-Bruhl, Jung appreciates primitive thinking (for Jung such thinking is genuine in the sense that it constitutes an expression of the operation of the unconscious).[16]

For Jung, getting rid of participation mystique is not, like for Lévy-Bruhl, a process linked to social transformations of the way of thinking, but a process associated with the establishment of the self, a hypothetical point between the conscious and the unconscious.[17] It is hard to find a better example of the difference between the goals of scientific inquiry and the goals of Jung's reflection describing a psychotherapeutic or even quasi-religious method.

Recognizing the work of the unconscious in the thinking of both primitive peoples and his contemporaries, Jung questioned the fundamental thesis of the French School of Sociology that the categories of the human mind were social in nature. This moment is decisive when it comes to the distinction between the way the notion of "collective" was used by Jung and by scholars from the French School of Sociology (it is worth noting that, given the reflection of "late" Jung, the collective unconscious evades even a psychological interpretation, moving towards the domain of metaphysics).

---

kulturologicznej" in: *Nieświadomość to odrębne królestwo..*, ed. I. Błocian, R. Saciuk, (Toruń: Wydawnictwo Adam Marszałek, 2003), 209.

14 K. Murawski, *Jaźń i sumienie*, (Wrocław;1987), 58.

15 See C. G. Jung, *Rebis czyli kamień filozofów*, (Warsaw: PWN, 1989), 254.

16 R. A. Segal, 641–649.

17 C. G. Jung, *Komentarz* in *Sekret złotego kwiatu*, trans. A. Sobota, (Wrocław-Warsaw: Thesaurus Press, 1994), 128. (Originally published as *Das Geheimnis der goldene Blüte* (*Ein chinesisches Lesenbuch*), Berlin, Dornverlag 1929); for a detailed analysis of the difference between Jung's and Lévy-Bruhl's positions on the thinking of primitive and contemporary people, see R. A. Segal, 649.

The difference between the ethnological and the Jungian approaches to the unconscious was articulated emphatically by Claude Lévi-Strauss, who referred to the legacy of the French School of Sociology, especially Marcel Mauss. When considering the notions containing the ideal of magic power, Mauss and Hubert reached a sphere in which the basic categories of the mind were unconscious and existed in the consciousness of individuals only thanks to society.[18] In their view the very fact that magical judgments were general and a priori in nature, preceding experience, suggested their collective origin.[19]

In expressing an ethnological understanding of the unconscious, Lévi-Strauss pointed to the structural and communicative nature of symbolic thought,[20] the products of which could be reconstructed by means of models analogous to linguistic models.[21] He stressed that the problem of the ethnological approach to the unconscious was a communication problem placed in the context of, on the one hand, the innate structure of the human mind, and on the other, of specific history of groups and individuals.[22]

Unlike Jung's concept, Lévi-Strauss's concept of the unconscious is structuralist and logocentric; symbols do not have individual meanings here, acquiring their sense from relations to other symbols (symbols here are more real than what they symbolize, while the signifying elements precede and define signified elements),[23] and the unconscious is not only linguistic in nature, but is also logical (for example, the logic of myth and the logic of scientific thinking are qualitatively equal).[24] The difference in the approach to the unconscious between Lévi-Strauss and Jung is also associated with their understanding of the symbolic. Both Jung and Lévi-Strauss treat the unconscious as a symbolic

---

18 H. Hubert, M.Mauss„ *Zarys ogólnej teorii magii,* trans. M. Król, in M. Mauss, *Socjologia i antropologia,* (Warsaw, Wydawnictwo KR, 2001), 135–6 (originally published as *Esquisse théorie générale de la magie,* in M. Mauss, *Sociologie et anthropologie,* Paris: Presses Universitaires de France, 1950); C. Lévi-Strauss, "Wprowadzenie do twórczości Marcela Maussa", in M. Mauss, *Socjologia i antropologia,* 23, originally published as "Introduction à l'oeuvre de Marcel Mauss", in M. Mauss, *Sociologie et anthropologie* (Paris: Presses Universitaires de France, 1950).

19 H. Hubert, M. Mauss, *Zarys ogólnej teorii magii,* trans. M. Król, in M. Mauss, *Socjologia i antropologia,* (Warsaw, Wydawnictwo KR, 2001), 141.

20 C. Lévi-Strauss, "Wprowadzenie do twórczości Marcela Maussa", in M. Mauss, *Socjologia i antropologia,* 35, Originally published as "Introduction à l'oeuvre de Marcel Mauss", in M. Mauss, *Sociologie et anthropologie* (Paris: Presses Universitaires de France, 1950).

21 C. Lévi-Strauss, *Antropologia strukturalna,* trans. K. Pomian (Warsaw: Wydawnictwo KR, 2000), 35–39, 58–59, (originally published as *Anthropologie structurale*).

22 Ibidem, 24, 35.

23 C. Lévi-Strauss, "Wprowadzenie do twórczości..," 24.

24 C. Lévi-Strauss, *Antropologia strukturalna,* 208.

system, but according to the latter, the unconscious is structural and communicative.

It is precisely because of the nonstructural nature of the unconscious in Jung's concept that, in Lévi-Strauss's view, symbols in the context of Jungism cease to be socially communicable as not being part of a language-like system.[25] Archetypal symbols understood in such a way are extra-social, and Jung's theses require the assumption that acquired traits are inherited or the acceptance of a theological hypothesis.[26]

Pointing to the mediating nature of the unconscious, Lévi-Strauss expressed the essence of his concept developed on the basis of the French sociological-anthropological tradition: the collective unconscious is communicative. It is an intermediary state between myself and the other (it could also be said, taking into account ethnological research, between myself and the alien, stranger), while in psychoanalysis we encounter a foreign or strange element of our Self.[27] This "foreign element" can be located in all dimensions united by the category of archetype: biological, psychological, anthropological, and metaphysical. In Jung's concept the subject communicates through the unconscious with the numinous aspect of itself and not with the other.

This "otherness," "foreignness" of the unconscious and its manifestations points to, especially in the context of Jung's late writings, a possibility of interpreting the notion of archetype in terms of religious studies and interpreting analytical psychology in terms of the sociology of religion.

Fascination with religious phenomena, which in the late 19th and early 20th century became the focus of intense research, in particular within the anthropological turn in religious studies (its contributors included the Cambridge School, J.G. Frazer, W.R. Smith, Émile Durkheim, Marcel Mauss) and phenomenological reflection, especially of the precursor of the phenomenology of religion Rudolf Otto, is an important context for the evolution of the Jungian concept of archetype.

The ontologizing of the concept of archetype linked to the concept of synchronicity (archetypes appear as transgressive; they can be found not only in the psychic aspect but also through meanings, in "external" circumstances, events)[28] may lead to metaphysical interpretations, which implicitly appeared already in Jung's writings preceding his study on synchronicity.

25 C. Lévi-Strauss, "Wprowadzenie do twórczości..," 24.
26 Ibidem, 24.
27 Ibidem, 24.
28 C.G. Jung, *Rebis*..., 533, 561–562.

An analysis of the notion of archetype reveals its links to the category of *numinosum* used by Rudolf Otto:[29] archetypes are pre-psychic; they are marked by fatalism; the unconscious appears as unknown (alien); it contains an element of *tremendum* and *mysterium*; it is irrational; it emerges vis-à-vis the conscious as an active, "objective" force as opposed to the passive object (these features are strongly emphasized especially with regard to the archetype of the Self).[30]

In the context of an analogy between archetypes, especially the archetype of the Self (worthy of note here is the self-saving nature of individuation)[31] and the numinous sphere, it could be said that Jung's concept in its late form contains premises for substituting religion understood, after Thomas Luckmann, as "invisible" religion, transferred from the sphere of the shared "sacred cosmos" to the private sphere—non-obligatory, characterized by a low degree of transcendence and subjective nature.[32]

The questioning by Thomas Luckmann and Peter L. Berger of the linear and unidimensional pattern of Weber's process of rationalization led to the identification of a number of secularization processes characteristic of industrial societies, including the transfer of religion from the public to the private sphere. Pushed out of the central sections of society associated with industrial processes (out of science, among others), religion began not only to move to the private sphere, but also to assume new social forms, hitherto not characteristic of religion. Based on the experiences of the private sphere, the new forms of religiosity draw on emotions and sentiments; they are volatile and highly subjective. As the traditional religious institutions lose the monopoly on delivering commonly accepted ways of defining the "sacred cosmos," there emerge fragmentary and private ways of establishing ultimate senses.[33]

The crisis of great nominizing social institutions led to the emergence of the "significance" of everyday life, and with it was opened a way to various secularized soteriologies.[34] In this case the privatization of religion is expressed in

---

29 See R. Otto, *Das Heilige: über das Irrationale in der Idee des Gõttlichen und sein Verhältnis zum Rationalen* (Munich: C.H. Beck, 1963), passim.

30 See E. Kwiatkowska, "Ponowne 'zaczarowanie...," 121–122.

31 The concept is a metamorphosis of the ancient gnostic mythologem of the self-saving saviour, see J. Prokopiuk, "C.G. Junga 'lapis philosophorum..", XXVII.

32 See T. Luckman, *The Invisible Religion. The problem of Religion in Modern Society,* (New York: Mac Millan Company, 1967, passim.

33 Ibidem.

34 P.L. Berger, Święty baldachim. Elementy socjologicznej teorii religii, trans. W. Kurdziel, (Kraków: Nomos, 1997), 172 (originally published as *The Sacred Canopy. Elements of a Sociological Theory of Religion,* Open Road Media, 2011).

individual experience of the archetype, while the process of individuation can undoubtedly be regarded as one of such private, individualized soteriologies. In this sense Jung's concept could be seen in its day as participating in the transformation of the historical forms of religious symbolization.

Sociologists of religion pointed to the hidden religious functions of psychoanalysis (not only Jungian psychoanalysis),[35] and generally a range of psychotherapeutic practices (with their characteristic direct accessibility of the "sacred cosmos" not mediated by the original public institutions), while scholars studying religion pointed to the gnostic nature of Jung's concept.[36]

Despite the fact that interpretations of Jungism from the perspective of the privatization of religion concern a stage in the development of Western societies that is already gone—and perhaps today it would be possible to place Jungian psychoanalysis in the context of some cultural practices other than religious practices (for example, in the practices of popular culture)—there are still grounds for perceiving analytical psychology not so much as psychology or philosophy of religion, but potentially, in specific social conditions, as a substitute forreligion.

It is worth noting that today the Jungian concept is associated with interpretations other than metaphysical interpretations, especially in the context of the so-called acausal phenomena, implicitly included in the concept of synchronicity.

Today the range of possible interpretations of acausal phenomena has widened considerably, especially with regard to the so-called paranormal phenomena, while explanations of these phenomena as natural, previously dominated by concepts drawing on physical aspects (for example, concepts proposed by Stefan Manczarski, Alexander Dubrov, David Bohm, Michio Kaku), are being replaced today by explanations referring to the biological paradigm, as is indicated by Michael Nahm referring to the concept of the morphogenetic field of Ruppert Sheldrake, and the field theory and theoretical biology of Jacob von Uexküll.[37] On the other hand, the naturalist dimension of Jung's concept is interpreted today mainly in terms of evolutionary psychology;[38] cognitivist approaches; and when it comes to inheriting acquired traits, potentially by

35 P.L. Berger, "Sociology and Psychoanalysis", *Social Research* 32, 1, (1965), 26–41.

36 See J. Prokopiuk, "C.G. Jung, czyli gnoza XX wieku", in C.G. Jung, *Archetypy i symbole* (Warsaw: Czytelnik, 1976), passim.

37 T. Sikora, "Zamiast wstępu; religioznawstwo i parapsychologia", in E. de Martino, Świat magiczny (Kraków: Nomos 2011), X–XI.

38 See A. Kuzmicki, "Developing Jung's Theory of Mind in the Light of Evolutionary Psychology", in *Contemporary Influences…*, 228–252.

epigenetics.[39] It seems that this last perspective in particular (rejected by the criticallyminded Lévi-Strauss at a time when the inheritance of acquired traits was rejected a priori as incompatible with the theory of evolution) is promising when it comes to explaining some aspects of psychoanalytical concepts (for example, unconscious inheritance of the memory of trauma), though not universal, as would be suggested by Jungism (it seems, although this is only a hypothesis, that the traceability of the epigenetic mechanism can be limited in time).

These naturalistic explanations are reductionist—that is unacceptable from the point of view of sociological concepts and cultural anthropology—with regard to the problem of, for example, the origin of the symbolic sphere or mythopoeic activity.

To sum up, in defining the relations between Jungism and social sciences, of key importance are the following aspects:

- The Jungian concept of the unconscious should be viewed in the context of the tradition of German idealism, especially metaphysical concepts of the unconscious.
- In Jung's concept the term collective does not mean "social" or "cultural" in the sense in which these notions function in social sciences but comes closer to the meaning of the terms supraindividual, inherited, generic, or universal.
- The nature of the unconscious in Jung's concept makes symbols non-communicable socially; their basis is instinctive, so interpreting cultural phenomena by means of the category of archetype leads either to a naturalist interpretation of culture or, given the concept of synchronicity (Synchronizität), to a metaphysical interpretation Jung's concept is not scientific, but rather, gnostic.

In view of the interpretations of the collective unconscious concept—metaphysical on the one hand and naturalistic on the other—it could be said that Jungian psychoanalysis and sociological and anthropological approaches to human beings and the culture they create are incommensurate with one another. With its therapeutic practices and cultural context, analytical psychology not only cannot provide social sciences with explanations, but can itself become their objects. Therefore, can the Jungian concept of the unconscious be in any way a point of reference for cultural studies today? Can the categories of the collective unconscious and archetype be used as heuristic tools in these studies?

---

39 See J. Cambray, "Jung in the Academy and Beyond: The Fordham Lectures – 100 Years Later", in *Contemporary Influences...*, 29–31.

When looking for an answer to these questions, an answer that avoids both the pitfalls of the metaphysical ontologization of the unconscious and reductionist perspectives, we could turn to the anthropological interpretation of the collective unconscious, primarily to the question of its nature: iconic versus linguistic.

2 The Iconic versus Linguistic Interpretation of the Unconscious

2.1 *The Psychoanalytical Approach to the Image and the Modern Dispute over Images*

Referring to the approach to the unconscious, we can distinguish two lines in the psychoanalytical tradition: one, drawing on the Jungian concept, recognizes the unconscious primarily through images, and the other, inspired by the language theory, attributes to the unconscious, like Jacques Lacan, a linguistic nature.[40]

Lacan's influential reflection combined two, previously separate traditions: psychoanalytical and structuralist, thanks to which the distance, explicated by Lévi-Strauss, between two concepts of the unconscious, ethnological and psychoanalytical, was abolished in a way. The combination of psychoanalysis and structuralism has its consequences both for the understanding of the image and the Imaginary (*Imaginaire*), and the unconscious itself, which is approached by Lacan, as well as Lévi-Strauss, in a logocentric manner.

The ethnological concept of the unconscious was formulated in semio-structuralism, the most influential strand of cultural anthropology and other cultural studies within the linguistic turn. What can be regarded as the essence of the linguistic turn is the belief that beyond the horizon of human cognition, we find language and linguistic description of the world. In psychoanalysis the linguistic turn led to Lacan's concept, which uses structuralist inspirations, especially Lévi-Strauss's reflection. In his Imaginary-Real-Symbolic (*Imaginaire-Réel-Symbolique*) triad, a fundamental categorial web of human reality,[41] Lacan juxtaposed two orders: the Imaginary (*Imaginaire*) and the Symbolic (*Symbolique*). Thus he openly expressed a tendency present in semio-structuralist concepts, which narrowed down symbolism to signification, without

---

40 On the iconic and linguistic interpretation of the unconscious, see E. Kwiatkowska, „Zwrot ikoniczny a psychoanaliza", in Z. Bitka et al., *Współczesne interpretacje koncepcji C.G. Junga*, (Wrocław: Wydawnictwo Uniwersytetu Wrocławskiego, 2018), 44–46.

41 F. Wörler, *Das Symbolische, das Imaginäre und das Reale. Lacans drei Ordnungen als erkenntnistheoretisches Modell*, (Bielefeld: transcript Verlag, 2015), 36.

being able to capture the visual symbol in his method[42] and consequently leaving out the imaginary aspect of culture (for example, both Lévi-Strauss and his continuators implicitly reduce the imaginary aspect of myth, paying attention only to its hidden meaningful structure).

The meanings of the concepts of the imaginary, the real, and the symbolic, the building blocks of the *Imaginaire-Réel-Symbolique* triad, are thoroughly redefined in Lacan's concept. In his understanding of the Symbolic, Lacan contradicted the tradition that saw symbolism in images, unequivocally identifying the Symbolic with the linguistic, that is, with what was a language or had a structure identical to a language, constituting the possibilities of establishing relations and distancingitself from the tangle of imaginary interconnections.[43] In his understanding of the Symbolic, Lacan presents the ultimate consequences of Lévi-Strauss's semio-structuralism: what is Symbolic corresponds in fact to the structuralist understanding of language.

The Imaginary as presented by Lacan in his concept leads to a negation of the previous, conventional use of the term *imaginary* as a world of representations, ideas, or internal images created by people.[44] In defining the Imaginary, Lacan combined various elements: phenomenological (the Imaginary as unreal, fictitious—a conviction taken over from Sartre's phenomenology of the imagination),[45] psychological (the Imaginary as illusions, hallucinations, phantasms),[46] and ethological (the Imaginary as a biologically functional

---

42 Which can be viewed as a consequence of Ferdinand de Saussure's attitude to the symbol, see T. Todorov, *Teorie symbolu*, trans. T. Stróżyński, (Gdańsk: Słowo/obraz terytoria, 2011), 303–305. (Originally published as *Théories du symbole,* Paris: Seuil, 1977).

43 H. Lang, *Język i nieświadomość. Podstawy teorii psychoanalitycznej Jacques'a Lacana,* trans. P. Piszczatowski (Gdańsk: Słowo/obraz teryroria, 2005), 151, 184 (originally published as *Die Sprache und das Unbewußte. Jacques Lacans Grundlegung der Psychoanalyse,* Frankfurt am Main, Suhrkamp Verlag, 1986).

44 F.Wörler, *Das Symbolische...,* 32.

45 The understanding of the Imaginary by Lacan is not identical with the understanding of the notion by Sartre. Sartre's image is an act of the imagination *sui generis* and, moreover, is a prerequisite of freedom (J.-P. Sartre, *Wyobrażenie. Fenomenologiczna psychologia wyobraźni,* trans. P. Beylin, (Warsaw: Aletheia, 2012), 23, 269–271 (originally published as *L'imaginaire,* Paris: Gallimard, 1960). In Lacan's concept the ontic status of the Imaginary (like that of the Real) is not defined; Lacan dissociated himself from ontological and in general philosophical interpretation of his concept (see J. Lacan, *Triumf religii,* trans. J. Waga, (Warsaw: PWN, 2017), 83–87. (Originally published as *La triomphe da la religion,* Paris: Seuil, 2004).

46 The notion of the Imaginary encompasses the phenomena of representation—as understood by Brentano—among them the blurry areas of experiences illusions and hallucinations, including everything that can be part of mental acts, but before judgment or emotion with regard to their content, see F. Wörler, *Das Symbolische...,* 156.

aspect occurring both in animals and in people; for example, it organizes mating rituals and feeding cycles).[47]

In this approach, the Imaginary appears as a pre-symbolic or extra-symbolic product of the subject,[48] a product shared by humans with animals, leading to a distortion of the image of the self and the other, a product that is illusory, chaotic, phantasmatic, disorderly, essentially uncommunicable and alienating.[49] What shapes and establishes the whole role of the Imaginary in human life is ultimately the symbolic order defined by its structure, the order with which the image is always more or less integrated.[50] The Imaginary is not subordinated to the structure of the symbolic, although it is permeated by it.[51]

Negative connotations associated with the imaginary order in Lacan's concept can have various sources (e.g., the understanding of the imaginary as unreal taken over from Jean-Paul Sartre), but it seems that the structuralist sources play a decisive role here. The negative attitude to the image in Lacan's psychoanalysis may revolve around Lévi-Strauss's juxtaposition of culture and nature. As Hermann Lang indicated, both Lévi-Strauss and Lacan were preoccupied by the problem of the development of the human being, their becoming in the process of exiting nature. The "unconscious is nothing other than the continuing effects, still present in the adult, of the extraordinary event [...]. That primordial symbolisation anchors the symbolic order which can be understood as the order of language (*ordre symbolique*) and the order of law (*ordre de la loi*)—order of culture. [...] With the emergence of symbolic meanings—be it in the form of language or law—nature becomes negated and in its place is established the human world of culture."[52]

---

47 See J. Lacan, *Seminarium III. Psychozy*, trans. J. Waga, (Warsaw: PWN, 2014), 18 (originally published as *Les PsychosLe Seminaire: Tome III; Les Psychos*, Paris: Seuil, 1981); idem, *Imiona - Ojca*, trans. R. Carrabino et al., (Warsaw: PWN, 2013), 21–22, 42–43 (originally published as *Des noms-du-père*, Paris: Seuil, 2005), see also F. Wörler, *Das Symbolische..*, 30–32, 119.

48 J. Lacan, *Imiona - Ojca*, 19–20.

49 See J. Lacan, *Seminarium III. Psychozy*, 272; H. Lang, *Język i nieświadomość*, 114, 184.

50 J. Lacan, *Seminarium III, Psychozy*, 18; cf. H. Lang, *Język i nieświadomość*, 186, 224. From the very beginning the Imaginary is permeated by language; it requires the perspective of some symbolic order. Lang points to a similarity of this thesis to Cassirer's thesis that language plays a decisive role in the process of perception (H. Lang, Język i nieświadomość, 224). Human behaviour can never be reduced to an imaginary relation (such a relation leads to a collision, a break-up); it requires a law, a symbolic order, an order of speaking that will prevent the situation from breaking up (J. Lacan, *Seminarium III. Psychozy*, 177–179).

51 J. Lacan, *Seminarium III. Psychozy*, 18.

52 H. Lang, *Język i nieświadomość*, 248–249.

In itself the Imaginary, understood by Lacan as an antithesis of the Symbolic, does not have and cannot have (to use the language of traditional terminology) a cultural and communicative status,[53] constituting, in fact, an internal, alienating instance of psyche,[54] linked to the mirror phase and experiences of the subject, serving as a defense against the Real.[55]

What is communicative and cultural comes from the Symbolic. Only thanks to the placement of a given object within a network of interconnections present within language is an analytical conversation possible, according to Lacan.[56] The Imaginary comes down here to generating successive phantasms (lasting imaginary creations) that can be confronted, which can be achieved thanks to the Symbolic, or rather, is never achieved.[57]

According to Lacan, in his concept Jung mixed the spheres of the Imaginary and the Symbolic, following the traditional thinking.[58] This accusation is very interesting from both the theoretical and therapeutic point of view. For it ultimately leads to a conviction that a confrontation with the sphere of archetypes is in some measure a confrontation with the sphere of the Imaginary, which, in Lacan's view, is not collective in nature.

An interpretation of Jung's concept through this remark by Lacan would have serious theoretical consequences. Separating and antagonizing the

---

53 In concepts in which the image is understood as a product of the imagination of the subjective subject; a phantasm; an uncertain, unstable product of the subject's imagination giving rise to illusions, it cannot be a medium for the I—the Other communication, although as a trace of memory it can be a medium for constructing the history of the subject.

54 See Lacan, *Seminarium III. Psychozy*, 272; H. Lang, *Język i nieświadomość*, 114; F. Wörler, *Das Symbolische...*, 30, 153.

55 S. Žižek, *Lacan. Przewodnik Krytyki Politycznej,* trans. J. Kutyła, (Warsaw: Wydawnictwo Krytyki Politycznej). 75 (originally published as *How To Read Lacan,* London: GrantaBooks, 2006). The boundary between the Imaginary and the Symbolic is the field of the Real. The "Real" is hard to define: in Lacan's concept the status of the Real is doubtful because the concept lacks an unequivocal, positive definition of the real order (F. Wörler, *Das Symbolische...*, 32–33, 242). Lacan himself points out that the notion of the Real is extraordinarily complex and cannot be captured in a way that makes up a whole (J. Lacan, *Triumf religii...*, 84).

56 H. Lang, *Język i nieświadomość*, 186. This position indicates another trace of the reception of concept of Lévi-Strauss, according to whom language (the symbolic) establishes the sphere of communication on the level of unconscious thinking (C. Lévi-Strauss, "Wprowadzenie do twórczości...", 24).

57 See P. Dybel, "Czy psychoanaliza Lacana jest hermeneutyką?", in H. Lang, *Język i nieświadomość*, 18, 28–29.

58 J. Lacan, *Seminarium I. Pisma techniczne Freuda*, trans. J. Waga, (Warsaw: PWN, 2017), 222–225 (originally published as *Le Séminaire. Livre I. Les ècrits techniques de Freud (1953–1954)*, Paris: Seuil, 1998.

Imaginary and the Symbolic implicitly challenges the foundations of Jungism, undermining its fundamental category, the notion of archetype, and splitting it into two aspects: imaginary and symbolic. This is only the ultimate conclusion of Lévi-Strauss's semio-structuralism, as well as Lévi-Strauss's criticism of Jungism referred to earlier.

By separating the Imaginary from the Symbolic, Lacan explicated the final consequences of the application of semio-structuralist methods, not only in psychoanalysis but also more broadly, in various humanistic disciplines, in which the application of these methods led to an important aspect of culture, the iconic aspect, being left out.

One of the consequences of the semio-structuralist approach is the impossibility of capturing the questions of the visual symbol, as was stressed already by Gilbert Durand. His answer to this deficiency contained references, though strongly transformed, to topics present in psychoanalysis, while the very question of imagination was presented by Durand explicitly as a plane for a polemic with structuralism. In this polemic Durand invoked the notion of archetype, which in the context of research into the cultural imaginary sphere, is obviously by no means accidental. Durand absorbed the Jungian approach to the unconscious as manifesting itself in the sphere of images and used it in anthropological studies of the cultural imaginarium.[59] This moment is heuristically important, for it constitutes a premise for enhancing the anthropological role of image phenomena in culture.

Historically speaking, the announcement of the modern iconic turn was preceded, in psychoanalysis among others, by an important revaluation of symbolic-pictorial phenomena as objects of cognition, be it with regard to dreams in Sigmund Freud's concept or with regard to the archetype, initially defined by Jung as a primordial image and later as a heritable possibility or even necessity of creating ideas.[60] Psychoanalysis also ascribed to images a number of qualities invoked by contemporary "iconoclasts": of an archaic, mythical, irrational (Jungian tradition) or possibly illusory, phantasmatic, and alienating (Lacanian tradition) character.

Thus both psychoanalytical perspectives, Jungian and Lacanian, so very different, have serious consequences for the understanding of the image and the imaginary in contemporary humanities. In the context of the Jungian concept, the archetypal image appears as a way of manifesting the autonomous activity

59 See G. Durand, *Les structures anthropologiques de l'imaginaire. Introduction à l'archétypologie générale* (Paris: Dunod, 1960). It was intended as a polemic with Lévi-Strauss' *Structural Anthropology*.

60 C.G. Jung, *Rebis czyli kamień filozofów*, 202.

of unconscious processes, a way connected with the anthropological mythopoesis (the link between myth and image was similarly pointed out by Ernst Cassirer, who, unlike semio-structuralism, perceived myth logocentrically, as a semiotic system similar to language). Lacan, on the other hand, attributed to the Imaginary (in addition to the above-mentioned negative connotations) the status of one of the three basic registers of reality, among which ran all relations of a human being between himself or herself, another human being, the world, and being.[61]

Both Lacan's and Jung's concepts can be regarded as important theoretical contexts of the current polemic over images,[62] carried out generally without any special emphasis being put on the link to psychoanalysis.[63] The connotations present in it and associated with the notions of image and the Imaginary influence the arguments used in the polemics, especially those indicating that imagination is reserved for variously conceptualized primordial or regressive aspects of human existence, while images, as products of illusions or hallucinations, are unreal and illusory.[64]

However, Jung's concept has rendered some services to the iconic turn. It is only now, in the context of the distinction between the iconic and linguistic concept of the unconscious and the juxtaposition between the iconic turn

---

61 See H. Lang, *Język i nieświadomość*, 183.

62 On the polemic surrounding images, see P. J. Bräunlein, "Bildakte. Religionswissenschaft im Dialog mit einer neuen Bildwissenschaft", in *Religion im kulturellen Diskurs. Festschrift für Hans G. Kippenberg zum. 65. Geburtstag*, B.Luchesi, S. Stuckrad (ed.) (Berlin: Walter de Gruyter, 2004), 197–203.

63 Although the volume inaugurating the iconic turn, *Was ist ein Bild?* edited by Boehm, contains two contributions by Lacan, and Boehm himself refers in it to Lacan's theory of regard or gaze, see G. Boehm, "Die Wiederkehr der Bilder", in *Was ist ein Bild?* ed. G. Boehm (Munich: Fink, 1994), 22–25. For more on the reception of Lacan's concept of gaze (*regard*) among representatives of various *Bildwissenschaft* disciplines, see R. Meyer-Kalkus, *Blick und Stimme*, in: *Bilderfragen. Die Bildwissenschaft im Aufbruch*, ed. H. Belting (Munich: Fink, 2007), 217–235, see also the references to Lacan's concepts made by W. J. T, Mitchell (idem, *What do pictures want? The lives and loves of images*, Chicago: University of Chicago Press, 2005).

64 The image understood in such a Jungian way was criticised by T. W. Adorno. He was worried by the possibility of hypostasizing archaic images, which he linked to the danger of mythical thought (see Adorno's letters to Walter Benjamin and Max Horkheimer, in W. Benjamin, *Pasaże*, trans. I. Kania (Kraków: Wydawnictwo Literackie, 2005), 1046–1051, 1082–1083 (originally published as *Das Passagen-Werk.* Frankfurt am Main, Suhrkamp Verlag, 1991). In today's image-centred polemics we see a recurrence of the motif of the regressive nature of images; what is criticized above all are images of the new media—they are criticized for depriving the viewers of a sense of reality, ability to maintain distance and carry out a critical analysis.

and the linguistic turn, that the heuristic significance of the Jungian tradition to culture studies is revealed. The Jungian concept of the collective unconscious cannot be "reconciled" in extenso with the scientific approach of contemporary cultural anthropology and other culture studies, if only because of its non-scientific assumptions referred to earlier.[65] It can, however, be placed among those reflections that, by raising the status of the symbolic image, opened up the prospects for research into the cultural visual sphere (cultural imaginarium, iconosphere).

References

Bellah R.N., *"Durkheim and History", American Sociological Review* 1959, t.24, nr 4, 457–458.

Benjamin W., *Pasaże,* trans. I. Kania, Kraków: Wydawnictwo Literackie, 2005. Originally published as *Das Passagen-Werk,* Frankfurt am Main, Suhrkamp Verlag, 1991.

Berger P.L., Święty baldachim. *Elementy socjologicznej teorii religii,* trans. W. Kurdziel, Kraków: Nomos, 1997. Originally published as *The Sacred Canopy. Elements of a Sociological Theory of Religion,* Open Road Media, 2011.

Berger P.L.,"Sociology and Psychoanalysis", *Social Research* 32,1, 1965, 26–41.

Błocian I., "Jung and Social Thought:" The Undiscovered Self", in *Contemporary Influences of C.G. Jung's Thought,* edited by I. Błocian, A. Kuzmicki, Leiden, Boston: Brill, 2018.

Boehm G., "Die Wiederkehr der Bilder", in *Was ist ein Bild?* edited by G. Boehm, Munich: Fink, 1994.

Bräunlein P. J., "Bildakte. Religionswissenschaft im Dialog mit einer neuen Bildwissenschaft", in *Religion im kulturellen Diskurs. Festschrift für Hans G. Kippenberg zum. 65. Geburtstag,* B. Luchesi, S. Stuckrad (edited by), Berlin: Walter de Gruyter, 2004.

Cambray J., "Jung in the Academy and Beyond: The Fordham Lectures - 100 Years Later", in *Contemporary Influences of C.G. Jung's Thought,* edited by I. Błocian, A. Kuzmicki, Leiden, Boston: Brill, 2018.

Durkheim É., Mauss M., "De quelques formes primitives de classification: contribution à l'étude des représentations collectives", *L'Année Sociologique,* t. VI, 1–72.

Durand G., *Les structures anthropologiques de l'imaginaire. Introduction à l'archétypologie générale,* Paris: Dunod, 1960.

Dybel P., "Czy psychoanaliza Lacana jest hermeneutyką?", in H. Lang, *Język i nieświadomość, Język i nieświadomość. Podstawy teorii psychoanalitycznej Jacques'a Lacana,* translatet by P. Piszczatowski, Gdańsk: Słowo/obraz teryroria, 2005.

65 See E. Kwiatkowska, "The Idea of Culture Image Confronted with Psychoanalytic Tradition", in *Contemporary Influences...,* 131–132.

Greenwood S.F., "Émile Durkheim and C.G. Jung: Structuring a Transpersonal Sociology of Religion", *Journal for the Scientific Study of Religion* 29, no. 4 (1990), 482–495.

Hubert H, Mauss M., *Zarys ogólnej teorii magii*, trans. M. Król, in M. Mauss, *Socjologia i antropologia*, Warsaw, KR, 2001. Originally published as *Esquisse théorie générale de la magie*, in M. Mauss, *Sociologie et anthropologie*, Paris: Presses Universitaires de France, 1950.

Jung C.G., *Typy psychologiczne*, trans. R. Reszke, Warsaw: KR 1997. Originally published as *Psychologische Typen*, C. G. Jung, *Gesammelte Werke*, Walter Verlag, 1994.

Jung C.G., *Wspomnienia, sny, myśli spisane i podane do drukiu przez Anielę Jaffé*, trans. L. Kolankiewicz, Warsaw: Wrota 1993. Originally published as *Erinnerungen, Träume, Gedanken von C.G. Jung*, Zürich - Düsseldorf, Walter Verlag 1993.

Jung C.G., *Rebis czyli kamień filozofów*, trans. J. Prokopiuk. Warszaw: PWN, 1989. Originally published as *Synchronizität:Einführung, Schlussfolgerung*, in *Naturerklärung und Psyche*, Zürich: Rascher Verlag, 1952.

Jung C.G., *Psychologia i religia*, trans. J. Prokopiuk, Warsaw: KR, 1995. Originally published in C.G. Jung, *Gesammelte Werke*, t.11, 17–125.

Jung C.G., *Podstawy psychologii analitycznej. Wykłady tavistockie*, translatet by R. Reszke, Warsaw: Wrota, 1995. Originally published as *Über Grundlagen der analytischen Psychologie. Die Tavistock Lectures 1935*, Walter Verlag, 1971.

Jung C.G., *Komentarz* in *Sekret złotego kwiatu*, trans. A. Sobota, Wrocław-Warsaw: Thesaurus Press, 1994. Originally published as *Das Geheimnis der goldenen Blüte* (*Ein chinesisches Lebensbuch*), Berlin: Dornverlag, 1929.

Kuzmicki A.,"Developing Jung's Theory of Mind in the Light of Evolutionary Psychology", in *Contemporary Influences of C.G. Jung's Thought*, eds. by I. Błocian, A. Kuzmicki, Leiden, Boston: Brill, 2018.

Kwiatkowska E., „Zwrot ikoniczny a psychoanaliza" in Z Bitka *et al.*, *Współczesne interpretacje koncepcji C.G. Junga*, Wrocław: Wydawnictwo Uniwersytetu Wrocławskiego, 2018.

Kwiatkowska E., "The Idea of Culture Image Confronted with Psychoanalytic Tradition", in *Contemporary Influences of C.G. Jung's Thought*, edited by I. Błocian, A. Kuzmicki, Leiden, Boston: Brill, 2018.

Kwiatkowska E., „Poszukiwanie kultury. O jungizmie od strony kulturologicznej", *in Nieświadomość to odrębne królestwo..*, edited by I. Błocian, R. Saciuk, Toruń: Wydawnictwo Adam Marszałek, 2003.

Kwiatkowska E., *Ponowne "zaczarowanie". Dwie nieświadomości*, in *Nieświadomość to odrębne królestwo..*, eds. I. Błocian, R. Saciuk, Toruń, Wydawnictwo Adam Marszałek, 2003.

Lacan J., *Triumf religii*, trans. J. Waga, Warsaw: PWN, 2017. Originally published as *La triomphe de la religion*, Paris: Seuil, 2004.

Lacan J., *Seminarium III. Psychozy*, trans. J. Waga, Warsaw: PWN, 2014. Originally published as *Le Seminaire: Tome III; Les Psychos*, Paris: Seuil, 1981.

Lacan J., *Imiona - Ojca*, trans. R. Carrabino *et al.*, Warsaw: PWN, 2013. Originally published as *Des noms-du-père*, Paris: Seuil, 2005.

Lacan J., *Seminarium I. Pisma techniczne Freuda*, trans. J. Waga, Warsaw: PWN, 2017. Originally published as *Le Séminaire. Livre I. Les ècrits techniques de Freud (1953–1954)*, Paris: Seuil, 1998.

Lang H., *Język i nieświadomość. Podstawy teorii psychoanalitycznej Jacques'a Lacana*, trans. P. Piszczatowski, Gdańsk: Słowo/obraz teryroria, 2005. Originally published as *Die Sprache und das Unbewußte. Jacques Lacans Grundlegung der Psychoanalyse*, Frankfurt am Main, Suhrkamp Verlag, 1986.

Lévi-Strauss C., *Antropologia strukturalna*, trans. K. Pomian, Warsaw: Wydawnictwo KR, 2000. Originally published as *Anthropologie structurale*, Paris: Plon, 1958.

Lévi-Strauss C., "Wprowadzenie do twórczości Marcela Maussa", in M. Mauss, *Socjologia i antropologia*, Warsaw: KR, 2001.Originally published as "Introduction à l'oeuvre de Marcel Mauss", in M. Mauss, *Sociologie et anthropologie*, Paris: Presses Universitaires de France, 1950.

Lévy-Bruhl L., *Czynności umysłowe w społeczeństwach pierwotnych*, trans. B.Szwarcman-Czarnota, Warsaw: PWN, 1992. Originally published as *Les Fonctions mentales-dans les sociétés inférieures*, Hachette Livre BNF, 2016.

Luckman Th., *The Invisible Religion. The problem of Religion in Modern Society*, New York: Mac Millan Company, 1967.

Main R., "In a Secular Age: Weber, Taylor, Jung" in *Contemporary Influences of C.G. Jung's Thought*, edited by I. Błocian, A. Kuzmicki, Leiden, Boston: Brill, 2018.

Meyer-Kalkus R., *Blick und Stimme, in: Bilderfragen. Die Bildwissenschaft im Aufbruch*, eds. H. Belting, München: Fink, 2007.

Mitchell W.J.T., *What do pictures want? The lives and loves of images*, Chicago: The University of Chicago Press, 2005.

Otto R., *Das Heilige: über das Irrationale in der Idee des Gõttlichen und sein Verhältnis zum Rationalen*, Munich: C.H. Beck, 1963.

Prokopiuk J., *C.G. Junga "lapis philosophorum: dyptych filozoficzno-alchemiczny"*, in Jung C.G., *Rebis czyli kamień filozofów*, translatet by. J. Prokopiuk, Warsaw: PWN, 1989.

Prokopiuk J., "C.G, Jung, czyli gnoza XX wieku", in C.G. Jung, *Archetypy i symbole*, translatet by. J. Prokopiuk, Warsaw: Czytelnik, 1976.

Sartre J.-P., *Wyobrażenie. Fenomenologiczna psychologia wyobraźni*, trans. P. Beylin, Warszawa: Aletheia, 2012. Originally published as *L'imaginaire*, Paris: Gallimard, 1960.

Segal R.A., "Jung and Lévy-Bruhl", *Journal of Analytical Psychology* 2007.

Sikora T. "Zamiast wstępu; religioznawstwo i parapsychologia", w: E. de Martino, *Świat magiczny*, Kraków: Nomos 2011.

Staude J.R., From Depth Psychology to Depth Sociology: Freud, Jung and Lévi-Strauss, *Theory and Society* 3, no. 3, 1976.

Todorow T., *Teorie symbolu*, trans. T. Stróżyński, Gdańsk: Słowo/obraz terytoria, 2011. Originally published as *Théories du symbole*, Paris: Seuil, 1977.

Wörler F., *Das Symbolische, das Imaginäre und das Reale. Lacans drei Ordnungen als erkenntnistheoretisches Modell*, Bielefeld: transcript Verlag, 2015.

Žižek S., *Lacan. Przewodnik Krytyki Politycznej*, trans. J. Kutyła, Warsaw: Wydawnictwo Krytyki Politycznej, 2008. Originally published as *How To Read Lacan*, London: GrantaBooks, 2006.

PART 2

Social Imaginarium

CHAPTER 4

The Lost Art of Personification

Vicky Jo Varner

Abstract

Personification has slipped in and out of fashion over the centuries. This paper looks at artistic representations of eccentric personified figures encountered by the author in archaic church settings and locates them in a historical context, looking at their antecedents and chronicled treatment, from iconoclasm to idolatry. It compares these objects with modern-day practices of active imagination. C.G. Jung encouraged his patients to draw or paint the imaginal figures they encountered in dreams or active imagination, just as he illustrated figures he encountered in *Liber Novus*. This paper concludes that the helping professions might benefit from an increased use of personification.

Keywords

personification, active imagination, Jung, iconoclasm, idolatry, misericords

1 Introduction

During the first half of 2019, I travelled around Europe and capitalized on the opportunity to visit several magnificent cathedrals: the Avignon Papal Palace, Exeter, Aachen, St. David's, and Rosslyn Chapel, along with a few less-renowned sanctuaries, such as the Cathedral of the Incarnation in Granada, the Basilica of Mary Magdalene in Provence, and the modest St. Mary's Church in Wales.

These excursions were enjoyable, educative, and psychoactivating. Some visitors to these sites become infatuated with church history, the royal politics, various religious matters, the architecture, engineering, and construction. I find myself irresistibly drawn to the fantastical medieval grotesques and funny little faces that peer out in ancient stone and wood carvings.

 | DOI:10.1163/9789004468757_006

2 The Rise and Fall of Personification

My fascination with these figures started in Great Britain's York Minster a couple of years ago when I happened to visit there. Contained within the Chapter House reside some of the world's finest medieval stone carvings. Dating from the 13th century, a riot of funny faces, animals, and mythical beasts grin and scowl down from the seat canopies a scant three feet above the stalls where the Dean and his canons once convened. These 237 sculpted heads and figures tease our imagination: men prying their mouths open with both hands; ferocious-looking monsters clutching human heads that grimace in pain; and one lone fellow is gleefully picking his nose (see Figure 4.1).

FIGURE 4.1 Carved head in York Minster Chapter House. (Photo by author)

Heads were presumed to be the center of power, a core of individual identity, and the primary vehicle for emotion, expression, and human character throughout the Middle Ages, in keeping with the ancient philosophy of Plato,[1] who had alleged that the soul was located inside this topmost part of the body.

The unidentified carvers who produced these figures were referred to as "imagiers" or "imaginators," and these artisans expressed a variety of different styles in their work. Those charming visages could be considered the peak of Gothic sculptural prowess, and they prompted me to seek out other

1 Plato, *Timaeus and Critias*, ed., T. Kjeller Johansen, trans., D. Lee, (New York, NY: Penguin Classics, 2008), 35.

such faces lurking in the corners. Once attuned to them, I began encountering faces glowering from the façades of private village homes, leering down from the ceiling in Castle Campbell, embellishing storefronts preserved from medieval times, even decorating Jung's hideaway tower at Bollingen. These odd countenances were surprisingly plentiful and appeared to be personifications of various kinds—some represented real people; several pictured story characters; and many were completely imaginary, existing only in the minds of those anonymous carvers. Incarnated figures such as these emanated from a long lineage of historical precedents: ancient alchemists personified the sun and moon with human faces, Greek and Roman artisans carved statues and bas reliefs representing their deities, monks transcribing holy texts adorned them with caricatures of angels and fantastical anthropomorphized creatures. It has been proposed that the stone circles at Avebury and Stonehenge are likewise comprised of ancient faces, contributing an additional layer of magic to these Neolithic ruins.[2] Unfortunately, pointing them out tends to attract accusations of anthropomorphism and pareidolia in their wake. But are such accusations merely forms of iconoclasm?

3 Iconoclasm versus Personification

The term *iconoclasm* comes from Greek words for "icon smashing" and is defined as "a breaking or destroying of images, especially those set up for religious veneration." Intolerance by iconoclasts was targeted at *iconolatry*, defined as "the worship or adoration of icons." *Icons* (from the Greek *eikones*, meaning *images*) are portrayals (might we say personifications?) of the saints, Christ, and the Virgin, as well as narrative scenes such as Christ's Baptism and Crucifixion, that are venerated as sacred.

Iconoclasts, iconophobes, and aniconists faced off against icon venerators, in turn referred to as iconolaters, iconodules, and iconophiles. Not surprisingly, it has been suggested that iconoclasts tended toward a rationalist bent while iconodules were mystical in their nature.

A vacillation between these two extremes of iconoclasm and idolatry extends throughout history, as all three major Abrahamic religions have struggled with ongoing tension between imagery and idolatry that at times involved the smashing of works of art. In Christian history, for example, two large-scale outbreaks of iconoclasm occurred in the eighth and ninth century Byzantine

2 T. Meaden, *The Secrets of the Avebury Stones: Britain's Greatest Megalithic Temple*, (Berkeley, CA: Frog, Ltd., 2000), 42.

Empire, lasting over 100 years and earning the title of the "Iconoclastic Controversy," and then arising yet again during the Protestant Reformation. Human history is rife with examples of tension between a love and hatred of art, which has been framed as a conflict between the veneration and hostility toward images.[3]

The arguments that raged between the iconoclasts and the iconodules were complex, bordering on hairsplitting, and are difficult to distill. As a technicality, the essential struggle between iconoclasm and iconodulism was predicated on contradictory messages that were given by God—on the one hand forbidding the making of "graven images" (as specified by the second commandment),[4] but on the other hand instructing Moses to create images in order to facilitate worship at the same time He gave him the previous commandment.[5] Thus, God prohibited all images and at the same time demanded their creation. Protracted and complicated arguments ensued over the matter as the iconoclasts claimed that religious icons were idols, and since the Christian iconophiles venerated icons—man-created objects—the iconoclasts branded them *idolators*, betraying rigid, literal, black-and-white thinking about the matter as they turned a deaf ear to the icon venerators' reasoned arguments that the word "image" has multiple shades of meaning and that elementary differences distinguish icons from idols and differentiate *veneration* from *worship*. As Avramidis noted,

> The iconoclastic controversy . . . spurred an intellectual and philosophical fervor within the church as both schools of thought, iconoclast and iconodule, were forced to develop and present convincing proofs to support their understanding of the same church fathers, and the same Holy Scriptures.[6]

The deep theorizing (both theological and philosophical) that emerged over the matter endowed this conflict with continuing significance that is still referenced with frequency today.

---

3 I confess my own proclivity toward the side of the iconophiles—I cannot maintain epoche in the matter, even while I appreciate the contrary views.

4 Exodus 20:4 states, "Thou shalt not make unto thee any graven image, or any likeness of any thing that is in heaven above, or that is in the earth beneath, or that is in the water under the earth." Exodus 20:5 continues, "Thou shalt not bow down thyself to them, nor serve them."

5 Exodus 25:18 instructs, "You shall make two cherubim of gold, make them of hammered work at the two ends of the mercy seat."

6 V. Avramidis, *The Image-less Idol: How Iconoclasm Leads to Idolatry*, (2019), 5.

Ironically, this scholarship was apparently overlooked at the onset of the Reformation and was seldom referred to, even as the iconoclasts and iconodulators traversed the same theological turf and reformulated arguments that echoed bygone disputes. Practically speaking, these disparate positions comprised overt attempts to regulate how others practiced their faith in a perpetual feud between those who celebrate imagery and those who distrust it. Or in the reductive view of Jungian Rafael Lopez-Pedraza, iconoclasm is "a struggle between two forces: the image on the one hand, and the forces that try to destroy it on the other."[7]

4 Icons as Symbolic Imagery

During the medieval period, the populace was illiterate, sermons were few, and masses were conducted in Latin. As a result, people lived in a highly visual culture, and images were vested with moral and spiritual meaning. Defenders of visual art advocated for the potency of images in moral education and religious devotion, arguing that an image recalls to memory what it represents more vividly and effectually than mere words. Writing around the middle of the 15th century, Bishop Reginald Pecock once again defended the use of images in churches in commonplace terms. Roughly translated, he explained:

> Seeing with the eye shows and brings into the imagination and into the mind within a man's head much information, and a great deal of information sooner and with less labor, work, and effort, than hearing with the ear does. And if this is true of a man who is able to read stories written in books, so much more is this true of those persons who are not able to read in books, since they shall easily find the painted walls of a church, a dyed cloth, or images spread throughout various parts of the church.[8]

In this he might have been one of the first to suggest "a picture is worth a thousand words," arguing that people remember a story they *see* more readily than one that is merely heard. Pecock emphasized that images might be regarded as "books of the unlearned," a view originally conveyed by Pope Gregory the Great in the sixth century, who relied on them for pedagogy, and suggested

7 M. A. Capriles, "Post-Jungian Movements: Conversations with Rafael López-Pedraza." *Spring* 77 (2007): 263.

8 P. Hardwick, *English Medieval Misericords: The Margins of Meaning*, (Woodbridge, UK: Boydell Press, 2011), 44.

"the image is the writing of the illiterate."[9] Because visual images could teach which virtues to be imitated and vices to be avoided, he wrote that "it is one thing to adore a picture and quite another to learn from narrative paintings what *should* be adored."[10] To illustrate how images could move a spectator to compassion and devotion, a recital was often invoked of how St. Gregory of Nyssen was moved to tears upon seeing a painting of the Sacrifice of Isaac. As a bishop from the Second Council of Nicaea commented, "Many times the father had read the story, but perchance he had not wept; but when once he saw it painted, he wept."[11]

Much of the Church's teachings began to be transmitted through pictures, which were spellbinding. Sculpture, stained glass, and wall paintings were the principal means for conveying faith inside churches, with images of saints arrayed alongside complex narrative scenes portraying events such as the life of the Virgin Mary or the Day of Judgment. In the view of C.G. Jung, these myriad metaphoric figures might be regarded as "personifications of psychic forces."[12]

In the late Middle Ages churches strove for overall decoration with few bare surfaces, and the predominant style in the 14th century has been called "decorated" for that very reason. Even the smallest of churches represented the Kingdom of God on earth, and its decor was created not only for the eyes of man but also for God, whose gaze could penetrate all spaces. Whenever possible, no hard, plain surfaces were left uncovered, and the minutest detail enhanced the splendor and glory of the church.

5 Imagery as an Inner Focus

Pope Gregory approved of images because "they arouse [people] from vain and worldly thoughts to more intent and frequent meditation on unseen things and the desire for them."[13] Graphic illustrations focused one's mind upon

9 M. J. Ramos, *Essays in Christian Mythology: The Metamorphosis of Prester John,* (Lanham, MD: University Press of America, 2006), 274.

10 H. A. Kelly, *The Middle English Bible: A Reassessment,* (Philadelphia, PA: University of Pennsylvania Press, 2016), 68.

11 M. Tassi, *The Scandal of Images: Iconoclasm, Eroticism, and Painting in Early Modern English Drama,* (Selinsgrove, PA: Susquehanna University Press, 2005), 30.

12 C. G. Jung, "Wotan." In *The Collected Works of C. G. Jung,* eds., H. Read, M. Fordham, G. Adler, W. McGuire, trans., R. F. C. Hull, Vol. 10: 179–193, (Princeton, NJ: Princeton University Press, 1970), 185.

13 J. C. D. Smith, *A Guide to Church Woodcarvings: Misericords and Bench-Ends,* (London, UK: David and Charles, 1974), 97.

spiritual matters. It was claimed that ruminating about Christ on the cross was the best weapon against sin, and figures of the Virgin and St. John mourning the crucified Christ in the church nave helped the faithful to conceive of that tragic episode and to contemplate its meaning.

In 1681, the Bishop of Worcester weighed in, composing in rhyme:

> A God the Image represents,
> But is no God in kind;
> That's the eye's object,
> It shows the object of the mind.[14]

We may take this to mean he condoned a *personification*[15] of God from the image, so long as the image itself was not venerated. However, even such support for images could not alleviate the continuous undercurrent of clerical anxiety about the dangers of idolatry.

Fear that the viewers misdirected their veneration toward the image rather than to the holy person represented in the image lay at the heart of this controversy. Bishop Ralph of Armagh, for example, fretted that people worshiped images named for those whom they were intended to represent, as if St. Mary the Virgin "was actually present in the statue."[16] This would make her worshipers idolaters because the Virgin was of course not inside the statue but in Heaven. Such apprehension on his part might understandably trigger the retort given previously in 814 by St. Theodore the Studite, who did not mince words when he wrote:

> No one could ever be so insane as to suppose that shadow and truth, nature and art, original and copy, cause and effect are the same in essence; or to say that each is in the other, or either one is in the other.[17]

6 Protestantism and Iconoclasm

The Protestant Reformation fractured the unity of Christianity and sparked a calamitous rise in iconoclasm. C.G. Jung viewed this event as disastrous,

---

14 T. T. Wildridge, *The Grotesque in Church Art,* (Glasgow, UK: Sagwan Press, 2015), 33.

15 Much debate has taken place among religious scholars about the degree to which an icon or image operates as a *personification* of the entity it represents. Steven Bigham (see references) details many of the nuances at issue, which are beyond the scope of this paper.

16 J. C. D. Smith, *A Guide to Church Woodcarvings: Misericords and Bench-Ends,* (London, UK: David and Charles, 1974), 97.

17 C. Roth, *On the Holy Icons,* (Crestwood, NY: St. Vladimir's Seminary Press, 1981), 31.

observing how "the iconoclasm of the Reformation . . . quite literally made a breach in the protective wall of sacred images, and since then one image after another has crumbled away."[18] He believed this to be the cause for "how the alarming poverty of symbols that is now the condition of our life came about,"[19] heralded by the destruction of so many carved treasures in continental Europe. Untold numbers of intricate and precious sculptures were lost. Our heritage of medieval artistry rendered in paint, glass, stone, and wood was decimated during the Reformation by a Protestant Church that harbored an aversion to images.

In 1550, during the reign of Henry the Eighth's son Edward the Sixth, England suffered through its own Reformation, culminating in the following century with the smashing of stained-glass windows, dismantling of church organs, and burning of hymnals. This destruction was vividly reported by Bishop Joseph Hall of Norwich:

> Lord what work was here! What clattering of glasses! What beating down of walls! What tearing up of monuments! What pulling down of seats! What wresting out of irons and brass from the windows! What defacing of arms! What demolishing of curious stonework! What tooting and piping upon organ pipes! And what a hideous triumph in the market-place before all the country, when all the mangled organ pipes, vestments, both copes and surplices, together with the leaden cross which had newly been sawn down from the Green-yard pulpit and the service-books and singing books that could be carried to the fire in the public market-place were heaped together.[20]

7 The Survival of the Misericords

An early church decoration that often escaped the iconoclasts was the misericord, a unique medieval innovation. A rule required monks to remain standing during daily offices of the church for as much as eight hours a day. Older monks had difficulty adhering to this rule, so in an act of pity, a device was

18 C. G. Jung, Archetypes of the Collective Unconscious. In *The Collected Works of C. G. Jung*, eds., H. Read, M. Fordham, G. Adler, W. McGuire, trans., R. F. C. Hull, Vol. 9, Part 1: (3–41). (Princeton, NJ: Princeton University Press, 1990), 12.

19 Ibidem, 13.

20 J. Hall, *The Works of the Right Reverend Father in God Joseph Hall, Lord Bishop of Norwich*, (London, UK: Thomas Hodgkin, 1714), XVII.

concocted. Called a "misericord" or "mercy seat," derived from a Latin phrase meaning "mercy of the heart," it consisted of a carved wooden bracket installed on the underside of the hinged seats of the choirstalls. Monks could tip their seats up and rest on the upper ledge of the misericord, all the while giving the appearance of standing whilst really sitting. The choir seat, ledge, and bracket were fashioned from a single piece of wood, typically oak. Medieval imagiers had an aversion to blank surfaces, and these craftsmen assuredly seized the opportunity to lavishly adorn these benches (see Figure 8.2).

FIGURE 4.2 Misericords showing the seat down and up. (Photo by author)

Many original misericord carvings can still be found today since they were hidden from view when the seat was folded down, thereby escaping the notice of the destructive iconoclasts when they wantonly vandalized the opulent edifices enclosing them. With their intricate decorations, these seats displayed a wide variety of subjects, ranging from biblical scenes to local references, with all manner of fanciful representations, including scriptural angels, saints, and the four evangelists, alongside various peculiar secular characters, animals, and monsters.[21] Gombrich wondered, "What prompted the artists to portray these bizarre figures? Was it a belief in some magic power to ward off the evil spirit, or just an innocent desire to indulge their sense of fun?"[22] Stylized

21 For more information, see the online database at http://www.misericords.co.uk/

22 E. H. Gombrich, and K. Kris, *Caricature,* (Harmondsworth, UK: Penguin Books, 1940), 6.

portrayals of most misericord subjects suggest they were copied from manuscript illustrations or other visual sources in the church. Bestiaries may have provided the most fertile derivations, since they were especially popular until the 14th century. Bestiaries united animal characteristics and behavior with allegorical tales, and thereby supplied carvers with a wealth of exotic creatures to imitate—from elephants and basilisks to mermaids and unicorns, alongside a wealth of depictions of the pagan "Green Man." Challis explained how "it is clear that those who were responsible for the wood carvings in our churches were not prepared to accept any strait jacket of strict Christian beliefs."[23] By offering comfort to the lower realms of the human body, misericords were on the down-to-earth side of matters, connecting the hallowed spiritual side with its opposite, *base* side. These craftsmen were observing what Ćurčić termed "the law of contrasts,"[24] and they heightened the experience by juxtaposing opposites within the same enclosed space. Life in the Middle Ages was an eternal struggle between the forces of good and evil, and—as with other images in the church—Gothic carvers were charged by their ecclesiastical employers to stress this contrast, and a tension of opposition could be experienced viscerally through these antithetical juxtapositions. As Gombrich characterized it, "If the portals of cathedrals were adorned with solemn statues and the windows glowed with tragic martyrdoms, on stalls and capitals, in ornaments and gargoyles, the world of grotesque[25] drollery lived its own life."[26]

Much of the humor on misericords contravened societal norms, displaying situations that inverted the world's natural state of affairs and contrarily upset the divinely rational order. Those whimsical reversals included mice hanging a cat, a rabbit boiling a dog in a pot, pupils whipping the teacher, and a fox in a cassock preaching to the barnyard—plus traditional gender roles were often switched around, such as women wearing pants or couples engaging in assorted marital combat, typically with a wife beating her husband. This recurrent theme of inversion harkened back to antiquity when early Christians bemoaned the destruction of rational order through the fall of Lucifer and

23 P. Hardwick, *English Medieval Misericords: The Margins of Meaning,* (Woodbridge, UK: Boydell Press, 2011), 20.

24 S. Ćurčić, "Aesthetic Shifts in Late Antique Art: Abstraction, Dematerialization, and Two-Dimensionality", In *Transition to Christianity: Art of Late Antiquity, 3rd–7th Century AD*, ed., A. Lazaridou. (New York, NY: Alexander S. Onassis Public Benefit Foundation, 2011), 68.

25 The term *grotesque* is a contraction of *grotto-esque*, referring to the fantastic decorations of ancient Roman private apartments unearthed during archaeological digs in the 15th century. It later morphed into its current definition as something odd or unnatural in shape, appearance, or character.

26 E. H. Gombrich, and K. Kris, 6.

Adam and Eve, resulting in sin and disorder. By this means, a moral ingredient was nested within the humor of topsy-turvy situations, concealing a nightmarish fear at the thought of the natural order becoming overturned without warning. On the whole, sinful human life was seen as an absurd reversal of the proper world of God, and so these "world-upside-down" scenes underscored the precariousness of human existence.

On many misericords, the artisan's accent was on humor, sporadically transgressing into lewd images of rudeness and outright bawdiness, such as showing couples flagrantly engaging in sex. Within the context of often overwrought expressions of spirituality within the church, the humor of the misericords likely offered a light and amusing escape from moral tales by providing a combination of sacred *and* profane exemplars. Some of the imagery found in these settings would be considered vulgar scatological humor by today's standards, such as portraits of people urinating, defecating, or collecting excrement, and perhaps they served as a reminder that our earthly existence is constantly beset by sin. This quintessentially medieval form of amusement may also have been a reaction to the Church's incessant preaching on the dangers of the flesh, conveying the ominous warning that rejoicing in animal nature and sin would incur subsequent punishments. Medieval artists might simply have employed levity to enforce their moral lessons, since fear and mirth are closely intertwined, and laughter frequently results from overcoming unconscious fear.

It is instructive to compare stylistic differences between these early medieval churches harboring profane images and the high-minded churches built during the Renaissance where only the ideal was celebrated, and every object aspired to express beauty and glorify God. While these latter cathedrals (such as the Cathedral of the Incarnation in Granada) are magnificent to behold, they lack the humanizing earthiness and warmth these earlier structures connote and may leave the visitor impressed but lightheaded from exposure to endless striving for purity and heavenly rapture framed in gleaming gilt. As Gombrich noted, "[We] all feel relieved once in a while to see the sublime reduced to the ridiculous."[27]

8 Opposition to the Grotesque

Whatever their purpose, these grotesqueries have been pronounced a "false taste"[28] (in poor taste) and undesirable to be perpetuated. The misericords are

27 E. H. Gombrich, and K. Kris, 5.

28 T. T. Wildridge, *The Grotesque in Church Art,* (Glasgow, UK: Sagwan Press, 2015), 25.

often kept off limits in the grand cathedrals, and when I toured York Minster, the docent did not even want to answer my questions about the curious stone figures in the Chapter House, seeming to resent their repulsive intrusion into holy space. She is not the only one. As early as 1125, St. Bernard of Clairvaux inquired:

> Why are there those ridiculous monstrosities in the monasteries where the monks do their reading, marvelous things at once ugly *and* beautiful? Why are there foul monkeys there? Why fierce lions? Why chimaerical centaurs? Why harpies? Why spotted tigers? Why fighting soldiers? Why hunters blowing horns within the cloisters? You see here under one head many bodies, and there one body with many heads. A serpent is seen with four feet, and a fish with a quadruped animal's head. There is a creature that is a horse in front, a goat behind; and another with horns and a horse's rear. There are so many there and of such diverse shapes that it is easier to read in the marble than in the books, spending the whole day gazing at each in turn, rather than meditating upon God's law.[29]

By this interrogation, Bernard questioned the practice of planting ridiculous monstrosities in the cloisters.

Yet one pertinent response to his question might be: *to honor diversity*. The church was an epitome of the world, and artists wished to place every living thing within it. To the unsophisticated medieval mind these weird creatures were representative of the amazing variety to be found in God's creation, which encompassed that which was ugly and dangerous directly alongside the beautiful and innocuous. As Barton observed:

> The contemplation of the divine understands God's creations in this world as part of the divine plan. Whether a creature is observed from life or is the product of the medieval imagination, it is … given equal weight on what is seen as the broad spectrum of God's creation, which stretches from the familiar to the monstrous.[30]

For the medieval viewer these freakish forms were, as Mittman explained,

> equal to images of Christ and the saints as images of God and his heavenly hosts, whose universal spectrum was broad enough to contain at

29 J. R. Sommerfeldt, *Bernard of Clairvaux on the Spirituality of Relationship,* (New York, NY: The Newman Press, 2004), 126.

30 P. Hardwick, *English Medieval Misericords: The Margins of Meaning,* (Woodbridge, UK: Boydell Press, 2011), 6.

> one end holy perfection and at the other the most wretched and abject, the vile, and the absolutely evil.[31]

Observers in medieval times would likely have positioned themselves somewhere between these two extremes, with the lower end of the scale no less salient than the higher end.

Within this spectrum, these part-human amalgams challenged the definition of the line between man and beast. Monsters[32] purportedly existed as a counter to normal humans; demons opposed angels, while pain and suffering encouraged better appreciation of good health. This theme is bound up with the sinful nature of human beings—of the animal side that sometimes takes over and the relentless battle between good and evil.

9 Psychomachia as Personification

This same contrast was graphically portrayed in the *Psychomachia*, a poem from the fifth century, whose ancient precedents derived from Greek philosophy. It seems our very earliest sages were obsessed with developing taxonomies of human strengths and shortcomings, starting with Plato enumerating several virtues in his writing. In similar fashion, Aristotle's *Nicomachean Ethics* lists positive, healthy human qualities, excellences, or *virtues*. He located virtue as a moderate point somewhere between the deficiency and excess of a trait, and so for each positive quality, two negative *vices* were to be found at the extreme ends of each scale.

The Roman lyric poet Horace (*c.* 20 CE) likewise extolled the value of virtue while listing and warning against vices. In his *First Epistle* he declared that "the beginning of virtue is to avoid vice; the beginning of wisdom is to depart from folly."[33]

But the *Christian* concept of vice seems to originate in the works of a fourth-century monk named Evagrius Ponticus, a theologian considered to be one of the "Desert Fathers," who catalogued eight evil thoughts, demons, or terrible temptations—nefarious evil forces from which all sinful behavior

31 A. Mittman, *Maps and Monsters in Medieval England,* (New York, NY: Routledge, 2006), 5.

32 Monsters belong to a tradition of moral allegory in which vices were portrayed as demonic forces, illustrating "the realm of the baser instincts," before becoming personified as human figures. See A. Katzenellenbogen, *Allegories of the Virtues and Vices in Medieval Art,* (Toronto, Canada: University of Toronto Press, 1989).

33 Horace, *Horace, the Greatest of Lyric Poets,* (Ann Arbor, MI: University of Michigan Library, 1907), 116.

springs. This checklist was intended to help people recognize their own areas of culpability, as well as providing the means to redress them.

Personifications of moral concepts had already materialized in antiquity, where human forms were used to represent sundry abstract concepts in the classical Greek tradition and the Roman concepts were personified as a host of numinous deities (including a female deity representing *Virtus* itself), and the Virtues thereby emerged in concrete and living form.

The fifth-century poet Aurelius Prudentius Clemens (Prudentius) developed the idea of personifying virtues and vices even further with a poem he authored titled *Psychomachia*,[34] which was a kind of spiritual drama that remained popular in England for several centuries and earned prestige as the first narrative poem in Europe written entirely as allegory.[35] In this epic poem, Prudentius described how the armies of the Virtues and Vices faced off against one another with champions from either side issuing challenges to single combat, resulting in a variety of duels (see Figure 4.3).

Fides Faith	⟷	*Veterum Cultura Deorum* Worship of Old Gods
Pudicitia Chastity	⟷	*Sodomita Libido* Lust of the Sodomite
Patientia Patience	⟷	*Ira* Anger
Mens Humilis Humility	⟷	*Superbia* Pride
Sobrietas Soberness	⟷	*Luxuria* Indulgence
Operatio Good Works	⟷	*Avaritia* Avarice
Concordia Concord	⟷	*Discordia* Discord

FIGURE 4.3
List of Virtues and their corresponding Vices. (Adapted from Prudentius by the author)

Approximately 1,000 lines in length, the poem portrays Christian virtues defeating pagan idolatry in the form of seven dramatic and action-packed military battle scenes waged between personifications of the Vices and Virtues. More sophisticated than the simple, personified abstractions in the style of the Greeks, Prudentius' characters are presented in ways that depict them as human beings evincing the particular qualities of the virtue or vice they allegorize. Lust attacks Chastity, who retaliates with a sword. Mortally wounded and

34 A. Pelttari, *The Psychomachia of Prudentius: Text, Commentary, and Glossary*, (Norman, OK: University of Oklahoma Press, 2019).

35 In scope and style, it has been compared to Virgil's *Aenid.*

vomiting blood, Lust expires while Chastity exults with a monologue about her victory. Patience is ineffectually besieged by Anger, who becomes frustrated and kills herself by thrusting a lance through her own breast. Greed and Love go head-to-head, but their incompatibility leads to a stalemate. Humility chops off the head of Pride after the latter stumbles into a pit that Dishonesty dug on the battlefield.

In comparable gruesome fashion, the remaining Vices fight their virtuous counterparts and are invariably thwarted, cheered on by a thousand Christian martyrs. It is a gory bloodbath that reinforces the deep-seated Christian faith in the power of goodness.

Christian literature often addressed the subject of virtue either explicitly or implicitly, and early authors singled out favored virtues as paramount. The *Psychomachia* was a crucial text in establishing key conflicts and iconographies, and to many minds, the virtues and vices became real as angels and demons, each flaunting their own distinct personality—the antecedent of the cartoon cliché of an angel on one shoulder and a demon on the other whispering into a hapless individual's ear. This allegory of good versus evil was decidedly popular in the medieval period and was widely copied and glossed in the Middle Ages with about 300 surviving copies, 20 of which were illuminated in a form that has been compared to the modern graphic novel. Personification likewise became especially popular during the Middle Ages because of its dialectic and didactic potential for providing visual expression to the battle between good and evil that was believed to transpire in the soul of every individual—an eternal preoccupation of the archaic medieval mind.

Were it not for Prudentius, we would not today think in terms of the Seven Virtues or the Seven Deadly Sins. While considered didactic and moralizing by many contemporary readers, this poem afforded endless pleasure to the age that followed him as it was felt that he provided a clear picture of the inner conflict. The turbulent heroines of Prudentius became frozen into sculptures of majestic immobility that can still be admired in some of the world's greatest cathedrals.

Initially, only the Virtues tended to be portrayed in representations, but as time went on, the Vices eventually outnumbered them. In keeping with this trend, the sculptures in the Chapter House at York Minster appear to be mostly representations of Vice. Reminding sinners of their faults might have been thought more relevant than exhibiting portrayals of model saints and their virtues. Additionally, the Vices were more realistically and humorously depicted, with every depravity associated with some type of animal, since animals personified human weaknesses. For example, the monkey was associated with *curiosita*, or a thirst for knowledge, warily regarded as a vice since it led to Adam and Eve being expelled from Eden. An additional unrelenting fear was that one sin would invariably lead to another. Drink in particular, in its association with gambling, might lead to fighting, which would then lead to the sin of Anger or Wrath. Life was thereby pictured as a constant cycling of tension between Good and Evil, with their conflict originating right from birth itself. As illustration, Rosslyn Chapel features the seven Vices and Virtues opposing one another on two sides of a single elaborately carved transom.[36]

10 Modern Personification

Ancient churches are marvelous allegories for our own psychic tasks. As Jung stated, "The relationship between religion and the unconscious is everywhere obvious: all religions are full of figures from the unconscious."[37] Whenever we consider good and evil with their associated personifications of shadow, psychomachia, or activation of the transcendent function, these archaic sanctuaries may be said to represent an image of the human self as a container of its myriad opposites. Are these images archetypes? I can only say they evoked something deep and archaic within me as I viewed them.

In modern times, C.G. Jung encouraged his patients to draw or paint imaginal figures they encountered in dreams or active imagination, just as he himself illustrated the figures he encountered during active imagination, carefully reproducing images of Salome and Philemon in *Liber Novus,* whom he personified and conversed with. Personifications are *image*, and Jung asserted that "everything of which we are conscious is an image, and that *image is psyche*."[38] Jung described how activated portions of the unconscious assumed the character of personalities when perceived by the conscious mind and suggested that our personal unconscious, as well as the collective unconscious, consisted of an indefinite number of fragmentary personalities. He touted the many

36 Note that two of the figures are juxtaposed. The carving showing the seven corporal works of mercy mistakenly includes "avarice," and the carving of the seven deadly sins mistakenly includes "charity." Whether this was erroneous or mischievously deliberate, no one knows; it is a mystery.

37 C. G. Jung, *Nietzsche's Zarathustra: Notes of the Seminar given in 1934–1939*, ed., J. Jarrett. (Princeton, NJ: Princeton University Press, 1988), 1351.

38 C. G. Jung, "Commentary on 'The Secret of the Golden Flower'", In eds., H. Read, M. Fordham, G. Adler, & W. McGuire, trans., R. F. C. Hull, *The Collected Works of C. G. Jung* (Vol. 13, pp. 1–56). (Princeton, NJ: Princeton University Press, 1983), 50.

advantages of personification, noting that "when a thing is personified it has autonomy and you can talk to it."[39]

James Hillman defined *personifying* as "the spontaneous experiencing, envisioning and speaking of the configurations of existence as psychic presences"[40] and described how personifying allows the multiplicity of psychic phenomena to be experienced as voices, faces, and names, such that "psychic phenomena can then be perceived with precision and particularity." According to Hillman, "What was once an affect, a symptom, an obsession, is now a figure with whom I can talk."[41]

Jung encouraged the exercise of active imagination, which he asserted was based on older practices such as crystal-gazing, automatic writing, hypnosis, and even the practice of alchemy. During a typical Jungian analysis session, if a patient triggered something psychoactive, the analyst would "invite them to draw the image using the paper and crayons or pencils that they keep available in their consulting room."[42] Analysts also traditionally "typed" imaginal figures using Jung's system of psychological types and affiliated each with a particular form of consciousness.[43] Following this tradition, Beebe has attempted to "type"[44] the figures profiled by Jung in *Liber Novus: The Red Book*.

In 2018, I conducted a workshop at a British conference for typology professionals and attempted to trigger a "type complex" in each of my attendees using simple guided imagery. I asked the participants to invite their unconscious to provide them with images representing their functions and then encouraged them to draw those images on cards that I supplied. They were asked to create four images: one for each of the functions, and then to characterize the one that gave them the most trouble on a fifth card, with no restrictions on which function that might be (see Figure 4.4).

39 C. G. Jung, *Nietzsche's Zarathustra: Notes of the Seminar given in 1934–1939*, ed., J. Jarrett. (Princeton, NJ: Princeton University Press, 1988), 1259.

40 J. Hillman, *Re-Visioning Psychology*, (New York, NY: William Morrow Paperbacks, 1997), 12.

41 J. Hillman, *Archetypal Psychology: A Brief Account*, (Woodstock, CT: Spring Publications, 1983), 52.

42 P. Goss, *Jung: A Complete Introduction*, (London, UK: John Murray Learning, 2015), 194.

43 See M. Milner, *The Hands of the Living God: An Account of a Psycho-analytic Treatment*, (New York, NY: Routledge, 2010), XLIII.

44 J. Beebe, "The Red Book as a Work of Conscience: Notes from a Seminar given for the 35th Annual Jungian Conference. C. G. Jung Club of Orange County, April 10, 2010." *Quadrant* XXXX, no. 2 (2010): 41–58. In this context, the "typing" of these characters follows Jung's original eight functions of consciousness as detailed in his book *Psychological Types*, and not an overall type code such as that generated by an assessment like the Myers-Briggs Type Indicator® (MBTI)®.

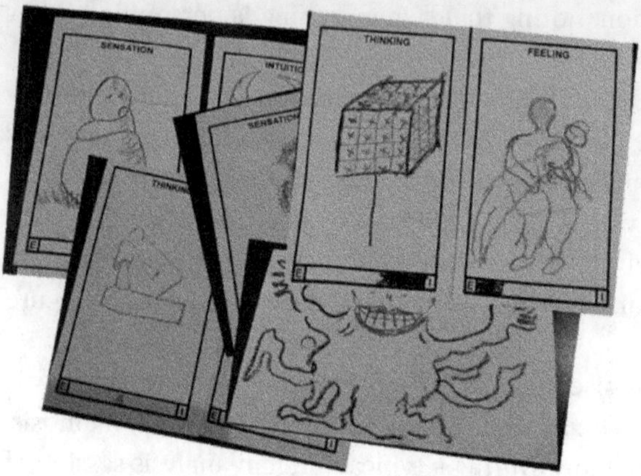

FIGURE 4.4 Images representing Type Complexes

Their drawings brought to consciousness some of the tensions that lived within the culture and within the psyche of each participant, and their results amply demonstrated how we all struggle with our own inner psychomachia. Each of us possesses our own cosmology, our own cast of characters, with our souls impatiently waiting for us to engage them as part of our individuation process.

11 Conclusion

Marion Woodman declared, "The unconscious image has to be brought into consciousness for you to see what's going on in the unconscious. That's what analysis is all about."[45] The act of personifying—whether through active imagination, chair-work in Gestalt, Transactional Analysis, psychodrama, sandplay, Dialogical Self, or Internal Family Systems (among others)—has proven to be efficacious as a form of mental health treatment. Exploring imaginal figures is thought to be especially effective, and Western culture might benefit from a greater embrace of this practice. Witnessing this superlative track record, I might echo the plaintive appeal of John Rowan, who addressed therapists and researchers: "My question to you is a simple one—why do you not use personification more in the actual therapy you conduct and research?"[46]

---

45 M. Woodman, *Marion Woodman and the Conscious Feminine: Marion Woodman in Conversation with Marlene Schiwy* [video recording], (Vancouver, Canada: Principia Productions Ltd, 2012).

46 J. Rowan, *Subpersonalities: The People Inside Us,* (New York, NY: Routledge, 1990), 4.

Despite Jung's wholehearted embrace and encouragement of using personification, nowadays people tend to talk about aspects of the psyche in terms of abstract principles, concepts, and qualities rather than encountering actual inner personalities.[47] Might this be a subtle form of iconoclasm against inner images? Perhaps it is time for us all to stock up on paper and crayons once again.

References

Avramidis, V., *The Image-less Idol: How Iconoclasm Leads to Idolatry*, Retrieved from https://www.academia.edu/7353973/The_Image-less_Idol_How_Iconoclasm_leads_to_Idolatry?source=swp_share, 2019.

Beebe, J., "The Red Book as a Work of Conscience: Notes from a Seminar given for the 35th Annual Jungian Conference. C. G. Jung Club of Orange County, April 10, 2010." *Quadrant* XXXX, no. 2 (2010): 41–58.

Bigham, S., "Allegorical Personification in Orthodox Iconography," *Sacred Art Journal* 13 (1992): 56–67.

Capriles, M. A., "Post-Jungian Movements: Conversations with Rafael López-Pedraza," *Spring* 77 (2007): 245–276.

Ćurčić, S., "Aesthetic Shifts in Late Antique Art: Abstraction, Dematerialization, and Two-Dimensionality", In *Transition to Christianity: Art of Late Antiquity, 3rd–7th Century AD*, ed., A. Lazaridou, New York, NY: Alexander S. Onassis Public Benefit Foundation, 2011.

Gombrich, E. H., Kris, K. *Caricature*, Harmondsworth, UK: Penguin Books, 1940.

Goss, P., *Jung: A Complete Introduction*, London, UK: John Murray Learning, 2015.

Hall, J., *The Works of the Right Reverend Father in God Joseph Hall, Lord Bishop of Norwich*, London, UK: Thomas Hodgkin, 1714.

Hillman, J., *Re-Visioning Psychology*, New York, NY: William Morrow Paperbacks, 1997.

Horace, *Horace, the Greatest of Lyric Poets*, Ann Arbor, MI: University of Michigan Library, 1907.

Jung, C. G., "Wotan." In *The Collected Works of C. G. Jung*, Vol. 10, eds., H. Read, M. Fordham, G. Adler, W. McGuire, trans., R. F. C. Hull, Princeton, NJ: Princeton University Press, 1970: 179–193.

47 Analyzing this curious and obstinate resistance, it might be argued that the ego is "iconoclast" (monotheistically opposed to images), while the Self is "iconodule" (polytheistic; creatively and perpetually offering images). The ego readily forfeits healing (wholeness) in order to preserve its singularity.

Jung, C. G. "Commentary on 'The Secret of the Golden Flower.'" In *The Collected Works of C. G. Jung*, Vol. 13, eds., H. Read, M. Fordham, G. Adler, W. McGuire, trans., R. F. C. Hull, Princeton, NJ: Princeton University Press, 1983: 1–56.

Jung, C. G., *Nietzsche's Zarathustra: Notes of the Seminar given in 1934–1939*, Princeton, NJ: Princeton University Press, 1988.

Jung, C. G., "Archetypes of the collective unconscious." In *The Collected Works of C. G. Jung*, Vol. 9, Part 1, eds., H. Read, M. Fordham, G. Adler, W. McGuire, trans., R. F. C. Hull, Princeton, NJ: Princeton University Press, 1990: 3–41.

Katzenellenbogen, A., *Allegories of the Virtues and Vices in Medieval Art*. Toronto, Canada: University of Toronto Press, 1989.

Kelly, H. A., *The Middle English Bible: A Reassessment*. Philadelphia, PA: University of Pennsylvania Press, 2016.

Meaden, T., *The Secrets of the Avebury Stones: Britain's Greatest Megalithic Temple*, Berkeley, CA: Frog, Ltd, 2000.

Milner, M., *The Hands of the Living God: An Account of a Psycho-analytic Treatment*, New York, NY: Routledge, 2010.

Mittman, A., *Maps and Monsters in Medieval England*, New York, NY: Routledge, 2006.

Pelttari, A., *The Psychomachia of Prudentius: Text, Commentary, and Glossary*, Norman, OK: University of Oklahoma Press, 2019.

Plato, *Timaeus and Critias*, ed., T. Kjeller Johansen, trans., D. Lee, New York, NY: Penguin Classics, 2008.

Ramos, M. J., *Essays in Christian Mythology: The Metamorphosis of Prester John*, Lanham, MD: University Press of America, 2006.

Roth, C., *On the Holy Icons*, Crestwood, NY: St. Vladimir's Seminary Press, 1981.

Rowan, J., *Subpersonalities: The People Inside Us*, New York, NY: Routledge, 1990.

Smith, J. C. D., *A Guide to Church Woodcarvings: Misericords and Bench-Ends*, London: David and Charles, 1974.

Sommerfeldt, J. R., *Bernard of Clairvaux on the Spirituality of Relationship*, New York, NY: The Newman Press, 2004.

Tassi, M., *The Scandal of Images: Iconoclasm, Eroticism, and Painting in Early Modern English Drama*, Selinsgrove, PA: Susquehanna University Press, 2005.

Wildridge, T. T., *The Grotesque in Church Art*, Glasgow, UK: Sagwan Press, 2015.

Woodman, M., *Marion Woodman and the Conscious Feminine: Marion Woodman in Conversation with Marlene Schiwy* [video recording], Vancouver, Canada: Principia Productions Ltd, 2012.

CHAPTER 5

The Wall: Object, Image, and Processes in the Individual and Collective Psyche

Monica Luci

Abstract

Walls have proliferated over the past 15 years, and quantitative analysis suggests they are a global phenomenon meriting further attention. Walls are more than simply barriers made of stones or bricks; they are made of a variety of materials and are often equipped with surveillance devices and military apparatus to control the movements of populations at borders. This chapter intends to present a study of walls and fences of the world from the perspective of analytical psychology, investigating both the empirical and symbolic facets of the erection of structures designed to keep away (and/or keep away from) the Other or others. Limiting the area of investigation to contemporary walls, the chapter will proceed with a typology of walls that is neither exclusive nor exhaustive but facilitates deeper investigation of the phenomenon. Here is advanced the hypothesis that the wall results from the activation of a group archetypal defense of Self in the face of a perceived threat. Walls separate space and people with the intention of conveying an idea of safety, and while providing this sense of safety, they design the geography of our Selves in large groups. It is proposed that they do that through our bodies (i.e., through perception of images that stimulate our senses, particularly tactile perception, if a barrier is seen or even just imagined within a group).

Keywords

Wall, borders, *participation mystique*, Hermes, states of identity, archetypal defense, psychic skin, group skin

1 Introduction

This chapter intends to present an initial study on walls and fences of the world from the perspective of analytical psychology, investigating both the empirical

 | DOI:10.1163/9789004468757_007

and symbolic facets of the erection of structures designed to keep away (and/or keep away from) the Other or others.

The *wall* is an interesting object that "embraces a heterogeneous range of structures built with diverse motivations on a variety of borders."[1] History and geography reveal a large variety of walls. Some were erected to protect or separate a culture or group from barbarians and/or the unknown and to delimit the territory of a kingdom, empire, or state, with these including the Great Wall of China, the Hadrian's Wall, and more recent political walls that delimit present-day states. Some walls of the past were deputed to create isolation from the surrounding environment, such as those enclosing the ghettos. This kind of wall today is more often designed to protect groups from terrorism. Then there are religious walls, such as the Western Wall in Jerusalem and the walls in Alsatian churches. Political walls placed at the borders of a State are generally to separate ethnic/religious/national groups and to control immigration.

At the end of the Second World War, there were seven border walls or fences in the world. According to Vallet's study, by the time the Berlin Wall fell in 1989, there were 15,[2] and today there are at least 77 walls or fences around the world, with many erected after the 9/11 attacks and others built after migration crises. Studying these various kinds of walls, you discover their different histories and functions and how those functions change over time.

Walls are made of different materials and conceived in different ways. Typically, they consist of much more than a barrier made of stones or bricks. Nowadays, these barriers are constructed of various materials surmounted by sharp edges that cut and injure; accompanied by sensors, cameras, and guard posts; flanked by border roads guarded by soldiers or police. Their existence is bolstered by an arsenal of laws and regulations determining the right to asylum and the aspects of residence, visas, and border procedures. Moreover, walls must be regarded not only as physical barriers but also as gateways, for they are punctured by official and unofficial openings through which people can cross from one side to the other. They also include apparatus, such as checkpoints, by which states can control the movement of populations.[3] In addition, a wall is not necessarily hermetically sealed. It is also a point of contact, an interface.

1 E. Vallet and C. P. David, "Introduction: The (Re)Building of the Wall in International Relations", *Journal of Borderlands Studies*, 27 (2012): 2, p. 115. DOI: 10.1080/08865655.2012.687211.

2 E. Vallet, *Borders, Fences and Walls. State of Insecurity?* (Abingdon, New York: Routledge, 2018).

3 See M. Sfard, *The Wall and the Gate: Israel, Palestine, and the Legal Battle for Human Rights* (New York: Metropolitan Books, 2018).

The aim of this study is to understand the function of the wall as object and image in the psychological processes of the individual and collective psyche. It seems reductive to think that walls are built only with a motivation of "defense" from enemies (often those who are targeted as such are very vulnerable people like migrants), or for the reasons that are officially put forward. Most walls were built in fact with a variety of functions, sometimes with a "symbolic" function to make the political program of a government evident or to make a state of segregation/separation between populations or factions concrete or even to annex territories or resources. In addition, many of these reasons go through a reshaping of the large group's psyche and the control that rulers can exercise over individuals and groups through such walls. My interest here is to understand why and how a wall performs all these functions (on a similar topic see Luci 2021).

This chapter offers a perspective that connects the *wall* as material object, with the somatic, psychic, and social *skin* as a means that has a crucial importance in the psychic and social processes involved in the dynamics of self and identity. In its material and symbolic forms, a wall seems to evoke a ubiquitous element of experience that regulates our complex relations with self and other, separating us from "different" others and enveloping us with "similar" others, thus influencing the modeling of individual selves within groups.

Limiting the area of investigation to contemporary walls, the chapter will proceed with a typology of walls, omitting the interesting and fascinating examples of the past.[4] Such a typology does not intend to be exclusive or exhaustive, and it maintains awareness that the functions of a wall overlap and may change over time. Only a few and well-known examples are provided.[5] However, they clarify that examining the historical conditions under which a wall was initially constructed is crucial to understand its nature or at least its initial function.

2 Ideological Walls

After the Second World War, the alliance between the United States of America and the Union of Soviet Socialist Republics, which was decisive in the defeat

4 For the walls of the past, see David Frye, *Walls: A History of Civilization in Blood and Brick* (New York: Scribner, 2018).

5 For much of the information that follows, I am indebted to Claude Quétel, *Histoire des Murs. Une autre histoire des hommes* (Paris: Edition Perrin, 2012) and Tim Marshall, *Divided: Why We're Living in an Age of Walls* (London: Elliott & Thompson Ltd, 2018).

of Nazism, quickly descended into crisis. Fear of the perceived expansionist aims of the Soviets led to Europe's dividing into two opposing blocs: the Western bloc, under the influence of the United States, and the communist bloc, under the hegemony of the USSR. Political and economic competition between the two superpowers, based on two contrasting economic systems and social development models, gave birth to a climate of continuous conflict and a threat to peace, characterized by an unstoppable race toward the development of nuclear weapons: the so-called Cold War. The "Iron Curtain," initially a metaphor for the divide, became a material reality and a militarized barrier erected between 1949 and 1989 from Lubecca to Trieste. These walls were points of accumulated tension between the two blocs, socialist and capitalist, representing an enormous threat looming over the world.

2.1 *The Berlin Wall*

After the Second World War, Germany was crushed by the weight of defeat and the division of its national territory, imposed by the winners, into two republics (the Federal Republic of Germany, a democratic and parliamentary state, and the German Democratic Republic [DDR], a communist regime). The old capital, Berlin, located in DDR territory, had also been divided into four zones placed under the control of the victorious powers. In August 1961, to mark this border line, the DDR began building a wall between the Soviet sector (East Berlin) and the western areas of the city (West Berlin) under allied control, as well as around West Berlin to isolate it from the rest of the DDR.

On August 13, 1961, under the astonished gaze of Berliners, the DDR authorities started constructing a wall that crossed the entire city and divided families, cutting off and separating streets, squares, and houses and interrupting underground and train lines. It soon became the symbol of the clash between the two opposing ideologies. Over time, the barrier was perfected with anti-personnel mines, high-voltage power lines, automatic firing systems, guard towers, and trenches in the so-called death strip. The exact number of people killed while trying to cross the Berlin Wall is not known. The official figure is 136, but from 1974 to 1979 there were 4,956 attempts, with 3,984 failing; 75,000 people were arrested and charged with the "crime of escape from the Republic." Between 1961 and its opening in 1989, the Berlin Wall was the symbol of a divided world and the enormous weight of suffering for the population.

In the early 1980s, the two blocs began to fall apart. The western bloc had repeatedly demonstrated its poor unity, especially questioning the so-called

Pax Americana. The communist bloc started to split particularly between Moscow and Beijing. The Polish unrest at the end of the 1970s, with its anti-communist and anti-Russian feelings, found support from the Catholic Church, and in September 1980, a wave of strikes led to the creation of a mass Catholic and anti-communist trade union, Solidarność.

In the Soviet Union, Mikhail Gorbachev, secretary of the Communist Party, tried to launch a series of reforms for political and economic renewal of the Soviet republics, especially to face the economic crisis of the time. His attempt, which had fed the hopes of a radical transformation throughout Eastern Europe, failed to prevent the now irreversible dissolution of communist regimes and of the USSR itself.

In May 1989, the German Democratic Republic began to suffer an unstoppable crisis. Tens of thousands of East German citizens started pouring westward through the Austro-Hungarian border, bypassing the very wall that, almost thirty years before, had represented the inviolability of the Iron Curtain. The East German authorities were forced to liberalize the expatriations. On November 9, 1989, the Berlin Wall, symbol of the Cold War, was attacked by the population, both from the East and from the West, and demolished.

2.2 *The Korean Wall*

A strip of land running across the Korean Peninsula serves as a buffer zone between North Korea and South Korea. In 1945, Korea was divided into two states along the 38th parallel, with North Korea protected by the Soviets and South Korea by the Americans. On June 28, 1950, North Korean troops crossed the divide. It was the beginning of a war that would last until 1953. On the Western side, 15 countries, led by the United States, participated in a crusade against communism. The war caused over two million fatalities. On July 27, 1953, an armistice was signed that provided for a line of demarcation coinciding with the front line where the fighting ceased and where it all began: the 38th parallel.

Since then, Korea has been cut in two by a fortified border 238 km long. Between the Democratic People's Republic of Korea (24.5 million inhabitants) and the Republic of Korea (48.7 million) there is a Demilitarized Zone (DMZ)—an absolutely improper name because it is anything but demilitarized—of 4 km in width. It is enclosed by a double wall from two to three meters high, rendered in concrete or reticulated and surmounted by barbed wire. It is one of the most hermetically sealed frontier in the world. Since 1953, 1,400 North Koreans have been killed while attempting to cross the DMZ.

3 Walls of Territorial Contention

This category of walls includes those erected in the context of territorial contention resulting from nationalistic politics of hegemony and/or appropriation of natural resources.

3.1 *Cyprus' Green Line*

The history of Cyprus is part of the historic rivalry between Greece and Turkey. Latinized for a long time, the island became an Ottoman province in the 16th century, although the community remained Greek. In 1878, Cyprus was ceded to Great Britain in exchange for its support to the Ottoman Empire against the expansionist aims of Russia. In the aftermath of the Second World War, three states had their eye on Cyprus: Turkey, Greece, and Great Britain.

Cyprus became an independent republic in 1960, with a Greek president and a Turkish vice president, and the United Kingdom, Turkey, and Greece as guarantors of the Constitution.

In 1963, the Greek president and archbishop of the island, Makarios, attempted to change the Constitution. Greek and Turkish Cypriots faced off, with both sides committing murder and rape in the name of ethnic cleansing. Turkey intervened militarily in July 1974. In two days it took over the entire northern part of the island. The kingdom of the Greek colonels collapsed, and with it went the coup leaders of Nicosia. The Turkish army forcibly imposed the partition of the island, establishing the border on the line where it stopped its campaign. To the north were Turkish Cypriots, and to the south were their Greek counterparts. Both communities, Turkish and Greek, living in opposing territory were driven out of their lands and homes, mostly without taking personal effects. A Green Line of 180 km in length and made of bins, sand blocks, and barbed wire was created, cutting the island in two from east to west, and separating the self-proclaimed Turkish Republic of Northern Cyprus from the southern Republic of Cyprus. Nicosia, situated on the front line, was also divided in two and remains so.

3.2 *The Sand Wall of the Western Sahara*

The Moroccan wall, or wall of the Western Sahara, is a berm longer than 2,720 km, built by Morocco in Western Sahara and designed as a means to defend itself against the Polisario Front. Polisario is a Sahrawi considered "rebel" national liberation movement aiming to end the Moroccan presence in the Western Sahara. The United Nations consider the Polisario Front to be legitimate representatives of the Sahrawi people, maintaining that they have a right to self-determination. The Polisario Front is outlawed in the part of Western Sahara under Moroccan control. This "defensive" structure is in effect a military area where special bunkers, moats, barbed wire fences, and minefields were installed. The minefield running along its entire length is the largest and longest in the world, and it is estimated to comprise around two million mines.

The construction of the Moroccan wall took place during different phases, with each aiming to expand the controlled territory for the defense of Morocco.

According to the Moroccan government, the wall has a strategic-defensive purpose, but according to the Sahrawi population, it serves to maintain control over a particularly profitable and strategic territory. The wall encloses phosphate mines, oil fields, and one of the most plentiful fishing areas of the Atlantic Ocean.

4 Anti-terrorism Walls

Anti-terrorism walls are officially built to protect a community from terrorist attacks, but some also have other functions such as appropriation of territory and segregation of populations.

4.1 *Israel*

Created in 1948, the state of Israel immediately found itself at war with neighboring Arab countries. In 1949, an armistice suspended hostilities, but Israel had already exceeded the territorial limits set by the partition plan of 1947, thus causing a Palestinian refugee crisis.

In 1967, the Six-Day War, again won by Israel against the Arab countries, aggravated the Palestinian situation. Israel conquered the Sinai Peninsula and the Gaza strip from Egypt, the strategic Golan Heights from Syria, and the West Bank from Jordan, as well as controlling the whole of Jerusalem. With the exception of the Sinai Desert, the Israelis have refused to relinquish these territories. Thus, the West Bank was, and partially remains, controlled and administered by Israel. Jewish colonies grew on these territories and led to the expulsion of the Palestinian families that lived there, exacerbating the feeling of being under siege.

Losing faith in their chances of ever becoming an independent state, Palestinians commenced the first Intifada (insurrection) in 1987. Failing to see results from the "international concert," the Palestine Liberation Organization (PLO), founded in 1964, proclaimed, in 1988, the birth of a Palestinian state in the West Bank and Gaza, with East Jerusalem as its capital. The peace process and negotiations carried out between Israel and the PLO during the 1990s were compromised by the activity of Israeli settlers in the West Bank and Palestinian suicide bombings in Israel.

As the second Intifada began, and the Al-Qaida terrorist network claimed responsibility for the 9/11 attacks, the toll of attacks in Israel left the Israeli population dismayed, with 1,000 dead and 6,000 injured. Deeply traumatized, Israelis demanded that their government enforce a radical separation from the Palestinians—not a border in the geopolitical sense of the term, but a barrier, a protective wall capable of preventing the passage of terrorists. The perception and language of the two people were markedly different, with Israelis speaking of Palestinian "terrorism" and Palestinians speaking of "armed resistance to occupation." Thus, the wall of Israel was created.

It was immediately clear that the construction of the wall was not just about fighting terrorism. Colonel Danny Tirza, appointed to trace the line of the wall, was a resident of a colony. He knew that the wall prefigured Israel's future eastern border and was supposed to grab the maximum amount of land with the minimum of Palestinians.

Nevertheless, despite the other elements motivating its construction, the wall did lead to a dramatic reduction in the number of suicide bombings.

4.2 *Baghdad Walls*

The 2003 invasion of Iraq by a military coalition of troops from the United States, the United Kingdom, Australia, Poland, and numerous other nations was the first stage of the Iraq War, lasting one month. Subsequently, the Coalition Provisional Authority (CPA) was established as the first of several successive transitional governments leading up to the first Iraqi parliamentary election in January 2005. U.S. military forces remained in Iraq until the official withdrawal in 2011.

The daily terrorist attacks that afflicted Baghdad during the coalition occupation and the transition phase produced two very different types of wall. First, classical walls protected the *Green Zone*, an area that housed most of the embassies, headquarters, and offices of the coalition forces, as well as the Parliament and Ministries of the new Iraqi government. In total, it was home to 5,000 people who never went out. The official name was the *International Zone*, but the population and journalists called it *The Bubble*, far from the reality of daily riots and attacks. Everything beyond it, the rest of Baghdad, was called the *Red Zone*, and for years it was at the mercy of attacks that killed more civilians than soldiers. Between 2008 and 2010, 900 children were killed and 3,200 wounded. The terrorists did not hesitate to target school buildings. The attacks culminated in 2006 and 2007, when the clashes became inter-denominational between

Shiites and Sunnis. The division between the two religious communities was much more profound than any sense of national belonging, which was created from nothing in 1932 after the British mandate since the end of World War I.

During the summer of 2006, the coalition forces, increasingly concerned about the civil war looming between Sunnis and Shiites, built walls to divide neighborhoods of Shia and Sunni communities, dividing Baghdad into ever-smaller areas. The city remained segregated for nearly a decade, with government officials partitioned away in the central zone. However, something changed in 2016, when the threat started coming from outside, from ISIS. Some of these concrete walls were dismantled in the districts that were no longer deemed under threat, and they were used to create a new wall around Baghdad. The walls and barriers around the so-called Green Zone remained until 2019, when security forces declared the Iraqi capital safe.

5 Segregation Walls

Segregation walls are intended to keep populations apart in order to temper tensions of various natures, often religious or economic.

5.1 *Northern Ireland Peace Lines*

Created in 1921 with the Government of Ireland Act that decided upon the partition of Ireland, Northern Ireland (six counties of the province of Ulster) remained part of the United Kingdom. It was just a stage in Ireland's long and bloody struggle to gain total independence from Great Britain. The *Peace Lines* are a series of barriers in Northern Ireland that separate predominantly Republican and Nationalist Catholic neighborhoods, where people support reunification of Ireland, from predominantly Loyalist and Unionist Protestant neighborhoods, where people tend to remain faithful to the United Kingdom. The stated purpose of the *Peace Lines* is to minimize inter-communal violence.

A movement for civil rights in Northern Ireland developed in the early 1960s, awakening a reaction of Protestant extremism. An escalation of clashes between the two communities overwhelmed the local (and predominantly Protestant) Royal Ulster Constabulary and led to British troops being deployed. Subsequent clashes between the paramilitary Irish Republican Army and the British Army, which included numerous atrocities such as *Bloody Sunday*—during which British paratroopers opened fire on unarmed protestors—and the deaths of scores of innocent civilians, marked the beginning of a civil war, dubbed the *Troubles*, which would last for almost 30 years. The clashes did not occur in the heart of community districts but in the interface areas that once housed mixed neighborhoods but were gradually abandoned by inhabitants of one or the other religious affiliations.

Barriers arose in the heart of the battle zones, and today they number about 40. Initially constructed of corrugated sheet metal and barbed wire, these barriers have gradually become more solid structures of bricks or sturdy metal panels topped by video surveillance cameras. They are up to eight or nine meters high, limiting the throwing of stones, bolts, and Molotov cocktails. Some barriers are opened by the police during the day but are closed at night and at the slightest alert.

Brexit has recently made this border sensitive again.

5.2 *Indian Walls*

India has two main fenced borders: one with Pakistan and one with Bangladesh. On August 15, 1947, the United Kingdom granted independence to the Indian Union (with a Hindu majority) and to Pakistan (with a Muslim majority). Pakistan had two separate territories: Western Pakistan and Eastern Pakistan (this would later become Bangladesh). Subsequently, there were huge population transfers (about 15 million people), with Muslims going to Pakistan and Hindus leaving Punjab for India. Violence and massacres had hundreds of thousands of victims.

The main border conflict between India and Pakistan concerned Kashmir. At the time of the 1947 division, Kashmir was an independent principality with a Hindu maharaja and a Muslim population. As the Maharaja of Kashmir was in favor of a reunion with India, Pakistan invaded a large western area of the country. The Maharaja called for help from India, giving rise to the first of the Indo-Pakistani wars. In 1948, the UN intervened, asking Pakistan to withdraw its troops from Kashmir and India and to hold a "free and impartial referendum," neither of which occurred.

The Indian "security barrier" is currently 550 km in length, along a disputed border of 740 km. Set back 1 or 2 km from the border, the Line of Control consists of a double row of electrified fences, three meters high and connected to a network of radar and thermal sensors. The thin strip of land between the two barbed wire fences is mined. The inhabitants, who have not been consulted on the issue, are hostages of this hidden war, with many separated from their families and being subjected to human rights abuses.

India has recently adopted the same formula for Bangladesh. After a long period of tolerance, when India began to take off economically, it began to worry about the problem of immigration, especially of illegal workers, extremists fighting for a "big Bangladesh," and the intensive smuggling of various goods. In Bangladesh, 12.9% of the population lives below the national poverty line. Life is very difficult for tens of millions of people: in rural areas, the work is very hard, and in the big cities, huge slums have arisen to accommodate people seeking jobs in factories. Minority groups such as Hindus and Christians are persecuted, and there is an overall growing religious intolerance fueled by radical Islamists. Furthermore, storms and floods afflict Bangladesh every year, so it is easy to understand why so many people decide to cross the border. However, the border between India and Bangladesh is now home to the longest border barrier in the world, 4,050 km long. Hundreds of kilometers of this barrier are double-layered: there are sections covered with barbed wire; walled sections; electrified sections; and sections illuminated by photoelectric cells, sensors, thermal imaging equipment, and night vision-enabled cameras that immediately detect intrusions and send emergency response units that are authorized to shoot to the area.

6 Anti-immigration Walls

Below are two examples of walls erected as a barrier against migratory flows. There are many others in the world, some of which were erected in Europe following the 2015 peak migration.

6.1 *Ceuta and Melilla*

Ceuta and Melilla are Spanish cities in North Africa, bordering Morocco and representing the only two land borders between the European Union and an African country.

The local Spanish and Muslim populations used to live in harmony. Each community participated in the religious festivals of the other, and the enclosure of the Spanish enclaves was not perfectly watertight, particularly from the nearby cities of Nador and Tétouan. Every morning, thousands of Moroccans with special permits arrived without visas with the intention to work or buy all sorts of tax-free goods.

The barrier erected to stop the recent growing influx of illegal immigrants coming from sub-Saharan Africa, the Maghreb (Morocco and Algeria), and Asia (India and Bangladesh) changed this precarious balance. The 2007 Lisbon Treaty called for a Schengen Area of freedom and justice, but also security. Policies related to asylum, immigration, and visas needed to be harmonized, and states on the borders of the Schengen Area were responsible for this new border.

In 1995 a first barrier was built to prevent illegal immigration and smuggling and drug trafficking. At 12 km long in Melilla and 8 km in Ceuta, it is a classic double barrier of metal surmounted by barbed wire, delimiting a rather large no-man's land that completely isolates the two enclaves. In the autumn of 2005, several hundred immigrants of sub-Saharan origin attempted to climb the barrier en masse using makeshift ladders. Some were successful, while others remained trapped within the barbed wire. In Ceuta, five people died, and the Spanish police, overwhelmed, were accused of having fired real bullets. Following these serious events, the Ceuta and Melilla barriers were drastically strengthened thanks in part to funding from the European Union.

6.2 *USA–Mexico Wall*

"Hispanic" immigration to the United States is an old problem that has become acute for some decades. At the end of the 19th century and in the first half of the 20th, American industrial and agricultural companies required a poorly paid and docile workforce, spurring an influx of immigrants from the south. Illegal immigration has always been tolerated in the United States, and any measure to curb it has always produced a drastic increase in the numbers of illegal immigrants. Paradoxically, the problem was accentuated by the start of negotiations in 1989 to create a free trade zone between the United States and Mexico. When the North American Free Trade Agreement (NAFTA) between the United States, Mexico, and Canada came into force in 1994, barriers had already begun to be erected on the Californian border, where the passage of illegal immigrants was becoming more frequent. The first section of wall was built with surplus military materials from the first Gulf War. As with all the other walls, such a barrier was not sufficient to stop illegal immigrants, but it facilitated their interception by the border police.

The trauma of the 9/11 attacks put an end to the benevolent attitude towards the border. George W. Bush, a former Republican governor of Texas, the largest U.S. state bordering Mexico, had just become president of the United States. Title IV of the anti-terrorism law, the Patriot Act on the protection of borders, was voted in during October 2001, and this legislation seemed to overlook the fact that the 9/11 terrorists had regular visas. The entire southern United States had become a sensitive area. On October 26, 2006, President Bush signed, with approval from Congress, the Secure Fence Act, a law authorizing the construction of a new barrier of 1,100 km divided into five segments along the U.S.-Mexican border.

Subsequent governments continued the work, in varying manners. The Democrat-controlled Senate passed a bill in June 2013 that offered further billions of dollars for policing, fencing, and deportations. According to the *New York Times*, with a winding down in Iraq and Afghanistan (however brief it proved to be), defense contractors were betting on a "military-style buildup at the border zone," hoping to supply even more helicopters, heat-seeking cameras, radiation detectors, virtual fences, watchtowers, and so on.

On June 16, 2015, Donald J. Trump descended an escalator in Trump Tower to announce his presidential campaign and denounce "Mexican rapists." "I will build a great, great wall on our southern border," he told Americans. "And I will have Mexico pay for that wall."[6]

7 Reflections from Analytical Psychology

If we look at the variety of walls and the political situations that generated them, we can see a number of themes that intertwine: the splitting of populations under areas of political, economic, and ideological influence; the protection of a safe space where a group can live in peace; the occupation of territory and appropriation of natural resources; the need of different (ethnic, religious, national, political, etc.) groups to be kept apart in order not to exacerbate conflicts; the exclusion of others from one's territory. Another very recurrent element is the presence of a dominating or colonizing superpower or country that appropriates territory.

There is a common element within this variety of stories: a wall seems to arise as a defense reaction against a perceived threat, which is sometimes concrete, sometimes imagined, sometimes experienced in the past through conflicts and wars, and sometimes experienced in the present and projected onto or into others. Can a wall be the materialization of a boundary determined by the activation of a group archetypal defense in the face of a perceived threat? Can it be the result of the stiffening of individual and collective defenses, following which individual selves and egos organize differently?

The archetype is a typical way in which mankind thinks and acts, an innate possibility of representation ("inherited representations," a form of instinct), which as such presides over imaginative activity, a disposition to reproduce typical representations, corresponding to humanity's experiences in the process of development of consciousness. It is a potential moment of synthesis

6 See G. Grandin, "The Militarization of the Southern Border is a Long-Standing American Tradition: Trump's Wall is just the latest incarnation of an old fixation", in *The Nation*, January 14, 2019. Available online at: https://www.thenation.com/article/the-militarization-of-the-southern-border-is-a-long-standing-american-tradition/.

between the conscious and unconscious. The archetype has the following characteristics:[7]

1. It is rooted in the experience of the *body*: The wall as an object concretely interacts with our bodies; it impedes sight; limits the freedom to move in space; and is conceived to reject, resist, and hinder any physical attempts to cross it.
2. It has a *formal* character (i.e., it regards the form of the psychic contents: a wall typically generates or stabilizes schizo-paranoid states of mind with massive use of projections on the "Other" and paranoid fears).
3. It has an *impersonal* and collective character, in the sense that its characteristics are not individual but universal or related to an entire group: This is observable in the similar and specular patterns of thinking and reacting of populations on both sides of a wall.
4. It has a *uniform* character, almost constant and immutable, like a scientific law: Walls, wherever they are erected, determine the same reactions in people.
5. It has a *congenital* character, in the sense of a preformed psychic heritage: Different kinds of threats may trigger the same reaction (i.e., building a wall, regardless of its functional utility for the specific social and political situation).
6. It has an *archaic-mythological* character in that its so-called "information" occurs in the language typical of myth and primitive psychology: This aspect can be retraced in the political discourse of many political leaders when they refer to a wall. The themes that revolve around this topic are those related to the myth of Hermes, which will be explored further below in this paper.
7. It has a *numinous* character: The wall, as an object that divides populations, owns and conveys a dynamic energy that dominates subjectivity. It has a strong almost religious or spiritual quality.

---

7 See C. G. Jung, "The Relations between the Ego and the Unconscious", in *Two Essays in Analytical Psychology*, Vol. 7. The Collected Works (Princeton, 1966). Originally published in 1928; C. G. Jung, "On Psychic Energy", in *The Structure and Dynamics of the Psyche*, Vol. 8. The Collected Works (Princeton, 1969). Originally published in 1928; C. G. Jung, "Archetypes of the Collective Unconscious", in *The Archetypes and the Collective Unconscious*, Vol. 9/1. The Collected Works (Princeton NJ, 1969). Originally published in 1934; C. G. Jung, "On the Psychology of the Unconscious", in *Two Essays in Analytical Psychology*, Vol. 7. The Collected Works (Princeton, 1966). Originally published in 1917; C. G. Jung, *Aion: Researches into the Phenomenology of the Self.* In The Collected Works, Vol. 9/2. (Princeton, 1968). Originally published in 1951.

The hypothesis here advanced is that a perceived threat is dealt with through an archetypal defense, which has all the mentioned characteristics and implies group investment in the erection of a concrete barrier. This barrier, by its very presence, leads other group members to reorganize their own selves so as to form certain links to ingroup members and certain other links to outgroup members. However, this reorganization at individual and group levels implies processes that are unconscious, because they are close to the somatic and perceptual level of experience. And they are mediated, I argue, by the relationship of humans with their environment, the group investment in a territory, an area in which a large group is living or intends to live and draw on resources. The archetypal nature of this defense would explain its ubiquity and the effectiveness of the object "wall" in organizing group mind, connecting and reshaping individual psyches in a way that sustains the political and social logics of the wall. Some kind of means has to connect inner and outer worlds, and I argue, it is the "psychic skin" in the inner world, which has some correspondence with the organization of space in the outer world.

The space we inhabit deals with our inner world as much as with our outer world. Groups are held together by culture, religion, practices, rituals, and values that orientate daily life and meanings in a complex intertwining of dynamics between families, subgroups, and generations composing the complex social matrix in which we live. However, our actual life as individuals and especially as members of groups happens in a material space with which we have a complex and largely unexplored relationship. The psychological function of walls can be better understood in the framework of a deeper understanding of the relationship between our psyche—individual and collective—and the space, the environment we inhabit. There is a deep level of our psychological functioning that is rooted in space and in our phantasy of that space for the stabilization of a sense of self.[8] And this stabilization has individual and group components.

Donald Winnicott was the first theorist to grasp, to some extent, the fact that the development of self has to do with processes that happen in a space and in the exchange between subjects and material "objects." The psychodynamics with the "transitional object" show that an object can be imbued with qualities of the subjects and that a subject, the mother, can play the role of "environment" to the infant.[9] He calls the result of good development in terms

8 L. Huskinson, *Architecture and the Mimetic Self: A Psychoanalytic Study of How Buildings Make and Break Our Lives*, (London & New York: Routledge, 2018).

9 D.W. Winnicott, "The Theory of the Parent–Infant Relationship", *International Journal of Psycho-Analysis*, 41: 585–595.

of "potential space" to refer to the development of some psychic abilities.[10] The way these skills are developed in infancy and childhood, and are used in adulthood, is crucial for the way we negotiate our way through life.

Walls separate space and people. They define who is with whom, and very likely how. Walls intend to convey the idea of safety, and while providing this sense of safety, they design the geography of our selves. But how do they do that? I propose this is done through our bodies, i.e. through the perception of images that stimulate our senses, particularly tactile perception, if a barrier is seen or even just imagined. The skin is a main door to access a very profound unconscious level of being for shaping and re-shaping the self. Tactile perception, visual perception, and imagination can stimulate the "skin," and the sense of "containment" has the power to open the self to a re-arrangement of self and ego and their relationships. This is because, as the work of many prominent thinkers in object-relations theory shows, the earliest experiences of this tactile encounter are the earliest experiences of self. They provide the infant with the required sense of containment and integration that stabilize the frenzied impulses that otherwise overwhelm it, gaining through development the capacity to gather itself together into a more coherent and self-reflecting being.

After Freud's first insights about the ego as "a mental projection of the surface of the body,"[11] Esther Bick[12] was one of the first to discuss the crucial role of the skin for "binding together" the infant's sensations, which enables them to overcome the "catastrophic anxieties" that otherwise arise from its unintegrated states. Significant for our investigation is Bick's suggestion that although the touch of the mother's skin is the "optimal object," any nonhuman object that is capable of holding the infant's attention will suffice to provide the infant with the containment and integration it requires. And when we are not feeling contained, we are hunting objects to provide such feeling of containment. Similarly, according to Didier Anzieu, the skin ego is not available to the infant from birth but is gradually achieved in response to stimuli impinging on the surface of their skin. These stimuli lead the infant to construct a mental image of themselves as a container that is capable of holding their experiences together.[13] The skin ego is the permanent support and ever-present backdrop of the thinking ego even in adulthood. The skin and tactile sensations continue their vital role in

---

10 D. W. Winnicott, *Playing and Reality*, (London: Tavistock Publications, 1971).

11 S. Freud, "An Outline of Psychoanalysis", in *Standard Edition of the Complete Psychological Works of Sigmund Freud*, vol. 23 (London, UK: Hogarth, 1938), pp. 144–207.

12 E. Bick, "The experience of the skin in early object relations", *International Journal of Psycho-Analysis*, 49, (1968): 484–486.

13 D. Anzieu, *The Skin Ego*, trans. C. Turner, (New Haven: Yale University Press, 1985), 61.

shaping identity, such that we continue to relate to objects and subjects through our imaginative perception of them, experiencing ourselves as if merged with them, with "shared skin." This process, I propose, is implied in the reshaping of the self induced by walls. Anzieu explains that the imagined merger of self and other, although repeatedly experienced throughout life, is itself a temporary experience, for the exchanges that occur through the skin surface of the subject lead them to become aware of the spatial boundaries of their body in relation to the other, and the subject comes to recognize it as a container for their own psychic contents, separate from the other. This awareness entails, he says, the "suppression" of the "common skin and the recognition that each has his or her own skin."[14] This temporary merger and perception of a common skin might also be a group phenomenon triggered by the presence of a wall delimiting the space of a group. The wall provides stimulation of a phantasy of merger with the same others and separation from different others that reshuffles group boundaries.

Jung refers to these psychic phenomena as the *participation mystique*, a term borrowed from Lévy-Bruhl to express a psychic relationship existent between the subject and an object, or two subjects in which the alterity between them is not acknowledged. This expression indicates all those cases in which the subject cannot be clearly distinguished from the object but is tied to it in a basic relationship of partial identity. Jung also uses the term "indistinction" to indicate the absence of psychological distinction among different objects or persons, or objects and persons.[15]

States of identity with objects, like walls, may have a re-structuring power for the self and for collective states of mind of groups, provided that a good number of group members identify with that object. Thus, I am supposing we can shape and reshape our belonging to groups going through these states of identity.

The concept of *participation mystique* is also correlated to that of *abaissment du niveau mental*. The expression of *abaissment du niveau mental* was first introduced by Janet to grasp the restriction of the realm of consciousness and the splitting of personality. In Jung's theory the *abaissment* triggers a restriction of conscious personality and, at the same time, compensates this latter with characteristic unconscious phenomena.[16] It has the following effects:

---

14 *Ibidem*, p. 63.

15 C.G. Jung, 'Psychological Types: Definitions', in *Psychological Types*, Vol. 6. The Collected Works (Princeton, 1971), par 781. Originally published in 1921.

16 C. G. Jung, "Concerning Rebirth", in *The Archetypes and the Collective Unconscious*, Vol. 9/1. The Collected Works (Princeton NJ, 1969), pars. 213f. Originally published in 1934.

1. It causes the loss of entire sections of personality normally in control.
2. It produces dissociated fragments of personality.
3. It impedes normal logical thinking.
4. It reduces the sense of responsibility and an adequate ego reaction.
5. It causes an incomplete representation of reality and triggers inadequate emotional reactions.
6. It lowers the consciousness level, allowing the unconscious contents to penetrate as autonomous invasions. For this reason, it has the meaning of a rite of passage and transformation of meanings.

This is how Jung describes a state of disintegration of self and ego, penetration of unconscious contents, and their following re-organization. This might be the work of a "wall" as an object and as a psychic image in the individual and group psyche, a work of redefining borders.

The myth of Hermes certainly pertains to this theme of borders. The name of this god is probably derived from *herma*, the Greek word for a heap of stones, such as was used in the country to indicate boundaries or as a landmark. Greek divinities were worshiped in the form of a heap of stones or a shapeless column of stone or wood. In many parts of Greece, there were piles of stones by the sides of roads, especially at their crossings, and on the boundaries of lands. The religious respect paid to such heaps of stones, especially at the meeting of roads, was shown by the custom of each passerby throwing a stone onto the heap or anointing it with oil. Later there was the addition of a head and phallus to the column, which became quadrangular. Among other functions, Hermes was the god of boundaries, both literal and figurative. He was also patron and protector of travelers, herdsmen, thieves, orators and wit, literature and poets, invention and trade (all expressions of crossing borders, traffic, and exchange of someone/something across borders), a creative function.

Here, where a wall is built to separate two territories and two peoples, the *function of Hermes* is frozen, impaired, or impeded to some extent. However, the wall also provides what Jung called a *primordial image*. Jung writes that the image is deemed *primordial* when it possesses an *archaic* character "in striking accord with familiar mythological motifs. It then expresses material primarily derived from the *collective unconscious*, and indicates at the same time that the factors influencing the conscious situation of the moment are *collective* rather than personal."[17]

---

17 C.G. Jung, "Definitions", in *Psychological Types*, vol. 6. The Collected Works Princeton University Press, 1971, par. 756.

If this image is able to activate a new process of a mercurial nature, it depends on Hermes' winged sandals. Murray Stein, commenting on Hermes, writes,

> Originally Hermes stood at the edge of known space (…). His sign marked the limit of consciousness. (…) When markers are created and limits set, however, curiosity and explorativeness are also excited and new spaces for exploration and discovery invite the bold and courageous traveler. If Hermes marks the boundary (…), we have to realize that this boundary is always shifting and in flux (…). Background and foreground may instantaneously reverse too, and generate new perceptions, novel insights.[18]

This chapter is a modest attempt to initiate a reflection on the topic of walls by posing some relevant issues. Many other questions remain open to further research. For instance, do walls change the way we think? If yes, then how? What exactly happens to our minds when we perceive or imagine the space of our ethnic, religious, or national group delimited by a wall? Do different kinds of walls have a different impact on people's thinking, and different meanings according to one's history? Such questions should be responded to through a deeper empirical investigation into the kind of intrapsychic and collective processes that are prompted by a wall's building, maintenance, and collapse, with the open mind that is suited to research.

References

Anzieu D., *The Skin Ego*, trans. C. Turner. New Haven: Yale University Press, 1985.

Bick E., "The experience of the skin in early object relations", *International Journal of Psycho-Analysis*, 49 (1968): 484–486.

Freud S., "An Outline of Psychoanalysis", in *Standard Edition of the Complete Psychological Works of Sigmund Freud*, vol. 23, London, UK: Hogarth, 1938, 144–207.

Frye D., *Walls: A History of Civilization in Blood and Brick*. New York: Scribner, 2018.

Huskinson L., "*Architecture and the Mimetic Self: A Psychoanalytic Study of How Buildings Make and Break Our Lives*, London & New York: Routledge, 2018.

Jung C. G., "On the Psychology of the Unconscious", In *Two Essays in Analytical Psychology*, in H. Read, M. Fordham, G. Adler, W. McGuire (eds.), *The Collected Works*, translated by R.F.C. Hull, v. 7. Bollinger Series XX. Princeton NJ: Princeton University

18 M. Stein, "Hermes and the Creation of Space", in *Soul: Treatment and Recovery. The Selected Works of Murray Stein*. London & New York: Routledge, 2016.

Press, 1966. Originally published in 1916. Sfard, M., *The Wall and the Gate: Israel, Palestine, and the Legal Battle for Human Rights,* New York: Metropolitan Books, 2018.

Jung C. G., "Psychological Types: Definitions", in *Psychological Types*, v. 6., *The Collected Works.* Princeton NJ: Princeton University Press, 1971. Originally published in 1921.

Jung C. G., "The Relations between the Ego and the Unconscious", in *Two Essays in Analytical Psychology*, v. 7. *The Collected Works*. Princeton, NJ: Princeton University Press, 1966. Originally published in 1928.

Jung C. G., "On Psychic Energy", in *The Structure and Dynamics of the Psyche*, v. 8. *The Collected Works,* Princeton, NJ: Princeton University Press, 1969. Originally published in 1928.

Jung C. G., "Archetypes of the Collective Unconscious", v. 9/1. *The Collected Works,* Princeton, NJ: Princeton University Press, 1959. Originally published in 1934.

Jung C. G., "Aion: Researches into the Phenomenology of the Self", In *The Collected Works*, v. 9/2. Princeton, NJ: Princeton University Press, 2nd edition, 1968. Originally published in 1951.

Luci, M. "The Psychic Skin between Individual and Collective States of Mind in Trauma", *Journal of Psychosocial Studies*, 14, no. 1 (2021): 33–45. DOI: 10.1332/147867321X16098253250019.

Marshall T., *Divided: Why We're Living in an Age of Walls,* London: Elliott & Thompson Ltd, 2018.

Quétel C., *Histoire des Murs. Une autre histoire des hommes,* Paris: Edition Perrin, 2012.

Stein M., "Hermes and the Creation of Space", in *Soul: Treatment and Recovery. The Selected Works of Murray Stein,* London & New York: Routledge, 2016.

Sfard M., *The Wall and the Gate: Israel, Palestine, and the Legal Battle for Human Rights* New York: Metropolitan Books, 2018.

Vallet E., David C. P., "Introduction: The (Re)Building of the Wall in International Relations", *Journal of Borderlands Studies*, 27, no. 2 (2012): 111–119. DOI: 10.1080/08865655.2012.687211

Vallet E., *Borders, Fences and Walls. State of Insecurity?* Abingdon, New York: Routledge, 2018.

Winnicott D.W., "The Theory of the Parent–Infant Relationship", *International Journal of Psycho-Analysis*, 41(1960): 585–595.

Winnicott D. W., *Playing and Reality*, London: Tavistock Publications, 1971.

CHAPTER 6

An Unconscious Source of Images: About How Bachelard Read Jung

Kamila Morawska

> We live directly only in the world of images.
>
> CARL GUSTAV JUNG

…

> Images are the first psychic realities. Everything starts, in the experience, from images.
>
> GASTON BACHELARD

∴

Abstract

Bachelard—in his works written between 1928 and 1960, situated on two mutually exclusive fields: science and poetics, reason and imagination—appoints the imagination responsible for the fundamental relationship between the psyche and the cosmos, between the man and the world. Reaching the depth of Me in contact with the elements of the world, the French philosopher is studying fire, water, air, and earth. The concept of elements of nature is related to the mental life of man, similar to the concept of C.G. Jung. The psychological energy of the subject, analyzed through the prism of the four elements, propagates in four different directions. If for Jung the symbolism (after the Hippocrates-Galen) of water was related to the personality type of melancholy, air to spitfire, earth to phlegmatic, and fire to sanguine, for Bachelard the classification of the four fundamental elements leads to the formulation of key points of the imagination concept. The imagined being, called the elementary and basic image, combines the material and dynamic dimension of the imagination. This means that the dreaming entity provides either; matter for dream (fire, water, air, or earth) and puts his consciousness in motion. Elemental analysis

 | DOI:10.1163/9789004468757_008

returns in Bachelard's "Rational materialism," when chemistry is confronted with alchemy, and then in "Poetics of dreams," when the philosopher shows the cosmic participation of I in Being. How does Jung appear in Bachelard's works? He refers to three works by a Swiss thinker: "Psychologie und Alchimie," "Psychologie der Ubertragung," and "Symbolik des Geites." The aim of the paper is to show the affinity between Jung and Bachelard. I think that you can capture them in three aspects. The first treats the importance of imagination in a mental life. For Bachelard, imagination is always defined as the ability, not to create an image, but to transform it; a new image is a creative transformation of the image-matrix. It is an anthropological reading of the imagination as an impulse, desire, will of man. The unconsciousness, which is necessary to explain this appearance of strength and psychological forms, cannot be determined solely by suppression (in the opinion of Bachelard, Freud's psychoanalysis). The unconscious is not only suppressed, but it is all that comes from the inside—from the depths—to nourish consciousness and that allows consciousness to remain permanently in connection with the deep sources of images. The second one is related to the fact that Bachelard accepts the concept of Jung's archetype to show that the unconscious is neither empty nor chaotic but that the images find in it their first potential of meaning and their dynamic source. Thanks to this, Bachelard enables universal sharing of the same image: Bachelard's books on the four elements are read in all languages as consistent with the experiences of their cultural imagination. The third one emphasizes the androgynous character of the imagination. In other words, the imagination spontaneously develops in two modes: the feminine and masculine modes, anima and animus.

Keywords

image, imagination, man, word, psyche, consciousness, unconscious, four elements, archetype, anima, animus

Gaston Bachelard (1884–1962) is probably one of the most recognizable French epistemologists of the 20th century in the world.[1] In his works written

---

1 Bachelard's epistemological works are extensive and well known. His most famous work, *La formation de l'esprit scientifique. Contribution à une psychanalyse de la connaissance objective*, had a huge impact on contemporary philosophical thought, mainly due to the concept of "epistemological rupture" (*la rupture épistémologique*) and "epistemological profile" (*le profil*

between 1928 and 1960, situated in two seemingly mutually exclusive fields (i.e., science and poetics, reason and imagination), Bachelard defines imagination (not reason) as the power responsible for the fundamental relationship between the *psyche* and the cosmos, between man and the world. This interpretation of Bachelardism is made in light of his reflection on the reality of images and their various relationships with human existence. Within it, man is defined as an "imagining being" (*l'être imaginant*), which constitutes his identity and develops his activities always in relation—negative or positive—to images present in the psyche, both in the field of consciousness and unconsciousness; images functioning within the framework of the collectively created discourse of science, as well as what is imagined, intimate, oneiric. In the anthropological paradigm, his works evoke important questions about man and his relationship with the world; awareness and unconsciousness, subjectivity, objectivity, illusiveness, giving sense and meaning to things, questions about happiness.

1 The World of Images

Bachelard's thought is part of the philosophy of the 20th century, which gives the image a new status.[2] The image is no longer depreciated (R. Descartes), suspect (E. Escoubas) or located on the periphery of philosophical discourse (F. Dagognet). Bachelard, however, does not propose a clear and monolithic interpretation of the image. As an archetypal image placed in the subject's unconsciousness functions simultaneously as a positive and negative category, these primary and universal images are filled with material content when the individual experiences the world through contact with the elements of nature. For scientific cognition they constitute an obstacle, while for poetry they are archetypes per se in the meaning of Carl Gustav Jung. Here, bachelardian thesis resounds strong: the images have unconscious roots. Another important moment in his reflection on the image is marked by phenomenology and ontology; Bachelard focuses on the phenomenon of the image. He asks about how the image appears in the field of subjective consciousness and what the image

épistémologique). This conception appeared in the philosophical discourses of the 20th century, inspiring Michel Foucault, Georges Canguilhem, Louis Althusser, Thomas Khun, Gilbert Simondon, and many others.

2 J.-J. Wunenburger, French researcher of the imagination, author of the work titled *Philosophie des Images*, calls Bachelard next to P. Ricoeur, G. Durand, and H. Corbin "the founding father of the concept of imagination." See J.-J. Wunenburger, *L'imaginaire*, (Paris: PUF, 2003), 18.

itself is. Regardless of the many interpretative perspectives of the concept of the image, we have in Bachelardism a clear anthropological dominant. It indicates that the images are rooted in man; it is the so-called "anthropological trajectory"—to use the formulation of the modern critic of Bachelardism J.-J. Wunenburger—running from "*a priori* image structures to the regions of the cultural noosphere."[3] The anthropological perspective captures the special power of images. They cannot be reduced to material artifacts (external images) or to laws associated with associating representations of the external world (reflections, phantasms). The images turn out to be equipped with "semantic and syntactic laws of organizations that allow them to participate in an orderly and meaningful representation of the world and life."[4] *Psyche* turns out to be a kind of palimpsest: new images are created on the first (archetypal) images. Reaching them through successive layers of imagery seems to be the most important experience for human existence.

"Images are the first psychic realities. Everything starts in the experience itself, with the images,"[5] writes Bachelard. Wunenburger adds that the *psyche* is "filled by the images," which are nonobjective projections of the unconscious and also conscious nature. Thus, they are both "unconscious phantasms" and "conscious performances preceding in most cases the perception act."[6] Regardless of their sources, they are recognized by Bachelard as "necessary intermediary transformations between man and the world."[7] His work shows that the human mind is "inhabited by powerful images, resistant, undetermined and overloaded with unconscious affects to such an extent that imagination precedes even all perception."[8] Thus, human existence and activity are anchored in a certain source order of images, which, like *arche*, in a genetic and ontological sense is prior to all our manifestations and ways of visualizing the world. Image, understood in this way, organizes and prepares perception and in the next step, prepares the concept. That is why it can be considered as the cause of the first errors of intellectual judgment, that is, expressed as an "epistemological obstacle" (*l'obstacle épistémologique*) on the path to scientific knowledge. It must be detected and eliminated thanks to the method of "psychoanalysis of objective knowledge" (*la psychanalyse de la connaissance objective*). However,

3 J-.J. Wunenburger, *Philosophie des images*, (Paris: PUF, 1997), 58.

4 Ibidem.

5 G. Bachelard, *La terre et les rêveries du repos*, (Paris: PUF, 1948), 324.

6 J.-J. Wunenburger, „O narodzinach obrazu: obecność czy zanikanie bytu?", transl. M. Ples-Beben, in *Idea -studia nad strukturą i rozwojem pojęć filozoficznych*, (Białystok, 2016), 378.

7 I. Błocian, K. Morawska, M. Ples-Bęben, *Gaston Bachelard i filozofie obrazu*, (Wrocław: Wydawnictwo Uniwersytetu Wrocławskiego, 2018), 97.

8 J.-J. Wunenburger, *La vie des images*, (Grenoble: PUG, 2002), 31.

the emotional and symbolic overdetermination of archetypal images becomes a privileged situation in the poetic dream.

2 Four Elements of Imagination

In 1938 Bachelard begins a systematic study of imagination. He describes his working method as follows: "We will analyze an attitude in which objectivity will never be realized, where the first seduction is so complete that it deforms minds by taking them to a poetic land where dreams replace thoughts and poems abolish theories."[9] Reaching the depth of the Self in contact with elements of the world, he takes fire, water, air, and earth into his research workshop. Alchemy is for him a mirror of poetic work. Full of unusual images and symbols, which are certainly obstacles from an epistemological point of view, alchemy becomes a real source for deep dreams. Substantial obstacles, which Bachelard rejects as an epistemologist, appear in a completely different light when he wants to understand the work of imagination. *La psychanalyse du feu* (1938) is the first attempt to transform what constitutes an obstacle to scientific cognition into a resource of imagination showing the depths of the Ego in contact with elements of the world. Bachelard will then examine water (*L'eau et les rêves*, 1942); air (*L'air et les songes*, 1943); and then after the war, an element of earth (*La terre et les reveries dur epos*, *La terre et les rêveries de la volonté*, 1948). This way, five books are created to describe the four elements. These analyses are strengthened in *La poétique de la rêverie* (1960), when he places the imagination in a "crevice of being," thus allowing a man to participate in it cosmically.

If the four elements were an *arche* in ancient cosmological concepts,[10] then in Bachelard's thought one cannot speak of an attempt to create a new cosmology. This philosopher analyzes water, air, earth, and fire, but refers only to the image of one element created by the imagination of a given artist. His purpose is to systematize four elements and show the laws according to which the images are arranged in sequences belonging to well-defined groups. Thanks to this, it turns out to be possible to show the life of emotions. The images of joy are as follows: "Earthly joy is wealth and heaviness, water joy is gentleness and rest, fiery joy is love and desire, air joy is freedom."[11] Bachelard's concept of

9 Ibidem, 12.

10 G.S. Kirk, J.E. Raven, M. Schofield, *The Presocratic Philosophers a Critical History with a Selection of Texts*, (Cambridge: Cambridge University Press, 1983).

11 G. Bachelard, *L'air et les songes*, (Paris: PUF, 1943), 156.

the four elements of nature is related to man's mental life. Jung does the same. The subject's mental energy, analyzed through the prism of four elements, travels in four different directions. If for Jung (after Hippocrates and Galen) the symbolism of water is associated with the melancholic personality type, air, choleric; earth, phlegmatic; and fire, sanguine; for Bachelard, classification of four fundamental elements leads to the formulation of key points in his concept of imagination. Imagined being, called the elementary and basic image, combines the material and dynamic dimension of the imagination. This means that the basic image provides the dreaming subject with "matter to dream" (fire, water, air, or earth) and sets his consciousness in motion. The value of the imagined being referred to its content implying unconscious valuations. It turns out to be a great means and a way by which man organizes and focuses his mental energy. Taming of this energy is associated with giving her direction. In this case, this energy is manifested through a literary image, hence, for Bachelard, the possibility of "objective literary criticism" (*la critique littéraire objective*), which is founded on the "law of four elements" (*le droit des quatre elements*). A given element of nature affects one creator; the creator becomes the translator of this element. This proclaims the so-called "theory of four poetic temperaments" (*la théorie des quatre temperaments poétiques*). For example, Novalis is a fire poet, just like Hoffman; Poe is a water poet, and Schelley and Nietzsche are air poets.

3 Jung and Bachelard

Gaston Bachelard primarily moves between Jung's three works, *Psychologie und Alchimie*, *Psychologie der Ubertragung*, and *Wandlungenund Symbole der Libido*. References to them appear in the texts entitled *La terre et les reveries du repos* and *La terre et les rêveries de la volonté*. In the context of the Jungian division of psychological types, Bachelard divides the imagination and images into those that are directed inward, which is to say, introverted (earth and dreams of rest), and those that are formed by outward-directed energy, action, extroverted (earth and dreams of desire). In *Le materialisme rationel* he returns to the topic of chemistry and alchemy, and in *La poétique de la rêverie* he writes about two dimensions of imagination and its androgyny. He directly refers to Jung in *La psychanalyse du feu*, when he describes what his own work is: "combining and extending Jung's observation in search of *libido* ingredients in all human psychic activities"[12] and when he recalls techniques for obtaining

12 G. Bachelard, *La poétique de l'espace*, (Paris: PUF, 1957), 47, 61.

fire in prehistoric times.[13] For Jung, *libido* is neutral and associated primarily with the "instinct for life," reproduction, and nutrition; it is energy, propulsion, vitality, *élan vitale.*[14] Thanks to such a broad term, he manages to escape the terminological and semantic reductionism that Bachelard attributes to Freud.[15] Then, in *L'eau et les rêves*, Bachelard mentioned the achievements of "new psychology" made by Jung, who showed and then proved that human drama is taking place in the limits of unconsciousness and consciousness.[16] It's about Jung's work *Wandlungenund Symbole der Libido*. There is no doubt that it is thanks to this work Bachelard considers the psyche as a processual being endowed with immaterial energy. For Jung, mental phenomena are autonomous in the sense of creating a separate world governed by its own rules. The

13 G. Bachelard, *La psychanalyse du feu*, (Paris: Gallimard, 1938), 43.

14 In Jung, libido is understood as mental energy in general. It determines the intensity of the mental process. "Psychological value" is expressed through its determining power, which manifests itself in certain psychic experiences. Jung used the term "libido" interchangeably with the term "energy." See C. G. Jung, *Psychological Types*, (London and New York: Routledge, 2019).

15 Bachelard interpreted the theory of the Viennese psychoanalyst in the following way: It is too strongly rooted in the pathological activities of the *psyche*, that is, either the suppression of such or other contents of consciousness or the mechanism of sublimation, which explains the genesis of poetic creativity. In his opinion, Freudian psychoanalysis does not attach sufficient importance to the positive and creative role of images (and therefore the one that interests the French philosopher most), but on the contrary, depreciates and degenerates it by reducing the image order to simple symbols of sexual *libido*. "The psychoanalytic symbol, to show it in its broadest dimension, (…) revolves around the concept of sexuality," writes Bachelard. Bachelard, *La terre et la rêverie de la volonté*, (Paris: PUF, 1948), 75. That is why, according to Bachelard, Freud's method, shows symbols and images only as an expression of libidinal energy. It causes images and symbols to become only conceptual instruments used during the analysis. The French author understands an image more deeply than a psychologist who just "understands" the image. "Psychoanalyst thinks too much and doesn't dream enough." G. Bachelard, *La poétique de la rêverie*, (Paris: PUF, 1960), 128. Then, Freudian inference about the existence of the complex in the perspective of the cultural prohibition applied by an adult to a child—this is how the complex in Freud's theory understands Bachelard—leads to a reduction of psychological strength to the socio-cultural symbolism, which has nothing to do with the first images. In addition, according to Bachelard, psychoanalysts do not distinguish between the image implicit and the image explicit. It should be clearly stated here that this is Bachelard's interpretation; in Freud's psychoanalytic hermeneutics, we deal with so-called cover memory and other forms of distinguishing between the explicit and the hidden. For Bachelard, classical psychoanalysis—and he always means Freud's psychoanalysis—neglects the most unconscious sphere in which deep complexes appear, and he understands the term "complex" non-psychoanalytically. Defining images only through their symbolization function, always referring to something else, somehow more important and more strongly existing, in his opinion in no way explains their essence.

16 G. Bachelard, *L'eau et les rêves*, 65.

psyche is a dynamic system of conscious and unconscious processes, the aim of which is to achieve fullness/unity (i.e., to combine the unconscious with consciousness). This is a state that Jung calls the Self (*Selbst*). It is characterized by integration, homogeneity, and a lack of divisions and dualism. Hence, for Bachelard, imaginal thinking, all relationships between psyche processes and images are dynamic and changeable. The energy in which the psyche is equipped is an expression of vitality. Mental energy finds expression in the form of imaginal representation—in a specific image. Further, in 1939, in *Lautréamont*, describing the life and work of Isidore Ducasse, Bachelard writes about primary and basic images, "from which one can hardly escape"[17] and which constitute a concept of archetype.

Inspiring Bachelard with Jung's thought is easiest to grasp in three aspects. The first of them deals with the importance of imagination in the mental life of man. Bachelard understands imagination as an ability not so much to create images but to transform them. In this sense, imagination is never a direct reflection and transformation of the real order. Imagination transforms images created in the *psyche*. It happens when it comes in contact with an object/world that evokes a dream and an imagination. In this way, imagination transforms archetypal images contained in the subject's unconscious, which may result in poetic works related to the imaginations of four elements of nature. It is different from the case of Sartre because according to his point of view, negation is an unconditional principle of all imagination because one has to imagine what is denied.[18]

Archetype/matrix images are "deformed" and "enriched" by the imagination: "the new image is grafted onto the old image."[19] Thanks to such a transformation, carried out through the imagination, a specific, imaginative domain is created that transcends all given reality. As Bachelard notes, "Imagination invents more things than dramas, invents a new life, a new mind; opens eyes to new types of view."[20] It is worth emphasizing that in this perspective an important definition of the image is shown as a creative transformation of the original image. In other words, the image is a creative variation on the unconscious matrix. The image here becomes a transformation of the archetype, not a copy of the mimesis of actual reality found. Thus, there is a deep agreement between Bachelard and Jung when it comes to the anthropological interpreta-

17 G. Bachelard, *Lautréamont*, (Paris: José Corti, 1939), 171.

18 See J.-P. Sartre, *L'imaginaire. Psychologie phénoménologique de l'imagination*, (Paris: Gallimard, 1986).

19 G. Bachelard, *L'eau et les rêves*, 24.

20 Ibidem.

tion of the imagination (i.e., as an impulse, desire, and human will). As such, imagination activates in all regions of the subject to ensure a continuous and endless metamorphosis of images. Thanks to this attitude, one can find in the Bachelard reflection a Renaissance and romantic philosophical tradition emphasizing the concept of "the power of imagination" (*Vis* in Latin, *Kraft* in German). Imagination is revealed as the power to animate images that arise from perception and are driven by human desire. Bachelard's approach to human will is related to the concept inherent in Schopenhauer and German Romanticism. Will is a vague force, close to what Freud calls impulses.

The unconscious, which is necessary to explain the appearance of forces and mental forms (i.e., images), cannot be determined solely by repression. It cannot be understood only in the category of suppression because it is everything that appears in the psyche from the inside, from the inside of man, to nourish and enliven the consciousness. In addition, thanks to it, consciousness can remain permanently in connection with deep/unconscious image sources. Bachelard is thus convinced that awakened consciousness is the "place" and moment of phenomenological understanding of the content of unconscious images. He devotes an important chapter in *La poétique de la rêverie* to what he calls the "dreaming *cogito*." The subject of the dreamer exists with the image (i.e., when he realizes the appearance of the image). This ontological relationship also applies to the poetic image. Without his creative transformation caused by the will of the subject, the image is not "renewed." Image analysis does not occur in the night activity of the psyche, where the role of the subject is negligible. The subject dreams of being unaware of his self. Let us repeat on this occasion the words of Paul Ricœuer from *On Interpretation. Essay on Freud:*

> Meanwhile, the very term "it"—borrowed from Groddeck (Das Buch vom Es), which in turn inspired Nietzsche—has countless implications that simple energy cannot exhaust. It is not only about some anti-phenomenology, but about a reverse phenomenology of the impersonal and neutral, which is never something I think, but something like That says, which is translated in abbreviations, shifts of significant accents and in the rhetoric of dreams and joke. This is the timeless kingdom, the order of what is premature.[21]

21 P. Ricœur, *O interpretacji. Esej o Freudzie*, transl. M. Falski, (Warsaw, PWN, 2008), 407. Ricœur dreams (*le rêve*) understands broadly: "It opens to all mental products—in insanity or culture—as long as they show some analogies to dreams, regardless of degree and the principles of this closeness; along with the dream has been established what I just

By dressing this thought in poetic words, Bachelard writes about the "metaphysics of the night" in which "ontological drama" occurs, because in the night mode of our being it is impossible to confirm the existence of *cogito*. The unconscious sphere is granted autonomous existence as well as an important role. It is a source of meanings and affects and determines as a matrix of images all oneirism. Universal and supersonic images are located in the unconscious, characteristic not for an individual but the whole of the human species, being the starting point for imagining or dreaming. For this reason, according to the French philosopher, it is better to analyze the moment of awakened consciousness—a daydream (*la rêverie*) and not a dream (*le rêve*). The daydream participates in the transformation of images through the linguistic dimension.

In Bachelardism, phenomenology has a special power: thanks to it, you can capture the imaginal novelty that is a creative transformation of the archetype, as well as capture and describe the subjective experience of happiness (so important for the *psyche* from the point of view of its mental functioning), resulting from the dazzle caused by the appearance in the consciousness of a new image. The activity of this experience—the experience of happiness—results from the activity of the subject (the creator and recipient take part in the creation of the image). During a reading, the reader creates images: The imagined and experienced image becomes his own image (this time, the phenomenological approach is to report on the appearance of the image in a different consciousness). The "axis of intentionality" connecting the imagining subject with the imagination connects the poet with the poem's reader in the domain of imaginations. The existence of the image in the perception of the creator and recipient—making him aware—is responsible in this case for his existence. Moreover, the image's ability to communicate (*la communicabilité*), the special relationship of various entities (e.g., creator and creator, creator and recipient, recipient and recipient), also has an impact on its ontic status: "The communion of a simple poetic image is a matter of great importance ontological,"[22] meaning "transmission of one soul to another."[23] Communication

described as 'dream semantics'. Well, this semantics revolves around the topic in a nuclear sense: as a man of wish, 'I follow the mask'—larvatus prodeo, above all and most often the language is distorted: he wants to express (*veut dire*) something other than he says, has a dual meaning, is ambiguous and further, 'Dreaming is what proves that we still want to say something other than what we are saying; there is an explicit sense that never ceased to refer to a secret sense; this fact makes every dreamer a poet. From this perspective, the dream is a personal archeology of the dreamer, sometimes intersecting the archeology of peoples." Ibidem, 17, 23.

22 G. Bachelard, *La poétique de l'espace*, 2.

23 Ibidem, 8.

between the recipient and the author's consciousness, where the poetic image becomes a source of new consciousness, affects the cogito of the recipient, and this new consciousness is the beginning of a new image.

The definition of the image in Bachelardism goes a long way. It goes from "negative sublimation" in the field of science, in which the role of sublimation is to clean the scientific material of "epistemological obstacles," to "positive sublimation of the imagination" (*la sublimation positive*) in the poetic field when enlarging image content occurs. In *La terre et les rêveries de la volonté*, the purpose of Bachelard's research is clearly outlined; it is "to find in the elements of the image of metapsychism, (…) by examining images that renew the archetypes of the unconscious."[24] However, in the 1960s, Bachelard no longer reduces man's creativity to his deep, dormant, obscure, and thus unconscious tendencies. In the field of imagination, it is not enough to follow the thought of classical psychoanalysis (Bachelard always thinks of Freud's psychoanalysis by thinking of "classical") and deduce, for example, as he writes, the image of "home" from the "belly" to the "cave" as the implementation of the archetype "return to mother." According to the French author, this interpretation of the image phenomenon is reductive. After all, it ignores the value and content of the "new" image. Also, the study of verbal images (and only such images interest him) as representatives of creative imagination, derived from the tendencies of psyche highly and exuberant (i.e., enlarging, taking over, spreading), needs a non-reductive method to be able to indicate and then define the entity itself image. The image, being something more than its counterpart given in sensory experience, transcends actual and perceptual reality. The difficulty associated with its definition is due to its very location between the senses and the mind, between the concrete and the abstract. Joining with perception brings the picture closer to the memory and places it in the memory order as a mnesic image; attribution to the mind, in turn, treats it as a mental datum, as a mental image, and therefore a thing studied in particular by the psychological sciences. Bachelard expresses this thought in the following words: "One always wants the imagination to be the power to form images. But it is rather the ability to deform images provided by perception, especially is the ability to trigger first images and change images."[25]

Image for Bachelard is primarily a product of imagination. So in defining this product, he starts by adding the adjective "young." Her youth is influenced by her essential features, which are openness, searching for new things, looking forward. He, in turn, sees the experience of "rejuvenation" in the dynamism

24 G. Bachelard, *La terre et les rêveries de la volonté*, 11.

25 G. Bachelard, *L'air et les songes*, 5.

of images. "By mixing the soul with the body in his imagination, the poet turns to the first mental reality: the image. He remains in dynamism and his life."[26] Bachelard refers to Shelley's poetry, and thanks to the images in *L'air et les songes*, proclaims "the law of not aging images,"[27] their remaining eternally young and fresh. Imagination in his opinion is "forever young." It is not surprising then to combine youth of imagination with "childhood," because the dream gains in value by circling its meaning around it. In *La psychanalyse du feu*, it is expressed in this way: "Childhood is certainly greater than reality, (...) on the set of dreams, not on the set of facts, childhood remains alive and poetically useful."[28] He is interested in the value, addition, and allowance brought with the picture. The translation and understanding of its value does not fit into the possibilities of data by facts and things. The reality tells us nothing about the values, meanings, and advantages of the image. Imagination works the opposite. Every novelty resulting from it always contains a reference to value. This is what happens with reimagined childhood memories. Imaginative action gives it a new meaning, a new value. "We have in mind micro-movies that cannot be read without receiving light from the imagination."[29] In this way, the philosopher introduces the force he calls "Memory-Imagination," which draws from the rich reservoir of our childhood. Similarly to archetypes—constant archetypal content renewed in new images—the memories of memories remembered are renewed in memory.

Unconsciousness, which is necessary to explain this kind of appearance of forces and mental forms, cannot be defined only in the category of suppression and complex, and in Bachelard's opinion it happens in Freud's psychoanalysis. Interestingly, thanks to the different understanding of the unconsciousness resulting from psychoanalysis of either Freud or Jung, Bachelard can see the difference between "nature" and "culture." In his reading, the more Jung is focused on the unconscious, the more natural he is and vice versa; the more Freud considers complexes, the more cultural it is. In this sense, the Jungian unconscious is associated with the species and the biological; on the contrary, in the prohibition of culture, unsatisfied and pushed unconscious drives are revealed. If, for Bachelard, in Jung the unconscious and what is present in it has a positive connotation, in the sense of, for example, dreaming by us (people here and now) of the same dreams that our ancestors dreamed, interspecies continuity given by means of unconscious content, which is to say, constant and unchanging

26 Ibidem, 62.
27 Ibidem.
28 G. Bachelard, *La poétique de l'espace*, 33.
29 Ibidem, 161.

archetypes, in Freud's case, unconscious content is negative and pathological as a result of a collision with culture, and then is displaced and banned by it. For this reason, Bachelard, after Jung, repeats that the unconscious is not only suppressed, but it is everything that appears in the psyche from the inside (i.e., from the depths of man). In my opinion, Bachelard's theory of imagination and image is the most interesting at the moment of showing constant tension between consciousness and unconsciousness. The unconscious constantly nourishes the consciousness; consciousness is permanently associated with deep image sources. However, this deep and unconscious dimension is not in itself the focal point of Bachelard research. Dream (le rêve)—"the royal road to the unconscious,"[30] as Freud wrote, according to Bachelard is too little understood by man. His investigations relate primarily to the negative impact of the unconscious on the development of scientific thought and its positive impulse in the field of poetic creativity. A dream derived from this area is a combination of the subject's elements and collective, supra-individual elements of the unconscious. Blending the unconscious with the conscious results in less deep images because they are marked by the presence of a dreaming cogito. The unconscious takes over the images of consciousness, and the images of consciousness follow the path of the originally unconscious image. Mixing, interlocking, and overlapping of two levels of psyche is of particular importance to Bachelard in creating the classification of images as collective images dictated by one of the four elements of nature.

The second relationship between Bachelard and Jung appears through the prism of the concept of "archetype." Jungian psychology of depth, according to the French philosopher, perfectly answers the question about the genesis and nature of the image resonating from the area of the unconscious. In Jung's concept, the psyche is a whole, continuity running from the unconscious to the conscious, and vice versa. However, the unconscious opposes the consciousness, eludes it. The subject must therefore reach it. For Jung, the domain of the unconscious part of the psyche is identified, according to a fairly widespread interpretation, with the ahistorical and universal structure of archetypes (which, however, is the foundation of the historical world)—images of the solid and unchanging, which are the basis of human existence. It is a

30 "Explaining dreams, however, is *via regia* to learn what is unconscious in psychic life," see: S. Freud, *Objaśnienie marzeń sennych*, transl. R. Reszke. Warsaw: KR, 1996), 509. "It is ('this') a dark, inaccessible part of our personality; the scant knowledge we have about 'this', we obtained thanks to research into the work of dreams and the formation of neurotic symptoms', because 'we' grasp approximately, comparing them to chaos, to a cauldron in which impulses stimulate," see: S. Freud, *Wykłady ze wstępu do psychoanalizy. Nowy cykl*, transl. R. Reszke. Warsaw: KR, 2015), 85.

collection of the most fundamental and common meanings of people, which, if they reach them, will allow to explain and describe various phenomena of conscious mental life. As Jung wrote in *Psychological types*:

> The original image can be expressed as a mnemic sediment, as an engram (Semon), which arose as a result of condensation of countless, similar processes. In this sense, it is a settlement, and therefore a typical form, a certain constantly recurring mental experience. As a mythological motive, it is always an effective, constantly re-emerging form of expression that evokes some psychological experience or forms it in the right way. If we look at it from this perspective, we recognize that it is a psychological expression of a specific physiological and anatomical disposition.[31]

The above description of the archetype undoubtedly shows more its anthropological than psychological character. He emphasizes the origin, genesis, and development of man; all phases of his development are recorded in the psyche (similarly Freud thought using the archaeological method). In this connection, the problems of the image are located in Jung and Bachelard in the sphere of the archetype, and not, as in Freud, the complex. By definition, the archetype is a basic, original, and typical form, given to all humanity through the use of collective ideas (*les représentations collectives*). In this way of understanding, the concept of archetype is inseparably assigned to the category of "collective unconsciousness"(i.e., the collective unconsciousness includes all archetypes): "These eternal images or archetypes, as I called them, constitute the main core of the unconscious psyche and cannot be explained as achievements individual. Together they form this psychic stratum, which I have called the collective unconscious."[32]

Besides, the archetype definition implies a synthetic form bringing together atavistic forces, energies, and instincts. The multidimensionality of understanding the archetype combines both the biological aspect as a model of forced and permanent action, as well as the psychological one appearing in the process of shaping the "spirit," in the individual experience and understanding of the world. This involves a broader understanding of the concept of unconsciousness, including instincts and traces of animal psyche beyond archetypes.

Archetype (from German *Urbild*) in the topology of J.-J. Wunenburger of the *Philosophy of images* is a matrix image (*l'image matricielle*). It refers to the Neoplatonic concept of intelligible forms (ideas) that are reflected in sensual

---

31 C. G. Jung, *Psychological types*, 465.

32 Cf. Z. Rosińska, [in:] Idem, *Jung*, (Warsaw: Wiedza Powszechna, 1982), 41.

reality (things). This image generates a representation system (i.e., has the ability to create derived images), and as the original, is the reference principle for identifying copies. The French image researcher emphasizes that, apart from the Neoplatonic interpretation of archetypes, they are associated with Jung's sphere of instincts belonging to the human species. The archetype is also an instinct that determines the content hidden from awareness. He is "a kind of psychic matrix, a pattern of creating images identical for the entire human species."[33] That's how Bachelard understands him. "The image originating in the most distant unconscious, coming from a life that is not our personal life, can only be studied by reference to psychological archeology."[34] And he emphasizes the phylogenetic conditioning of ontogenetic development. The concept of archetype in Bachelard's theory of the picture becomes its basis as a manifestation of the subject's unconscious in symbolic forms moving the world of imagination. Thanks to it, he is able to show that, firstly, the unconscious is not empty; images find their first potential of meaning and their dynamic source in it. Secondly, it is not chaos, temporal or spatial, but a field of already organized and even ordered images, in the sense of archetypes. This treatment allows Bachelard to show universal sharing of the same image; Bachelard's books with four elements are read in all languages as consistent with the experience of their cultural imagination. In other words, when they read Bachelard's books about the elements, they recognize the significance of their symbolic values. This proves that Bachelard perfectly understood, from his experience of his provincial world—I would like to remind you that he valued nature and provinces more than culture and civilization—universal archetypes of images of nature.

The third aspect of affinity between Jung and Bachelard emphasizes the androgynous nature of the imagination. In other words, the imagination spontaneously develops in two modes: female and male, *anima* and *animus*. Bachelard devotes many pages to this issue in *Le materialisme rationel*, in which he focuses on scientific rationality dictated by animus and its rigor. In the chapter *La poétique de la rêverie* entitled *Anima and animus*, according to J.-J. Wunenburger "is a delight for a Jungian."[35] There are really many references in it to both Jung and the texts cited by Jung. Rooted in the unconscious, masculinity and femininity patterns determine the tension between the poles of sexual differentiation. According to Jung, the anima—corresponding to

33 J.-J. Wunenburger, *Philosophie des images*, 41.

34 G. Bachelard, *La terre et les rêveries du repos*, 263–264.

35 J-J. Wunenburger, "Jung et l'école française de l'imaginaire: Gaston Bachelard et Gilbert Durand", *Cahiers Gaston Bachelard*, 2015, no. 13, 21.

the maternal eros—directs the man, among others, towards artistic activity and towards the sphere of emotions and relationships.[36] On the other hand, the Animus, corresponding to the paternal logos, inclines a woman towards independence, independence and activity.[37] Bachelard contrasts this with the oneiric situation in which he separates the dream (*le rêve*) from the daydream (*la rêverie*). He assigns the animus sign to the first one, and the anima to the second. An in-depth analysis of the concepts and phenomena of oneiric life is preceded by an analysis of language, proving the abovementioned, special relationship of Bachelard to words, which otherwise permeates the whole chapter. Le rêve (dreaming, dreaming) is a masculine noun in French, while la rêverie (day dream, daydream) is a feminine noun. The act of dreaming is therefore thoroughly feminina.

Bisexuality in the psyche is important in Bachelard's anthropology. Considering human motor skills, it turns out that movement is ultimately the most decisive energy element of the imagination. For imagination, which in itself is not the right source of movement, we must look for its source in the body. For this reason, for Bachelard, there are two types of imagination studied in the last two books on the element of the earth—anima imagination generating dreams of fullness, center, center, security and depth, and animus imagination, which Bachelard will illustrate with craftsmanship, especially handwork (i.e., kneading bread, forging metal, engraving or carving in stone).

4 Going beyond Jungism

This does not mean, however, that Bachelard's philosophy of imagination is a continuation or development of Jung's thought. In the most general perspective, one can see the similarity between these positions in terms of two-prongedness or bipolarity of the conceptualization of psyche activity. In Symbols and transformations, Jung separates acceptable, present, and well-rooted thought from imaginative thought. These are two types of thinking: targeted and conscious,

---

36 "Anima is a personification of all female psychological tendencies in a man's psyche such as: foggy feelings and moods, prophetic insights, susceptibility to irrationality, the ability to personal love, feelings related to nature and not an important attitude towards the unconscious from them". M-L. von Franz, "The process of individuation", in *Man and His Symbols*, ed. C. G. Jung (London: Aldus Books Limited, 1971), 243.

37 "Her [woman] animus can transform into an invaluable inner companion who will give her such masculine qualities as initiative, courage, objectivity and spiritual wisdom". Ibidem, 266.

directed "to others" and undirected and fanciful, "free play of fantasy," "for me." The first follows consciousness and is ordered, specific, functions in the real world; second, following the unconscious is characterized by spontaneity and lack of control, as such moves away from reality. Fantasy, however, is not assigned a hierarchically lower position. Her retreat from reality is a manifestation of the need to follow her own path, which is determined by the subjectivity of the subject. As such, detached from concreteness, it can afford unfettered freedom. This freedom is placed in the sphere of dreams and complexes.

The above Jungian division into the real and unreal world, objective and subjective, concrete and fanciful finds its counterpart in Bachelard's separation of discursive thought assigned to scientific cognition from the expansive poetic dream. Despite this demarcation, scientific thought is never pure thought. There is no cognition that would not be disturbed by unconscious, imaginary, or oneiric elements. It should be emphasized once again that Bachelard cogito is not recognized as "pure." *Cogito* in its most basic or source form coexists with the order of the unconscious and is shaped under its influence. One may even be tempted to define it as inherently emerging from the unconscious (*l'inconscient*); thanks to self-reflection, *cogito* extracts and separates itself from the field of the unconscious. This thread is considered in more detail together with Bachelard's Prometheus complex. Fire is associated with the meaning of "dispersing darkness," "knowledge overcoming ignorance," "the arrival of consciousness / light," and so on.

Bachelard's concept of "thematic criticism," in addition to pre-Socratic theories about the four elements of nature, includes the theory of complexes (Freud) and archetypes (Jung). The poet's response to the call of one of four elements results in a work written under the sign of fire, water, earth, or air. Then, analyzing the example of the earth's intimate dreams, images of the nest, grotto, house as "archetypes of happy childhood," deepest roots, warmth, interior, and security appear. Bachelard uses the term "archetype" but understands it differently from the way Jung does. For him, he determines a specific reference given to man in a natural way, in the sense of a programmed imagination that will create such and no other image. The image form is one—like a fixed and unchanging matrix—that is then restored and renewed in the creative work of the imagination. Each element has its own elemental form updated through the imagination appearing through a poetic image. Compared to the archetype, Bachelard's complex is a pattern of cultural creation—production and reproduction—to which the former cannot be subjected. In this context, the term "culture complex" (*le complexe de la culture*) appears and means a space in which poetic impressions and emotions are permanently included in the cultural order. The specific definition of such a complex is introduced in Lautréamont as follows:

> Our thesis suggested that the cultural adolescence was painful, intellectually neurotic for Isidor Ducasse. Generally speaking, psychoanalysis considers intellectual culture more specifically than classical psychoanalysis. The psychoanalysis of cognition does not delay the discovery in the sedimentary layer—below the primitive layer studied by Freudian psychoanalysis—specific complexes, cultural complexes resulting from premature embedding.[38]

According to Bachelard, Ducasse's violence and aggression bear signs of cultural complexes. They are a reaction of a young poet to socialization and education, to problems resulting from failure to comply with the system. Competition, intimidation, corporal punishment, all this had a huge impact on the shaping of the young Isidor's imagination. His greatest drama took place in the walls of the "rhetorical class" disciplining "free imagination." Bachelard considers lautreamontism as a group of cultural complexes in which the poetic diagram is based on the drama of culture and the drama of life in society. Education aiming to create a "corrected man" always stands in opposition to the poet who writes in the spirit of autonomy and freedom of language. Imaginatively, the most fertile individuals elude socialization and education that limit them. Then, as Maryvonne Perrot[39] when considering the status of the cultural complex in Bachelard, the Freudian "principle of reality" and "principle of pleasure" become respectively: either adaptation to social reality or functioning in the domain of the imagination. Imagination in this way of understanding, disconnecting the subject from reality, connects him to the depth and intimacy of things (thus only then really situating man in the world).

Bachelard writes about the complex in such words: "The complex is essentially unaware. If it rises to the centres of language, it will be given the possibility of exorcism."[40] The cultural complex turns out to be linguistic content rooted in tradition and custom, well-known content that, if purified, will show its source/natural element. In this way, for example, the element of the earth that is the content of the archetype of the "house" subjected to cultural development takes specific forms, appearing, for example, as a complex of Jonah

38 G. Bachelard, *Lautréamont*, 62.

39 M. Perrot, "Autour du complexe de culture. La place du Lautréamont dans l'oeuvre de Bachelard", *Cahier Gaston Bacheard. Bachelard et l'écriture*, 215–221.

40 G. Bachelard, *Lautréamont*, 83.

talking about the desire to be inside the object ("inside the whale"). His matter is earth, and his intimate dream is the desire to go inside/to be inside. This complex may also take a false form, although it may well be preserved. Such images Bachelard calls "school and banal," satisfying only professors of rhetoric. They are images of nymphs, flying fish, bird wings, blue sky, and Ophelia. As such, they are "empty," devoid of matter, "dead."

To define a cultural complex, one must de facto depart from its psychoanalytical understanding—the necessary content and constituting the human mental apparatus. In Bachelard, the complex is by definition associated with culture. As the philosopher himself writes: "In the area of what we do, to get to know the man we have only reading, wonderful reading judging a man after what he wrote."[41] Therefore, he subjects psychoanalysis to the human psyche by dividing the poetic image into prime factors. The complex understood in this way is said when "culture put a mark on nature."[42] For Bachelard, material imagination is rooted and culturally instilled. On the contrary, the psychoanalytical complex, which comes from nature, is understood as an order of instincts/desires whose satisfaction would be met with cultural depreciation—according to Bachelard. The Bachelard complex is already developed, dressed in words; in this sense it is already rationalized. As such, it is within the domain of *natura naturata*, not *natura naturans*. This location of the complex on the surface allows it to be known and understood. Imagining subject situates himself in the order of reproducing nature; his imaginations are certainly works of culture. The art he made will always be nature that has already been planted (*la nature greffée*). The Bachelardian characterization of the complexes does not differ much from Freud's understanding of them. The complex in Freud is not placed solely in the sexual sphere, as Bachelard thinks, and perhaps that is why he calls the Oedipus complex an "intellectual life complex"[43]—it arises at the intersection of (sexual) desire and (cultural) prohibition. It is possible that Bachelard's attribution to the adjective *cultural* is to indicate that they are less immersed in the unconscious than psychoanalysts thought. In my opinion, it is also his way of emphasizing the difference between the semantic content of the archetype and the complex. The first has an unconscious genesis and is a deep source of meanings and meanings. It is created by images shared by all people—matrices. The other, from the rational and cultural order, is constructed, individual, intellectual. Thus, it seems more and more likely that the French philosopher would use such and not other names. In *La psychanalyse*

41 G. Bachelard, *L'eau et les rêves*, 14.

42 Ibidem.

43 G. Bachelard, *La psychanalyse du feu*, 31.

du feu calling the Prometheus complex a "desire to intellectualize,"[44] a desire to surpass the master in terms of intellect, seems to confirm this hypothesis. The Oedipus complex in the intellectual sense allows it to function well in culture. The Freudian desire to kill his father is transformed into the Bachelardian desire to have more and more knowledge/power; this is a figure of intellectual authority.

Contrary to understanding the complex, Bachelard approaches "unconsciousness." It plays an overpriced role when it comes to creativity. Without unconscious archetypes, which then reveal themselves as complexes in symbolic order, a work of art cannot exist. Archetypes are general patterns and sources of imaginary actions. From this order man derives his creative potential and his creative development. Archetypes are patterns of transmission between man and the world. Thanks to them, man is in the world, and the world speaks to man through it. Being a dream is the final moment of creation (i.e., a creative development of one of the four elements of nature). It is done by reference to both archetypal and cultural order. In this way a theory appears, according to which art subordinates itself to fundamental archetypes, and its basic question is the question of *arche*. The archeology of imagination is based on the opposition of the aesthetics of matter to the aesthetics of form, elemental aesthetics, and natural formal or artificial aesthetics. Therefore, the psychoanalyst looks well because he looks deeply. He sees clearly the foundation of being/work.

> The comprehensive philosophy of language must combine teaching psychoanalysis and phenomenology. To psychoanalysis should be added poetic-analysis, where all the adventures of the language will be organized, where all possible ways and talents of expression will be shown. (…). Poetic-analysis must therefore be an intimate deepening of the joy of imagining.[45]

This method will then be able to show the "absolute image" renewing the "old" man through the newly created image—it will be able to revive a permanent archetype.

In this way, Bachelard develops a theory of creative imagination based on language, which, however, will constantly be a kind of transition between the expression of the unconscious and consciousness. In Jungian, the unconscious is structured by archetypes and projections to be vaccinated on the materials

44 Ibidem, 30.

45 G. Bachelard, *Fragments d'une poétique du feu*, (Paris: PUF, 1988), 53–54.

of the world in Bachelard style. Imagination, according to Bachelard, does not work in a vacuum but is always associated with specific matter. The natural element becomes its intended material, always ready for processing. This means that the image is a kind of medium located between the individual psyche and one of the four elements of nature. There is no doubt that both, Jung and Bachelard, gave us exhaustive information about the structures and creative processes of the *psyche*.

References

Bachelard G., *La psychanalyse du feu*. Paris: Gallimard, 1938.

Bachelard G., *Lautréamont*, Paris: José Corti, 1939.

Bachelard G., *L'eau et les rêves. Essai sur l'imagination de la matière*, Paris: José Corti, 1942.

Bachelard G., *L'air et les songes*, Paris: PUF, 1943.

Bachelard G., *La terre et les rêveries du repos*, Paris: PUF, 1948.

Bachelard G., *La terre et la rêverie de la volonté*, Paris: PUF, 1948.

Bachelard G., *La poétique de l'espace*, Paris: PUF, 1957.

Bachelard G., *La poétique de la reverie*, Paris: PUF, 1960.

Bachelard G., *La formation de l'esprit scientifique. Contribution à une psychanalyse de la connaissance objective*, Paris: Vrin, 1972.

Bachelard G., *Fragments d'une poétique du feu*, Paris: PUF, 1988.

Błocian I., Morawska K., Ples-Bęben M., *Gaston Bachelard i filozofie obrazu*, Wrocław: Wydawnictwo Uniwersytetu Wrocławskiego, 2018.

Franz M-L., von, "The process of individuation", In *Man and His Symbols*, edited by C. G. Jung. London: Aldus Books Limited, 1968.

Freud S., *Objaśnienie marzeń sennych*, transl. R. Reszke. Warsaw: KR, 1996.

Freud S., *Wykłady ze wstępu do psychoanalizy. Nowy cykl*, transl. R. Reszke. Warsaw: KR, 2015.

Jung C.G., *Psychological Types*, transl. H. G. Baynes, revision R. F. C. Hull. Londo and New York: Routledge, 2016.

Kirk G.S., Raven J.E., Schofield M., *The Presocratic Philosophers a Critical History with a Selection of Texts*, Cambridge: Cambridge University Press, 1983.

Perrot M., "Autour du complexe de culture. La place du Lautréamont dans l'oeuvre de Bachelard", In *Cahier Gaston Bacheard. Bachelard et l'écriture*.

Ricœur P., *O interpretacji. Esej o Freudzie*, transl. M. Falski. Warsaw: PWN, 2008.

Rosińska Z., *Jung*, Warsaw: Wiedza Powszechna, 1982.

Sartre J.-P., *L'imaginaire. Psychologie phénoménologique de l'imagination*, Paris: Gallimard, 1986.

Wunenburger J-J., *Philosophie des images*, Paris: PUF, 1997.

Wunenburger J.-J., *La vie des images*, Grenoble: PUG, 2002.

Wunenburger J.-J., *L'imaginaire*, Paris: PUF, 2003.

Wunenburger J-J., "Jung et l'école française de l'imaginaire: Gaston Bachelard et Gilbert Durand", In *Cahiers Gaston Bachelard*, 13, 2015.

Wunenburger J.-J., "O narodzinach obrazu: obecność czy zanikanie bytu?", transl. M. Ples-Bęben. In *Idea -studia nad strukturą i rozwojem pojęć filozoficznych*, Białystok, 2016.

CHAPTER 7

In the Quest for *Temenos*: Metaphors for the Origins of Serbian Cultural Complexes

Bojana Stamenković Rudić

Abstract

This paper is concerned with images of life in the Balkan region, inspired by conversations the author has had with foreign supervisors and colleagues in the Serbian Developing Group, and by my clinical work. These images have included: permanent tension, wars, horrible devastation and destruction; then, revival, in a burst of life, like a Phoenix. Taking into consideration concepts of Analytical Psychology, this text presents metaphors for the origin of Serbian cultural complexes. It explores how the mutual impact of historical events and a deeply rooted belief system form collective experience. The focus is on the challenges for the survival of *temenos*, understood as an analytical concept, in a secure and relatively permanent space where the psychological maturation of the social group could be achieved. With this aim, the content of events and meanings in the Balkan region, which for centuries was designated "Limes," is explored. Due to dislocation and vast migrations caused by persecution, political decree, and economic hardship, changes in context prevailed over stability and persistence. The velocity and turbulence of the changes influenced a mode of life where the only permanence was impermanence. The mercurial quality of events in this region, also evident in the form and the content of the group's experiences, evokes an archetypal image of Hermes. Here, he is conjured in all his different aspects, with particular emphasis on the Trickster. The paper questions the collective tendency in our culture to identify with some aspects of this god and discusses the risks of this sort of inflation. In conclusion, the existence of some possible remedies is discussed. With no clear answer, the question of the mutual impact of historical events and the behaviour of our groups, which is governed from the realm of the psyche, is emphasized. The dynamics of the archetypal field are offered as one of the possible explanations.

Keywords

Balkan Peninsula, Temenos, Hermes, Trickster, cultural complexes, migrations, metaphor, home, archetypal field

 DOI:10.1163/9789004468757_009

1 Introduction

> This is a book about a wave which forgot it was the sea; about we who dream that the Balkans will one day become a pleasant piece of Europe.
>
> ISIDORA SEKULIĆ, *The Balkans*[1]

Fifteen years ago, an eminent Jungian analyst Mario Jacoby visited Belgrade as asupervisor of the Serbian Developing Group. This was a great privilege for us. In our inspirational, informal conversations, he was asked about his images of the Balkan Peninsula. After brief pauses, he responded: "Permanent tension, wars, horrible devastation and destruction, ashes and more ashes; then, revival in a burst of life, like a Phoenix (…)" It was deeply touching to imagine that fantastic, mythological bird on our poor Peninsula. At the same time, his images evoked our associations with a plant called Ramonda Serbica. It was a Serbian national symbol from World War I: a plant which, even after being completely dried out, miraculously revives when watered. It can survive even if frozen over long periods of time. That's why it is also called the Serbian Phoenix Flower.

Miracles and "breaks" belong to the space of liminality, as do contradictions and paradoxes. I focused on this topic of our social life, occupying myself with the enigmas in our culture through time. How is it possible to survive such inhuman conditions in difficult historical periods, including an enormous loss of citizens, and to persistently desire to develop a state? At the same time, why do we have such short periods of civilian organization and prosperity, and why do we always repeat the same mistakes? Where is our container, our common inner space of resilience? Is our capacity to internally manage the troubling thoughts and feelings appropriate enough? Why do we have difficulties incorporating what could have been learned from past experience, and why do we live the same old narratives as though they had never been integrated maturely into our current life? It is as if there has never been a time of stability and security long enough to enable us to devote ourselves to the conjunction of the opposite realms of our experiences from historical and mythical times. This guided me to focus my thoughts on the concept of *temenos,* a holy place in Jungian terms, whose existence could support auto realization. Jung wrote about *temenos* as an inner quality of the individual: "a magical furrow around the centre, the temple or *temenos* (sacred precinct) of the innermost

1 I. Sekulić, *Balkan* (Beograd: Plavi jahač, 2012).

personality." He further explained that a specific ritual in *temenos* could serve to "prevent an 'outflowing' or to guard by apotropaic means against distracting influences from outside."[2]

Presuming that the concept of *temenos* might be applied on a group level (rather than the individual with which Jung concerned himself), this paper hypothesizes that a lack of *temenos* would be more easily noticed in Balkan societies. Recognition that the energy in social events has such a huge power and that the dynamics of it frequently don't have a rationally predicted outcome, guided the author's thoughts toward the field of unconscious and archetypal powers. The author concerned herself with a search for *temenos* at the group level: a sacred place which could help us "to break free by a force that did not stream down from above (…). but come up with tremendous pressure from below and increased strength as consciousness detached itself from the darkness and climbed into the light."[3] This was seen as a desirable statement which, of course, is not easy to achieve.

It is evident that people in this region are in a quest for something they miss. The first question might be, How did we have so many difficulties in keeping more persistent conditions of *temenos*? In the short periods of time when it was temporary established, beautiful artworks used to appear: the icons in monasteries and churches with their warm and secure places that followed "tender" architect constructions. National poetry and music, full of deep emotions, as well as newer art, presented the urge to surround the Balkans and to cut it out from turbulent space. Nonetheless, even a superficial view of our cultural history could point to change being far more predominant than stability. It could be said that, during the centuries, we were literally living the change, trying to explore more deeply this condition of life. We were not observing the change; we were living it. There was no "point" of view; it couldn't be made because of the velocity, frequency, and turbulence of changes in this place of "storm winds." The Balkan is, as Isidora Sekulić wrote, "The place where no one has yet cultivated a field and seen the fruits of their labour."

Of course, there were many changes for other groups of people. Smaller groups could be even more sharply disturbed. Balkan groups survived due to some permanent aspects of cohesion which were through centuries represented in church, army, language, and mythology. Each of these aspects is undergoing its own process of reconsideration nowadays.

---

2 C. G. Jung, "Commentary on 'The Secret of the Golden Flower'", in *The Alchemical Studies*, v. 13, The Collected Works (Princeton NJ: 1977). Originally published in 1959.

3 C. G. Jung, "The Spirit Mercurius", in *Alchemical Studies*, v. 13, The Collected Works (Princeton NJ: 1977). Originally published in 1959.

This paper presents an attempt to create integrative narratives from this material. It is dominantly essayistic in the sense that it is based on metaphors which could inspire imagination. Its aim is to open new perspectives on this topic and to allow fluidity in conclusions. One might also aim to improve therapists' sensibilities in this domain, which would have high value in therapeutic work.

2 Limes

We are in the middle of a very important crossroads between East and West, North and South. That's what my generation was taught in school. We were proud to learn this because it gave this region special value, and we could presume that we were honoured and privileged to live here. Going back through history, the Balkan Peninsula (where Serbia is located) was part of a region that was named Limes in Roman times.[4] It was a border (what *limes* means in Latin) and at the same time, a space between great, historically well-known kingdoms, empires, and cultures. In contrast to them, this region was seen as chaotic, unstructured, undeveloped, and with high inner diversity.

To foreigners and those just passing through, it seemed settled by unknown gods and numerous, diverse mythological beings. Among the population since ancient times, some groups of people disappeared, some were removed, some settled as refugees or conquerors, and all more or less mixed with "domestic" groups. In the sense that Limes is a border, the next quotation gives an essential description:

> Limes pervades the history of Southeast Europe. The dimension of the border of civilizations and the sense of the marginal space between East and West are constantly repeated throughout the anthropologies and cultures of this part of Europe, through the rise and fall of states and peoples, over the course of the past two millennia.[5]

Transit across the limes-stones (borders) could be dangerous throughout historical times—asindeed nowadays. This danger could apply as a description of the psychological transition in ahuman life. Passing the separation from a

---

4 N. Samardžić, *Limes: istorijska margina i poreklo posebnosti Jugoistočne Evrope* (Beograd: HERAedu, 2017).

5 E. Ivetic, book cover comment on *Limes: istorijska margina i poreklo posebnosti Jugoistočne Evrope,* by Nikola Samardžić (Beograd: HERAedu, 2017).

well-known world, in front of the entrance to the unknown (as we know from our personal lives) could be full of fear, tension, and sorrow. We can imagine that for someone standing exactly on the border or on the cut stone, their point of view of the world at large is very specific. Their experience of time is not the same as it would be in outer reality, nor are their attitudes about identity. Strong emotions paint their attitude toward the world, and it could be difficult to obtain a harmonized rational and emotional view of the structure, distinctiveness, organization, and maps of the outside and inner life, as long as we are contained in what is neither known nor unknown. Dislocated from the structure and from the rules, deeply rooted in the place of liminality, either between borders or psychological boundaries between states of being, we experience uncertainty and disorientation. Transit through Limes is a metaphor for transition through the *liminal space* and vice versa. For people who lived in Limes, it could be experienced as though living "in-between" and not clearly belonging anywhere. Thinking of a parallel in biological system theory, Limes might be designated as "intercellular space," where the dynamics of diffusion and osmosis govern, supporting the development of a multicellular system. Between the cells, physical forces would not be controllable from inside this space, and movements could seem more like flow, like motions that react strongly on changes from multicellular system arrangements. If we develop this thought, we can recognize that although these dynamics are controlled from outside, intercellular space has a spectrum of deep impacts on the cells around them. It could damage their membranes or supply them. In Limes, which was not a small space, the topic of borders was always as questionable as the issue of boundaries in liminal space. We are focused on Limes, which was a space where the "inside and outside" were not united in the magical way of the Moebius strip. They were mixed, indiscriminate, and undifferentiated.[6]

This was the context where Serbs and other Slavic groups were present, among others, from medieval times. Slavic mythology also contained universalities about horizontal and vertical axes in the map of the space. The visible and invisible worlds were seen in dichotomies; as confined-uninhibited, tame-wild, conquered-not conquered, organized-chaotic, social (in which the sound of the axe and the voice of the rooster is heard)-the world beyond (the world of the thousand, gods, souls of the deceased, and demons). Communication with the outside world took place through rites at borders: the threshold

6 M. Stein, "Hermes and the Creation of Space", in *Soul: Treatment and Recovery, The Selected Works of Murray Stein,* (London: Routledge, 2015).

of the house, the fence of the yard, the border of the village, the river bank.[7] The theme of belonging—or, we could say, looking for the possibility to be contained—continued. Life in social liminality, between not easily recognizable thresholds of reintegration and reintegration itself, was contained with the great risk of losing identity and with permanent searching for home (concretely and metaphorically) and new roads on the way to salvation.

3 The Home

In my wish to present part of our history, I will not restrict myself to historical facts. We can have an equally worthy experience of knowing through metaphors and following our images and evoked emotions. To this aim, the title of the book of the well-known Serbian poet Vasko Popa is inspiring: "The house in the middle of the road."[8]

Let us stay with this image for a while—the house in the middle of the road. We might imagine that this house is unsecure, unprotected from the outside. Is it comfortable? No, not in the least. It's stormy all around. Could you be calm and relaxed inside? No, not at all. Are you afraid of the danger which could come from outside or of the high tension inside?

"The house in the middle of the road" could be a bothersome, disturbing object for powerful groups. "Let's just destroy it!" And so it happened, many times. For those who were desperate and miserable, even one of these houses (they were made again and again) could be seenas a shelter. "Let's enter!" What about inner voices? One of them could be, "Is it only chaos, or is this hell? Let's go live somewhere else, or let's go conquer something else!"

The aim of this imaginative exercise is to prepare us for understanding the complexity of defining and experiencing "home" in this region of horrible devastation. The feeling of home, as one of the central human realities, was distorted all too many times, not only by the loss of the concrete object, but also in the totality of all the dimensions of home.[9] As Papadopoulos explains, the loss of home is a very complex concept, full of challenges and sorrow and suffering.

In the Balkan region, the lack of home was common, due to destruction, dislocation, and huge migrations caused by persecution, political decree, and

---

7 Lj. Radenković, "Prostor", *in Simbolika sveta u narodnoj magiji Južnih Slovena* (Niš: Prosveta, 1996).

8 V. Popa, *Kuća nasred druma,* (Beograd: Prosveta, 1975).

9 R. K. Papadopoulos, "Refuges, home and trauma", in *Therapeutic Care for Refugees. No Place Like Home*, (London: Karnak, 2002).

economic hardship. Becoming a refugee "whose primary common characteristic is their lack of home"[10] could happen at the ashes of the place where someone previously lived, or far away from their former landscape. For those who were dislocated or who migrated, a feeling of sorrow and guilt for having abandoned their ancestors and land of origin became one of the most widespread narratives. This also influenced poetry, one of the rare "channels" offering the possibility to "communicate" these feelings. Having new rulers in your land or being a refugee or immigrant in the new environment, your memories of this type of loss would need to be frozen. Tortures, annihilations, and humiliations had to be annulated; grieving became forbidden. Even nostalgia, which could be very helpful in passing through the early phases of grieving,[11] was seen as an opportunistic or "extremist" tendency. We could say that nostalgia was poisoned here, through circumstances which "prevent loss from progressing gradually and undergoing change, so that one cannot get used to the fact that they have become a refugee or displaced person, unable to establish an internal distinction and continuity between the past, present, and future."[12] Within our society, we were always governed by the rule, the command, or even the proclamation that the "former" was wrong, in contrast to the descendants of great empires who can share romantic memories of glorious days. We cannot share these feelings with them because we were affirmed through the experiences of the Shadow of great monarchies, living through very dark parts of their history.

We can suppose that missing the former home gave strength to the development of one of the most present "intangible" forms of belonging. It is the family ritual, the *slava,* dedicated to the saint who protects the family. This solemn celebration, which is inherited from one generation to another, marks one of the most important days in the Christian calendar.

A lot of pre-Christian rituals were practiced here. The threshold of the home was one of the most frequently used places for this, with the intention of connecting the horizontal and vertical division of the space. There were also forbidden behaviors, regarding the threshold, with the aim of "keeping peace" with the invisible world. It was not permitted to sit on a threshold, or to cut wood on it: it had to be respected. Shaking hands above it was also undesirable behavior.[13]

10 Ibidem.

11 V.D. Volkan, *Imigranti i izbeglice* (Beograd: Clio, 2018).

12 Ibidem.

13 Lj. Radenković, „Semantika kućnog prostora (na primerima tradicionalne srpske kuće)", in *Graditeljsko nasleđe u Srbiji, Zbornik u čast Dr Dobroslava Bojka St. Pavlovića* (Beograd: Zavod za proučavanje kulturnog razvitka, 2014). pp. 20–43.

Reintegration, as an internal, psychological path of "returning" home or redeveloping a new home was commonly interrupted. The cause lies in the fact that the "new" was experienced as unfriendly, persecutory, and exploitative. The collective experience of this developed into a very specific personality trait named "inat." It is similar to "in spite of," but has wider implications. It means that you would do something which might not be beneficial for you—and might even be auto-destructive—with the strong feeling of pride and of hate for the other, to make someone feel the other, unsatisfied or obstructed, even at your own expense. I believe it is connected with depressive feelings, in connection with and compensation for feelings of inferiority.

There was no time for healing and recovery;as our famous writer Isidora Sekulić once said, "The Balkan is a huge cemetery of various lordships and civilizations."[14]

> We never had the time to build and shape our culture in peace. Wars, escapes, wandering, devastation, building on ruins, that's our history. And even when we were creating, everything was at a dizzying pace, it broke people (...) We always start from scratch, like grass. After every uprising, every war, every dynasty, from scratch (...) Every beginning is marked not only by building, but by sacrifice as well.

4 Temenos

One of the inspirations for imagining *temenos* as a container for culture was Anish Kapoor's Middlesbrough work named Temenos.[15] The world's largest public artwork looks like a vast butterfly net with two loops. There are two poles, a circular ring and an oval ring, all held together by a net. It is obvious that butterflies couldn't be captured by this net. They would fly through the space between those two hoops—two boundaries—entering into the tender hug of this net, feeling secure. They could rest there; they could also recover and maybe gather strength for the next stage of their flight. This artwork is dedicated to the regeneration, healing, and transforming of society and culture.

What about the Balkan region? Even a seemingly permanent (if ultimately temporary) life in the same geographical area, for Serbs, saw frequent changes in the name of the state. People who are now around 70 years of age have lived

14 I. Sekulić, Balkan, (Beograd: Plavi jahač, 2012).

15 M. Wainwright, "Anish Kapoor sculpture nets high price", in *Guardian Weekly,* (London, 2008). https://www.theguardian.com/artanddesign/2008/jul/10/art (Accessed: 18 May 2019).

in at least seven states, even as they might never have left their home. These changes, which have involved not only changes to borders but also forced adaption to ever-changing official rules and to myriad new and strange value systems, have hindered the general feeling of security. As discussed earlier, a "container," a "magic circle," or a "vessel" in which psychological growth inherent to our group condition could take place, was painfully missing through time. We know that the origin of the term *a yard around a temple* presented a space clearly marked between two boundaries. One was the boundary of everyday life or the outer world; the second was toward the world of divines. We have already mentioned some circumstances from the outer world that interrupted the existence of *temenos* for groups of Balkan people. On the other hand, we are at great risk if we do not consciously recognize the necessity of the appropriate boundary toward the center, toward the vertical axis of the world; if we allow ourselves to identify with the divine. When *temenos* is missing, it is like being permanently stuck in a liminal state, full of dangers, as described in Jung's writing:

> It does not seem to occur to anyone that there might be something valuable in between. The "other" may be just as one-sided in one way as the ego is in another (…) What fearful abysses of doubt would then be opened? What madness should we not then have to fear? One can also understand why that inner friend so often seems to be our enemy, and why he is so far off and his voice so low.[16]

5 Trickster

As it is known, our inner "other" could easily be projected upon external others, frequently on those with whom we are familiar. Neighbours or "siblings" in the Balkan groups could have archetypal dynamics in their misunderstandings and conflicts. From one point of view, it could be explained as a quarrel between Olympian siblings. Metaphorically told, we all could be easily seduced by the idea that we are children of the main Olympian god. It is so attractive to be Apollo, god of light, healing, and prophecy, one who protects truth and fairy music and poetry. It is no less attractive to recognize some appreciated aspects of the Hermes archetype in the same domain. Among Balkan siblings,

16 C. G. Jung, "Concerning Rebirth", in *The Archetypes and the Collective Unconscious*, v. 9, I, The Collected Works (Princeton, NJ: 1977). Originally published in 1959.

superficial quarrels are always like that between Apollo and Hermes.[17] They include expectation or even invitation of the supreme god to make a judgment. However, the cruel siblings' wars contain a rather different, gloomy, and cruel part of interactions, connected with the darkest aspects of Trickster. It could be very disturbing for the individual and group "owners" of the shadow to recognize this "primitive 'cosmic' being of divine-animal nature; on the one hand superior to man because of his superhuman qualities, and on the other hand inferior to him because of his unreason and unconsciousness (...) older even than the Greek Hermes."[18] We all deny this figure in our siblings groups, and this content is one of the most frequently projected into the "other." We don't see each other because we always see Trickster. We can't see ourselves because we don't recognize Trickster in us. Full of tricks and full of danger, childish, fluid, temporarily charming and temporarily disgusting, without any sense for boundaries, Trickster cannot find a point of view to introduce "himself." Without conscious effort, it could be very easy to be engulfed by this figure.

Considering the devastations of civil wars in the Balkans, these reflections can neither annul and disguise human aggressiveness, nor equalize the darkest side of our reality—the evil—with Trickster's traits alone.

6 Hermes

Having described life in Limes and found connections with existence in liminal space, we might introduce some thoughts about the archetypal figure that governs in this world, the world of Hermes. How does he affect collective life in Limes?

He is not permanently settled here because he cannot be contained anywhere. There are no boundaries which could be an obstacle for his fluid presence. At the same time, wherever he appears, the boundary is assigned. Could we notice that people who live in his "land" have difficulties respecting borders and boundaries? Coincidentally, they were frequently collateral damage because of turbulent border changes, yet they also created many new borders. From the perspective of time, those borders seem fluid and changeable, almost like vivid organisms. They change their graphics, as well as their qualities, like cell membranes.

---

17 R. Grevs, *Grčki mitovi* (Beograd: Nolit, 1987).

18 C. G. Jung, "On the Psychology of the Trickster-Figure" in *The Archetypes and the Collective Unconscious*, v. 9, 1, The Collected Works (Princeton NJ: 1977). Originally published in 1959.

How much did Hermes' traits affect events on this landscape? Did his readiness to protect so many different types of people invoke all who needed protection? All those on the roads—passengers, shepherds, thieves, traders, robbers, civilians, and soldiers who were passing away to the other world, people who had an intense need to gamble, to cheat, to make jokes, to imagine a beautiful life or something else—during short breaks between battles—did they all, existing in the outer reality, evoke the presence of this mythic character of Hermes? He was, and is, definitely still involved in life here in his different aspects, Trickster among them. This sort of influence could be detected in the way we think, feel, and behave in either a good or a bad manner. Here, we might conclude that "discovering" those mythological figures refers to a psychological reality which is larger than the individual. When we suppose that our culture is embedded in a specific archetypal field, we also suppose that there are tangible representations of this archetype in the outer world. We recognize them in the repetition of strongly expressed specific behaviors, supposing that they are governed by an archetypal pattern. Let me illustrate this dilemma with a new question: Did this region, full of winds, known as the crossroads of pleasant Mediterranean winds, and those who came from the north-east parts of the continent, deeply rooted in our cold and humid Karpathos mountain cradle, invite Hermes? Or did Hermes, who was also known as "a wind," just present himself, attracting them all here?

Looking for the "presence" of Hermes-Trickster traits in our common life, the author analyzed patterns of behavior, expressed emotions, and styles of communication, using sequences from a short documentary recorded during a garden party for children, in 1992.[19] In the video, it is early summer, 27 years ago. The embargo had begun a week before.

The author was deeply touched by a clip from the video in which two girls spontaneously took the shape of Hermes: they took sticks, they had hats, they wore "wings," and they walked as though two passengers on the road, or two little shepherds. This image is a contemporary variation of the deeply rooted pattern. This and similar clips presented playfulness, joy, imagination.

Cheating was also in evidence. Children competed in a game of eating doughnuts that were hung on two sides of a long string, without using their hands. In circumstances in which you wish to eat, but your hands are bound behind your back, and the food is not easily available, you easily become a Trickster "in training." Quickly or slowly, you start to cheat. We can recognize

19 Video material was presented, with the permission of those filmed, at the Jungian Conference: "Collective structures of imagination - image - myth - society," University of Wroclaw, Poland, 6–8 June, 2019.

cooperation in playing the game, in sport, or just for fun. There were also clips about noncooperation, about a tendency to be a solo player, to perform tasks in your own way. Some of the sequences presented a permeable boundary between the game and the dangerous, a cunning fight with intensification of disguised anger. Strange, changeable coalitions and temporary alliances were made there.

Using this material for exploration, the author neither forgot that it is common to find Trickster's traits in a group of children, nor did she want to "infantilize" the adults in our culture; this was a search for metaphorical illustrations. These clips also reveal dangerous, archaic traits of division, splitting the "as if" behavior in adults at these circumstances of fragmented life, in the presence of the "ghost from the bottle" in the Balkan region. The group of adults in the clip is frozen; they worry, but they are sincerely vivid in protecting and playing with the children. There is no separation between parents and children, and everything is festive in group interactions. Amongst themselves, the adults show their "dark" mood. It is as though each group's behavior emerges from their two personalities.

A helicopter approaches, spooky in its very existence because, as the adults know, flights are cancelled (because of the embargo), and the passengers in this helicopter are wounded soldiers and civilians on the way to the military hospital. The flying object comes from the Hell of War. Fifty-seven seconds of this clip gave the author the chance to observe, and perhaps understand, the primary archetype around which we are gathered. The conclusion is that deeply archaic psychological defense, splitting in this case, has important meaning. Its existence here gives clear meaning to its original function: defense. It gives support to (no less than) the survival of mutual relations and social life, continuing the existence of each person in our culture. It is a defense on the edge of breakdown, theoretically—pathologically, existentially—unavoidable and meaningful. It serves as a platform which temporarily keeps particles from fragmented life and preserves them as a condition to unity between themselves. Nowadays, children who participated in this party, metaphorically named the children of Hermes, have grown up influenced by him, as the descendants of people who were frequently dislocated unwillingly but who also liked to travel a lot, to discover, to try something new. Most of them live abroad now, three quarters, in fact. It is an illustration of a migration rate which is among the highest in Europe.

Continuing with the tendency to create division, it is worthy to mention a contemporary book, written by a famous playwright, about 20 divisions among Serbs. Some of them are Serbs and Yugoslavs, chetniks and partisans, pro-Western and pro-Eastern Serbs, and so on.[20] The language that was the same for several groups around us is now divided into four languages, by political decision and contrary to the findings of philologists. The joking trickster part in us could say, "What a privilege! We all became polyglots in a day!" Maybe even now, writing this text, the influence of Trickster on the author could be recognized. At the same time, the awareness of Trickster's presence in the context of collective trauma is not ignored. His function here could be recognized as self-defense,[21] with all the complexities that its existence could present, since collective recovery from traumas was never begun.

Dušan Kovačević has been one of the most prolific and popular playwrights in the ex-Yugoslav region during the last half of the century. It could be said that in his work, he "sculpts" our culture, looking for the most logical prominent paradoxes within. His eye is focused on the collective features that we don't like to see in ourselves. As a rule, we recognize them clearly in the "other." Even the titles of his plays sound like dramatic oxymorons: *Claustrophobic Comedy*, *Uproarious Tragedy* (subtitled *Tragedy Burlesque*), *Five-Star Dumpster*, *Doctor Shuster*, and so on. These contradictions are harmful opposites whose unity cannot be sustained emotionally. They are a bitter presentation of a reality—our reality—which is not easy to live. In our society, the acceptance of paradox in the Jungian sense has yet to be achieved; there are no glimpses of harmonization and the acceptance of paradox as a wise, unavoidable, inherent part of life which represents, as Jung wrote, "the most valued spiritual possessions. The paradox (…) reflects a higher level of intellect and, by not forcibly representing the unknowable as known, gives a more faithful picture of the real state of affairs."[22] What comes to mind when thinking about some of Kovačević's plays is that he is the master of the grotesque, itself a colorful presentation of the world.

> The simplest explanation for why the grotesque is so effective is that it makes contrasts more obvious while juxtaposing the ugly and the beautiful, the divine and the unholy, the sublime and the ordinary, the romantic and the dull (…) and we don't take it for granted.[23]

---

20 D. Kovačević, *20 srpskih podela (Srba na Srbe)*, (Beograd: Nin, Novosti, 2008).

21 D. Kalsched, *The Inner World of Trauma, Archetypal Defences of the Personal Spirit*, (London and New York: Routlege, Taylor & Francis Group, 1996).

22 C. G. Jung, "Transformation symbolism in the mass", in *Psychology and Religion: West and East*, v. 11, The Collected Works (Princeton, NJ: 1977). Originally published in 1954. Pg. 275.

23 B. Mikašinović, *Selected Serbian Comedies* (New Avenue Books) https://openlibrary.org/publishers/New_Avenue_Books (Accessed: 18 May 2019).

We could accept this state as a basic starting point, as the first step toward true recognition of opposites and a deeper emotional connection with each. This could be an unavoidable condition for making conscious connections between them and for founding a more mature and socially engaged attitude toward our culture.

7 Conclusion

Could we conclude that our historical destiny has become our psychological faith? Or could we suppose that living in the archetypal field of Limes predestined events on both sides—the outside and the inner realm?

In any case, the differentiation of consciousness includes the task of recognizing the archetypal streams in which we are all involved, and the task of diachronic connections with the contents of life in this region. This could produce the conditions for reorganization in our life in liminality, as a first step toward the next, presumably more mature, stage of life. As Jung wrote,

> Every new stage in the differentiation of consciousness to which civilization attains, (we are confronted) with the task of finding a new interpretation appropriate to this stage in order to connect the life of the past that still exists in us with the life of the present, which threatens to slip away from it.[24]

The history of "friendships and betrayals"[25] of the Balkan groups of people, as a conscious interpretation of our long-lasting circumstances, could present a solid foothold and firm support for future planning in our culture.

What could be a pessimistic outcome?

Continuing the inflation, being so deeply engulfed with the archetype of Hermes, could force a melting of the particles in the suspension we live in. Identification with Hermes, who resists the gravitational forces, could guide our inner fluidity toward deeper loss of structure, toward disappearance. As scientists say, most people enjoy being in an anti-gravitational field. With the repetition of this experience, human beings develop a sort of dependency. But, as human

---

24 C. G. Jung, "The psychology of the child archetype", In *The Archetypes and the Collective Unconscious*, v. 9, I, The Collected Works (Princeton NJ: 1977). Originally published in 1954. Pg. 157.

25 J. Hillman, "Betrayal and Friendship", in *Loose Ends*, (Washington: Spring publication, 1989).

beings, we start to suffer in a short period of time. The loss of bones and muscle tissue manifests itself as a medical problem of the connective tissue. Analogically said, if we refuse to live on the ground (continuing with psychological identification with Hermes), we lose our inner psychological connections; we lose coherency, structure, boundaries between the inside and the outside.

We need *temenos* as a space where the world of humans and the world of gods could communicate. Without the recognition of its structure—of two boundaries (toward the outer world and toward the world of the Divine)—borderline experiences could be repeated all over again. The least we could do as therapists is not only to spread knowledge and acknowledge various points of view, but also to develop our imagination to recognize slow and fast motions of social groups, to recognize their risks and immobility. Our sensitivity for the differences that are embodied in different cultures is a matter of urgency.

References

Grevs R., *Grčki mitovi,* Beograd: Nolit, 1987.

Hillman J., "Betrayal and Friendship", In *Loose Ends.* Washington: Spring publication, 1989.

Ivetic E., Book cover comment on *Limes: istorijska margina i poreklo posebnosti Jugoistočne Evrope,* by Nikola Samardžić. Beograd: HERAedu, 2017.

Jung C.G., "Concerning Rebirth", In *The Archetypes and the Collective Unconscious*, v. 9, I. *The Collected Works*, Princeton NJ, 1977. Originally published in 1959.

Jung, C.G., "On the Psychology of the Trickster-Figure", In *The Archetypes and the Collective Unconscious*, v. 9, I. *The Collected Works*, Princeton NJ, 1977. Originally published in 1959.

Jung C.G., "The Psychology of the Child Archetype", In *The Archetypes and the Collective Unconscious*, v. 9, I. *The Collected Works*, Princeton NJ, 1977. Originally published in 1959.

Jung C.G., "Commentary on 'The Secret Of the Golden Flower'", In *Alchemical Studies*, v. 13. *The Collected Works*, Princeton NJ, 1977. Originally published in 1959.

Kalsched D., *"The Inner World of Trauma, Archetypal Defences of the Personal Spirit",* London and New York: Routlege, Taylor & Francis Group, 1996.

Kovačević D., *"20 srpskih podela (Srba na Srbe"),* Beograd: Nin, Novosti, 2008.

Mikašinović B., *"Selected Serbian Comedies",* New Avenue Books, 2016. https://openlibrary.org/publishers/New_Avenue_Books (Accessed: 18 May 2019).

Papadopoulos R.K., "Refugees, home and trauma", In *Therapeutic Care for Refugees. NoPlace Like Home.* Edited by Renos K. Papadopoulos. Tavistock Clinic Series. London: Karnac, 2002.

Popa V., *Kuća nasred druma*, Beograd: Prosveta, 1975.

Radenković Lj., „Prostor" in *Simbolika sveta u narodnoj magiji Južnih Slovena*, Niš: Prosveta, 1996.

Radenković Lj., „Semantika kućnog prostora (na primerima tradicionalne srpske kuće)" in *Graditeljsko nasleđe u Srbiji, Zbornik u čast Dr Dobroslava Bojka St. Pavlovića,* Beograd: Zavod za proučavanje kulturnog razvitka, 2014.

Samardžić N., *Limes: istorijska margina i poreklo posebnosti Jugoistočne Evrope*, Beograd: HERAedu, 2017.

Sekulić I., *Balkan.* Beograd: Plavi jahač, 2012.

Stein M., "Hermes and the Creation of Space", in *Soul: Treatment and Recovery, The Selected Works of Murray Stein,* London: Routledge, 2015.

Stein M., *In Midlife, A Jungian Perspective*, Dallas, Texas: Spring Publications, 1983.

Volkan V.D., *Imigranti i izbeglice,* Beograd: Clio, 2018.

Wainwright M., "Anish Kapoor sculpture nets high price." In *Guardian Weekly* (London, 2008). https://www.theguardian.com/artanddesign/2008/jul/10/art (Accessed: 18 May 2019).

CHAPTER 8

Therapy of Shadow in Film and Literature: Introductory Remarks

Maria Kostyszak

Abstract

The article will concentrate on selected examples of potentially successful therapy of shadow. Apart from awakening of one's awareness of shadow's presence, they may help to find constructive solutions. Both artistic domains—film and literature—do not cure anything in a direct way. The metaphorical quality of literary codes and the symbolic space of cinema creations demand knowledge and experience on how to interpret their messages. The more opening books one has read, the more creative films one has watched, one's place of understanding of what is going in the world transforms more radically into a richer one. On the other hand, both literature and film also try to develop simple and universal codes of communication that can appeal to anybody, even an inexperienced person, on the condition that appeal to human imagination and emotional sphere will be psychologically relevant, and that is why it is finally effective. The article considers such chosen examples.

Key words

therapy, shadow, fictional imagination, filmosophy

1 Powerful and Sensitive Women in Contemporary Contexts

When, in the 1930s, Virginia Woolf was asked by a respected British lawyer how to prevent culture from the threat of war, her answer was a complex one. In her book *Three Guineas* (1936–8), she offers a similar project of social reconstruction that some years earlier Bertrand Russell provided.[1] Egalitarian education and social peace-building may be pointed out as the essence of both proj-

1 B. Russell, *Principles of Social Reconstruction*, (London: Routledge 1997).

 | DOI:10.1163/9789004468757_010

ects. Treating women as less developed and mentally weaker was, according to Woolf, connected with the lack of women's access to education. Once they can acquire education and be able to earn money, they can demonstrate equal intelligence, creativity, and inventiveness.

If in the following examples the article points mainly, although not exclusively, to heroines, it is because it happens more frequently that women are not satisfied with the social status quo. They strive to change some aspects of experienced reality.

As these selected examples I have chosen Olga Tokarczuk's short story entitled "Transfugium" from her anthology *Bizarre Stories,* as well as Svetlana Alexijewicz's *Chernobyl Prayer: The Chronicle of the Future.* These are two literary specimens. From the vast space of the multitude of artistic films,[2] my choice refers to Agnieszka Holland's *Spoor a*nd Tom Tykwer's *Heaven.* We know from Carl Gustav Jung's research that there may be various kinds of shadow when we approach the process of individuation. "The first stage leads to the experience of the shadow" as Jolande Jacobi describes the process.[3] In Jung's *The Practice of Psychotherapy* there appears a powerful emphasis on the relevance of that first stage. "Assimilation of the shadow gives a man body, so to speak."[4] The moment of getting a sort of ground from which to begin psychic transformation empowers a patient with energy to continue the shadow work.

In my analyses the focus is on the collective shadow produced by some cultural, unexamined, but systematically reproduced assumptions. In general I mean here our attitude to the so-called weaker ones: to children; to persons with disabilities; to animals; to people of lower positions in the social hierarchy; to people of a different religion, nation, skin color, gender (any otherness discerned as lower quality). Even when, in the sphere of declared views, one claims to be tolerant and affirmative, nonverbal and very often unconscious treatment of these enumerated categories of people, things, or meanings may be observed as hiding double standards.

When one becomes more and more aware of how limited and hypocritical one proves to be in numerous situations despite declared systems of values, one may undertake the process of transformation. But the adaptive mechanisms operate not only on younger people who are sometimes completely dependent

---

2 When our conference took place, the film based on Svetlana Alexijewicz's *War's Unwoman Face,* directed by Kantemir Balagov was not yet shown in Poland. Now I would recommend watching that difficult, but very valuable in a therapeutic sense, film, its title being *Beanpole* (2019).

3 J. Jacobi, *The Psychology of C. G. Jung,* (London: Routledge 1946), 102.

4 C. G. Jung, *The Practice of Psychotherapy,* (London: Routledge 1993), 63.

on common acceptance. Also adults, working within established systems, must adapt some rules or values which are not in agreement with their conscience. European art becomes more and more conscious of the pathological consequence not only of colonization of continents, but also of colonization of one's head, colonization of nature in general. The fundamental lack of imagination in the European attitude to nature, exposed nowadays also by intense ecological movements, uncovered that connection not so transparent before. An improper attitude to nature results from reification of the natural processes that are treated as repeatable and able to be observed in laboratories.

For approximately three centuries, the false theses of strong opposition between culture and nature deformed healthy relations among various factors concerning human life (body, feeling self-respect, not humiliating one another in chains of generations). Philosophical emphasis on the strong opposition between the subjective and the objective has also caused a lot of unnecessary exclusions and conflicts. Finally, the lack of balance between technoscience and nature,[5] as well as various forms of turbocapitalism, seem to support the growth of culture's shadow instead of reducing it.

2 Olga Tokarczuk's *Transfugium*

As in Tokarczuk's *Drive Your Plow Through the Bones of the Dead*, William Blake appears in *Transfugium* directly and indirectly. Czesław Miłosz appreciated in his book *The Land of Ulro* the great role of Blake's poetry. The poet expressed the danger of the scientific worldview that gradually replaced imagination and dreaming with rational, logical thinking. Both Blake and Miłosz opposed the one-sidedness of such a type of rationality, resulting in a reduced and barren culture.

In *Transfugium* there is a clinic in which transformation into an animal is possible. After her children have left the house, and her husband has died, the sister of the narratorundertakes the decision to change into a wolf. The clinic that specializes in this transforming process seems to operate in a way similar tothe ritual ofthe traditional funeral. The clinical aspect of the process, as well as the sterile atmosphere created by the ceremony master, suggests it is a form of escape from life. Loneliness remains unbearable, especially when all the interpersonal relations have become devoid of empathy and marked with social atomism. Tokarczuk does not emphasize the passive role of family, but

5 D. F. Noble, *The Religion of Technology. The Divinity of Man and the Spirit of Invention*, (New York: Knopf 1997).

it may be marginally observed that there are no communities within which women could realize their creative potential apart from serving within a family.

In her anthology of bizarre stories, Olga Tokarczuk offers constructions based on the hypothetical "what if." Can we imagine such a possibility? Can we realize it? Does such a transformation signify a step backward, or is the continuity between animals and humans regained in that symbolic way?

I consider the possibility of asking all these questions as the unique adventure of involving both imaginations—the authoress's and the reader's—into a sort of cooperation. The discerning and hypothetical experience of such imaginary cooperation may develop into an investigation of one's boundaries. Self-awareness is not sufficient to cure shadow, but it forms the first step in the process. How may therapy be achieved? Through fiction—due to the fantastic fictional imagination that may help to produce a proper distance toward one's habits.

3 Svetlana Alexijewicz's Voices of Chernobyl Prayer: The Chronicle of the Future

My second literary example is *Voices of Chernobyl Prayer: The Chronicle of the Future*[6] by Svetlana Alexijewicz. She is a Belarusian journalist who is most famous for her book entitled *War's Unwomanly Face* (1995) and *Zinky Boys* (1985). The former tries to build the feminine idiom of experiencing and speaking about war. Alexijewicz noticed that the Russian celebration of war memory is formulated in victorious masculine language in which certain qualities of experience are not articulated, not even touched. While collecting various stories about war she has two purposes: to write the story of the human soul in historical events, not just to report the so-called facts; the second one is to make war so disgusting that even generals would hate it. After being awarded the Nobel Prize in Literature for 2015 (the first time it was given to a journalist), her creativity became more known, unfortunately not commonly but only within some circles. Justification of the award emphasized "her polyphonic writings being a monument to suffering and courage of our time."[7]

6 In Polish the book was translated with the title: *Chernobyl Prayer: The Chronicle of the Future.* It suggests the rich sense of promise that in the future, the singular, personal voice will be treated more seriously than it is treated now. Thus from the great tragedy and despair of the victims of the nuclear catastrophe, who speak in the book with their own voices, Alexijewicz can derive an affirmative message for the future. I consider it to be a precious case of care ethics in journalism and literature.

7 Cf. https://www.goodreads.com/pl/book/show/357486.Voices_from_Chernobyl (Accessed: 29.10.2019)

Her book *Zinky Boys* (1995) contains her own experience of being a witness in Afghanistan. She considers the war there to be immoral on both sides and concludes that it is tragic that young Russian soldiers and nuns are encouraged to participate in the war that is supposed to introduce democracy but is only thoughtless murdering of people on both sides. Instead of promised profits, they are coming back to their homeland either in zinky coffins or as cripples without any support from the state.

Alexijewicz's book about children's fates during the Second World War, entitled *Last Witnesses* (1985), belongs to the stream of accusing war of producing the effect of an unbearable burden on our common psyche. All the books by Svetlana Alexijewicz belong to the category of therapeutizing individuals and collectivity.

In many of her interviews she confesses how much time and effort she devotes to the issue of seeking the proper style. How not to exaggerate? How to arouse empathy and avoid the risk that readers cannot bear so much despair, so they would react with resistance? How to provoke responsibility for the future? The narrative in *Voices of Chernobyl* is guided between the cry of despair and a prayer. The unique way of combining individual life stories with the chaotic actions of the state to organize the unexpected effects of the radioactive catastrophe seems to produce room for future responsibility, awareness that anticipates and avoids what may be too dangerous for humanity. Confrontation with the unpredictable consequence of a nuclear reactor accident revealsa complete lack of safety when human exploitation of natural sources trespasses its borders. The critics claimed that S. Alexijewicz's journalism creates a new quality. I would call it ecological journalism because the authoress is very responsible in describing, in a very moving but not grandiloquent way, numerous difficult issues: women and children being witnesses of or participants in wars, and Soviet soldiers in Afghanistan who had been deceived into believing that they were to introduce democracy whereas it was just a Soviet occupation.

For the first time the Nobel Prize in Literature was awarded for journalism. It was appreciated that this sort of literary creativity seemed to stand so close to life and death, ultimate experiences that its therapeutic effect may be amplified.

4 Agnieszka Holland's *Spoor* (in Polish: *Pokot*, 2017)

Film art, like great literature, may influence the development of imagination and thus cure the gradual effect of the reduction of the human imaginary dimension caused by the growth of rational mentality.

Agnieszka Holland's *Spoor*, based on Olga Tokarczuk's *Drive Your Plow Through the Bones of the Dead*, may be pointed out as one among such cinematic masterpieces. The convention of Tokarczuk's crime story was criticized by those who consider murdering animals too important a moral issue to be conveyed in such a "light" literary genre. The additional moral issue is connected in Tokarczuk's short story with the Catholic Church officials supporting hunting and a reified attitude to animals. The Christian interpretation of the human attitude toward animals is not so simplified. Although there is a hierarchy, the lower creatures should be under the care of those that are higher on the existential ladder. Unfortunately, a less ethical interpretation of the assumption of hierarchy seems to allow lower creatures to be treated as objects without feelings.

Despitethe critical tendency of murdering animals and the Christian church's justification of hunting, one can say that the convention of the crime story appeals to numerous readers. That is why it can expose the problem as something that should not be commonly accepted. Hunting has become a kind of sport without rules. *Spoor* is not a just, intersubjective presentation of the social issue. Agnieszka Holland interprets Tokarczuk's short story in an even more radical way, because neither of the hunters is a responsible man who truly takes care of animals. All the hunters are presented in the film as bad, insensitive persons. Such interpretation is biased. Perhaps one of the film's messages was to expose the argument that not only evil is effective, but also goodness; empathy to animals, love and respect for nature, friendship among people and mutual helping—all these signs of solidarity among people may be effective, not weak. In contrast to the thoughtless killing of wild animals, the film introduces the figure of a Czech entomologist who comes to Polish forests because a rare, protected kind of beetle may be foundthere. Although science examines and influences law to offer protection to some species, the lack of moral rules covered by customs and false, hypocritical interpretations leads to complete indifference. Legal protection of a rare kind of beetle in *Spoor* is brought from our southern neighbors, because the forest workers in Poland sometimes either do not know or do not observe the rules.

In the context of Tokarczuk's short story on which Agnieszka Holland based her film, as well as of the film itself, the issue of crime that seems not to be punished was much debated. Some critics called the short story and the film unethical because Mrs. Duszejko is a murderer of hunters, and the mysterious ending of the film suggests she has avoided punishment.

It is necessary to remember that no literary text or film can be treated as an unambiguous mirror to reality. As Daniel Frampton, in his *Filmosophy*,[8] claims, every film creates a world of its own. That obvious principle also concerns lit-

8 D. Frampton, *Filmosophy*, (London, New York: Wallflower 2006).

erature, contemporary literature even more strongly than older ones. Artistic codes must be decoded through the competent practice of combining particular parts with the sense of the whole. Frampton introduces special categories: "filmmind," "filmbeing," "filmthinking" invented to realize at least two purposes. On one hand, they are to point to the specific character of artistic reality that is in the process of being constructed by these categories. On the other, they are meant to connect what is going on in the film with one's own "subjective" experience. The way we exert that connection uncovers our attitude to the world in general. Thus film becomes a sort of training in self-awareness. According to Frampton, when we watch cinematic methods of creating sense, we can presume that recreation of one's life conditions is also possible.

In the case of the film *Spoor*, the fruitful cooperation of Olga Tokarczuk and Agnieszka Holland reminds one that tenderness towards nature and shared identity with animals, together with empathy following as the consequence, are still accessible. The contrast between the beauty of nature and the ugliness of human behavior in the film surely has therapeutic resonance.

5 Tom Tykwer's *Heaven* (2002)

The script of the film was written by Krzysztof Kieślowski and Krzysztof Piesiewicz. The interdependencies within the plot are so complex and meandric that any simplification of the meaning contained in the title is blocked. The essence of the film consists in the human impatience of evil reaction to evil. Franz Kafka once said that because of impatience we were expelled from paradise and that because of it, we do not return there.

In the film, an English teacher becomes a suffering witness of the drug addiction of her very young pupils. She knows that the businessman who had previously involved her husband in drug addiction, resulting in his death, now influences her pupils. She wrote letters to the city council and police to inform them about the crime, but nobody reacted. Finally, in the opening scene of the film, she prepares a bomb and decides to kill the businessman. She has just returned from the funeral of the next addicted child, who had left a letter addressed to her parents saying that they could throw away her body to the rubbish because it meant nothing to her. The teacher felt it was the ultimate limit she could bear. Random circumstances change her intentions, and instead of the evil man, she kills four innocent people, including two children.

As in the *Decalogue*, in which each part offered a very labyrinthine interpretation of a given commandment, here, the symbolic quality of Heaven as the peak of love and justice, together with the way individuals interpret that pure dimension and how legal procedures execute it, similarly provides a maze. Neither linear theories nor simple solutions, but the thick, dense layers of complex life have become introduced here to produce a sort of therapeutic catharsis. The Jungian idea of enantiodromia helps one to understand that mental divisions do not have to lead into a battle of struggling forces but into a more peaceful state. They must be monitored with awareness to become accepted, but not identified with, the conscious parts of the human psyche. Film art and literary experiments do not follow a strict philosophical road separating sensual perception and intellectual understanding. Art in general and perhaps especially film and literary forms—as was exposed here—mix elements of documentary report (*Voices of Chernobyl Prayer*) with fiction (*Transfugium*) to open paths of possible psychic exchange to achieve comparable successes in collective shadow therapy, as in proper, long-lasting individual shadow work.

6 Conclusions

The article pointed to the double dimension of shadow as described by Jung and as exposed in works of art. It was conceived as an individually dark side of one's psyche, as well as a certain quality of European-American (Western) culture. The first aspect was examined in detail by Jung and his followers. The second aspect, also on the various levels described and exposed, I would diagnose as deriving from the feature that could be called the **overabundance of negativity.** That factor reveals itself in different phenomena and in a surprising way but may be recognized easily once the vector of discernment is sharpened. When I emphasize in the article a lack reflection, lack of responsibility, and the rule of one-sidedness, they may be treated in a circular way as causes and effects of that overabundance of negativity.

The evident phenomenon that we all may observe of that overproduction of negativity[9] is the **decline of culture.** The clue is that therapy of shadow in an individual and in culture is a long and complex process, whereas we live in the epoch of quick truth. In a logocentric epoch people imagine that knowledge, information may substitute for one's own transformation process and effort, whereas knowledge may be helpful only within it. What is more urgently

9 It could be treated as pathology of critical thinking. When criticism is being reduced only to recognition of merely negative sides of the situation (of one's thinking, behavior, action, etc.), the essence of critique about which the Greeks thought of as the art of placing everything in its own place, that Greek essence, that Immanuel Kant tried to recover, becomes annihilated.

needed is a constant awareness of what is going on—inwardly and outwardly. Also, reflection on one's own experience seems to be the best guide.

And finally, art, whether it is literature or film, may contribute to the process, on the condition it correlates, refers to, or explains something to the readers or the film goers of what they experience themselves.

References

Alexievich S., *War's Unwomanly Face*, Moscow: Progress Publishers, 1988.

Alexievich S., *Chernobyl Prayer: A Chronicle of the Future*, London: Penguin Modern Classics, 2016.

Frampton D., *Filmosophy*, London, New York: Wallflower, 2006

Jacobi J., *The Psychology of C.G. Jung*, London: Routledge, 1946.

Jung C. G., *The Practice of Psychotherapy*, London: Routledge, 1993.

Noble D. F., *The Religion of Technology. The Divinity of Man and the Spirit of Invention*, New York: Knopf 1997.

Russell B., *Principles of Social Reconstruction*, London: Routledge, 1997.

Tokarczuk O., *Drive your Plow Through the Bones of the Dead*, transl. A. Lloyd-Jones, London: Fitzcarraldo Editions, 2018.

Tokarczuk O., *Transfugium* [in:] eadem, *Opowiadania bizarne* (*Bizarre Stories*), Kraków: Wydawnictwo Literackie, 2018. https://www.goodreads.com/pl/book/show/357486.Voices_from_Chernobyl [Accessed: 29.10.2019].

CHAPTER 9

Archetypal Feminine in *Kaxinawá*'s Stories: A Decolonizing Option to Jungian Approach

Hannah Armbrust

Abstract

Myths are archetypal stories present throughout the world. Those archetypal stories have the power to guide our individuation path, even when we are not fully conscious of them. In this debut of the *Kaxinawá* mythology applied to Jungian studies, I present *The Story of the Origin of Remedies from the Woods* along with the powerful goddess *Yushã Kuru*, or the Purple Female. The choice of an Amazonia mythology epitomizes a decolonizing option to analytical psychology, as it brings voices and perspectives other than the Eurocentric view of the world.

Keywords

Kaxinawá, Amazonia, mythology, archetypal feminine, decolonizing option

1 Introduction

Myths express in a symbolic language a wealth of archetypal material valuable to the knowing of the unconscious process,[1] and for this reason, the study of myths holds a notable place in Jungian studies. Due to being timeless narratives that belong to primordial times, myths comprise significant psychic contents.[2] They are stories with no definite author[3] emerged from a process that involved gathering[4] of emotionally charged experiences. Those narratives, forged in

1 C. G. Jung, *Two Essays on Analytical Psychology*, ed. W. McGuire, The Collected Works of C. G. Jung (Princeton, NJ: Princeton University Press, 1966).

2 M. Eliade, *The Myth of the Eternal Return,* (Princeton: Princeton University Press, 2005).

3 M. Eliade, *Myths, Dreams, and Mysteries*, (New York: Harper & Row, 1975).

4 M. Eliade, *Images and Symbols: Studies in Religious Symbolism,* (Princeton: Princeton University Press, 1991).

 | DOI:10.1163/9789004468757_011

the mind during challenging times, are for C. G. Jung a leading force directing one's life: "What is the myth you are living?"[5] I have been particularly moved by Jung's self-inquiry, due to my growing up listening to Amazonian myths. Thus, I propose a change of venue in this paper. Based on Jung's question and my personal background as an Amazonian woman, I suggest an archetypal story from the *Kaxinawá* people to contribute to our collective archive of myths. This is a debut of their mythology in Jungian studies, which in itself epitomizes a decolonizing option[6] to analytical psychology. A decolonizing option, in this case, means to open epistemological doors to indigenous wisdom and worldview. Hence, I will explore how the archetypal feminine manifests in the *Kaxinawá*'s myth titled *The Story of the Origin of Remedies from the Woods*.[7]

The analysis will begin with my exploring of the basic emotions underlying the story. I will then look at the symbols associated with the archetypal feminine. Emotions make us human[8] and are in the background of myth creation. We are natural storytellers, autobiographical *Selfs,* says the neuroscientist Antonio Damasio.[9] The brain, according to him, holds several images that have been stored but often forgotten; from those conglomerations of images, a narrative is created. In this editorial brainwork, some images are left out; others are prioritized in the creation of a story. After this coherent story is created and edited in the brain, to consciousness "only a small number of images"[10] are projected in those narratives. Emotions, in turn, are archetypal for their natural, transcultural, and universal characteristics.[11]

Lastly, the memories of what we are have been recorded in thousands of narratives throughout the world. Those archetypal stories are humankind's most important resource to unveil the depths of our collective soul. Timeless narratives with a mythos-logical comprehension of human experience, they hold memory of ancient interactions with others, recurrent archetypal values,

---

5 C. G. Jung, *Symbols of Transformation,* ed. W. McGuire, *The Collected Works of C. G. Jung* (Princeton, NJ: Princeton University Press, 1956), XXIV.

6 W. Mignolo, *The Darker Side of Western Modernity: Global Futures, Decolonizing Options,* (Durham, UK: Duke University Press, 2011).

7 Organização dos Professores Indígenas do Acre, OPIAC, *Shenipabu Miyui: História dos Antigos*, ed. O. Souza (Belo Horizonte, Brazil: Editora UFMG, 2000).

8 R. C. Solomon, *True to our Feelings: What our Emotions are Really Telling us,* (New York, NY: Oxford University Press, 2007).

9 A. Damasio, *Self Comes to Mind: Constructing the Conscious Brain,* (New York, NY: Vintage Books, 2010).

10 Ibidem, 185.

11 J. Panksepp and L. Biven, *The Archaeology of Mind: Neuroevolutionary Origins of Human Emotions,* (New York, NY: Norton, 2012).

and thus a pattern of our cultural traits stored in the depths of our collective unconscious.

2 Who Are the *Kaxinawá*?

The *Kaxinawá*, self-described *Huni Kuin*,[12] occupy a vast territory on the basin of the *Juruá* and *Purus* Rivers, an area in the Western Amazonia between Brazil and Peru. The total population is close to 6,000 people where 75% of it is on the Brazilian side.[13] They used to live far deep in the Amazon jungle in constructions made of woods and palm leaves called *malocas* or *Xubuwan*, in the *Kaxinawá* language. The *malocas* house several *Kaxinawá* families. Each family has its own space marked by tent pegs. Herein this space, they have their own fire, which is used to keep bats and other animals away. The space is also reserved for their family belongings. In addition, each family has their own path leading to an outside place reserved for privacy. Men and women have different roles in their tribe, which are part of the *Kaxinawá* learning system. While men learn to work in external activities, the women are responsible for creating the tribe's crafts and cooking. Both men and women have the right to obtain two spouses if they fulfill their obligations accordingly.

In the past, the *Kaxinawás* practiced the death ritual of endocannibalism, something that has been extinct among them. For the *Kaxinawás*, the process of dying begins with human intervention. For them, one is likely to be poisoned by an inside enemy of someone in their own tribe who is jealous of one's hard work before falling ill. Nowadays, there are few who openly attribute disease to the action of their own people. The disease usually comes from an outside source, as "white disease." The healing process, though, includes mourning before the actual death happens in order to counterbalance a second and final form of intervention in the process of dying, which is that of the spirits of the dead, gods, and demons.[14]

3 The Story of the Origin of Remedies from the Woods

In the myth, *The Story of the Origin of Remedies from the Woods*, the first *Kaxinawás* are together wondering about how life will be from now on since they

---

12 OPIAC, *Shenipabu*.

13 E. Camargo and D. Villar, *Huni Kuin Hiwepaunibuki: A História dos Caxinauás por Eles Mesmos*, (São Paulo, Brazil: Edições Sesc São Paulo, 2015).

14 Ibidem.

are in this world. They begin the narrative with the following question: What will it be like when people get sick? How are we going to heal the sick?

Indians of ancient times, right after coming into the world, thought and discussed in an assembly what their life would be like going forward: "What are we going to do when people get sick? How are we going to heal the sick? A bunch of us will die to come out of the woods as remedies, thus others will continue to live by having these remedies." *Yushã Kuru*, a woman called Purple Female, then addressed the assembly: "I think your idea is very important. The best we can do is to become remedies. You all can do it, so I'm going to teach you and our relatives all about it." Everyone agreed with her idea: "That's true. If you know it well, you will teach us. You will teach our children and grandchildren."

Yushã Kuru, the Purple Female, gave much advice, and the remedies came out. Some were poison and could kill things, such as strong eye, *Beru Paepa*, bitter urine, *Isu Muka*. Other remedies were good for itching, *Nuĩ*. The old Purple Female observed all the tree leaves closely, as well as the trees' feet (roots): "This herb is not a good remedy," she said. And so it was. Several remedies came out, all the remedies they have in the woods. Good remedies for healing people. Good remedies for snake bites, scorpion stings, spider bites, rheumatism, and the liver.

The Purple Female, *Yushã Kuru*, knew all the leaves of these remedies well. But then she began to hold this knowledge to herself and taught no one else. She used all these remedies while hiding from everyone. Then one day, the old Female began to teach her grandson, the son of her daughter. She taught him all the remedies of the forest she knew. She also taught him how to prepare the remedies and how to prepare strong and poisonous remedies to put spells on others. And she experimented with him to find out if he had learned everything his grandmother knew. He learned to prepare the poison to put a spell on others and sometimes, with poisonous bush, to take away the spirit of the person.

When the young woman or the young man grew beautiful, she put a spell on her or him. When there was a hardworking man, the woman made handicrafts, and when they insulted the old Purple Female, she also put a spell on them so they would die. The people in the *aldeia* did not know about the Purple Female's doings. For a long time no one realized what was going on. One day, old *Yushan Kuru*'s son-in-law went hunting in the woods. Upon finishing hunting, he decided to get clay to make pots and bowls. The place where they were used to taking clay to make pottery was the same one they used to go hunting. There, the son-in-law saw old *Yushan Kuru* and had sex with her. The son-in-law hid himself to take the old woman without warning and did the job on her, who shouted: "Let me go! Who did this evil thing to me?"

Upon finishing with the old Female, the son-in-law placed her into the hole where they took the clay and ran through the woods. *Yushã Kuru* struggled trying to leave the place, but then she finally got it. When she was about to leave the deep hole where she had been placed by her son-in-law, the old Female was able to see him leaving the place without being noticed and then said: "It is a dead man who has done me wrong." She left crying, and on her way back home, she took the poisonous bush that grows on the road with the intention to kill her son-in-law. When she got home, she went fishing in a nearby stream (*igarapé*). She picked up fish called *piaba* and a soft *mandim*, and then she seasoned the fish with the poison she got on her way back home and wrapped them up in the straw of *sororoca* to cook (*muquinhar*).

When her son-in-law arrived from hunting, she gave him fish to eat. The next day, he died. Everyone was crying until her grandson realized what happened to his father and announced: "Look, my father died because my grandmother poisoned him. Our father is dying, and it's my grandmother's fault. She is the one who knows how to put a spell on others." The grandson then took his grandmother's basket. The basket was full of hearts arranged on a small line. When the old Female picked up a heart to cast a spell and poison it, the targeted person would soon die. She tucked the hearts into the basket neatly on a small line. Each one of them had a name: there was a heart for the hardworking man, another one for the pretty girl. There were several lines in the old Female's big basket, *Yushã Kuru*. The grandson discovered all the old woman's secrets and disclosed them to the people, who by listening to those secrets, felt scared, "Oh, this old witch! She cannot live among us. If she, herself, doesn't die, she will destroy our people."

So the people from the aldeia decided to kill *Yushã Kuru*. Many men got their weapons ready, but when the old Female heard about it, she fled into the woods. They kept on hunting but could find no sign of *Yushã Kuru*. So, after speaking to another boy, whose name was Cross-Eyed Cricket (*Tawa Xini Bexta*) and who was very smart and could see far away, they found out where she was. Cross-Eyed Cricket jumped into the yard, looked around, and said: "There she is; old Yushã sitting. You can go in this direction to find her."

Following Cricket's hint, they kept on searching until they could find Old Female. She was well hidden, sitting. The folks from her *aldeia* spoke and convinced her to return with them. She believed in their story and agreed to accompany them back home. When they were close to her house, Old Female said: "I'm going to shit in the woods." And she ran away again. People hunted and searched for her again with no luck. They then returned home.

Over and over again the *aldeia* folks asked Cricket to give information about the old woman, to which he always answered accurately. They went to the old woman many times, and many times she was able to escape from them. Thus, after several repeated unsuccessful attempts to get *Yushã Kuru*, they agreed on a plan to fool her. So one of her sons-in-law decided to tell her a lie. When he finally met the old woman again, he said: "Look auntie, I came to get you because I'm going to baptize your grandchildren, and I need you to sing our *aldeia*'s songs to them."

After hearing that, Old *Yushã Kuru* became excited. She accepted her son-in-law's invitation and returned home. Right upon her arrival, the waiting crowd killed the old Purple Female. They say that was so.

4 The Kaxinawá Goddess Yushã Kuru

Yushã Kuru is the Kaxinawá's old wise woman who incorporates opposing archetypal energies. She is a goddess of healing who holds the power of sickening people. In this sense, *Yushã* represents the soul of the*Kaxinawá* people. The Jungian analyst James Hollis[15] says that the archetype of mother "is both the source of life and source of death,"[16] qualities clearly manifested in the image of *Yushã Kuru*. Dr. Hollis goes on arguing that "the same Great Mother who has given us life is speeding us toward extinction and all in service to a great mystery."[17] *Yushã Kuru*, like the Egyptian goddess Isis, manifests the life and death powerful energies of what most Amazonian indigenous people call *A Cobra Grande*, the big snake. The ambivalence of serpents is described in cosmological myths of several parts of the world.[18] "The cobra is nevertheless as much an emblem of deathlessness as it is of death."[19] Its power to see beyond the obvious comes from an acute intuition, which is also a quality found in the archetype of the old wise woman present in some of the Brothers Grimm's fairy tales[20] and in this *Kaxinawá* myth.

Yushã Kuru, or Purple Female, first appears as the *aldeia*'s hero, the one who promises to teach them powerful healing lessons. She's the hope in the midst of fear, "How are we going to heal the sick?" In Brazil the color purple (*Yushã*'s alternate name *Purple Female* appears several times in the story) is associated

15 J. Hollis, *Mythologems: Incarnations of the Invisible World*, (Toronto, Canada: Inner City Books, 2004).

16 Ibidem, 48.

17 Ibidem, 49.

18 M. Eliade, *The Myth of Eternal Return: Cosmos and History*, Bollingen Series XLVI, 2nd. ed. (Princeton, NJ: Princeton University Press, 2005).

19 The Archive for Research in Archetypal Symbolism – ARAS, *The Book of Symbols: Reflections on Archetypal Images*, ed. K. Martin (TASCHEN, 2010), 198.

20 J. Grimm and W. Grimm, *Grimm's Fairy Tales*, ed. George Stade, (New York, NY: Barnes & Nobles Classics, 2003).

with death, grieving, but also with nurturance, warmth, strength. Purple represents two of Brazilian's treasures: the super fruit *açai* and the gem amethyst, both local symbols of physical and spiritual health. Purple also incorporates two primary colors, the red and the blue, representing the royal couple, the union of the opposites.[21] Thus, *Yushã* possesses the knowledge and intuition required to lead her people toward a collective healing, but they have forgotten that it includes death, then rebirth: *A bunch of us will die to come out of the woods as remedies; thus others will continue to live by having these remedies*. The Amazon forest has plenty of medicinal plants, trees which, according to the *Kaxinawá* mythology, represent one of their own at the service of healing.

5 Archetypes

Jung describes archetypes as archaic forms or images that are common to all of humankind and that can be observed through their expressions in myths and fairy tales, among others.[22] The word *archetype* comes from the Greek *arkhe* (primitive) and *tupos* (a model); therefore, archetypes are primordial forms imprinted in the psyche. According to Jung, the archetypes of the collective unconscious when constellated can act upon consciousness in an arbitrary way, thus the importance of investing in a process of increasing consciousness, which he called individuation process. It seems to be evidence now that "without consciousness things go less well."[23]

The process of integrating unconscious contents into consciousness seems to be an urgent matter these days, where so much has been projected into minorities throughout the world. The changes, or rather, a dialectic process of integration, arrive from a constant communication between conscious and unconscious processes, either in a compensatory form or in opposition to one another.

In postcolonial countries like Brazil, a re-reading of C.G. Jung regarding the concept of collective unconscious and archetypes is urgently needed. Although I firmly believe in Jung's theories, and knowing that these are being gradually confirmed by neuroscience, I question the validity of a collective unconscious

---

21 C. G. Jung, *Mysterium Coniunctionis: An Inquiry into the Separation and Synthesis of Psychic Opposites in Alchemy*, ed. W. McGuire, *The Collected Works of C. G. Jung*, (Princeton, NJ: Princeton University Press, 1970).

22 C. G. Jung, *Archetypes and Collective Unconscious*, ed. W. McGuire, *The Collected Works of C. G. Jung*, (Princeton, NJ: Princeton University Press, 1959).

23 C. G. Jung, *The Structures and Dynamics of the Psyche*, ed. W. McGuire, *The Collected Works of C. G. Jung*, (Princeton, NJ: Princeton University Press, 1960), 361.

forged in prejudice, fear, and racial discrimination. To bring awareness about the archetypal energies emerging from such unconscious is one of my major concerns in Jungian studies. In this sense, I want to advocate for the emergence of the primitive and savage as equal voices in our consciousness. They have spoken but always in comparison to the dominant voice of the civilized man; in other words, they are primitive only in contrast to the one considered "superior" when in fact, "Primitive man simply has a different theory."[24]

Mircea Eliade argues that the repetition of an archetypal model constitutes its reactualization. Hence, by experiencing the symbolic without awareness means the perpetuation of old patterns not always helpful to the coming of a new and higher collective consciousness. Jung came to this conclusion after observing behaviors and analyzing hundreds of the dreams of his patients. He found that certain archetypal symbols and patterns were common to peoples of other regions of the world at different times. Archetypes are manifested not only in patterns of behavior, but also in cultural and religious paradigms, and mainly in archetypal stories also known as myths, fairytales, legends, and so on. The word *archetypal* in this case refers to the common psychological (feeling-toned psychic imprints) aspect of those stories.

Archetypes seem to encompass the sum of ancient cultures and psychological adaptations that are now unconscious. They are ahistorical, meaning, all our gains in social justice and changes in how we perceive race, gender, and minorities are oblivious to the archetypal paradigm. In this sense, archetypes possess a transpersonal aspect, which I believe is their most relevant characteristic. However, we need to understand archetypes with a critical sense so that we do not fall into what Franz Fanon calls symbolic crystallization. In this case, the concept can also be used to feed prejudice, racism, and violence, as Fanon ponders in this passage:

> Darkness, obscurity, shadows, gloom, night, the labyrinth of the underworld, the murky depths, blackening someone's reputation; and on the other side, the bright look of innocence, the white dove of peace, magical heavenly light. A beautiful blond child—how much peace there is in that phrase, how much joy, and above all how much hope! No comparison with a beautiful black child: the adjectives literally don't go together.[25]

---

24 C. G. Jung, *Civilization in Transition,* ed. W. McGuire, *The Collected Works of C. G. Jung,* (Princeton, NJ: Princeton University Press, 1964).

25 F. Fanon, *Black skin, white masks,* (New York, NY: Grove Press, 1967), 166.

The words selected in Fanon's text are examples of how archetypes can be a source of controversial statements, especially when taken out of a transpersonal context and used in the political and economic sphere. In Fanon's perspective, the archetypes are another source of enslavement of the black man, and the collective unconscious "is quite simply the repository of prejudices, myths, and collective attitudes of a particular group." It is hard to argue against Fanon's ideas in our current economic and political context. According to Edinger, though, those archetypal projections are a consequence of "no adequate container such as an established religious structure" for unconscious contents (archetypes). They are then "projected into banal or secular matters"[26] losing their transpersonal characteristic.

Edinger's take on the religious aspect of the psyche should be understood in a generalized way and not in relation to a specific religion. In fact, this religious characteristic of the psyche manifests itself in several fields of knowledge; it can turn into fanaticism or other "isms" of our time. Thus the concept of archetypes, when serving as a political and cultural projection, can support oppressive systems perpetuating a collective trauma of the politically and economically oppressed.

The implications of repeating a myth, or in other words, of reactualizing an archetype, is that they carry a type of knowing that might have been formed during a period when humankind experienced a different type of physical and psychological reality. Hence, a type of collective consciousness that sees a certain group of people as primitives or dangerous have no place in today's world. The symbol has an ancient form; it's archetypal, which doesn't mean that it cannot gain a new meaning.

6 The Archetypal Feminine

The term *archetypal feminine*[27] represents an unconscious arbitrary form of symbol creation, which is particularly feeling-toned and emotional-driven. It manifests through a wide range of paradoxical attitudes and behaviors represented symbolically in the form of witches and fairies, good girls and bad ones, virgins and prostitutes when in fact, they are all part of the same archetypal force. It is important to notice, though, that consciousness cannot be divided into masculine and feminine. And thus, the symbol representing the initial

26 E. Edinger, *Ego and Archetype*, (Boston, MA: Shambhala, 1972).

27 E. Neumann, *The Great Mother: An Analysis of the Arhetype*, Bollingen Series XLVII, (Princeton, NJ: Princeton University Press, 1963).

psychic state of the original situation where the ego was not fully developed is the Ouroboros, or the circular snake biting its own tail. The evolution of consciousness, says Neumann, begins with the mythological stage "when the ego is contained in the unconscious" and by becoming aware of its own position, struggles like a hero to free itself and broaden its horizons. The Ouroboros thus represents a chaotic and unconscious state of the psyche. In this psychic state, all these undifferentiated elements that can potentially become conscious are present and will eventually emerge into consciousness.

The myths of the archaic man teach us that in the beginning we were one in connection with the Divine energy of creation. This ouroboric state still works on the background of our psyche and manifests itself through dreams, fantasies, and projections. It was a time when we lived in the darkness of our unconscious being at the same time creator and creation, as Mary Shelley's novel *Frankenstein; Or, the Modern Prometheus* reports. In this novel, the creator lost perspective of his own self because in the process of creating a monster, he became one with his creation. The creator then begins a deadly projection: All the evil was taken from his soul and placed in his creation.

We still attribute to the other fellow all the evil and inferior qualities that we do not like to recognize in ourselves and therefore have to criticize and attack him, when all that has happened is that an inferior "soul" has emigrated from one person to another. "The world is still full of *bêtes noires* and scapegoats, just as it formerly teemed with witches and werewolves."[28] *Yushã*'s story reveals the dynamism of the mother archetype and how we have the natural inclination to return to the same ouroboric state, a type of paralyzing paradise for the spirit. Creation myths also explain the archaic man mentality, which from time to time erupts in the modern man. Jung said that archetypes are the contents of the collective unconscious, which possess an arbitrary nature forming an intrinsic component of our soul. The archetype of the mother is certainly the most important of all, for it brings to the spirit a transcendent energy that has the power to kill us and at the same time build us from inside out. Such reality is clearly expressed in the *Kaxinawá* myth.

The mother archetype is death and rebirth in a constant, endless process that Jung named individuation. To individuate is to become conscious of who we are in relation to the archetype of the Great Mother. This archetype is what the alchemists called the *anima mundi*.[29] Neumann argues that the Great Mother emerged from the primordial archetype and that parts of this arche-

28 Jung, *Civilization*.

29 C. G. Jung, *Psychology and Alchemy*, ed. W. McGuire, *The Collected Works of C. G. Jung*, (Princeton, NJ: Princeton University Press, 1953).

type can be perceived by consciousness in three forms: the good, the terrible, and the good-bad mother. The first two are one-sided elements of the archetype while the third expresses wholeness, and it is called the Great Mother.[30]

According to Neumann, we can experience those archetypal energies through their manifestations in the physical world represented by mythic figures or persons. Neumann argues that the Good Mother is the manifestation of the virtuous characteristics of male and female aspects of the archetype; *Yushã* presents both traits, even expressed in her alternate name, Purple Female. The same incompleteness is found in its opposite character, the Terrible Mother, which manifests its vicious characteristics, such as *Yushã* jealousy and vengeance that we see in the *Kaxinawá* myth. Thus the Great Mother incorporates both, the Good Mother and the Terrible Mother psychic structures.

The symbolic expressions of this psychic energy can be found in literature, the arts, religious artifacts, historical events, and several other archetypal motifs. Edinger[31] clarifies that "a symbol has a subjective dynamism which exerts a powerful attraction and fascination on the individual."[32] This interaction with the symbolic is a constant psychological reality that I defined as archetypal intersubjectivity. I borrowed the term *intersubjectivity* from psychoanalysis to express my belief in the archetypal transformative living experience. The mother archetype is a consciousness that guides the individual towards the integration of opposite forces in the psyche. Humankind and the individual "have the same task, namely, to realize themselves as a unit,"[33] thus the relevance of studies on this topic to promote a liberating knowledge that can transform the world through the individuation process.

7 An Explanation of the Meaning of the Word "Myth"

In Ludwig Wittgenstein's *The Blue Book*, the author argues that one can find the meaning of a word by first asking for an explanation of the meaning of a word.[34] Thus, rather than asking "what is myth?" one may ask, "What is an explanation of the meaning of myth?" And so now I present an explanation of the word *myth* by using Mircea Eliade's words:

30 E. Neumann, *The Origins and History of Consciousness*, Bollingen Series XLII. (Princeton, NJ: Princeton University Press, 1953).

31 Edinger, *Ego*.

32 Ibidem, 109.

33 Ibidem, 417.

34 L. Wittgenstein, *The Blue Book*, in *Major Works*, (New York, NY: Harper Perrennial, 2009).

> What exactly is a myth? In the language current during the nineteen[th] century, a "myth" meant anything that was opposed to "reality". But the researchers of the ethnologists have obliged us to go behind this semantic inheritance from the Christian polemics against the pagan world. We are at last beginning to know and understand the value of the myth, as it has been elaborated in "primitive" and archaic societies—that is, among those groups of mankind where the myth happens to be the very foundation of social life and culture. In those societies the myth is thought to express the *absolute truth*, because it narrates a *sacred history*. Being *real* and *sacred* the myth becomes exemplary, and consequently *repeatable*, for it serves as a model, and by the same token as a justification, for all human actions.[35]

Myths are guiding models to human behavior. The absolute truth expressed by myths means that they are archetypal, ancient, and arbitrary in nature. Due to their literary structure, it's fair to say that myths are the crystallization of archetypes. They express an ideal form that can serve as a reference through generations to come. They have in common with fairytales the fact that both are archetypal expressions of the collective unconscious, fairytales being closer in structure to the dream experience than myths. The latter being more complex, it has been under cultural influences and is not even immune to time and fashion. It's a story rooted in ancient knowledge; it preserves its form, but it has changed its contents. Myths are archetypes in themselves, the best literary expression of the contents of the collective unconscious. They are living stories, archetypal tales whose guidance no one walking through the individuation path can afford to miss. Myths incorporate several archetypal manifestations in one single image (the story itself). They are suppliers of archetypal energy to the psyche, which makes them very powerful. Myths are timeless and their primordial form unchanging, but their energy can influence the physical world and—change it. The era of quantum physics is here to present this undeniable truth: Everything is energy, and in this light, myths hold creative energies that continue to shape the world as we know it.[36]

Creation myths,[37] as the *Kaxinawá*'s, are of great importance to the grasping of the concept of archetype. They are, according to von Franz, "the deepest and

35 M. Eliade, *Myths, Dreams, and Mysteries*, (New York, NY: Harper Torchbooks, 1960), 23.

36 A. Mindell, *Quantum Mind: The Edge Between Physics and Psychology*, (Portland, OR: Deep Democracy Exchange, 2012).

37 M. L. von Franz, *Creation Myths*, (Boston, MA: Shambhala, 1972).

most important of all myths."[38] Each one of us carries within an archetype of God, the Creator, and we continuously repeat the myth of creation throughout our lives. Myths are symbols of meaningful experiences shared by humankind and translated into narratives by man's intuitive mind. They represent a subjective and collective experience, a transcendent form of reality. Obviously, myths cannot be reduced to a scientific explanation, but when a mythical narrative voices man's deepest aspects of the soul, they become his reality:

> Our outward-oriented consciousness, addressed to the demands of the day, may lose touch with these inward forces; and the myths, states Jung, when correctly read, are the means to bring us back in touch. They are telling us in picture language of powers of the psyche to be recognized and integrated in our lives, powers that have been common to the human spirit forever, and which represent that wisdom of the species by which man has weathered the millenniums.[39] (Campbell, 1972, p. 12)

Campbell makes an excellent assertion of how myths are still (and will continue to be) present in our everyday life. The forces and power of the heroes are part of our reality, which becomes more evident when we read those stories in the light of a psychic phenomenon. For instance, if we return to the phenomenological question, "What is this archetypal manifestation an archetypal manifestation of?" and apply it to a myth such as the one that tells the story of *Yushã Kuru*, we will find answers regarding a type of the collective consciousness of the people living in the Amazon region, in this case, the *Kaxinawás*.

Jung studied in depth how myths are associated with the psychic phenomena, to which he states that "mythological man perceived the unconscious in all the adversities and contrarieties of external nature without ever suspecting that he was gazing at the paradoxical background of his own consciousness."[40] And from the study of ancient mythology in connection with unconscious contents, Jung explains how archetypes were created: "The archetype is essentially an unconscious content that is altered by becoming conscious and by being perceived, and it takes its color from the individual consciousness in which it happens to appear." It is important to note that archetypes have a "transubjective" and "autonomous" character as well.[41]

Identical mythological motifs as the ones found in this *Kaxinawá*'s myth have been found in different parts of the world, indicating an unconscious

38 Ibidem, 1

39 J. Campbell, *Myths to Live by*, (New York, NY: Penguin Compass, 1972).

40 Jung, *Symbols*, 260.

41 Jung, *Two Essays*.

sharing of experiences with our fellow human beings. The way one engages with myths is conditioned to one's temperament, but the content is common to all humankind in an inclusive system that concedes to a White American the sharing of identical mythological motifs with an African American living near or in different regions in the world, and people from the depths of the Amazonia alike.

8 Conclusion

I wrote this paper in the year of my mother's physical demise, and in a way, my own. All creative process also involves death in order to flourish. The ones who don't want to weep for a while are also prevented from celebrating a rebirth. *Yushã Kuru* became a remedy to her people. The Self is wholeness, and the archetype of the Great Mother can help us to graciously embrace all the pieces of our own psychology. The Self is the Great Mother with plenty of unconditional love and acceptance but also with a bitter, salty, and furious transformative attitude. I wanted to demonstrate how the archetypal feminine, here symbolized by the Amazonian goddess, *Yushã Kuru*, can lead us towards and throughout the individuation path. I invited the reader to consider the Amazon forest as the place where it happens.

Psychology is about emotions, feelings, energy, soul, and spirit. Its scientific meaning finds nurturance in the connection with the Great Mother. Hence, studies concerned with the psyche outside the phenomenological standpoint tend to fall into a dry world of statistics and brain images: "Through scientific understanding, our world has become dehumanized."[42] The Great Mother as an archetypal manifestation of creation, death, and rebirth can help to develop a collective consciousness that can reach out to individuals from a more diverse background. We are all *prima materia*, great matter of the Divine, the Great Mother Earth, *LaPachamama*. This assumption is inclusive, for it dismisses the things that set us apart; instead, the Great Mother archetype looks at what makes us one.

References

Camargo E., & Villar, D., *Huni Kuin hiwepaunibuki: A história dos Caxinauás por eles mesmos,* São Paulo, Brazil: Edições Sesc São Paulo, 2015.

42 C. G. Jung, *The Symbolic Life*, ed. W. McGuire, *The Collected Works of C. G. Jung*, (Princeton, NJ: Princeton University Press, 1976), 225.

Damasio A., *Self Comes to Mind: Constructing the Conscious Brain*, New York, NY: Vintage Books, 2010.

Edinger E. F., *Ego and Archetype*, Boston, MA: Shambhala, 1972.

Eliade M., *Myths, Dreams, and Mysteries*, New York, NY: Harper Torchbooks, 1960.

Eliade M., *Images and Symbols: Studies in Religious Symbolism*, Princeton, NJ: Princeton University Press, 1991.

Eliade M., *The Myth of the Eternal Return: Cosmos and History*, Princeton, NJ: Princeton University Press, 2005.

Fanon F., *Black Skin. White Masks*, New York, NY: Grove Press, 1967.

Jung C. G., *The Collected Works of C. G. Jung* (2nd. ed.), v. 5: *Symbols of Transformation*, Bollingen Series XX. Princeton, NJ: Princeton University Press, 1956.

Jung C. G., *The Collected Works of C. G. Jung* (2nd. ed.), v. 8: The *Structure and Dynamics of the Psyche*, Bollingen Series XX. Princeton, NJ: Princeton University Press, 1960.

Jung C. G., *The Collected Works of C. G. Jung* (2nd. ed.), v. 9i: *The Archetypes and the Collective Unconscious*, Bollingen Series XX. Princeton, NJ: Princeton University Press, 1959.

Jung C. G., *The Collected Works of C. G. Jung* (2nd. ed.), v. 10: *Civilization in Transition*, Bollingen Series XX. Princeton, NJ: Princeton University Press, 1964.

Jung C. G., *The Collected Works of C. G. Jung* (2nd. ed.), v. 7: *Two Essays on Analytical Psychology*, Bollingen Series XX. Princeton, NJ: Princeton University Press, 1966.

Hollis J., *Mythologems: Incarnations of the Invisible World*, Toronto: Inner City Books. 2004.

Mignolo W. D., *The Darker Side of Western Modernity: Global Futures, Decolonizing Options*. Durham: Duke University Press, 2011.

Mindell A., *Quantum Mind: the Edge Between Physics and Psychology*, Portland: Deep Democracy Exchange, 2012.

Neumann E., *The origins and history of consciousness*, Bollingen Series XLII. Princeton, NJ: Princeton University Press, 1954.

Neumann E., *The Great Mother: an Analysis of the Archetype*, Bollingen Series XLVII. Princeton, NJ: Princeton University Press, 1963.

OPIAC, *Shenipabu miyui: História dos antigos* (2nd ed.), Belo Horizonte, Brazil: Editora UFMG, 2000.

Panksepp J., Biven L., *The Archaeology of Mĩnd: Neuroevolutionary Origins of Human Emotions*, New York, NY: Norton, 2012.

CHAPTER 10

The Hero as a Dominant Mythical Motif in Western Culture and Its Relevance Nowadays: The Postulates of Jung and His Followers

Patrycja Neumann

Abstract

The paper presents Jung's postulates about the imaginative psyche and the hero myth, which is interpreted as a manifestation of the archetypical psyche. According to the psychologist, the figure of the hero is one of the most significant mythical images, which has an influence on the human psyche. Jung wrote about many different variants of the hero myth in every major culture. This issue inspired, among others, such thinkers as J. Hillman. He wrote about the presence of myths in culture, society, religion, and their effect on the human psyche. He created his own intellectual positions, but they were based on Jung's theory of archetypes. Jerzy Grotowski, a theater director and theater anthropologist, was also interested in these problems. He attempted to verify the relevance of the myth of Christianity in the second half of the 20th century and the figure of Christ as hero. The aim of this paper is to indicate common features of the hero figure as described by Jung and the thinkers inspired by his psychological conception. Furthermore, I present how these thinkers transgress Jung's conclusions concerning the hero myth. In the conclusion, I address the issue of the possibility of the hero myth's influence on modern society and the individual human psyche.

Keywords

C.G. Jung, J. Hillman, J. Grotowski, myth, hero, psychology, culture, ego, archetype, pop culture

 | DOI:10.1163/9789004468757_012

1 Introduction

In Carl Gustav Jung's opinion, every civilization created its own mythology.[1] Such representatives of archetypical psychology as Jung and James Hillman saw the source of myths in people's natural and unconscious need to create them. Such psychoanalysts as Freud and Jung turned to mythology because of its ubiquity. They observed similarity between myths, dreams, and schizophrenic visions. This similarity is visible especially between symbolic motives. According to psychoanalysts, dreams contain a hidden message. They are carriers of meaning and similarly to myths, they are created by the collective unconscious.[2] The meaning of myths refers to humankind as a collective entity and concerns existential and mental problems. Jung, as opposed to Freud, concluded that myths and dreams are more than a source of knowledge about mental disorders. Their meaning concerns people's inner lives. Myths are conditioned by psychological tendencies. In this way, he transferred myths into the area of the human psyche. The myth can be a source of psychological and anthropological cognition, as well as an instrument for interpreting visions, which are a subject of psychological analysis.[3]

According to Jung, the reason for the convergence of myths in different cultures lies in the construction of the human psyche.[4] He observed the recurrence of such topics as fratricide, flood, and an unusual birth of a hero. Mythical thinking manifests itself by symbols, images; its language is not literal.[5] However, it has a rationality of its own, which has a source in the order constituted by archetypal patterns. Jung identified the most popular symbolic motifs and recognized that they illustrated basic mental properties. He called them dominants.[6] What belongs to them are the archetypes of anima; animus; shadow; ego; and the organizing dominants: the self, the circle, and

1 C. G. Jung, "Symbols of transformation. An analysis of the prelude to a case of schizophrenia", in *The Collected Works*, v. 5, translated by G. Adler and R. F. C. Hull, (New York, Princeton University Press, 1965).

2 Ibidem, 280.

3 C. G. Jung, "The Theory of Psychoanalysis", in *The Journal of Nervous and Mental Disease Publishing Company*, No. 19, (New York, 1915), 55.

4 C. G. Jung, *Contributions to analytical psychology*, trans. H. G. and C. F. Baynes, Kegan Paul, Trench, Trübner & Co, (London, Trübner & Co, 1942), 46–47.

5 Ibidem.

6 C. G. Jung, "Symbols of transformation. An analysis of the prelude to a case of schizophrenia", in *The Collected Works*, v. 5, trans. G. Adler and R. F. C. Hull, (New York, Princeton University Press, 1965), 391.

the quaternity.[7] By indicating these types, Jung provided a base for explaining mythical symbols. He created the foundation for reading myths as manifestations of the unconscious, but he did not want to develop a single interpretation scheme.[8] He recognized his theory as an open system and the manifestations of archetypes in mythological images as having many possible variants. Jung used myths to interpret the archetypal unconscious psychic ground and interpreted myths through the prism of the unconscious at the same time.[9] He considered them to be mental projections. Because of their archetypal source, he saw their relationship with the collective experience of all humanity, reflected in mythological stories.

The nature of symbol as described by Jung is different from the one of allegory or sign because the latter functions as markers of what is conventional, whereas symbol is an expression of what is unrecognized in its entirety.[10] Symbol consists of integrated rational and irrational content and corresponds to the sphere of inner and outer life. Sign and allegory originate from consciousness, whereas symbol comes from the collective unconscious and is not intentionally created; it arises spontaneously.[11] Symbols, however, are an imperfect message of unconscious content because there is no direct way from the unconscious to consciousness. It is not possible to read the symbols exhaustively.[12] This gives the impression that they are indicative of a kind of secret, as which the unconscious is regarded.[13]

The nature of archetype is paradoxical.[14] It is expressed in symbols that have many meanings, and the more of them they have, the more fully they illustrate the nature of an archetypal pattern. This exact issue is described by Jung's words from *The Archetypes and the Collective Unconscious*:

> The discriminating intellect naturally keeps on trying to establish their [archetypes—P.N.]singleness of meaning and thus misses the essential point; for what we can above all establish as the one thing consistent with

7 C. G. Jung, "Aion. Researches into the phenomenology of the self", in *The Collected Works,* v.9 *Part 2,* translated by R. F. C. Hull, (New York, Pantheon Books, 1959), 42.

8 R. Segal, *Theorizing about Myth,* (Amherst, University of Massachusetts Press, 1999), 71.

9 Ibidem, 70.

10 Z. Rosińska, *Jung,* (Warszawa, Wiedza Powszechna, 1982), 70.

11 Ibidem, 70–71.

12 R. Segal, *Theorizing about Myth,* (Amherst, University of Massachusetts Press, 1999), 72.

13 C. G. Jung, *Memories, Dreams, Reflections,* translated by R. F. C. Hull, (New York, Pantheon Books, 1961), 160–170.

14 C. G. Jung, "The Archetypes and the Collective Unconscious", *in The Collected Works* v. 9, *Part 2,* trans. R. F. C. Hull, (New York, Princeton University Press, 1981), 38.

> their nature is their manifold meaning, their almost limitless wealth of reference, which makes any unilateral formulation impossible. Besides this, they are in principle paradoxical, just as for the alchemists the spirit was conceived as "senex et iuvenis simul"—an old man and a youth at once.[15]

According to Jung, one of the basic functioning principles of the psyche is the coexistence of opposites and the self's tendency to integrate them. This process, the process of individuation, is desired on the level of personal development, but it is also necessary for maintaining mental health.[16] Jung clearly interprets myths not only for therapeutic purposes, but also in order to describe the nature of the human psyche; its development; and how it determines human life, culture, and religion.

In his analyses, he often used motifs from several different myths. Guided by the conviction of the universality of myths's meaning, he juxtaposed them with each other irrespective of the culture from which they originated or the time of their creation. In order to decode the message of a given symbol, he juxtaposed its various meanings with each other. As he pointed out, meanings that are symbolized by a particular image, an image derived from mythologies of various cultures, often coincide. An example of such coincidence are the symbols of the sun and the moon as portrayals of male and female energy,[17] or the symbolism of a serpent as a crafty nature, possessing secret power or knowledge.[18] Sometimes the symbol functions in many contexts; it can be characterized positively or negatively depending on the time and place in which it functions.

Jung described the myth as "a collective dream that humanity dreams of."[19] He regarded all religious stories as equally important because they contain symbols from the sphere of the collective unconscious. The most significant literary works, such as Goethe's *Faust* or Nietzsche's *Thus SpokeZarathustra,* were also considered significant in terms of the presence of mythical symbols.[20]

The way in which Jung analyzed motifs from different stories is visible in the work from 1912 titled *Symbols of Transformation. Analysis of the Prelude to a Case of Schizophrenia*. It contained a description of the psychiatric analysis

15 Ibidem.

16 C. G. Jung, "Psychological Types or The Psychology of Individuation", in *The Collected Works*, v. 6, trans. by H. G. Baynes and H. G. Cantab, Phanteon Books, New York, 1953), 207.

17 Z. Rosińska, *Jung*, (Warszawa, 1982), 70.

18 Ibidem, 82.

19 C. G. Jung, "Symbols of transformation", 21.

20 Ibidem, 410.

of a patient, Miss Miller, made on the basis of her dreams and schizophrenic visions. This description is not only about Miller's disease; it is primarily an analysis of the relationship between the psyche and the myth. Jung noted the convergence between his patients's dreams and mythical motifs. When he analyzed Miller's dreams and chose the key characters or events from her life, he was guided by the conviction that these images contained a timeless sense. The interpretation of dream images through myth was possible due to the assumption that myths have a common source, that is archetypes.

Jung regarded the myth as "the most precious creation of the primitive mind."[21] According to him, there is a difference between the mentality of modern people and that of our ancestors, who lived in ancient times. This postulate stems from the assumption that consciousness is still evolving along with the development of humanity. The ancient myths allow one to "return to the roots" to find an area that combines the contemporary mentality with the primitive one.[22] In his opinion, basic human internal conflicts remain the same, regardless of time and place. Myths remain universal, especially in relation to morality, whose dilemmas were important for our ancestors.[23] The research into the content of myths created in the past is aimed at deepening the contemporary consciousness.

Thus, Jung attempts to combine two approaches. Firstly, he assumes the existence of archetypes in the psyche of a human being as a universal sphere. Secondly, he assumes the evolution of the collective unconscious, which is in constant historical flux and therefore, subject to changes. The development of consciousness is determined by archetypes; at the same time, however, the area of the unconscious is subject to changes occurring throughout history. The heroic myth as an object of interpretation should be considered as the product of unchanging psychological conditions, and at the same time many contexts, resulting from changes at the level of social life, should be taken into consideration. According to Jung, myths over time cease to be valid, partly or completely. They lose their impact on the psyche because they no longer bear the content relevant for the collective unconscious. This issue is connected to his interpretation of the myths of Christianity.[24] The transformation of the Old Testament image of Yahweh, the omnipotent ruler, into the merciful God of the New Testament, is a reflection of the transformation in the collective

21 Ibidem, 45.

22 Ibidem, 23–24.

23 Ibidem.

24 C. G. Jung, "Antwort auf Hiob", in *Gesammelte Werke,* Bd. 6, (Stuttgart-Zürich, Rascher-Verlag, 1963).

unconscious.[25] The development taking place in the area of myths indicates the need to express the processes of a psychological nature.

The evolutionary nature of psychological tendencies consists in the transformation on the grounds ofcollective experience through the accumulation of certain conscious content. If we recognize that the very process of the development of the psyche is not accidental and proceeds out of a certain necessity, then it would indicate that the consciousness has been in the unconscious from the beginning. This means that any content that is a component of the unconscious is by nature subject to the possibility of becoming conscious. Consciousness complements the unconscious; the former is an aspect of the latter. We should ask whether consciousness and the unconscious, as opposing areas, determine each other's content—that is, does the development of consciousness affect the unconscious? Jung did not give a concrete answer to this question, although if we treated archetypes as formal structures, we would suppose that their forms remain unchanged, even if consciousness becomes richer by assimilating some new content.

2 The Hero as a Dominant Mythical Motif in Western Culture

One important researcher of the myth was Lord Raglan, who created the anthropological concept of the myth of the hero. His comparative analysis of myths from different cultures was aimed at identifying those features that are repetitive. He devoted a lot of attention to the myth of the hero's journey. This concept is anthropological, not psychoanalytic; however, Raglan described the universal features of the hero. He believed that these myths reflected a common cultural pattern. The development of psychoanalysis had an impact on his work, especially since he initially collaborated with Otto Rank, who was inspired by Freud's psychoanalysis. What Raglan postulated was that heroic figures were not treated as historical, but above all, mythical. He did not question the existence of some of the characters but drew attention to the universalistic aspect inherent to their image. In his opinion, this is indicated especially by the repeating motifs in the stories of their fate. An important accomplishment of Raglan was pointing out the myth of the hero as commonly occurring not only in the Western cultural circle.[26]

The views of such thinkers as Hillman and Grotowski (he was not a myth theorist, but he adopted Jung's concept of studying the interactions of collective

25 Ibidem.

26 L. Raglan, *The Hero. A Study in Tradition, Myth and Drama,* (London, Watts & Co, 1949).

ideas during paratheatrical activities) are rooted in Jung's idea of the archetypal source of myths. They all share his view that the myth is alive and has the power to influence the psyche at the collective and individual level. Both Jung and Hillman considered the hero as one of the most popular mythical figures.

Jung considers the phenomenon of the presence of the hero myth in a multidimensional way. He specified the essential characteristics of the hero as a symbolic character, which include the desire for independence, overcoming one's own limitations, often transgressing socially constructed boundaries, and persistently pursuing one's goals. The hero's desire is to perform a task that is to serve the good of the community and lead to its redemption, healing, or saving. His effort is usually accompanied by miraculous circumstances, indicating the action of supernatural forces, but an aspect of his heroic courage is necessary. The hero does not shy away from the challenge. Through courage, he takes all the risks and thus overcomes his own limitations.[27] In the image of a hero figure, the action for the common good is combined with his personal transformation and overcoming himself.

In Jung's psychological interpretation, the image of the hero is a transference of the process of psychological development.[28] The constant tendency of the development of consciousness corresponds to the aspirations of the mythical hero to overcome the hardships of self-determination. Consciousness, in a similar manner to the hero, makes a constant effort, on the one hand, to overcome oneself in the process of integrating the unconscious, and on the other, to continually build one's independence from the unconscious.[29]

The state of the unconscious is sacrificed for the development of consciousness. Cosmogonic myths show the loss of the original state and the emerging diversity that symbolizes mental diversity.[30] The cosmic sacrifice myth symbolizes the sacrifice of the unconscious state of being in the womb of the Great Mother.[31] The mythical hero symbolizes the ego, which is the center of consciousness; he is like a son (most often the mythical hero is male) of the great mother symbolizing the unconscious.[32] Jung thought that the unconscious is undifferentiated and that individuality comes from differentiating the unconscious content, which is general and common to each psyche.[33] In spite of one's striving for development, the human being longs for the state described

27 C. G. Jung, "The Archetypes and the Collective Unconscious", 21.

28 Ibidem, 6–7.

29 C. G. Jung, "Symbols of transformation", 310.

30 Ibidem, 333.

31 Ibidem, 327.

32 R. Segal, *Theorizing about Myth*, (Amherst, University of Massachusetts Press, 1999), 85.

33 C. G. Jung, "Symbols of transformation", 327.

by Jung as "being in the womb of the Great Mother," that is, at the source of one's psychic experience of reality. A dramatic situation arises: the psyche simultaneously follows two directions—toward consciousness and toward the unconscious. The psyche development is determined by the need for returning to the unconscious state, instincts, being only and exclusively in the present but at the same time going beyond this state, gaining knowledge, achieving self-awareness and independence of self-determination. Rational consciousness seeks power and control over one's self and external circumstances. According to Jung, the nature of the psyche is reflected in the image of hero myths; the hero strives for independence and self-determination and at the same time, is eager to return to his homeland, beloved one, mother. In myths, the figure of a woman as an image of the unconscious often manifests itself as a force of nature or mother earth.[34] This is a transference of the relationship taking place between the unity of the unconscious and differentiation.[35] This situation is paradoxical. The hero-consciousness wants its own independence and self-determination, and at the same time it seeks its source, which is the Great Mother, the unconscious, as the primary source of experience of the world and knowledge.[36]

The multidimensional character of Jung's approach to this problem lies in the fact that he relates the meaning of the image of the hero also to the tension between the basic opposites, namely, male and female.[37] In this context, it would be important not only to pursue self-awareness and self-determination, but to remain in a state of equilibrium, resulting from the constant interaction of these two opposites.[38]

Another type of Jung's interpretation of this figure oscillates around the unconscious self and the unity of all archetypes. Hero myths expressing the total self are solar myths. The symbol of the sun as a representation of divinity is also a representation of completeness as fullness of mind. Jung compares sunlight to the light of self-consciousness.[39]

Despite the drama generated by the paradoxical tendency of the psyche, the two move in two directions at the same time—toward consciousness and the unconscious—Jung saw a chance to achieve harmony as a result of

34 Ibidem, 337.

35 Ibidem, 280.

36 Ibidem, 325.

37 C. G. Jung, "Aion", 14–15.

38 C. G. Jung, "Mysterium Coniunctionis, an Inquiry into the Separation and Synthesis of Psychic Opposites in Alchemy", in *The Collected Works*, v. 14, translated by G. Adler and R. F. C. Hull, (New York, Princeton University Press, 1970).

39 C. G. Jung, "Symbols of transformation", 315–316.

the integration of opposites. Self-development that leads to the integration of opposing complexes, and therefore to psychological fullness, is the most important dimension of human existence.[40] The Christian myth of Christ's sacrifice as the price of deliverance from the power of instinct, treated as a mental projection, has a strong, positive dimension of the ability to overcome one's nature, and at the same time constitutes one of the most important representations of the hero, next to Buddha or Shiva. The heroic image of the sacrifice of God-man is an archetypal reflection of the effort that is associated with the development of personality and inner transformation. In the psychiatrist's opinion, the mythical hero is an illustration of the most basic and important directions of the psyche development on personal and collective ground.

James Hillman also recognized the popularity of the hero's myth as a reflection of trends at the collective level. The psychologist pays special attention to the need for fantasy, which is the basis of the imaginative tendency of the psyche. Myth as fiction is an expression of imaginary truths, inexpressible in a literal and conceptual way.[41] He does not see the phenomenon of the hero's myth as a progressive development of consciousness but as a clear expansiveness of the archetype of the ego and its dominance over other mental images. He rejects Jung's position according to which the ego is the center of consciousness and recognizes it as one of many archetypes. It is the drive to act and conquer. He uses the words *hero archetype*[42] to describe the ego.

Jung defines the ego as the center of consciousness. Although both psychologists agree that the psyche itself is archetypal, the difference between their ego definitions is clear. Jung builds his system on the basis of the opposition between the consciousness and the unconscious. This archetype plays an important role in orienting in external reality.

According to Hillman, the domination of one of the archetypes does not mean that consciousness is centralized but only that the area of self-determination, the sense of individuality and one's own identity exceeds the activity of other archetypes. The center of the psyche is determined in an extra-conscious way. The ego, in a similar manner to the mythical hero, manifests the pursuit of struggle and does so in relation to other parts of the psyche.[43] The state of mental stability is understood by him as different from the monotheism of ego and consists in a manifestation of multiple archetypes. Hillman draws attention to the prevalence of the archetypal pattern of individualism and

---

40 C. G. Jung, "The Archetypes and the Collective Unconscious", 175.

41 J. Hillman, *Re-visioning psychology,* (New York, Harper & Row, 1997).

42 Ibidem.

43 Ibidem, 105.

heroic courage, especially in the Western world. He believes that the mythical character of the hero is represented by both Heracles and Christ.[44] The psychologist describes the hero's disposition as built on the sense of indivisible unity, which is a reflection of a united internal force, ready to be directed outside. He also recognizes the connection between the nature of the ego and the tendency to monotheism on the ground of religion. In both cases there is a tendency towards unity resulting from the ego archetype activity.[45] According to Hillman, this aspiration is a kind of disorder eliminating the potential of other parts of the psyche, which are the source of the content that affects the development of the internal human world. Other archetypes do not exhibit such expressive expansiveness in their essence; that is why the ego perspective tends to dominate and construct an adulterated and scarce image of the individual personal psyche, which is convinced that it controls its inner world.

Hillman's interpretation of the hero image is undoubtedly axiologically negative. He considers the dominance of one of the archetypes as likely to threaten the psyche, which is polymorphic in nature. Jung also perceived the ego's domination over other archetypes, but he considered the direction of its tendency to development to be its natural aspiration as the center of consciousness.[46] In addition, Jung, unlike Hillman, combined the hero myth with the development of the self—the psychological integrity, in which he saw the source of religious monotheism.

Hillman's interpretation of the hero myth has further consequences. He believes that the archetype theory is another mythical story, created in times when the world became disenchanted, and gods or other wonderful images of fantasy were not needed anymore. According to Hillman, the fact that psychoanalysts are interested in mythical characters is not accidental. He claims that "in a secular world, one should seek gods where mental illnesses are."[47] The reason for this is an impoverishment on the ground of symbolism, including religious symbolism. The world is deprived of the spiritual and mythical dimension. However, it is still images, not concepts, that appeal to the human psyche. The language of the myth enables one to form a relationship with one's own spirituality. Such a relationship is not expressed in linguistic structures, but by a metaphorical—symbolic and pictorial—message. The process of losing images of divine characters, heroes, miraculous events in the

---

44 J. Hillman, *The soul's code. In search of character and calling,* (New York, Bantam Edition, 1997).

45 Ibidem, 87.

46 C. G. Jung, "Symbols of transformation", 348.

47 J. Hillman, *Re-visioning psychology,* (New York, Harper & Row, 1997), 206.

surrounding world leads to the loss of contact with the psyche and builds a sense of alienation, since some realms of inner life have been neglected. Hillman believes that metaphor has the ability to connect the world of matter and external life with the world of psychological acts.[48] In the modern world, however, it ceases to serve as a tool for personifying mental forces. The model of the world explained by science, entrusted to rationality, demythologizes reality. At the same time, another myth is created—a myth of science and reason which can grasp the reality at all levels of existence but in a one-sided way, losing the multitude of perspectives typical for fairy tales or myths. This myth has its source in the power of the ego that overcomes other archetypes, displaces their content more and more into the area of the unconscious.[49] From Hillman's postulates it follows that the Enlightenment legacy exacerbates certain symptoms that threaten the fullness of mental life. Hillman blames heroic tendencies underlying the nature of the ego archetype for providing grounds for the attempt to encompass the whole world of phenomena and build an adequate system of explaining it.

Jerzy Grotowski's anthropological, cultural, philosophical, and artistic explorations are yet another example of the interest in the presence of myth, including the hero myth, in life and culture. He was described as a philosopher working in the field of art or a philosophizing artist. He believed, however, that art should not be subordinate to philosophy, psychology, andthat it should not be a tool for presenting one's views. By the same token, philosophy should not be separate from the work. He postulated an action in which philosophy and art are combined.[50] He created on the border of various fields, and his activity is difficult to specify under existing classifications. Grotowski claimed that what was most interesting for him, from the beginning to the late period of his work, when he moved on from the field of theater to paratheatrical experiments,[51] was the philosophy of man. What he meant by that was philosophy as the art of living, a practice. In one of his speeches, he pointed out that he is not interested in creating theoretical systems butin acting. He often referred to Jung's concepts. He was primarily an explorer who wanted to verify to what extent myths common in a given society determine various areas of life and how it is possible to transfer those myths from the collective

48 Ibidem, 53.

49 Ibidem.

50 Z. Osiński, *Grotowski i jego Laboratorium*, (Warszawa, Państwowy Instytut Wydawniczy, 1980), 268–269.

51 Ibidem, 266–272.

unconscious to consciousness.[52] As part of his theatrical and paratheatrical projects, he tried to reach the actors' and audience's real psychical and physical reactions in order to extract the archetypical images that have a profound effect on them. The way he worked consisted in acting on the basis of precise movement and voice structures, combined with texts of literature. At the same time, these compositions were not artistic projects; they were a result of a persistent search for personal reactions, initially improvised. Thanks to this, the archetype was to be "shaped"[53] and subject to profanation; it was to become the object of the mystery of the performance.[54] The archetype "stripped in contradictory aspects"[55] was at the same time affirmed and problematized;[56] it fulfilled cognitive functions.[57]

In 1961, Tadeusz Kudliński, a theater critic, formulated the phrase "the dialectic of ridicule and apotheosis"[58] in the review of the play *Dziady*. It was adopted as a description of the way of acting that was characteristic for the Laboratory team then called the Thirteen Rows Theater; this way of acting, consisting of an "attack on the archetype," was a form of play that combined profanity and adoration.[59] In the play *Apocalypsis cum figures*, such a procedure consisted in showing the image of Christ's martyrdom, which was composed of heroism and humility in a way that was grotesque, pathetic, and tragic at the same time. This was not a stage device but "putting the archetype into motion," reviving it by acting in order to transfer its meaning from the collective unconscious into consciousness. The goal was not to invite the viewers to reflect or make their own interpretations but to bring their participation in the performance to a deep level, enriching the personality of all the participants, actors, and spectators.[60] The director appealed not to intellect or feelings but to unconscious patterns of perception and understanding of life that are present in every person. His work shares common ground with primitive rituals. He appealed to instincts and intuition but with the baggage of experience and the consciousness of the modern man, which were not present in distant times.

52 J. Grotowski, „Teatr Źródeł", in *Tekst zebrane* (Wrocław, Wydawnictwo Instytutu Grotowskiego, 2012), 973.
53 J. Grotowski, „Możliwości teatru", in *Teksty zebrane* (Wrocław, Wydawnictwo Instytutu Grotowskiego, 2012), 212.
54 Ibidem.
55 Ibidem, 213.
56 Ibidem, 219.
57 Ibidem, 213.
58 Ibidem.
59 Ibidem.
60 Ibidem.

In his every project, Grotowski sought "the totality of the image" so that what took place on the stage was holistic as an archetype.[61] The actor was involved on many levels in the act in which he undertook a confrontation with himself using text scores or cultural symbols taken from them. According to him, the nonverbal message was the asset of stage activity, thanks to which the archetype could be experienced and explored. As he claimed, the experience of wholeness as integrity and consciousness described by Jung was possible in the space of interpersonal relations, in a meeting with another human being.[62] He mentions that the verbal transmission of psychoanalysis is its limitation, even though the therapeutic process also takes place on the ground of relation between the therapist and the patient.[63] The dialectics of ridicule and apotheosis were based on the principle of opposites, their coexistence in relation to a specific stage event or character. As Jung and Hillman believe, from a psychological point of view, every reason that directs a behavior, as archetypal in its essence, has an equivalent representing an exactly opposite pattern. The reality of the collective unconscious is paradoxical, dual, based on the coexistence of opposites.[64]

In the theatrical works of Jerzy Grotowski, a hero returns, a martyr who is full of humility toward his own suffering. He devotes himself to the salvation of freedom and humanity.[65] The above-described figure was embodied in the characters of Kordian, Faust, Prince the Indomitable, and Dark from *Apocalypsis cum Figuris*; it appears then in all significant performances that were created over the years of the theater's activity.[66] The director often based his plays on Polish Romantic texts. His intention was not to recreate the world from the past on the stage but to find what is still alive and archetypical in the texts and to confront it with the contemporary context.[67] Grotowski defines an archetype as an image that is not unknowable and does not exist outside of historical time. In his opinion, an archetype functions as a metaphor that takes a concrete form in the circumstances of an epoch.[68] His interest in the works

61 J. Grotowski, „Nie jestem cały, jeśli Ty nie jesteś", in *Teksty zebrane* (Wrocław, Wydawnictwo Instytutu Grotowskiego, 2012), 1027.

62 Ibidem, 1026.

63 Ibidem.

64 C. G. Jung, "The Archetypes and the Collective Unconscious", 230.

65 Z. Osiński, *Grotowski i jego Laboratorium*, (Warszawa, Państwowy Instytut Wydawniczy, 1980), 102.

66 Ibidem, 102.

67 J. Grotowski, „Możliwości teatru", in *Teksty zebrane* (Wrocław, Wydawnictwo Instytutu Grotowskiego 2012), 211–213.

68 Ibidem, 212.

of Polish Romantic literature stems from his conviction that they contain the pattern of Polishness, which has an influence on the collective unconscious of the society shaped by certain shared social experiences. For this reason, they affect the imagination of the Polish, and not another cultural community.[69]

The heroes portrayed in his performances exhibited the traits of heroic sacrifice and martyrdom that resulted from the experience of the Second World War. What connected them was the fact that each of them struggled to save humanity and human dignity. They were lonely heroes, acting in the circumstances of a stage reality that was full of contradictions. The dialectics of ridicule and apotheosis consisted in introducing them to the world in which they were glorified and humiliated at the same time. What they were able to save was innocence. They themselves exhibited opposite features, displaying knowledge and naivety, an internal rebellion against the destruction of values and submission to perpetrators. They patiently endured the yoke of the two-faced society, but they defended their ideals in silence. They were strong and gentle, and the way other people reacted to them made them funny and tragic at the same time.[70]

From these stage works emerges an image of the "Polish hero," or as dramatic director of the Laboratory theater Ludwik Flaszen put it, the mythical fate of the Pole.[71] The performances were made in the 1960s and 1970s, in the reality of communist governments, not long after the war and Holocaust experiences, and they brought up the Polish national experiences that were still painful for the society. What is typical of the characters created by the actors of the Laboratory Theater is their messianism and "Christ-likeness." According to Grotowski, the Christian myth had an influence on how the Polish collective unconscious was shaped.[72] In the performance *The Tragical History of Doctor Faustus*, based on the play by Marlowe, whose premiere took place in 1963, Mephistopheles plays a double role: he tempts against God and praises the work of His creation.[73] Grotowski consciously used the principle of the influence of opposites as an element that triggers authentic psychological reactions. He built his message on them, waking non-conscious patterns in actors. In the modern version, the heroic traits typical of messianic characters are aimed

69 Z. Osiński, *Grotowski i jego Laboratorium*, (Warszawa, Państwowy Instytut Wydawniczy, 1980), 298–301.

70 J. Grotowski, „Możliwości teatru", 212–213.

71 J. Grotowski, „Nie jestem cały, jeśli Ty nie jesteś", in in *Teksty zebrane* (Wrocław, Wydawnictwo Instytutu Grotowskiego, 2012), 1026.

72 Z. Osiński, *Grotowski i jego Laboratorium*, (Warszawa, Państwowy Instytut Wydawniczy, 1980), 114–115.

73 Ibidem.

not as much at establishing new values, as Campbell puts it, but at saving the existing ones. According to Jung, the principle of contradictions is fundamental; it constitutes psychic experience and the way the collective unconscious functions. He mentions the opposition of the heroic quest for independence and the return to the "matrix of the unconscious at the same time."[74] Jerzy Grotowski enlarged the image of the hero figure because he pointed not only to the direction of the hero's aspirations, but to the complexity of his relationship with others; he was transferred to the ground of interpersonal relations.

Kazimierz Dąbrowski, the creator of the theory of positive disintegration, participated in one of Grotowski's para-theatrical projects called "Beehives." He described the imaginary, emotional, irrational, intellectual, intuitive, and animistic "dynamisms" that arose at the time in the group activities. As the psychologist observed, one of the basic and authentic aspirations that were provoked by these psychophysical activities was the desire to survive danger and experience heroism.[75]

Jerzy Grotowski explored the problem of heroic myths based on the principle of the coexistence of opposites in what we could call "high culture." It was a deep, thoughtful, and demanding process. One of his goals was to enrich the personality of both the viewers and the creators on the basis of the Jungian concept of personality integration and making the unconscious conscious.[76] The image of the hero figure emerging from the work of Grotowski and Flaszen is slightly different from the one derived from the descriptions made by Jung. It is dominated by the scapegoat aspect. According to Flaszen, that is the archetypal image of a hero specific to the Polish nation, marked by its specific cultural heritage and collective experience.

Furthermore, the way the hero's myth functions in the dimension of mass culture can be described by Hillman's interpretation, who attributed the universality of this motif to the ego archetype. One of the features of mass culture, which is noticeable in films, books, and comics, is the appeal to human emotionality based on a simple, repetitive pattern, for example, the struggle between good and evil. The construction of the world presented in mass productions of this type is simple, based on unambiguous solutions. The recipients of popular culture products strengthen their egos by getting excited about the image of the hero coming out of many predicaments and defeating his opponents. This hero sometimes acts on behalf of some higher idea, but each time it is his personality, persona, that comes to the fore. The main emphasis of the story is placed on his

---

74 C. G. Jung, "Symbols of transformation", 301.

75 Z. Osiński, *Grotowski i jego Laboratorium*, 227.

76 J. Grotowski, „Możliwości teatru", 212.

image, which is built on the basis of the confession of egoism. This kind of story does not encourage reflection but evokes admiration.

Hillman noticed the disturbing prevalence of the hero's myth. One can wonder whether this desire results from the need to confirm the pursuit of one's own ego. The image of the hero would then be a reference to the need for self-acceptance. Or maybe there is an unconscious need to portray the effort of the psyche towards the integration of opposites—as Jung claimed. Certainly, the dominance of popular culture does not serve the development of an individual personality and the process of individuation. Simplification is the domain of mass culture; the mass culture hero image is not problematized but appears only in the spotlight of his own successes. Mass culture is devoid of complexity and paradoxicality resulting from the ambiguous nature of many matters, the integral part of which is the coexistence of opposites.

The above examples show that the myth of the hero functions on many levels, not only psychological and cultural, but also anthropological. Two variants of the hero myth in contemporary culture were mentioned: the one present in Jerzy Grotowski's Laboratory Theater and another one present in pop-cultural products. Regardless of whether we consider the pursuit of the integration of opposites or the ego's need to reflect its own drive for development as the cause of the present occurrence of this symbol, this myth still meets the needs of the community. Nowadays, this figure appeals to the imagination, which indicates that the psyche still works in accordance with the same pattern, according to Jung—ego, libido, or the self, according to Hillman—the archetype of the ego. In Jung's opinion, myth evolves together with the development of the self. One may ask: Are we moving away from internal development as a civilization, and the archetype of the hero exerts more and more dominance over other archetypes, or does the admiration for the mythical image of the hero figure express the unchanging direction of the psyche toward the archetype of integrality? This problem is still relevant, and the analytical tools developed by Jung and his follower J. Hillman are certainly applicable not only to psychological work, but also, as shown in the example of J. Grotowski's research, to contemporary social, cultural, and artistic problems.

References

Grotowski J., „Teatr Źródeł", in *Tekst zebrane*, Wydawnictwo Instytutu Grotowskiego, Wrocław, 2012.

Grotowski J., „Możliwości teatru", in *Teksty zebrane,* Wydawnictwo Instytutu Grotowskiego Wrocław, 2012.

Grotowski J., "Nie jestem cały, jeśli Ty nie jesteś", in *Teksty zebrane*, Wydawnictwo Instytutu Grotowskiego, Wrocław, 2012.
Hillman J., *Re-visioning psychology*, Harper & Row, New York, 1997.
Hillman J., *The soul's code. In search of character and calling*, Bantam Edition, New York 1997.
Jung C. G., "Aion. Researches into the phenomenology of the self", in *The Collected Works*, v. 9, *Part 2*, trans. R. F. C. Hull, Pantheon Books, New York, 1959.
Jung C. G., "Antwort auf Hiob", in *Gesammelte Werke*, Bd 6, Rascher-Verlag, Stuttgart-Zürich, 1963.
Jung C. G., *Contributions to analytical psychology*, trans. H. G. and C. F. Baynes, Kegan Paul, Trench, Trübner & Co, London, 1928.
Jung, C. G., *Memories, Dreams, Reflections*, translated by R. F. C. Hull, Pantheon Books, New York, 1961.
Jung C. G., "Mysterium Coniunctionis, an Inquiry into the Separation and Synthesis of Psychic Opposites in Alchemy", in *The Collected Works*, v. 14, trans. G. Adler and R. F. C. Hull, Princeton University Press, New York, 1970.
Jung C. G., "Psychological Types or The Psychology of Individuation", in *The Collected Works*, v. 6, trans. H. G. Baynes and H. G. Cantab, Phanteon Books, New York, 1953.
Jung C. G., "Symbols of Transformation", in *The Collected Works*, v. 5, trans. G. Adler and R. F. C. Hull, Princeton University Press, New York, 1965.
Jung C. G., "The Archetypes and the Collective Unconscious", in *The Collected Works*, v. 9, *Part 2*, trans. R. F. C. Hull, Princeton University Press, New York, 1981.
Jung C. G., "The Theory of Psychoanalysis", in *The Journal of Nervous and Mental Disease Publishing Company*, No. 19, New York, 1915.
Osiński Z., *Grotowski i jego Laboratorium*, Państwowy Instytut Wydawniczy, Warszawa, 1980.
Raglan L., *The Hero. A Study in Tradition, Myth and Drama*, Watts & Co., London, 1949.
Rosińska Z., *Jung*, Wiedza Powszechna, Warszawa 1982.
Segal R., *Theorizing about Myth*, University of Massachusetts Press, Amherst, 1999.

CHAPTER 11

What Only They Could See: A Comparative Analysis of Hilma af Klint's Swan Paintings and C.G. Jung's Mandala Sketches

*Kathrin Schaeppi**

Abstract

In this paper, I will illuminate the striking parallels in the life and art of the contemporaries Hilma af Klint and C.G. Jung through a comparative analysis of their art—specifically af Klint's swan paintings and Jung's mandala sketches. Hilma af Klint and C.G. Jung, who never met during their lives, were informed by several shared factors. Particularly their sustained dedication to self-experimentation and connecting with a similar stream of archetypal images would result in their works' uncannily echoing the other. What is it about their art that resonates with us a century after it was produced? In this comparative analysis of their life and art, I attempt to illuminate how Hilma af Klint and C.G. Jung inadvertently offer structures through which it is possible to better imagine what each has brought into the world and how it took extremely individual journeys to achieve this. In essence, af Klint's commission was to paint "the immortal aspects of man" while Jung conceived representations of Self.

In particular, I will examine af Klint's swan paintings and Jung's mandala sketches and illuminate how each series—curiously similar in both development and in length—is a whole reflecting the other. I will demonstrate how it is the archetype, and specifically the archetype of number, that lies at the basis of the human psyche—and the individuation process, as Jung revealed—that binds these images together.

* Grateful acknowledgment goes to the contribution of friend and colleague Bettina Kaufmann from The Foundation of the Works of C.G. Jung Zurich for her contribution and assistance in research. My gratitude to Johan af Klint, great-nephew of Hilma af Klint, for his thoughtful review and insights.

 | DOI:10.1163/9789004468757_013

Keywords

Jung, Hilma af Klint, comparative analysis, parapsychological experiences, mandala sketches, swan series, parapsychological experiences, alchemy, Rosarium Philosophorum

1 Introduction

When Hilma af Klint died in 1944 at the age of 81, she left more than 1,200 works; 123 notebooks; and 26,000 neatly handwritten and partly typed pages[1] to her nephew, Eric af Klint, a vice admiral in the Swedish navy.[2] Firm in her belief that the world was not ready for her work, she even stipulated in her Notebook (Hak 1049) that Works carrying the sign "+x" were not be released until 20 years had lapsed after her death. In October 2018, the Guggenheim Museum, NY, featured Hilma af Klint in a curation titled "Paintings for the Future." The exhibition ran until April 2019 and drew more than 600,000 visitors—the largest crowd in the history of the museum. This spectacular turnout also begs reflection. What has been vivified in the collective?

The art of C.G. Jung was similarly fated. Jung—who was a contemporary of af Klint—would write *The Red Book* between 1915 and 1930, but it was made available to the public only in 2009, nearly 80 years after he completed it. During his lifetime, Jung would show the book to a small circle of trusted analysands and members from the Psychology Club, Zurich.[3] In an English-Language sem-

1 All Paintings and Notebooks are jointly called "the Works." Written communication with Johan af Klint.

2 In his will, Eric af Klint in turn bequeathed all of Hilma af Klint's works to his son, and Hilma's great-nephew, Johan af Klint. It was Erik and Johan af Klint who recovered the paintings from the attic of Kalavägen 56 where they had been housed during the 20-year wait period. Written communication with Johan af Klint.

3 He later revealed that it was Maria Moltzer who had most actively attempted to persuade him to follow in the footsteps of the Swiss psychiatrist, Franz Riklin, and publicly share his creative work. There is an indirect connection between Jung; af Klint; and the three Dutch Moltzer sisters: Peggy, Johanna, and Maria. In Amsterdam af Klint met Peggy Kloppers-Moltzer, a trained Eurythmist and member of the Anthroposophical Society. Peggy supported af Klint with English correspondence when af Klint exhibited and gave a talk at the 1928 World Conference of Spiritual Science in London. (Okkultismus und Abstraktion die Malerin Hilma af Klint (1862–1944), exh. cat. (Vienna, Graphische Sammlung Albertina, 1991–1992, p. 28.) Peggy was the sister of Maria Moltzer, a client, student, and friend of Jung. She belonged to the small circle of trusted persons from the Psychology Club to whom Jung had shown his works in *The Red Book*. Johanna, the third sister, was in Dornach during this time as af Klint. See B. Kaufmann, K. Schaeppi, "Illuminating Parallels in the Life and Art of Hilma af Klint

inar in 1925, Jung would disclose that it was only with great difficulty that he was able to overcome an inner voice that told him not to show his work. He never shared his pictures from within an art context. Since its publication in 2009, *The Red Book*, like Hilma af Klint's exhibition, has reached an acclaimed number of people.[4]

2 Arriving at the Occult

Even at the young age of 17, af Klint became interested in the Spiritist Society and was drawn to the idea that there existed unseen spirits who could communicate with living beings. After the death of her sister Hermina in 1880, her interest in the occult increased. At age 27 she became a member of the Swedish branch of the Theosophical Society in Stockholm. In her early 30s, (1896), she was part in forming a group, De Fem—or The Five—with four other women,[5] who all had met at the Edelweiss Association; a Rosicrucian Order.[6] For 10 years, they would meet every week in each other's homes to conduct séances in order to communicate with spirit guides. To be noted is that these spirits were of two different classes. One class were those spirits on the astral level, named Ananda, Amaliel, Gregor, and so on. The second class of spirits were merely called De Höga Mästarna—High Masters, as these spirits communicated ideas and messages from higher levels but could not be individually identified by humans and thus, had no names.[7]

In any case, the meetings had a Christian connotation as they started with a prayer and meditation, followed by a sermon in front of an altar with a cross

---

and C.G. Jung." ARAS.org (publication pending: first presented at Art and Psyche Conference Santa Barbara, April 2019).

4 Hammer Museum, Los Angeles, The Red Book of C.G. Jung, April 11, 2010–June 6, 2010; Library of Congress, Washington, DC, The Red Book of C.G. Jung, June 17–September 25, 2010; Museum Rietberg, Zurich, C.G. Jung: Das Rote Buch, December 18, 2010–March 20, 2011; Musée des arts asiatiques Guimet, Paris, Le Livre Rouge de C.G. Jung, September 7–November 7, 2011; Fondation Bodmer, Geneva, C.G. Jung: Le Rouge et le Noir, November 26, 2011–March 25, 2012; La Biennale di Venezia—55. Esposizione Internazionale d'Arte, Venice, Il Palazzo Enciclopedico, June 1–November 24, 2013; Auf dem Weg zur Erleuchtung. Der Indien-Mythos in der westlichen Kultur 1808–2017, Lugano, Museo d'arte della Svizzera italiana (MASI), September 24, 2017–January 21, 2018; "The Illuminated Imagination: The Art of C. G. Jung" at the Art, Design & Architecture Museum University Santa Barbara.

5 The Five were Hilma af Klint, Anna Cassel, Cornelia Cederberg, Sigrid Hedman, and Mathilda Nilsson.

6 https://www.hilmaafklint.se/about-hilma-af-klint/ (Accessed: 8 May 2019).

7 af Klint, Hilma. Notebook HaK 1162, 158.

and on the wall, a reproduction of Bertha Valerius's painting of Jesus. Thereafter followed an analysis of a text from the New Testament. De Fem recorded their activities and results "in a way that recall[ed] scientific research,"[8] documenting everything from who had acted as medium, which spirits were contacted, and what messages were received. This was done in five Notebooks (HaK 1159–1163) constituting 630 pages. Thirty years before the Surrealists, they were producing automatic drawings by recording the movement of the pencil held by the medium.[9] In 1904, at age 42, af Klint joined the Swedish Lodge of the Theosophical Society-Adyar.[10] Three years later she also became a secret member of the Rosicrucian Society (Hak 556).

This 10-year period (1896–1906) with The Five was vital for Hilma af Klint's spiritual and inward development, which resulted in her great works of late 1906. For on January 1, 1906, af Klint received a commission from the spirit-being Amaliel, to "perform a work, which she immediately accepted." In her notebook she wrote that this was the most impressive work of her life (HaK 555, p. 8). The result was the "Paintings for the Temple," about which she would later write: "The pictures were painted directly through me, without any preliminary drawings, and with great force. I had no idea what the paintings were supposed to depict; nevertheless I worked swiftly and surely, without changing a single brush stroke" (HaK 556, p. 274).

Jung also dialogued with inner voices and figures such as Elias, Philemon, and Salome.[11] His deep inner work, "Septem Sermones ad Mortuos," or "Seven Sermons to the Dead," were dictated to him in the form of a trance by a figure named Basilides of Alexandria. In *Memories, Dreams, Reflections* Jung would go on to describe the process of working on his mandala sketches as follows:

> My mandalas were cryptograms concerning the state of the self which was presented to me anew each day. In them I saw the self—that is, my whole

8 Müller-Westermann, I. "Hilma af Klint in Her Time and Ours" in The Art of Seeing the Invisible. (Stockholm, Sweden: Axel and Margaret Ax:son Johnson Foundation, 2015) 184. In general, in this time séances were primarily performed by women giving the feminine voice space to be heard.

9 This has prompted the question "Could af Klint have been the pioneer before the pioneers (namely Wassily Kandinsky and Kazimir Malevich)? Yet art historian Susan Tallman asks a different question in her article "Painting the Beyond," in the *New York Review of Books*, "To what degree does celebrating these things as works of art, and celebrating af Klint as their creator, invalidate everything she was hoping to achieve?" https://www.nybooks.com/articles/2019/04/04/hilma-af-klint-painting-beyond/ (Accessed: 8 May 2019).

10 http://tsmembers.org/ (Accessed: 20 July 2019). Theosophical Society General Membership Register, 1875–1942; See book 2, entry 25919 (website file: 2C/66).

11 see for ex. C. G. Jung, *The Red Book: Liber Novus*, fol. vi (r), translation, 248f.

> being—actively at work. To be sure, at first I could only dimly understand them; but they seemed to me highly significant, and I guarded them like precious pearls.[12]

When af Klint produced the swan paintings, and Jung the mandala sketches, each worked as a medium and transcriber of something deeply connected to their inner lives—af Klint's notebooks even contain elaborate codes through which to read her art; a system that has not necessarily made the task of decoding the Work any easier (HaK 1040).[13]

3 The Swan Series and Mandala Sketches

It was af Klint's time with De Fem when she matured spiritually, enabling her to produce the "Paintings for the Temple" from 1906 to 1915, of which the Swan paintings is one series within this sequence. The Swan Paintings is a series of 24 paintings made between 1914 and 1915 (HaK 149–HaK 172). For af Klint, whose training at the Royal Academy of Fine Arts (1882–1887) in Stockholm, had primarily been in the naturalistic style, her work on the "Paintings for the Temple" marked the beginning of a new form. As of 1912 she would no longer produce art by working as a medium to something beyond herself; but her years spent working on the series would transform her artistic language, delivering her into the more abstract, less figurative style that characterizes her later work.

There are specific circumstances that influence this series. First, af Klint's mother had lost her eyesight, and af Klint therefore stopped painting for four years to care for her mother. Second, in 1908 there had been a discouraging encounter with Rudolf Steiner, then the head of the Theosophical Society in Germany (and later the founder of Anthroposophy). Steiner clearly articulated his disapproval of her producing art through mediumship promoting that spiritual truth would only be found by looking inward. Third, during the four years that she did not paint in abstract form (though she did paint conventional landscapes for sale and at least one portrait) she devoted much time to studying a wide range of religious and philosophical subjects and writers including

---

12 C. G. Jung, *Memories, Dreams, Reflections*, ed. Aniela Jaffé, trans. R., C., Winston, (New York: Pantheon Books, 1963), 221.

13 Notebook HaK 1040 has been translated into English and is published in C. Burgin (ed.) and The University of Chicago Press (co-publication), *Hilma af Klint: Notes and Methods* (London: The University of Chicago Press, 2018), 246.

Annie Besant, H.P. Blavatsky, Franz Hartmann, Nizda and Carl du Prél. And finally, she painted the series during the early part of World War I.[14]

Like af Klint, Jung's interest in the spiritual and the occult began at an early age. Born into a family already oriented towards the spiritual—his father and six uncles were theologists; his mother, maternal grandfather, and aunt[15] all had had experiences with spirits—a 21-year-old Jung would attend séances with his cousin, Helene Preiswerk. Helene, who had mediumistic abilities, had read Justinus Kerner's "The Seeress of Prevorst"—an account of Kerner's research on Friederike Hauffe, a young German clairvoyant and somnambulist—and with Helene Preiswerk, Jung would record the séances the way Kerner had with Hauffe, eventually writing his dissertation, "On the Psychology and Pathology of So-Called Occult Phenomena." In his dissertation Helene is anonymized as S.W.[16]

At the age of 26, he would meet and get to know Théodore Flournoy, a professor of psychology at the University of Geneva who had studied the mediumistic abilities of one of the best-known automatic writers, a Swiss woman named Hélène Smith who was also known as Catherine Elise Müller. When he studied with Pierre Janet in the following year, he would be introduced to Janet's proposition that automatic writing was a form of somnambulism, a condition in which a part of the personality is dissociated.

At age 40, from 1915 to 1928, Jung would pursue a self-experimentation that was later referred to as his "confrontation with the unconscious," through which he developed his technique of active imagination—letting inner fantasies and images rise up, then recording them in writing. Some of these fantasies were put into raw drawings—to which the mandala sketches bear witness—that he would later carefully redraw into *The Red Book*. The Mandala Sketches can be considered his *prima materia* upon which his entire opus grew.

Although af Klint and Jung were introduced to automatic drawing differently—Jung became acquainted with it through the empirical sciences—the works they produced as a result of it contain parallels that demand a thorough analysis of the recurring symbols and themes.

In 1907, before she began work on the "Paintings for the Temple," af Klint would receive a message from the High Masters concerning the sound of the letters that appeared in her paintings. The message revealed that "the purpose

---

14 Within the Swan Series there are abstract objects that may point to propellers, apertures, and color checks that may be interpreted as linked with the widespread use of propeller fighter airplanes and the introduction of moving pictures at the turn of the century.

15 Gustele Preiswerk was credited with bringing "the occult strain" into the family. D. Bair, Jung: *A Biography*. (Boston: Little, Brown and Co, 2003), 15.

16 S. Shamdasani, "'S.W.' and C. G. Jung: mediumship, psychiatry and serial exemplarity", *History of Psychiatry*, 26, 3, (2015): 288–302.

of these letters is to prepare the way for a language that *has already existed forever* and that has now been given to humanity by the creative spirits."[17] In their pursuit of that which lay beyond, did af Klint and Jung both arrive at that which had "already existed forever"? It is possible that the question of the curious similarities in their works is most successfully pursued both through an understanding of where they came from and from an archetypal view.

4 The Alchemical Bond

Using the third century alchemical precept, the Axiom of Maria, which Jung himself used to describe the process of individuation, I will consider the parallels between af Klint's swan series, Jung's spontaneous mandala sketches, and the Rosarium Philosophorum[18]—a series of woodcuts printed and produced in Frankfurt in 1550. As stated in the Axioma Maria: "One becomes Two, Two becomes Three, and out of the Third comes the One as the Fourth." Starting with One, here are the first images from three different works—the Rosarium Philosophorum (the 16th century alchemical treatise), Jung's mandala sketches, and af Klint's swan paintings. In this section I will perform a comparative analysis of six corresponding images from each work and show how the archetype of number informs and binds these images to each other. Beyond C.G. Jung, this section has also been informed by writings on number by Marie-Louise von Franz,[19] Gary Sparks,[20] and Alain Negre.[21] Comparative analysis with images in *The Secret of the Golden Flower*[22] have been made previously and will not be further explored here.[23]

---

17 C. Burgin (ed.) and The University of Chicago Press (co-publication). Hilma af Klint: Notes and Methods (London: The University of Chicago Press, 2018), 246. Hilma af Klint, Notebook HaK 431. (emphasis author).

18 *Rosarium Philosophorum: Ein alchemisches Florilegium des Spätmittelalters.* Faksimile der illustrierten Erstausgabe (Frankfurt 1550. ed. and comm. by Joachim Telle. Weinheim: VCH Verlagsgesellschaft, Vol. 1&2. 1992).

19 M.L. von Franz. *Number and Time: Reflections Leading Towards a Unification of Psychology and Physics*, (London: Rider & Company, 1974).

20 G. J. Sparks, *Valley of Diamonds: Adventures in Number and Time with Marie-Louise von Franz*, (Toronto: Inner City Books, 2010).

21 A. Negre, *The Archetype of the Number and its Reflections in Contemporary Cosmology*, (North Carolina: Chiron Publications, 2018).

22 R. Wilhelm (trans.). *The Secret of the Golden Flower: A Chinese Book of Life.* (with a European Commentary by C.G. Jung; Eleven Plates and four text Illustrations) (London: Kegan Paul, Trench Trubner & Co., Ltd., 1931).

23 B. Kaufmann, K. Schaeppi, *Illuminating Parallels in the Life and Art of Hilma af Klint and C.G. Jung*, (ARAS.org, 2019) (publication pending: first presented at "Art and Psyche Conference", Santa Barbara, April 2019).

5 One: Initial Wholeness

Rosarium Woodcut 1

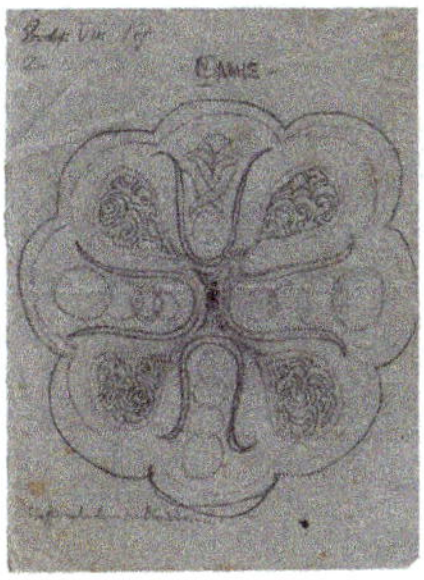

Jung Sketch 1

Jung Red Book 80

Af Klint 1 (HAK 149)

In most creation myths, One represents an initial, undifferentiated state of archetypal wholeness before creation and the separation of all things—what in psychological terms is the undifferentiated state of consciousness—and which each of the above images depicts.

In the rosarium woodcut "The Mercurial Fountain," the image contains the knowledge of the alchemy of the time. The then-known four elements: earth, water, air, and fire, indicated by the four stars in the corners, meet the three mercurials: mineralis (inorganic), vegetablis (organic), and animalis (animated), which then meet the sun (mineral gold) and the moon (mineral silver). In the "Psychology of the Transference" Jung himself would describe the image as "going straight to the heart of alchemical symbolism, for it is an attempt to depict the mysterious basis of the opus."[24]

The five-pointed star represents *quint essentia*, or the quintessence; the basin of water represents the *vas hermeticum*, where the transformation takes place; and the streams from the flowing fountain point to circular pouring and to containment by the basin, representing the cyclical ouroboros (that which fertilizes, rebirths, devours, and kills). In psychological terms, the fountain represents the unconscious psyche, holding the polar tensions of chaos and wholeness.

Jung's first image holds the symmetry of a mandala while simultaneously depicting asymmetry in the filigree within the red droplet forms, thus holding the tension of asymmetry within symmetry. This first mandala sketch is called "Phanes" and described by Jung as the divine child and new God; the Shining One; cosmogonic principle; the cosmic, comet-like eight-rayed star.[25] "At the bottom of the sketch, Jung wrote 'Stoffwechsel im Individuum' (Metabolism

24 C. G. Jung, "Psychology of the Transference", in *The Collected Works*, W. McGuire (ed.), v. 16, (London: Routledge, 1969), § 402.

25 C. G. Jung, *The Red Book: Liber Novus*, 354, 356, 370–371.

in the individual), to emphasize that the mandala is an energic image of the metabolism required for the birth of the new God in the individual."[26]

Af Klint's swans resemble the Eastern yin-and-yang symbol, holding the ancient wisdom of unity in duality; with their color juxtaposition, the birds are mirrors that evoke the feeling of an eternal flow. The work of af Klint suggests that opening the veil to higher dimensions would allow one to see that polarity or duality is an illusion and that on a higher level, all is one consciousness.

6 Two: Opposites Meet

Rosarium Woodcut 2

Jung Sketch 5

Jung Red Book 83

Af Klint 1 (HAK 149)

The above images represent a coming together of opposites. Two involves division, separation from the original unity. They are depicted in the form of masculine and feminine—the king and the queen; the flower; and black and white swans touching beaks and wingtips. The swans represent both unity and duality, the opposite energies striving to be in contact, and reminiscent of yin-and-yang, masculine and feminine, spirit and matter, and even of the fingertips of Adam and God, as imagined by Michelangelo in the Sistine Chapel.

Two represents a development of consciousness that begins through mirroring and relationship as a couple. Through the archetype of Two, in all the images, separation, differentiation, and dissociation from the One is implied. At this juncture, relationship, communication, and transformation as a creative process begins. "More specifically, two is associated with the threshold of

26 D. F. Zervas, "Intimations of the Self: Jung's Mandala Sketches for the Red Book", in *The Art of C.G. Jung. Edited by the Foundation of the Works of C.G. Jung.* (London, New York: Routledge, 2018), 182.

consciousness that is reached by psychic content—which, through the tension of opposites, drives differentiation and conscious realization."[27]

7 Two: Union of the Opposites

Rosarium Woodcut 5

Jung Sketch 9

Jung Red Book 85

Af Klint 3 (HaK 151)

These images show the *coniunctio*, or the coming together, of opposites in sacred marriage. In "Mysterium Coniunctionis," the first chapter of his collected works, Jung writes, "The factors which come together in the *coniunctio* are conceived as opposites, either confronting one another in enmity or attracting one another in love."[28] Jung refers to the masculine-feminine antithesis in the long and round objects: cigarform and circle that "may be sexual symbols."[29]

In Jung's image,

> The chthonic force has reached the mandala, forcing open its receiving vessel. The thrust has scattered seed from the hollow of the top vertical axis. A hexagram star presides over the cosmic union unfolding below, its opposing triangles symbolizing the union of fire and water, male and female.[30]

---

27 A. Negre, *The Archetype of the Number and its Reflections in Contemporary Cosmology*, (North Carolina: Chiron Publications, 2018), 53.

28 C. G. Jung, "Mysterium Coniunctionis", in *The Collected Works* v. 14. (London: Routledge, 1963), § 1.

29 C. G. Jung, "Civilisation in Transition", in *The Collected Works*, ed. by W. McGuire and trans. R.F.C. Hull, v. 10 (London: Routledge, 1964), § 772.

30 Zervas presents a sequential description of the mandala sketches using image and word. Zervas in The Art of C.G. Jung, 179–210. On p. 192 Zervas references C.G. Jung CW 12, fig 160 (Symbol of the art as union of water and fire); CW 10 § 771 (central archetype of self, fire and water, "star of David").

In af Klint's image, the white swan covers the black swan. Their necks intertwine, heads align, and beaks touch in a new way. Wings hold and enfold the other as one. Pink pours from the heart region of the white swan. White radiates from the heart region of the black swan. Blood and milk, the ultimate fluids of life meet.

Through the entwining and coming together of opposites in carnal and spiritual intercourse, a new being or symbol is in the process of being created. This union of the opposites is an archetypal step in individuation.

8 Three: Creation of the Uniting Symbol

Rosarium Woodcut 7

Jung Sketch 12

Jung Red Book 87

Af Klint 4 (HaK 152)

In all three of the above images, there is an emergent third. The tension of the opposites seeks resolution in a third thing. In the woodcut, a divine child or soul symbol arises out of the hermaphrodite incubating in water. In the mandala series, the star emerges out of the mandala, immersed and gestating in water. In the swan series, the swan couple tumbles into the lower chthonic mother earth while a young swan is birthed and emerges in the upper spiritual realm.

In alchemy this image represents sublimation, where through heating, a solid has passed into a vapor state. On an image level it represents symbolic death. The "soul" element (homunculus, divine child, anima and/or animus) separates from the hermaphroditic decaying body shell and unites with upper powers and spirit realm (clouds).

In Jung's image, following the *coniunctio* there has been a separation. From Jung's sketch 12 to his *Red Book* painting, the star has transformed from six-pointed to eight-pointed and is now cushioned in "clouds" or "dew" above. The fertilized and gestating mandala floats in water where four lotus flowers are developing. The chthonic phallic energy is present yet has receded. In *The Red Book* in several places, Jung describes the blue star as man's Pleroma and his divinity.[31] In quintessence, the emergent eight-rayed blue star is a symbol that leads[32] and unites.

In af Klint's image, in the upper left, pink square, a young swan with one yellow foot and one blue arises and hovers like the phoenix arising from the ashes, witness to its own incarnation. This new swan carries parts of the old: a fully pink wing; a black wingtip, one blue and one yellow foot and blue-yellow beak. As in Mendelian inheritance and Darwinian evolution, the new carries part of the old. The young swan appears to represent a (re)birth out of the original two swans who are now falling into the depths, the primordial chaos.

9 Three and Birth of the Fourth: Integration of the Uniting Symbol

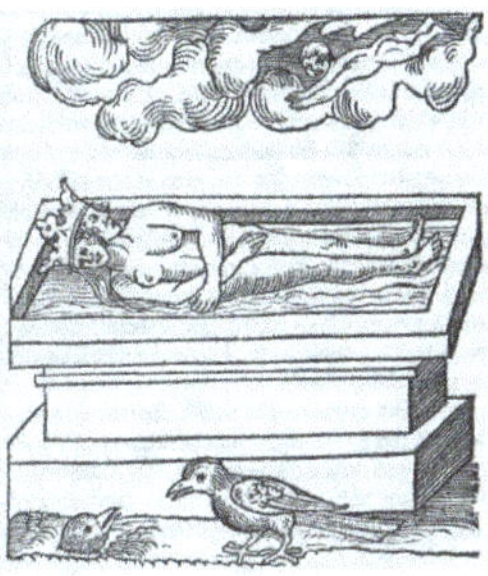
Rosarium Woodcut 9

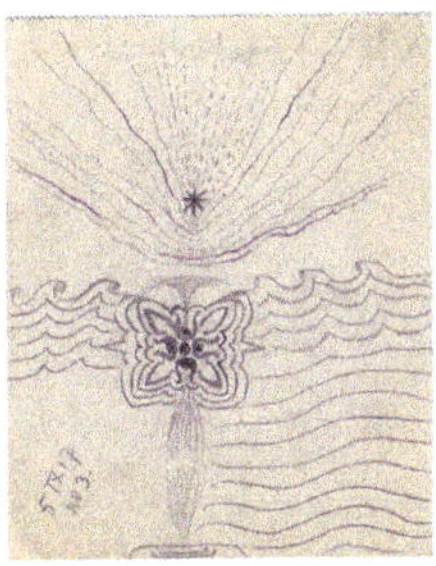
Jung Sketch 20

Jung Red Book 91

Af Klint 6 (HaK 154)

From the point of number symbology, these images show a pull of the transcendent third to be re-integrated into something new. The three is coming into relation with the four. The four cardinal points fixed in the middle change to something else, and new symbols emerge.[33] In dynamic chemical terms this is sublimation where the gas condenses back into solid form. The Rosarium Woodcut 9 depicts the third, returning and replenishing the androgynous body, which has gone through an (inner) death process.[34]

In Jung's sketch, the blossoming lotus or "golden flower" is visible for the first time. The eight-rayed star (self-symbol) "descends toward the mandala, generating an energy field that whips up crest-capped waves on the watery

31 Jung, *The Red Book: Liber Novus*, 354.

32 J. Dourly, "Jung, the Nothing and the All", in *Jung's Red Book for Our Times*. vol. 2. eds. Murray Stein and Thomas Artzt (Chiron Publications: Asheville, North Carolina, 2018) 95.

33 Negre, *The Archetype of the Number and its Reflections in Contemporary Cosmology*, 59.

34 Jung considers the soul or Anima archetype to be the "archetype of life itself" including the life force as well as the archetype of meaning (i.e., the wise old person/senex). Jung, CW 9, § 44–66; particularly § 66.

surface."[35] Phanes is bisexual and akin to the god of love.[36] In af Klint's image, the vertical and horizontal merge in the center of the cross and spiral where a tiny heart—a new symbol—is held by four ethereal swans' beaks. The spiral is a symbol of being and becoming. Number, time, and the intimate (heart symbol) merge.

In the analytic setting, the analysand may now find inside himself/herself what he/she has previously been seeking in a partner of the opposite sex in the outer world. In this way, the unconscious may mediate with its inner partner. Relations to others may gain depth and become more truly felt and experienced. As witnessed above there may be a birth of new consciousness (return of the soul, birth of Phanes, birth of a connection to the heart).

10 Four: The New Birth/Totality/Self-Symbol

Rosarium Woodcut 10

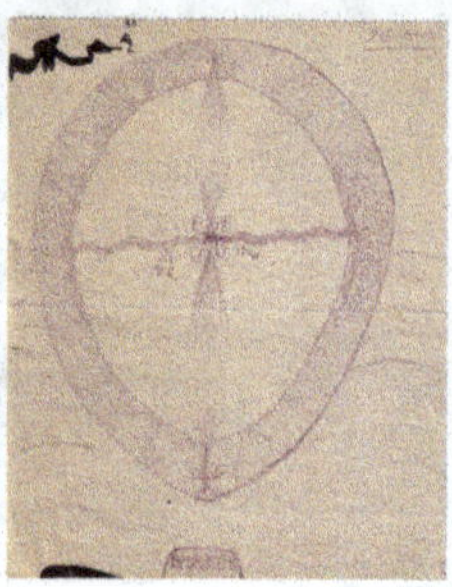

Jung Sketch 29

Jung Red Book 97

Af Klint 24 (HaK 172)

According to the Axiom of Maria: "Out of the One comes Two, out of Two comes Three, and from the Third comes the One as the Fourth." In nature four is encountered in the four cardinal directions and quadrants; the four elements (air, fire, earth, water); the four moon phases; the four seasons; and the four human limbs (two arms, two legs). At the same time, four is a symbol of wholeness such as the mandala, egg, and balanced personality. In fairy tales, the hero's completion of the third and final task most often leads to increased stability and completeness as represented in images of marriage and vivified life.

---

35 Zervas, *The Art of C.G. Jung*, 199.

36 C.G. Jung, "Symbols of Transformation", in *The Collected Works*, ed. by H. Read, M. Fordham, G. Adler, trans. R.F.C. Hull, v. 5. (London: Routledge, 1956) § 198; L. Corbett, *"The Red Book as a Religious Text"* in *Jung's Red Book for Our Times*. v. 2. eds. M. Stein and T. Artzt, (Chiron Publications: Asheville, North Carolina, 2018), 60.

In the last of the first series of the *Rosarium Philosophorum*, the 10th woodcut, an androgyny is born and rises on a quarter moon. This image represents the integration of the feminine (anima, soul) as evidence of standing on the moon and the moon tree. Jung's sketches 26 to 29 depict the "cosmic egg" to be fully constellated in the final sketch 29. Within the egg's thick shell, at the center of the mandala is the blue star described by Jung as the mystery of the self and soul that holds the oppositions together, connecting micro and macrocosm.[37]

In "Alchemical Studies," Jung cites Gerhard Dorn: "Nothing is more like God than the center, for it occupies no space, and cannot be grasped, seen or measured. Such too, is the nature of God and the spirits. Therefore the center is 'an infinite abyss of mysteries.'"[38]

This exploration of Jung's mandala sketches is indeed an individuation process that culminates in "visual representations of Jung's direct experience of the Self and the birth of the new God."[39]

Although af Klint's paintings 8 to 23 depart from the figurative, the last image returns to the swan bodies. This intuitive and emotional 24th image completes the sacred geometry of the swan series. The canvas is square and divided into four sections upon which the swan wings form a delicate cross. The swans' necks and beaks merge in a delicate kiss forming an oval, like an Ouroboros (the snake biting into its own tail) and also form the symbol of infinity. The commission that af Klint received from the spiritual-being Amaliel had been to represent the "immortal aspects of man." This final image of her series radiates the aura and mystery of the infinite and transcendent and thus, successfully "fulfills" her commission. The final image is reminiscent of the first painting yet points to infinity, the eternal held in an image. This closing image points to the completion of a deep personal process. As in the first image where white wingtip meets black wingtip, here too a meeting space is created—where the sacred and human come together.

Four is the number of Jung's archetypal Self symbol, which is also the archetype of ordering of the contents of the psyche[40]—a symbol of wholeness signifying balance and centeredness of the personality.

---

37 see also Dourley, *Jung's Red Book for our Times*, 95–99.

38 see Dorn, "De Vita Longa": An Exposition of the Secret Doctrine. in *The Collected Works*, ed. W. Mcquire, trans. R.F.C. Hull, v. 13 (London: Routledge, 1968), 186.

39 Zervas, *The Art of C.G. Jung*, 207.

40 T. Abt, *Introduction to Picture Interpretation According to C.G. Jung*, (Zurich: Living Human Heritage Publications, 2005), 129.

When the state of four is reached, the opposing forces in the Self have reached a new state of balance, symbolized by the four sides of a square. Its center, where all opposites are resolved is the quintessence, the fifth element of alchemy that Plato and Aristotle explained in relation to the elements and the qualities. Five is, therefore, the center of four, the center of the unfolding oneness, i.e., the "one who is not" or superessential nothingness that was to be replaced by zero when the latter found its way to Europe around the 12th century.[41]

11 Conclusion

As I discover the works of Hilma af Klint and C.G. Jung, it is important to investigate the manner in which they resonate with us nearly a century later. What is it about their art that reaches through time and allows us to be moved by it? Is it the uniqueness that holds our attention, or the sheer authenticity of two deeply personal representations of the discovery of the Self? In studying their art together, I have attempted to show how af Klint and Jung inadvertently offer structures through which it is possible to better understand what each was individually attempting to bring into the world—"the immortal aspects of man"—and "the Self" and how it took extremely individual journeys to achieve.

References

Abt T., Introduction to Picture Interpretation According to C.G. Jung, Zurich: Living Human Heritage Publications, 2005.

Bair D., Jung: A Biography, Boston, MA: Little, Little, Brown and Company, 2003.

Burgin C. (ed.) and The University of Chicago Press (co-publication), Hilma af Klint: Notes and Methods, London: The University of Chicago Press, 2018.

Corbett L., "The Red Book as a Religious Text", in: Jung's Red Book for Our Times, v. 2. eds. Murray Stein and Thomas Artzt. Asheville, North Carolina: Chiron Publications, 2018.

Dourly J., "Jung, the Nothing and the All", in: Jung's Red Book for Our Times, v. 2. eds. Murray Stein and Thomas Artzt. Asheville, North Carolina: Chiron Publications, 2018.

41 Negre, *The Archetype of the Number and its Reflections in Contemporary Cosmology*, 63.

Foundation of the Works of C.G. Jung, The Art of C.G. Jung, Norton, 2018.
https://www.hilmaafklint.se/hilma-af-klint-foundation/ - [Accessed: 16 April 2019].
http://tsmembers.org/Theosophical Society General Membership Register, 1875–1942; book 2, entry 25919 (website file: 2C/66) – [Accessed: 20 July 2019].
https://www.nybooks.com/articles/2019/04/04/hilma-af-klint-painting-beyond/ - [Accessed: 8 May 2019].
https://www.nybooks.com/articles/2019/04/04/hilma-af-klint-painting-beyond/ - [Accessed: 8 May 2019].
Jung C.G., "Alchemical Studies. 'De Vita Longa': An Exposition of the Secret Doctrine", in: The Collected Works, ed. W. McGuire and trans. R.F.C. Hull, v. 13. London: Routledge, 1968.
Jung C.G., "Civilisation in Transition", in: The Collected Works, ed. W. McGuire, trans. R.F.C. Hull, v. 10, London: Routledge, 1964.
Jung C.G., Memories, Dreams, Reflections, ed. A. Jaffé, trans. R. and C. Winston, New York: Pantheon Books, 1963.
Jung C.G., "Mysterium Coniunctionis", in: The Collected Works, ed. W. McGuire, trans. R. F. C. Hull, v. 14. London: Routledge, 1963.
Jung C.G. "Psychology of the Transference", in: The Collected Works, ed. W. McGuire, trans. R. F. C. Hull, v. 16, London: Routledge, 1969.
Jung C.G. "Symbols of Transformation", in: The Collected Works, eds. H. Read, M. Fordham, G. Adler, trans. R.F.C. Hull, v. 5, London: Routledge, 1956.
Jung C.G., The Red Book: Liber Novus, ed. S. Shamdasani, trans. J. Peck, M. Kyburz, S. Shamdasani, New York: W. W. Norton & Company Inc., 2009.
Kaufmann B., Schaeppi K., Illuminating Parallels in the Life and Art of Hilma af Klint and C.G. Jung, ARAS.org [publication pending: first presented at "Art and Psyche" Conference Santa Barbara, April 2019].
Müller-Westermann I., "Hilma af Klint in Her Time and Ours", in: The Art of Seeing the Invisible, Stockholm: Axel and Margaret Ax:son Johnson Foundation, 2015.
Negre A., The Archetype of the Number and its Reflections in Contemporary Cosmology, North Carolina: Chiron Publications, 2018.
Rosarium Philosophorum: Ein alchemisches Florilegium des Spätmittelalters. Faksimile der illustrierten Erstausgabe, Frankfurt 1550, ed. and comm. J. Telle, Weinheim: VCH Verlagsgesellschaft, Vol. 1&2, 1992.
Shamdasani S., "'S.W.' and C.G. Jung: mediumship, psychiatry and serial exemplarity", History of Psychiatry, 26, 3, (2015): 288–302.
Sparks G. J., Valley of Diamonds: Adventures in Number and Time with Marie-Louise von Franz, Toronto: Inner City Books, 2010.
von Franz M.-L., Number and Time: Reflections Leading Towards a Unification of Psychology and Physics, London: Rider & Company, 1974.

The Secret of the Golden Flower: A Chinese Book of Life (with a European Commentary by C.G. Jung. Eleven Plates and four text Illustrations), trans. R. Wilhelm, London: Kegan Paul, Trench Trubner & Co., Ltd., 1931.

Zervas, D. F., "Intimations of the Self: Jung's Mandala Sketches for the Red Book", in: *The Art of C.G. Jung*, Foundation of the Works of C.G. Jung (ed.), 2018.

CHAPTER 12

Traces of Psychological Impact Found in the Drawings by Cancer Patients

Norifumi Kishimoto

Abstract

Although great progress has been made in the treatment of cancer, it remains the leading cause of death. In this article, three cases are presented to demonstrate a practical application of a psychotherapeutic approach to cancer patients from the viewpoint of Jungian psychology.

The first case was a woman in her thirties with leukemia, whose Baumtest showed the structure of the Möbius tree. The Möbius tree was initially found in the Baumtest of patients with schizophrenia and was considered an indicator of schizophrenia, but it was later revealed that the Möbius tree was also found in the Baumtests of cancer patients, reflecting a common vulnerability between cancer and schizophrenia patients. This may reflect, in Jungian psychology terms, a situation in which the deep barriers of the mind become fragile, allowing the contents of the collective unconscious to flow easily into the ego.

The second case was a man in his 50s with lung cancer; his disease was advanced, and he complained of intense agitation and insomnia. With the help of the Baumtest and the landscape montage technique, he began to draw spontaneously and came out of his strong agitation and regained himself. Based on the ideas of Jungian psychology, Bach used free drawings to approach children with cancer in a psychotherapeutic way. Although she emphasizes that signs of physical illness can be seen in the drawings, we could pay more attention to the therapeutic power of the drawing itself, just as Jung came out of his crisis with a drawing he later called a mandala.

The third case was a 48-year-old woman with leukemia who had a profound experience during a bone marrow transplant that was comparable to a near-death experience. Her course of treatment was compared to a series of pictures in the Rosarium Philosophorum, and it was suggested that transplantation needs to be regarded as a treatment that goes through to the point of death and rebirth, rather than simply replacing a sick organ with a healthy one. In conclusion, the contemporary usefulness and applicability of Jung's idea can be sought in the field of cancer treatment.

 | DOI:10.1163/9789004468757_014

Keywords

cancer, Baumtest, drawing, death and rebirth, Rosarium Philosophorum

1 Introduction

Cancer is a disease caused by abnormal cells that continue to grow without control so that not only is the organ from which they derive damaged, but they also spread to other parts of the body, causing various dysfunctions. If the treatment is not effective, it will eventually lead to death. Despite remarkable advances in medicine in recent years, many people are still dying of cancer. In 2016, there were 17.2 million incident cancer cases worldwide and 8.9 million cancer deaths. The number of cancer patients increased by 28% between 2006 and 2016.[1] Cancer is estimated to account for 16% of all causes of death worldwide.

While cancer is no longer considered incurable, it is still the leading cause of death, and having cancer can't help but remind us of our own mortality, to a greater or lesser extent. At first glance, it may seem that the impact of having cancer is temporary and that many people are getting over it. However, deep down inside, it is often a profound shock. We can glimpse the depth of that shock in the fact that a cancer patient may be hurt by a casual word, get annoyed by a small thing, or have a recurring bad dream. I believe that we need to take into account this less visible shock in our treatment. And often, I have experienced that drawing helps to visualize that hard-to-see shock.

Before I get to the subject, let me give the reader my personal background. I am an internist, not a psychiatrist or psychotherapist. I started my career as a hematologist and then worked in the fields of psychosomatic medicine and palliative care after being trained in psychotherapy. The following discussion is based on my clinical practice as a physician.

In 1965, Hayao Kawai became the first Japanese person to qualify as a Jungian analyst, and in 1975 he became a professor at Kyoto University, where he laid the groundwork for psychotherapy in Japan. As a result, Jungian psychology has deeply permeated throughout psychotherapy in general, not just as a single school of psychology. His influence was so great that not only specialists,

---

1 Global Burden of Disease Cancer Collaboration, "Global, Regional, and National Cancer Incidence, Mortality, Years of Life Lost, Years Lived With Disability, and Disability-Adjusted Life-Years for 29 Cancer Groups, 1990 to 2016. A Systematic Analysis for the Global Burden of Disease Study", *JAMA Oncology* 4, no. 11 (2018): 1553–68.

but also the general public became interested in Jungian psychology. Thus, as I became a medical student at a time when Jungian psychology was flourishing in Japan, I too became interested in and greatly influenced by Jungian psychology. Moved by Kawai's monograph, I had and recorded some 700 or so dreams during my medical studies, and although I never had the opportunity to have a dream analysis, I personally struggled with my dreams.[2] My practice would not have been possible without my encounter with Jungian psychology. I hope that this paper will be taken as a presentation of the clinical practice of a physician deeply influenced by Jungian psychotherapy.

2 The Baumtest

First, I take up the Baumtest.[3] *Baum* means "tree" in German. The Baumtest is a type of projective technique in which the subject is asked to draw a picture of a tree. All you need for the test is a pencil and paper. A 4B pencil and A4-sized paper are usually used. The test can be applicable easily and safely to almost everyone who can draw a picture, including patients with schizophrenia and patients with cancer, although a good relationship between the tester and the subject must be established before the test.

It was a Swiss psychologist, Karl Koch, who raised it to a psychological test. He published a textbook, "Der Baumtest," in 1949[4] and revised it in 1954[5] and 1957.[6] In his interpretation of the Baumtest, Koch was heavily influenced by Jung's idea of the symbol. In the 1960s, the Baumtest was introduced into Japan and has been widely used as a therapeutic medium and as a psychological assessment tool.[7,8,9] Depending on how you use it, the Baumtest can be a

2 N. Kishimoto, *Cancer and Psychotherapy (in Japanese)*. (Tokyo: Seishin Shobo, 1999).

3 K. Koch, *Der Baum-test*. (Bern: Hans Huber, 1949).

4 Ibidem.

5 K. Koch, *Der Baumtest, zweite Auflage*, (Bern: Hans Huber, 1954).

6 K. Koch, *Der Baumtest, dritte Auflage*, (Bern: Hans Huber, 1957).

7 K. Koch, *Baumutesuto (Der Baum-test)*, trans. K. Hayashi, M. Kuniyoshi, T. Ichitani, (Tokyo: Nihon Bunka Kagakusha, 1970).

8 There were many problems with translation because it was a double translation of the English translation of the German original. Only recently, the direct Japanese translation from the original third edition was published by us and made available.

9 K. Koch, *Baumutesuto Dai Sanpan (Der Baumtest, dritte Auflage)*, trans. N. Kishimoto, N. Nakashima, T. Miyazaki, (Tokyo: Seishin Shobo, 2010).

vehicle that promotes treatment.[10] To bring out the therapeutic power of the Baumtest, the following points should be noted:

1. It may work as a trigger of communication.
2. It may work as a fine hook of projection and open a way to express oneself.
3. It may function as a kind of mirror that encourages the subject to reflect oneself.

I have used the Baumtest, paying attention to these points, but at the same time, through form analysis and index analysis, I have been able to keep an eye on the psychological characteristics of the patient. From here, we will proceed with the discussion while showing actual cases.

3 The Case of Mrs. White

Mrs. White (a pseudonym), in her thirties, was diagnosed with leukemia. When I took over treatment from the previous doctor, the patient had been receiving chemotherapy for more than one year, but it was ineffective. She looked very depressed and often sobbed. One day I asked her to draw a tree. Several days later, she handed a picture of a tree to me (Figure 1, p.223). When asked, "A cherry tree?" she replied, "Yes. There is a cherry tree in my parental home. There are also cherry trees with a lot of fruits in the kindergarten where my son attends. To my great regret, birds eat them up. Only a few remain." I said to her, "So it is covered with something like a net." She replied, "Yes. I have been unlucky since I came here two years ago. My son had a car accident. Soon I was repeatedly admitted to the hospital. I can't sleep well recently." I asked, "Do you have a bad dream?" She answered, "Not these days," and then she abruptly shed tears for a while. She continued, "When I was hospitalized for the first time, I had many terrible dreams. There is a tomb, and I prayed." Thus, with the drawing as a trigger, she began to talk about things she had never spoken of before. I felt as if drawing a tree opened a new communication channel.

4 Möbius Tree

While listening to her narratives, I realized the therapeutic power of the Baumtest that facilitated her to start talking, but at the same time I was surprised

10 N. Kishimoto, *Baumutesuto Nyumon* (*Introduction to the Baumtest*), (Tokyo: Seishin Shobo, 2015).

to find a strange structure called the Möbius tree (Figure 2, p.223). In order to understand the Möbius tree, we need to refer to two papers. One is the research of Fujioka and Yoshikawa, and the other is that of Yamanaka. Fujioka and Yoshikawa[11] studied 511 pictures obtained from preschool children and elementary school students and proposed a classification based on the configuration of the top of the trunk. They found that the trunk apex of a tree drawn in the Baumtest is usually closed by itself with or without ramification, or if it remains open, is usually covered with a crown. They are called radial type, fir type, and crown type, respectively. All of these trees have a kind of boundary that separates the inside of the tree from the outer world, and I call these three types "closed type apical termination." They also pointed out that an open-ended trunk without any cover (Open type apical termination) was rarely observed in the normal population (less than 5%).

Following this study, in 1976, Yamanaka[12] reported that some schizophrenic patients leave the apex of the trunk open. Moreover, several patients draw the tree in a way that the line that forms the trunk becomes a single-track branch line without notice. Thus, the space inside the trunk seamlessly changes over to the space outside the tree. Even if you are in the trunk at the bottom of the tree, you find yourself out of the trunk without knowing it, if you go up. Yamanaka called this type of tree the Möbius tree because its structure is similar to a Möbius strip. A Möbius strip can easily be created by taking a paper strip, giving it a half-twist, and then joining the ends of the strip together to form a loop. Consequently, a line drawn from a point on one side can run through seamlessly to the other side and then rejoin the starting point, making it impossible to distinguish between the front and the back. Yamanaka suggested that the Möbius tree might be regarded as visualizing patients' delusions that intrude from the outside without notice or the ego-leak in which the ego content leaks from the inside unwittingly. In other words, it may reflect the situation in which the ego boundary was broken, and the inside and outside worlds contacted each other unknowingly. The following studies showed that around 30% of chronic schizophrenic patients draw the Möbius tree and that it is significantly more than normal people.

---

11 Y. Fujioka, K. Yoshikawa, "Jinruigakuteki ni mita baumu niyoru imeiji no hyogen" (Image Representation of Baum from the anthropological point of view)", *Kikan Jinruigaku (Quarterly Anthropology)*, 2, vol. 3 (1971): 3–28.

12 Y. Yamanaka, "Seishinbunretsubyo ni okeru baumutesuto no kenkyu (Study of Baumtest of Schizophrenic patients)", *Shinri sokutei jahnaru(Psychometric journal)*. 12, vol. 4 (1976): 18–23.

5 A Hole in the Psyche

It was, therefore, a great surprise to me that I found the Möbius-like structure in the Baum[13] of Mrs. White, who was not schizophrenic. The finding suggests that she had some weakness shared with schizophrenic patients, although she was not schizophrenic. She used to be susceptible to her surroundings, deeply hurt by a casual remark, and easily moved to tears. She had nightmares frequently. Looking back on her symptoms again, all of them could be regarded as a consequence of the thin boundary pictorialized in the Möbius tree. Leukemia, as it were, had left a big hole deep in her psyche, which might allow the contents that are usually retained in the mind to easily intrude into consciousness and overflow. I came to be able to understand her better through this image of the tree.

Later, others and I investigated the configuration of the trunk apex of Baum in different groups separately.[14] It was revealed that open-type apical termination, especially the Möbius type of processing, was used significantly more often, not only in patients with schizophrenia, cancer,[15] diabetes mellitus,[16] hyperthyroidism,[17] etc., but also normal people over the age of 70[18] and several African people.[19] In contrast, the Möbius tree was hardly or rarely found in groups of patients with dementia,[20] atopic dermatitis, and benign breast tumor and most normal people.

From a Jungian psychological perspective, the Möbius tree may be seen as a depiction of the vulnerability of the bulwark that prevents the contents of the collective unconscious from flowing into consciousness. This is suggested by

---

13 Hereafter, the picture of the tree drawn in the Baumtest will be called Baum.

14 N. Kishimoto, "Apical Termination in Baumtest and Blurred Outline Syndrome", Journal of Japanese Clinical Psychology 20, no. 1 (2002): 1–11.

15 N. Kishimoto, "Boundary in the Tree Test and Dream Recall", [presentation at the 30th Annual Conference of the International Association for the Study of Dreams, June 22, 2013].

16 M. Tomita, "Psychological characteristics of patients with diabetes in poor glycemic control", *Japanese journal of clinical psychology* 11, no. 6 (2011): 860–868.

17 M. Yamamori, "Basedou Byo Kanja no Shinrigakuteki Byotai ni tsuite (On the psychological characteristics of the patients with Basedow disease)", *Proceeding of the 17th Annual Conference of the Association of Japanese Clinical Psychology*, 546–547, 2013.

18 T. Kobayashi, "Aging study in Baumtest", *Psychiatria et Neurologia Japonica,* 92, no. 1 (1990): 22–58.

19 K. Hamano, T. Sugioka, "Jumokuga to Fudo (Baumtest and Climate)", *Clinical Practice of Baum* (*Baumu no Shinririnsho*), ed. Y. Yamanaka, (Osaka: Sogensha, 2004).

20 T. Kobayashi, "Aging study in Baumtest", *Psychiatria et Neurologia Japonica,* 92, no. 1 (1990): 22–58.

the relative prevalence of the Möbius tree in schizophrenic patients. As we can see from the actual drawing of the tree, the shape of the trunk tip is the most energy-intensive part of the process of drawing the tree. It takes a conscious effort to close the tip of the trunk, no matter what shape it is, but if you leave it open and don't care about it, it means that you have left a hole in your consciousness, so to speak, and because of this hole, it seems to me that the inside and outside of your mind are unconsciously connected to each other.

6 The Case of Mr. Land

Mr. Land (a pseudonym), a man in his 50s, was admitted to the hospital due to a relapse of lung cancer. He complained of serious insomnia and depressed mood and was referred to me. When I saw him for the first time, he repeatedly said, "I can't sleep at all. Please let me sleep." I sensed that his thought went round and round and got nowhere.

After listening to him for a while, I asked him to draw a tree. He stopped thinking and stayed silent for a while. Suddenly he seemed to come up with an image and slowly began to draw a tree. The Baum showed trunk and branch with their tips opened. Then I asked him to draw a landscape using ten items in the order I say. First, I asked him to draw a river, and he drew it. Second, a mountain, third, a rice field, and so on. This is a method called Landscape Montage Technique developed by Nakai. The picture shows that he could not anticipate and construct the one scene as a whole from the ten items. This means that his sight became extremely narrow. Despite being asked to draw a landscape with 10 items in advance, he couldn't think of anything other than the river when he was told to draw a river. As a result, items were drawn separately instead of building a landscape.

While I watched him draw the Baum and the landscape, I sensed that something changed within him. He seemed to start thinking about the image he had drawn. The image of the tree might have provided something to reflect on about himself. Then, he began to talk about his hometown. I arranged to see him once a week.

The next week, he seemed a little relieved and began to talk a lot. Gradually he relaxed. A month later, he said that he wanted to be a painter when he was young and started drawing again after the first session with me. He brought the picture he had just drawn and showed it to me. I was so surprised; I hardly imagined that he could draw so excellently. Cancer has the destructive power of breaking down patients physically and mentally. Consequently, even those who can draw well can draw only very poorly. The Baumtest and

Landscape Montage Technique might give him a medium to reintegrate himself. He recovered rapidly and was discharged. He was a leader of carpenters and returned to that work. He kept drawing. A few months later, he suddenly died of arrhythmia due to the cardiac invasion of lung cancer. Mr. Land taught that patients have the potential to recover from a severe hurt that generates the Möbius structure.

Susan Bach showed that the pictures drawn by seriously ill children, such as those with leukemia or brain tumors, can reveal not only their psychological features, but also the physical features of their diseases.[21] I admire her pioneering work, and I myself have experienced no small amount of unconsciousness manifestation of the body image in the Baumtest, in which images that implicate cancerous lesions are represented. However, rather than overemphasizing the sign aspect of the drawing, I am more interested in the therapeutic power that exists in the drawing itself, as Jung himself overcame a psychological crisis by painting a series of pictures, later called mandalas, in the midst of the crisis. The case of Mr. Land is a good example of this healing power of drawing.

7 The Case of Mrs. Light

Mrs. Light (a pseudonym), a 48-year-old woman, had an extraordinary experience that could be regarded as an extreme manifestation of the Möbius type of vulnerability. On May 1 of X, she was admitted to our hospital. She was a calm, middle-sized woman but looked exhausted because of anemia. She was diagnosed with acute myelogenous leukemia. Chemotherapy started the next day. On the night of admission, she had a dream of seeing a growing, small white light at the upper left corner. She felt that the light would save her. Chemotherapy was successful and resulted in complete remission.

Chemotherapy lasted for a year. Although complete remission was maintained, she became allergic to one of the key drugs of chemotherapy. We recommend bone marrow transplantation to her, and she agreed.

High doses of anticancer drugs were administered from August 21 to 26 of X+1. On August 27, she got utterly confused. She seemed obsessed with something and said,

> Why are there so many nurses? And Dr. A. Ah, he has disappeared. Look! I feel like being watched by many things, such as snakes, ghosts, monsters,

21 S. Bach, *Life paints its own span*, (Switzerland: Daimon, 1990).

> and so on. There were more beautiful images. Buddha prepared a chair for me and told me to sit down. I refused because I don't want to go there.

She seemed to forget herself, and I told her to take a rest. I gave her an intravenous drip of a sleeping drug. I stayed with her until she fell asleep.

The next day, the confusion continued. She said,

> Your face seems dreadful. The nurse and everything I see seem dreadful. I feel as if I have been watched all day. Why do I see so many things today? The baby face turns into an elder or scary one. I see. This is an experiment. You are watching me over there.

From a medical point of view, she was diagnosed with delirium. At the same time, from my experience of the Baumtest of cancer patients, I considered that the barrier deep in the psyche became so thin that the content of collective unconscious overflowed into her. So I tried to do two things at the same time. On the one hand, I administered sedative drugs for safety and watched over her objectively. On the other hand, metaphorically speaking, I dove into the world where she was so that she could feel that she was not alone.

On August 29, the day of bone marrow transplantation, her expression improved. I felt the lost soul returned to her. While she was receiving the donor's bone marrow cells in the clean room, she told me what she had experienced.

She said,

> Yesterday I did not know whether I was in reality or in dream. I did not feel your presence, and I just heard your voice. I hold a syringe for injection in the right hand and an intravenous drip in the left hand. The doctor repeats, 'Syringe, syringe, syringe, drip, drip, drip,' and I reply, 'I hold, I hold, I hold.' I walk around. I say goodbye one after another and go out. I sense flow, and I cannot resist it. A voice says that I should see the water falling from the high rocks. But I cannot see. For a moment I come across the entry of Paradise, but I am pushed back. Then I enter the cave. I feel like I'm in the stomach or intestine. The red and white stripes are arranged by turns to make two walls. I step into the passage between them, saying,'the correct direction or not?' I repeat, 'medicine, medicine, medicine and taken, taken, taken.' I came to an open space, and there is a doll in the shining light. It looks like Buddha. I am asked to draw the face, but I cannot. The doctor's voice of syringe and drip continues. At last I find an exit. When I come out, there is my brother's exit next to me. I think I have to wait for my brother there. Beside it there is a dome, and

> at the foot of it there is a hell. I am almost taken away, but I refuse because I must live. On this side of the river, doctors and nurses are saying, 'Come here.' A voice tells, 'Look at yourself.' I answer, 'I do not know how to do it.' A voice says,'Like this,' and then a lot of smiles and anger faces appear in the sky. A figure like Buddha appears and emits light and joins the palms together.

In this way, she told in detail what she had experienced immediately after recovering from the state that would be diagnosed as delirium. Her words left a strong impression on my mind. She recovered smoothly.

A year after the transplantation, she sent me a series of pictures depicting the experience. I was very moved by the fact that she kept the vision so vividly that she could draw a series of pictures even one year after the transplantation.

No. 1; there is no sound. The light was very bright. No. 2; there are faces in the air. No. 3; it is like a plastic container. No. 4; in the clean room, there is a bed and objects glittering with fluorescent lights. No. 5; the water flows, and she cannot resist it. No. 6; on the edge of the cliff. Concentrate! See the tip of the ribbon and fly into the air! No. 7; she goes forward into the tunnel with a syringe and a drip. No. 8; vertical stripes of red, yellow, and white. She felt as if she were in a blood vessel. No. 9; it is a doll like Buddha. What is transmigration? I am almost taken away.

She was completely cured from acute leukemia.

8 Death and Rebirth

We can recognize several traits that are said to be characteristic of a near-death experience:[22] a sense of peace, an out-of-body experience, a tunnel experience, an encounter with "the existence of Light," an approach to the border and the decision to return to your body by yourself or others. Thus I began to consider that bone marrow transplantation could be regarded as a process of death and rebirth.

For a deeper understanding of bone marrow transplantation, I will discuss the series of pictures of Rosarium Philosophorum[23] that Jung took up in his

22 R. A. Moody Jr., *Life after Life*, (CA: Mockingbird, 1975).

23 Due to the limited space, the series of pictures cannot be shown here, but they can be easily found on the Web.

"The Psychology of the Transference."[24] The series of pictures in the Rosarium can be regarded as an excellent depiction of what happened in the case of Mrs. Light.

Jung named the first picture of Rosarium Philosophorum the *Mercurial Fountain*. It depicts the secrets of alchemical work. The stars in the four corners represent the four elements, and the stars in the upper center signify the first and fifth elements arising from the four. The lower basin is an alchemical vessel, and on the rim of the fountain is written, "Unus est Mercurius mineralis, Mercurius vegetabilis, Mercurius animalis." (*Vegetabilis* should be translated as "living" and *animalis* as "animate" in the sense of having a soul, or even as "psychic.")[25] In modern medicine, intensive research at the in vitro and in vivo levels has contributed significantly to the realization of transplantation. At the level of minerals and plants, we have made tremendous progress. However, as Bosnak reported, heart transplant recipients have lost their minds, as it were, as they suffer from feelings of depersonalization after transplantation, or are frightened by recurring nightmares and ghosts, even though their bodies have been saved by the transplantation.[26] Transplant medicine requires all three of these pillars: minerals, plants, and animals.

The top center depicts the sun and the moon, and the two-headed serpent above it has two smoking columns. There are conflicts in transplantation: recipient and donor, mind and body, healthy and diseased parts; Jung recognized the "axiom of Maria" in this progression from the number 4 to 3 to 2 to 1, and the creation of the therapeutic space and the therapeutic process are cohesive here.

In the second picture, a king and a queen appear, and Edinger points out that the primordial chaos seen in the first picture was split into two persons, light and darkness, which shows the budding of consciousness, as well as a similarity to the Annunciation.[27] Behind the telling of the diagnosis there is the idea of the Annunciation, but what has descended into the patient's body is a leukemia. Edinger reminds us that such an announcement is not happy news, but rather the notification of a difficult process, and this is true in the case of Mrs. Light. Furthermore, Edinger identifies this dove with the serpent of temptation in the Garden of Eden. We need to reflect on whether we are

---

24 C. G. Jung, "Psychology of the transference", in: *The Collected Works*, v. 16, ed. G. Adler, trans. R.F.C. Hull, (Princeton: Princeton University Press, 1985. Originally published in 1946).

25 Ibidem, 402.

26 R. Bosnak, "Integration and Ambivalence in Transplants", in: *Trauma and Dreams*, ed. D. Barrett, (Cambridge: Harvard University Press, 1996).

27 E. Edinger, *The Mystery of the Coniunctio*, (Toronto: Inner City Books, 1994).

tempting our patients easily by saying that transplantation will save you. Also, the union of the left hand seen in this picture indicates that it is an ominous, unconscious union. The left is also the side of the heart, from which not only love, but also malice, which is morally against human nature, is born. Although bone marrow transplants cannot be performed without an HLA (white blood cell type) match, it is extremely important to recognize the fatalistic and transcendent aspects beyond the human intent at work in transplantation.

What is noteworthy in the third picture is that words have arisen.[28] The stars seen in the second picture have disappeared, but they are not yet grounded. This corresponds to the time when Mrs. Light, who had been overwhelmed by images of lights, ghosts, and monsters immediately after her hospitalization, began to relax and began to tell her own story.

The fourth picture is the descent into the bath. On a physical level, it would correspond to the administration of large doses of anticancer drugs to annihilate both normal and pathological white blood cells, leaving them unprotected. The theme of this picture is dissolution. Edinger sees here the dissolution of the old ego,[29] which is often accompanied by great fear. It is possible to think that Mrs. Light's delusions on the day before transplantation, especially the frightening looks on the faces of her doctor and nurse, reflect her fear of lysis.

The fifth picture is the union, which is essentially an invisible process in water, but we are peeking in through a little window cut through the wall of the basin. According to Edinger, a short circuit to the first picture often occurs here.[30] In other words, even if the union is achieved, as the later diagrams show, if there is no reincarnation after death, the same thing will happen again. Even after transplantation, if death and rebirth are not sufficiently accomplished psychologically, the situation will revert to the first picture as shown in the Bosnak case. Forced union alone is not the solution.

Death comes in the sixth picture, which Edinger relates to the fifth picture's composition of peering into the process of invisibility, stating that it's an insight that can literally kill.[31] Confronting the negative aspect, one's own shadow, would be psychologically experienced as death. The experience of death is extremely important, with the difference that it is experienced as one's own death in bone marrow transplantation, whereas in heart transplantation it is projected in the form of the donor's death. When I look back on my experiences with bone marrow transplants, I am reminded of the fact that each of

28 Ibidem, 50.
29 Ibidem, 54.
30 Ibidem, 65–66.
31 Ibidem, 68.

these patients has gone through a place of death in one way or another, and as Bosnak remarks, we cannot remain the same after a transplant. We have to die to be born again.

The themes from seventh picture onwards are the ascent of the soul, purification, the return of the soul, and the new birth. This corresponds to Mrs. Light's itinerary of the soul on the day of the bone marrow transplant. Transplantation creates a new psychological amalgam, and the series of pictures in the Rosarium illustrates this process well.

The treatment of transplantation is not a treatment that removes the diseased part of the body and restores it to its former health, but rather a treatment that suffers death and rebirth. Therefore, the medical profession must be prepared to be involved in the process of death and rebirth, rather than trying to remove the bad parts of the body as if they were repairing a broken machine. While Jung found the essence of transference and countertransference in the Rosarium pictures, we could also recognize that they offer a different therapeutic paradigm to transplant medicine to the traditional "removal" of diseased parts.

FIGURE 1
Baum (a picture of tree) by Mrs. White. With favor of Mrs. White

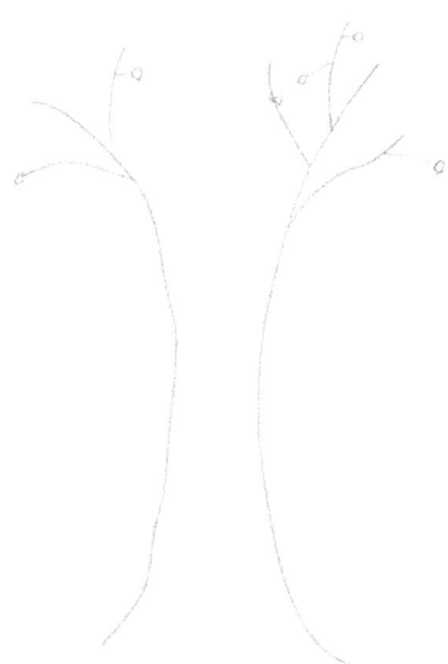

FIGURE 2
Möbius tree. No permission needed.

9 Conclusion

Jung differentiated between the personal unconscious and the collective unconscious.[32] According to the idea, the ego is protected by, as it were, a double wall. If the barrier between the ego and the personal unconscious is preserved, some degree of ego integrity is maintained. However, in the case of cancer patients, the defense in the depth, or the defense between the personal and collective unconscious, is often weakened or broken down in some places. As a result, unconscious contents easily penetrate into the personal unconscious, which prepares the condition that a few words can make emotions overflow or words have unexpected meanings by phonological association. The Möbius tree is a form of visualization of such a situation.

However, because most cancer patients previously had a normal social life, they also have the potential to recover from it, as the case of Mr. Land demonstrated, even if they had a strong impact from suffering from cancer. Nonetheless, the Möbius tree indicates that if you do not pay attention to the state that the defense is weakened deep in the mind, even if you are in good faith, you may hurt the patient. The Baumtest not only tells the state of the patients, but also helps heal their minds. The case of Mrs. White illustrates that drawing a tree invites narratives and triggers a new story. The Baum functions as a hook of projection and becomes a mirror wherein the patients look back on themselves. Mrs. Light fell into extreme mental confusion just before the bone marrow transplantation. Medically, she was diagnosed with delirium, but even in such circumstances, it was demonstrated that patients subjectively might have a significant experience. Jungian psychology paved the way for bone marrow transplantation to be considered as a process of death and rebirth. It gives valuable tips for understanding such subjective experiences. The cases presented here are good examples of how Jung's idea can be applied in the field of contemporary cancer treatment.

References

Bach S., *Life paints its own span*, Switzerland: Daimon, 1990.

Bosnak R., "Integration and Ambivalence in Transplants", in: *Trauma and Dreams*. ed. D. Barrett, Cambridge: Harvard University Press, 1996.

Edinger E., *The Mystery of the Coniunctio*, Toronto: Inner City Books, 1994.

32 C. G. Jung, "The Relations between the Ego and the Unconscious", in: *The Collected Works*, v. 7, ed. G. Adler, trans. R.F.C. Hull, § 437–507. (Princeton: Princeton University Press, 1953. Originally published in 1916).

Fujioka Y., Yoshikawa, K., "Jinruigakuteki ni mita baumu niyoru imeiji no hyogen" (Image Representation of Baum from the anthropological point of view)", *Kikan Jinruigaku (Quarterly Anthropology)*, 2, vol. 3 (1971): 3–28.

"Global, Regional, and National Cancer Incidence, Mortality, Years of Life Lost, Years Lived With Disability, and Disability-Adjusted Life-Years for 29 Cancer Groups, 1990 to 2016. A Systematic Analysis for the Global Burden of Disease Study." *JAMA Oncology* 4, no. 11 (2018): 1553–68.

Hamano K., Sugioka T., "Jumokuga to Fudo (Baumtest and Climate)", in: *Clinical Practice of Baum (Baumu no Shinririnsho)*, ed. Y. Yamanaka, Osaka: Sogensha, 2004.

Jung C.G., "The Relations between the Ego and the Unconscious", in: *The Collected Works*, v. 7, G. Adler (ed.), trans. R.F.C. Hull, §§ 437–507, Princeton: Princeton University Press, 1953. [Originally published in 1916].

Jung C.G., "Psychology of the transference", in: *The Collected Works*, v. 16, G. Adler (ed.), trans. R.F.C. Hull, Princeton: Princeton University Press, 1985. [Originally published in 1946].

Kishimoto N., *Gan to Shinriryoho (Cancer and Psychotherapy)*, Tokyo: Seishin Shobo, 1999.

Kishimoto N., "Apical Termination in Baumtest and Blurred Outline Syndrome", Journal of Japanese Clinical Psychology 20, no. 1 (2002): 1–11.

Kishimoto N., "Boundary in the Tree Test and Dream Recall", presentation at the 30th Annual Conference of the International Association for the Study of Dreams, June 22, 2013.

Kishimoto N., *Baumutesuto Nyumon (Introduction to the Baumtest)*, Tokyo: Seishin Shobo, 2015.

Kobayashi T., "Aging study in Baumtest", *Psychiatria et Neurologia Japonica* 92, no. 1 (1990): 22–58.

Koch K., *Der Baum-test*, Bern: Hans Huber, 1949.

Koch K., *Der Baumtest, zweite Auflage*, Bern: Hans Huber, 1954.

Koch K., *Der Baumtest, dritte Auflage*, Bern: Hans Huber, 1957.

Koch K., *Baumutesuto (Der Baum-test)*, trans. K. Hayashi, M. Kuniyoshi, T. Ichitani, Tokyo: Nihon Bunka Kagakusha, 1970.

Koch K., *Baumutesuto Dai Sanpan (Der Baumtest, dritte Auflage)*, Trans. N. Kishimoto, N. Nakashima, T. Miyazaki, Tokyo: Seishin Shobo, 2010.

Moody R. A. Jr., *Life after Life*, CA: Mockingbird, 1975.

Tomita M., "Psychological characteristics of patients with diabetes in poor glycemic control", *Japanese journal of clinical psychology* 11, no. 6 (2011):860–868.

Yamamori M., "Basedou Byo Kanja no Shinrigakuteki Byotai ni tsuite (On the psychological characteristics of the patients with Basedow disease)", *Proceeding of the 17th Annual Conference of the Association of Japanese Clinical Psychology*, 546–547, 2013.

Yamanaka Y., "Seishinbunretsubyo ni okeru baumutesuto no kenkyu (Study of Baumtest of Schizophrenic patients)", *Shinri sokutei jahnaru(Psychometric journal)*. 12, v. 4 (1976): 18–23.

CHAPTER 13

Return to Indigenous Art Forms: Potential for Healing

Josefa Bayes-King[†]

Abstract

In a pre-verbal society, the body was the pen and paper. This paper addresses issues of how different cultures manifest psychological issues at the collective and individual levels, with a focus on the role of dance as a means of deep communication. Indigenous Australians embrace the collective, traditionally gathering together with their tribe or "mob" for both celebrations and mourning, whereas Western psychology has focused upon the individual. Dancers such as Mary Starks Whitehouse and Martha Graham, who analyzed with Jung, incorporated his work into their creativity, including aspects of active imagination. Indeed, Martha Graham found that dance provided body/mind healing for those who had been traumatized by war and rape. The central theme of dance as an important and primal form of communication is further elaborated in the context of Indigenous Australians, who developed complex means of communication based on dance, which were passed on through generations and transcended barriers of oral language. One of the advantages of dance is the ability to combine and adapt patterns of expression dependent on context, including emotional nuance and response to current environmental or societal circumstances. Over the past 200 years into the present, many Indigenous communities and individuals have suffered various trauma and loss of soul as a result of the principle and reality of White Australia. These fundamental human means of expression are accessible to modern societies but require guidance in their interpretation and assignment of meaning, particularly in relation to structured description of unconscious responses to the complexities of contemporary life.

Keywords

Jung, trauma, dance, collective, Indigenous culture

 | DOI:10.1163/9789004468757_015

1 Introduction

Recent history has reminded us that dance transcends geographic, cultural, and linguistic boundaries. This has manifested in various forms during the current COVID-19 pandemic. Perhaps more poignantly, following the 2019 mass murders in Christchurch, New Zealand, that targeted a single community, a spontaneous and prevalent response confirmed the power of the collective, with dance specifically providing the most powerful form of communication within the multicultural population, demonstrating its value as a medium for healing and bonding. The Haka is the traditional Maori ceremonial dance, these days most widely associated with the New Zealand rugby team, and was observed being performed unprompted as the natural response throughout the country in the days following the shootings.[1] The Haka has evolved within New Zealand as increasingly diverse cultures have integrated into the modern population, and it is taught to all school children from an early age. This gift from the Indigenous Maori has allowed it to be adopted without concerns of cultural appropriation.[2] It was originally performed only by men who were about to go to a war from which they might not return and was therefore regarded seriously as a possible last rite, as well as a means of providing collective energy for the man to perform whatever was required of him, even unto death.

2 The Individual and the Collective

Indigenous Australians traditionally gather together with their tribe or "mob" for both celebrations and mourning. Funerals are very intricate and conform to a specific ritual particular to the specific tribe.[3] In some communities, the mourners must present themselves in a specific order, based upon the relationship to the deceased, and cry in public. In Ballina, in the Northern Rivers area of New South Wales, the mourners do not follow this practice, but all present and cry as a collective.

In contrast, Western psychology has focused upon the individual rather than the collective. Jungian psychology, in keeping with most Western traditions, has focused upon a face-to-face interaction based largely upon the spoken word. However, Jung recognized the importance of the collective unconscious and encouraged his analysands to share dreams and experiment with art

1 Maxwell, Te Kahatau, quoted in *The Straits Times*, March 19th, 2019.
2 *Te Ara. Encyclopedia of New Zealand*, https://teara.govt.nz/en.
3 *Death and Sorry Business*, https://www.commonground.org.au/learn/death-and-sorry-business.

forms.[4] Dance did not feature in his own psychology, although he recognized the role of dance in Indigenous cultures, including the Wachandi of Australia[5] and the Taos Pueblo.[6] As an intuitive type, he experienced the inferior function through art and clay modeling. In her paper on the Inferior Function, von Franz notes:[7]

> The rare form of dancing I have usually seen is when feeling is the fourth function. Sometimes thinking types, when they have to assimilate their feeling function, have a genuine wish to express it by dancing in certain primitive rhythms.

3 Professional Dancers

Many dancers, most notably Martha Graham, who was one of the foremost pioneers of modern dance, analyzed with Jung and incorporated his work into their creativity. Miss Graham said: "There are always ancestral footsteps behind me, pushing me, pushing me when I am creating a new dance, and gestures are flowing through me."[8] This appears to be a concept that Westerners need to relearn. Another pioneer, Mary Starks Whitehouse, analyzed with Jung and then took dance classes with Martha Graham, from whence she moved on to develop a branch of active imagination, which she named Authentic Movement.[9,10] She specialized particularly in using this form with people who had been traumatized by war and/or rape. This provided body/mind healing, regardless of the ethnicity of the patient.

4 L. van der Post, *Jung and the story of our time*, (New York: Pantheon, Random House, 1975).

5 C. G. Jung, *The Collected Works*, H. Read, M. Fordham, G. Adler, W. McGuire (eds.), trans. R. F. C. Hull, v. 8 § 83, (London: Routledge, 1973).

6 Ibidem § 86.

7 M.-L. von Franz, *The inferior function*, in: *Lectures on Jung's typology*, eds. M.-L. von Franz and J. Hillman, (Woodstock, CT: Spring Publications, 1989), 77.

8 M. Graham, *Blood Memory: An autobiography*, (New York: Doubleday), 1991.

9 M. Starks Whitehouse, *Physical Movement and Personality (1963)*, in: *Authentic Movement: A Collection of Essays by Mary Starks Whitehouse, Janet Adler & Joan Chodrow*, ed. P. Pallaro, (London: J. Kingsley, 1999), 51–57.

10 M. H. S. Farah, "Jung's active imagination in Whitehouse's dance: notions of body and movement", *Psicologia USP*, 27(3) (2016): 542–552.

4 Dance as an Important Form of Communication

In certain Indigenous cultures in Australia, dance was a primal form of communication because each individual tribe had its own spoken language, and they needed to migrate according to the seasons. Therefore, individual tribes used specific dance forms in order to communicate with each other and between tribes.[11] This was particularly important in the Northern Territories, which is desert land and was populated by many different tribes who all had their own languages, hence the need to communicate nonverbally regarding sources of food.[12] They formulated certain routines, primarily to indicate sources of food. These were important and extremely intricate because it was often the case that it was a dry season and that people needed to walk a long way, sometimes for many days, without sustenance. Dance was therefore an extremely practical way of communication regarding location and sources of food and safe water. There was no GPS back then!

5 Evolution of Dance from Communication to Celebration

Once the various semi-nomadic tribes became sufficiently comfortable in their temporary environment to establish a settlement, they needed to communicate with other tribes who used a different verbal language. As has been recognized elsewhere, dance was an effective means of approach,[13] signifying whether they came in peace or war. If in peace, many times intermarriage took place, and bonds between communities were formed. This was especially important in the desert regions.

6 Diversity within Australia

Within individual communities, dance, music, and visual art became adopted as a major form of spiritual expression. Amongst the Bundjalung people in what is now northern New South Wales, food was plentiful, and the tribes

---

11 F. Sharifian, "Cultural conceptualisations in intercultural communication: a study of Aboriginal and non-Aboriginal Australians", *Journal of Pragmatics* 42, (2010): 3367–3376.

12 M. C. Ross, "Australian Aboriginal oral traditions", *Oral Tradition* 1, (1986): 231–271.

13 V. E. Sanchez, "Intertribal dance and cross-cultural communication: Traditional pow-wows in Ohio", *Communication Studies* 52(1), (2009): 51–69.

mostly collaborated in order to celebrate and mourn. This was a collective activity, although the genders were distinguished with selected dances and musical instruments designed as the property associated with either men or women. This was not a question of discrimination but of specific functions. The males were better equipped to go out and hunt, whilst the women were often gestating or lactating, but could work around the home and the garden.

7 Loss of Soul in Indigenous Males

There was considerable diversity in terms of spiritual activities that evolved within different Indigenous communities, where males and females also had different roles to play. Young males were taken into the bush with older males in order to be initiated into manhood, after which they could not be with young females until marriage.[14]

Many Aboriginal Australians have suffered various trauma as a result of the principle and reality of White Australia. Indigenous communities have been traumatized by the invasion of the "white fella," to the extent that children were snatched from parents. This resulted in Aboriginal children being torn away from their families in what has become recognized as "the Stolen Generation."[15] Their identity is also precarious and confronted by the fact that at the first outbreeding generation, their appearance is often closer to white. This is a genetic phenomenon not yet fully understood.[16]

Most of those who were deemed to pass as white were sent to a white family and told that they were not black. These children were forbidden to speak their own language, although they often communicated secretly through dance. In a pre-verbal society, the ***body was the pen and paper***.

In contemporary Australia, many Indigenous people have lost their culture due to forcible abduction and/or assimilation from intermarriage. This has often led to a loss of soul and unawareness of one's place in the world.[17]

---

14 G. Curran, "The 'Expanding Domain' of Warlpiri Initiation Rituals", in: *Ethnography & the Production of Anthropological Knowledge. Essays in honour of Nicolas Peterson,* eds. Y. Musharbash, M. Barber, (Canberra: ANU Press, 2011).

15 C. Bird, *The Stolen Children: their stories,* (New York: Random House, 1998).

16 R. R. Gates, "The genetics of the Australian aborigines", *Acta geneticae medicae et gemellologiae: twin research,* 9(1), (1960): 7–50.

17 J. Atkinson, *Trauma trails: recreating songlines.* (Geelong: Spinfex Press, 2002).

Although this is by no means confined to Aboriginal Australians, the problem has been recognized and programs established to address this.[18]

Jung felt that everyone should be connected with their ancestral land[19]—in Australian Indigenous idiom "with Country."

8 We Al-Li

There are examples in which Indigenous communities have been healed by rediscovering aspects of their heritage. Programs have been established by people such as Prof. Judy Atkinson, who herself is an Indigenous Australian—in order to use dance, music, and art to help bring people back to their roots.[20] However, these programs are nonexclusive, are open to white fellas, and represent an opportunity to return to the psycho-social roots of Australia. This helps form a sense of healing for all who live here and feel an association with the Land.

For one particular group of workshopscalled *We Al-Li*, which means "fire and water," there is immersion in Country, coming together as a collective—sharing dance forms, music, clay modeling, finger-painting, and art—all expressions of the unconscious. In the evening there is opportunity to share in the process of talking about dreams around the fire—a very primal experience. These workshops, based on Indigenous principles, are also a locus for a wider sense of healing, bringing together both White fellas and Indigenous peoples.[20]

Mary Whitehouse stated that in her practice, women were more receptive than were men with regard to using dance as a form of active imagination.[21] However, in the Australian workshops the reverse appears to be true. Aboriginal men have suffered more than have women from loss of culture. The women continue to maintain the home and the children and often take action within the broader community. Many of the men are uneducated and unable

18 *Council for Aboriginal Reconciliation. Walking together: the first steps. Report to Federal Parliament*, Canberra: Australian Government Publishing Service, 1994.

19 C. G. Jung, *The Collected Works*, eds. H. Read, M. Fordham, G. Adler, W. McGuire, trans. R. F. C. Hull, vol. 12 § 171, (London: Routledge, 1973).

20 J. Atkinson, "Recreating the Circle with We Al-Li: A program for healing sharing and regeneration", *Aboriginal and Islander Health Worker Journal*, 18(6), (1994): 8–13.

21 M. Starks Whitehouse, *Physical Movement and Personality (1963)*, in: *Authentic Movement: A Collection of Essays by Mary Starks Whitehouse, Janet Adler & Joan Chodrow*, ed. P. Pallaro, (London: J. Kingsley, 1999, 51–57).

to provide for their families. Relearning some of the dances related to war or to hunting has been a true release for them.[22]

In principle, Jungians who explore the unconscious could benefit greatly from the Indigenous traditions associated with Country. In the context of Indigenous rituals, Jung cited the example of *yaibichy* dances that represented healing ceremonies for the Navaho in Arizona.[23] However, many Indigenous people have also lost their spiritual base, and so there is opportunity for all cultures to learn from each other.

There are key differences in the way in which Western psychology is applied from an individualistic perspective, compared to the collective manner in which trauma is confronted and healing is managed in Indigenous communities. We Al-Li is a useful tool that combines both and that also allows cultures to learn from each other.

9 Conclusion

Over millennia, Indigenous cultures have used dance, music, and visual art as a means to express complex and deep thoughts associated with the unconscious. Various forms of visual representation have developed, using different media, that are able to communicate and contribute to developing conscious, unconscious, and emotional thoughts. For Australian Indigenous peoples, various forms of the visual medium developed in which were embedded a formalized figurative language. This is seen in ancient examples of rock art that have survived to the current time.[24] These can embody complex cognitive networks from the ancestral generations, which are revered today both for their spiritual content and more prosaically as roadmaps. Likewise, dance transcends and pre-dates oral linguistic boundaries, with the body representing both pen and paper. Australian Indigenous peoples developed complex means of communication based on dance, which were passed on through generations. One of the advantages of dance is the ability to combine and adapt patterns of expression dependent on context, including emotional nuance and response to current environmental or societal circumstances. These fundamental human

22 V. J. Atkinson, J. Graham, G. Pettit, L. Lewis, "Broadening the focus of research into health of Indigenous Australians", *The Medical Journal of Australia*, 177(6), (2002): 286–287.

23 C. G. Jung, *The Collected Works*, H. Read, M. Fordham, G. Adler, W. McGuire (eds.), trans. R. F. C. Hull, v. 18 § 1225, (London: Routledge, 1976).

24 R. Layton, "The Cultural Context of Hunter-Gatherer Rock Art" *Man* (*New Series*), 20(3), (1985): 434–453.

means of expression are accessible to modern societies but require guidance in their interpretation and assignment of meaning, particularly in relation to structured description of unconscious responses to the complexities of contemporary life.

References

Atkinson J., "Recreating the Circle with We Al-Li: A program for healing sharing and regeneration", *Aboriginal and Islander Health Worker Journal* 18(6), (1994): 8–13.

Atkinson J., *Trauma trails: recreating songlines*, Geelong: Spinifex Press, 2002.

Atkinson, V. J., Graham J., Pettit G., and Lewis, L. *Broadening the focus of research into health of Indigenous Australians*. The Med. J. Aust. v. 177. No.6, (2002): 286–287.

Bird C. *The Stolen Children: their stories*, New York: Random House, 1998.

Common Ground. Death and Sorry Business, https://www.commonground.org.au/learn/death-and-sorry-business.

Council for Aboriginal Reconciliation. Walking together: the first steps. Report to Federal Parliament, Canberra: Australian Government Publishing Service, 1994.

Curran G., "The 'Expanding Domain' of Warlpiri Initiation Rituals", in: *Ethnography & the Production of Anthropological Knowledge. Essays in honour of Nicolas Peterson*, eds. Y. Musharbash, M. Barber, Canberra: ANU Press, 2011.

Farah M.H.S., "Jung's active imagination in Whitehouse's dance: notions of body and movement", *Psicologia USP*, vol. 27, no. 3. (2016): 542–552.

von Franz M-L., *The inferior function. In. Lectures on Jung's typology*, by M.-L. von Franz and J. Hillman, Woodstock, CT: Spring Publications, 1989.

Gates R.R., "The genetics of the Australian aborigines", *Acta geneticae medicae et gemellologiae: twin research*, 9(1), (1960): 7–50.

Graham M., *Blood Memory: An autobiography*, New York: Doubleday, 1991.

Jung C.G., *The Collected Works*, H. Read, M. Fordham, G. Adler, W. McGuire (eds.), trans. R. F. C. Hull, v. 8, London: Routledge, 1973.

Jung C.G., *The Collected Works*, H. Read, M. Fordham, G. Adler, W. McGuire (eds.), trans. R. F. C. Hull, v. 12, London: Routledge, 1973.

Jung C.G., *The Collected Works*, H. Read, M. Fordham, G. Adler, W. McGuire (eds.), trans. R. F. C. Hull, v. 18, London: Routledge, 1976.

Layton R., "The Cultural Context of Hunter-Gatherer Rock Art", *Man* (*New Series*) 20(3), (1985): 434–453.

The Straits Times, March 19th, 2019.

Post van der, L., *Jung and the Story of Our Time,* New York: Pantheon, Random House, 1975.

Ross M.C., "Australian Aboriginal oral traditions", *Oral Tradition* 1, (1986): 231–271.

Sanchez V.E., "Intertribal dance and cross-cultural communication: Traditional pow-wows in Ohio", *Communication Studies*, 52(1), (2009): 51–69.

Sharifian F., "Cultural conceptualisations in intercultural communication: a study of Aboriginal and non-Aboriginal Australians", *Journal of Pragmatics*, 42, (2010): 3367–3376.

Starks Whitehouse M., *Physical Movement and Personality (1963)*, in: *Authentic Movement: A Collection of Essays by Mary Starks Whitehouse, Janet Adler & Joan Chodrow*, ed. P. Pallaro, London: J. Kingsley, 1999.

Te Ara Encyclopedia of New Zealand, https://teara.govt.nz/en.

CHAPTER 14

Erich Neumann's Great Mother, André Green's Dead Mother, and Ecopsychology

Lidar Shany

Abstract

Based on Erich Neumann's perception of the archetypal nature of human psychological development, which indicates the affinity between the collective and the individual, this paper suggests the creation of an ecopsychological cultural complex based on what we understand about an individual's psychology.

The paper will synthesize Neumann's writings about the Feminine and the Earth archetype and his theory about children's psychological development with André Green's notion of the dead mother complex. Doing so, this paper will suggest an ecopsychological perspective through which the development of consciousness in Western culture led to a bias toward the patriarchy and the masculine, which created a collective experience of alienation from nature and a deprivation of the feminine qualities of containment, nourishment, and relatedness. This paper will also suggest that Western culture's alienation from nature is experienced as a deprivation of the love of Great Mother Earth and thus forms a cultural complex of the dead mother and its central pathology as a loss of meaning, which calls for ecopsychological healing.

Keywords

Archetype, Earth, ecopsychology, ego-Self axis, dead mother complex, Feminine, Great Mother, *participation mystique*, primal relationship, uroboros

1 Introduction

Leading ecopsychologist Andy Fisher, in his book *Radical Ecopsychology*, wrote that it is only the modern and Western mind that needed and created the discipline of ecopsychology. Indigenous and aboriginal people, who lead their lives in reciprocal relation with the natural world, do not need it. He described the task of ecopsychology: to present and describe the human psyche as a natural

 | DOI:10.1163/9789004468757_016

phenomenon, within nature and an integral part of the natural world. Fisher also states ecopsychology's vision as "that of humans healing and flourishing in concert with the healing and flourishing of the larger natural world, in one great celebration of life."[1] This indicates ecopsychology to be both a perspective of living and a perspective of healing souls, personal, and as this paper will show, collective.

Although the term *ecopsychology* was coined by Theodore Roszak in 1992, the foundation for a psycho-ecologically oriented theory may be found in Jung's thought in the early 20th century, when the notion of an earth-spirit was first put forth by Jung: "The earth has a spirit of her own."[2] The idea of the earth-spirit was further elaborated by Erich Neumann, Jung's most promising disciple, as expressed in various of his writings, particularly in the article "The Meaning of the Earth Archetype for Modern Times."[3] Neumann used the symbolism of the "first parents" to establish the connection between the Earth and the feminine and theorized that man's patriarchal perspective, which overemphasized consciousness and spirit, diminished the Feminine unconscious, and thus matter and earth, as if it were spiritless. Neumann indicated that this perspective of earth as concrete and spiritless leads modern man to a sense of deprivation from meaning, which becomes pathological.

Traces of Jung's psycho-ecological perspective are also found in the way he described his travels around the world as an expedition, of which he wrote: "The purpose of my travels was not to investigate only the differences, but also the similarities between the civilized and the primitive mind."[4] In these words, Jung expressed a vital aspect of his theory, referring to the archaic sphere alive in modern man's psyche, known in Jung's theory as the archetypal realm. Theorizing that modern man's psyche holds the archaic imprints within it, Jung compared the nature of the archaic and modern man's relationship to the land, and he pointed to the advantage he believed primitive man had over modern man. He wrote:

1 A. Fisher, *Radical Ecopsychology: Psychology in the Service of Life* (Albany: State University of New York Press, 2002), XIV.

2 Th. Roszak, *The Voice of the Earth: An Exploration of Ecopsychology* (Grand Rapids, MI: Phanes Press, 2001); C. G. Jung, from *The Visions Seminars Zurich*, cited by Meredith Sabini, ed., *The Earth Has a Soul: C. G. Jung on Nature, Technology and Modern Life* (Berkeley, CA: North Atlantic Books, 2008), 2.

3 E. Neumann, "The Meaning of the Earth Archetype for Modern Times," in *The Fear of the Feminine and Other Essays on Feminine Psychology* (Princeton, NJ: Princeton University Press, 1994).

4 C. G. Jung, "A Radio Talk in Munich," in *The Symbolic Life*, v. 18, *The Collected* Works, (Princeton, NJ: Princeton University Press, 1976), § 1290.

> Thus does primitive man dwell in his land and at the same time in the land of his unconscious. Everywhere his unconscious jumps out at him, alive and real. How different is our relationship to the land we dwell in! Feelings totally strange to us accompany the primitive at every step.[5]

Jung understood and recognized the psychological importance of closeness to nature, body, and soul. He therefore stressed that archaic man's closeness to nature manifested in his closeness to his psychic nature, rather than being estranged to it. Accordingly, Neumann—while theorizing ego-conscious' development—described the initial stages of human consciousness' development as a phase of *participation mystique* of humans and nature. The term *participation mystique*, which Jung and then Neumann borrowed from Lévy-Bruhl, refers to the relationship between both, mother and baby and humankind and earth, and expresses the experience of oneness and unity of humans and nature.[6]

Neumann elaborated Jung's assertion that the unconscious is Feminine and theorized that the archetypal Feminine is the core from which all later psychological development proceeds and from which the archetype of the Great Mother Earth emerges.[7] Neumann, in his theory, maintained a constant movement between the personal and the collective when he denoted both the psychological development and its possible disturbances to the close affinity between the two layers that coexist within psychic reality, the personal and the archetypal. As an implication of this perspective he wrote, "Ontogenetic development may … be regarded as a modified recapitulation of phylogenetic development."[8] Therefore, his description of the development of an individual's consciousness relies on world mythology as a way to describe the development of humanity's consciousness. Neumann theorized that in the initial stages of conscious development, at the dawn of humanity as well as of personality, mother represents the world, and the natural world is the mother of all things. For the human child, the relationship with the personal mother becomes a prototype of its relationship with the world, and thus with nature, as there is yet no differentiation between inner and outer worlds. Neumann explained that as humanity's consciousness

5 C. G. Jung, "The Role of the Unconscious," in *Civilization in Transition*, v. 10, *The Collected Works*, (Princeton, NJ: Princeton University Press, 1964), § 44.

6 C. G. Jung, "The Relations between the Ego and the Unconscious," in *Two Essays on Analytical Psychology*, v. 7, *The Collected Works*, (Princeton, NJ: Princeton University Press, 1972), 206.

7 C. G. Jung, "Symbols and the Interpretation of Dreams," in *The Symbolic Life*, v. 18, *The Collected Works*, (Princeton, NJ: Princeton University Press, 1976), para. 484; E. Neumann, *The Great Mother*, trans. R. Manheim (Princeton, NJ: Princeton University Press, 1991), 18–23.

8 E. Neumann, *The Origins and History of Consciousness*, trans. R. F. C. Hull, (Princeton, NJ: Princeton University Press, 2014), xx.9.

developed, and man was able to scientifically explain the phenomenon of rain or fire, rather than perceiving them through projection, he gradually differentiated himself from nature, and consequently from his unconscious femininity. Therefore, it is suggested that Western culture's alienation from nature, and thus from human nature, became a collective experience of deprivation from what was previously a maternal containing experience and a *participation mystique* with the natural world, and thus it manifests as an eco-psychological wound. Here we will use the same movement laid down by Neumann between the personal and the collective to describe a cultural complex based on psychoanalysis's understandings of individual's psychology and pathology. Holding a Jungian archetypal perspective, and examining the issue through the lens of Neumann's theoretical stance, the dead mother complex, coined and described by André Green as a complex created under the mother's emotional withdrawal within her positive relationship with her baby, may be seen as Western culture's archetypal wounding, calling for ecopsychological healing.

2 An Overview of Neumann's Formulation of Archetypal Development

Neumann's theory describes the archetypal stages of psychological development as well as the archetypal psychic structure that is a result of the fulfillment of each of these stages. He asserted that human psychological development, as well as humankind's conscious development, proceeds and progresses inherently while it follows the path of archetypal stages. Each stage of conscious development is anchored in and stems from an archetypal layer, which is, in Neumann's terms, a "world related" in the sense that each archetypal layer comprises a field of relatedness, that is, the preconditioned perspective through which the world is perceived.[9] Neumann also emphasized that the sequence of the layers is nonreversible, from the uroboros to the archetype of the Great Mother as the matriarchate, followed by the archetype of the Great Father as the patriarchate; the uroboros is always prior to the matriarchate, which in turn is always preceded by the patriarchate.[10] The progression between the stages ensures a natural and healthy development of psychic structure, which was theorized by Neumann as a progression of the ego from an initial ego germ, through

9 E. Neumann, *The Child: Structure and Dynamics of the Nascent Personality* (London: Karnac Books, 1973), 84.

10 E. Neumann, "The Significance of the Genetic Aspect for Analytical Psychology," *Journal of Analytical Psychology* 4, no. 2 (1959): 125–37, 128.

several developmental stages, to finally become an independent integral ego.[11] The transformation of the Self, which initially is experienced by the baby only as body-self (while the functional, relatedness aspect of the self is deposited with and carried by the mother), gradually becomes a unitary Self.[12] As an implication of the layered base structured and based on Jung's differentiation between the archetype as such and the archetypal image, Neumann theorized that the deeper the layer is, the older it is in time, and the younger it is in development and thus less differentiated. Therefore, the archetype as such is the deepest and oldest layer, which is the youngest on the conscious developmental line, and therefore it is preconscious and not perceivable.[13] Neumann called this layer a "purely effective phenomenon," meaning it is sensory and affects but is not perceivable by the conscious.[14] The first layer Neumann described is the uroboros, in which no differentiation yet exists and the world parents are still united. As consciousness develops, the archetype gradually becomes a perceivable image by the phenomenon of the opposites, and accordingly, the first differentiation that humankind's conscious was able to perceive is that of the world parents, described in myth as the opposites of Sky and Earth.[15] Therefore, the archetypal Feminine is the first partially perceivable archetypal layer. As consciousness grows, and further differentiation is enabled, the archetypal Feminine differentiates into more specific archetypes. First, it becomes the image of the Great Mother Earth, then differentiates to the Good and the Terrible Mother, and then it manifests as the anima, which, if fully differentiated and integrated, reaches the evolved image of Sophia, the archetype of feminine wisdom. As mentioned, Neumann uses world mythology to demonstrate the symbolism of each of these images, and he described Great Mother Earth in her positive aspects as containing, holding, and comforting, as well as nourishing and fertilizing. It is evident that the ecopsychological perspective, in which humans's psyche is seen as in reciprocal relation with Earth, is embedded in Neumann's theory.

3 Neumann's Theory about Mankind's Relationship with Earth

In the preface of his volume *The Fear of the Feminine*, Neumann wrote that his essays about the feminine "belong in the context of a depth psychology of culture

11 Neumann, *The Child*, 56.
12 Ibidem, 28.
13 Neumann, *The Origins and History of Consciousness.*
14 Neumann, *The Great Mother*, 19.
15 Neumann, "Meaning of the Earth Archetype," 165–66.

and of cultural therapy ... understanding the Feminine is an urgent necessity ... to heal the collective."[16] This important statement is based on his perception of Western culture's bias toward the Masculine, leaving the Feminine neglected. Neumann theorized that while the development of consciousness is an innate process for mankind as a species, Western culture currently is situated in a pivotal phase, in which the development of the masculine ego, which had accumulated in the patriarchal layer, had now diminished and oppressed the feminine and its maternal values.[17] When describing the Earth and accordingly the Feminine from the point of view of Western culture, Neumann effectively described a cultural wound, in which Western man's experience is symptomatically and pathologically similar to that of a deserted and a forsaken child, suffering from a dead mother complex, resulting in the loss of meaning.[18]

Neumann suggested that creation myths, which appear in different versions, describe the initial psychological state from which humankind's conscious developed and also manifest a description of human relationship with the Earth. Neumann saw these mythologies as the prototype of the beginning of things, when consciousness lights the darkness of unconsciousness. The psychological characteristic of the beginning, prior to light, is nonexistence, in which psyche and world are one and the same, inner world and outer world are not differentiated, and man *is* nature. The symbol of this perfect state, which is to be found in different world mythologies, is the round, the circle, in which no opposites yet exist and the world parents Sky and Earth are still united. This round is the uroboric snake, eating its own tail, of which Neumann wrote, "It is man and woman, begetting and conceiving, devouring and giving birth, active and passive, above and below, at once."[19] The Uroboros thus represents "the infancy both of mankind and of the child," and it is the ultimate container, the womb from which all later existence will be born once psychological life begins and experience is enabled.[20] Existence in the uroboros is experienced as a *participation mystique*, whether between a mother and her baby, or between humankind and Mother Earth. Humanity, at that developmental stage, was still primitive, fully submerged in nature, and this is

16 E. Neumann, *The Fear of the Feminine and Other Essays on Feminine Psychology* (Princeton, NJ: Princeton University Press, 1994), XI.

17 E. Neumann, "Narcissism, Normal Self-Formation and the Primary Relation to the Mother," *Spring* (1966): 95–103.

18 Neumann, "Significance of the Genetic Aspect"; Neumann, *The Child*; Neumann, "Narcissism, Normal Self-Formation"; André Green, "The Dead Mother," in *On Private Madness* (New York: Routledge, 2018).

19 Neumann, *The Origins and History of Consciousness*, 10.

20 Ibidem, 11.

the initial phase of the relation between humankind and Earth, an experience prior to any perception.

Once the first differentiation between Sky and Earth took place, humankind was able to perceive these opposites, and our perceptible relationship with Earth began. In his essay "The Meaning of the Earth Archetype for Modern Times," Neumann described the development of mankind's perception of the Earth archetype as a representation of the Feminine. He theorized that the first differentiation granted Sky with everything that is masculine, spiritual, and light, while Earth was granted the feminine, matter, and darkness. Whether the subject is humanity in its early conscious development or an individual in the early stages of his or her psychological development, Neumann asserted that the negative projections onto the Feminine and the Earth are evident of a weak conscious. In terms of human history, Neumann referred to this developmental stage as the time of the Middle Ages and wrote, "The Christian patriarchal image of the Earth was unambiguously negative, while the positive archetype of Heaven was dominant."[21] Therefore, from the current Western perspective, the Middle Ages were an early stage of consciousness development, in which the opposites are perceived as those between spirit and nature, which implies that nature is spiritless.

The next segment of humankind's relationship with Earth, according to Neumann, is that of the Renaissance and the beginning of modern science. Man discovered new continents of the world as a projection of his psyche's need to discover inner continents. Art, science, and empiricism began to view the world objectively, and accordingly, what had been until then an entirely negative projection onto the feminine during the Middle Ages, now became less intense.[22] This time is indeed a renaissance of humankind's perception of the Earth, which came to be perceived through her beauty as a subject of curiosity and inquiry and as the life-giving mother of humankind.[23] On the other hand, the allegedly objective perception of Earth left man separated from Earth, which he "confront[s] at a distance and handle[s] by means of developed instrumental techniques."[24] That is, man and Earth now became separate sides confronting one another; man was no longer a part of nature but rather was investigating it and observing it from a distance.[25] The ascendant dominance and value now denoted to Earth diminished the previous dominance

---

21 Neumann, "Meaning of the Earth Archetype", 169.

22 Ibidem, 179.

23 Ibidem, 177.

24 Erich Neumann, "The Psych and the Transformation of the Reality Plans" (1952), in *The Essays of Erich Neumann*, v. 3, *The Place of Creation* (Princeton, NJ: Princeton University Press, 1989), 9.

25 Ibidem, 10–13.

of the Sky spirit but nevertheless kept Earth objective, concrete, and thus distanced and still spiritless.

Neumann then described the relationship of modern man and Western culture to Earth: "The Earth archetype ... today fills all our horizons ... represents a danger in the immense superiority of its powers. ... The embracing Mother has become a devouring Mother."[26] He referred to the overflow of objective information, of concretization, of details and collectivization, which orients modern man in his extraverted direction to the outer world, while abandoning his inner Mother Earth. Here we should remember we are talking of the same Mother Earth to which primitive man, due to his lack of consciousness, was so close and bonded within a *participation mystique* experience. At the same time, another thing happens to modern man in Western culture: the abundance of information binds him to a fragmented perception of reality in which he specializes in one aspect and remains illiterate in another.[27] Unlike animals, which are still embedded in the natural world and cannot differentiate between inner and outer, modern man sees the world as "outside," external to himself.[28] This situation of fragmented perception prevents a unified experience of the world and thus causes a loss of meaning.[29] Neumann wrote, "Since science refuses the human quest for meaning, it drives us to search for it in collective movements, even though in reality these hollow us out from within or destroy us from without."[30] This wound affects Western culture's collective psyche and calls for depth psychology's introverted orientation, which may lead to a sense of wholeness. It is at this point that Neumann became an eco-psychologist, when he described the intelligible identity of mankind in relation to the Earth archetype within and without. What is broken and wounded in our relationship to the Earth is also broken and wounded in relation to the inner Mother Earth, inner Femininity, and its qualities.

4 Neumann's Concept of the Primary Relationship and the Earth Archetype

Neumann described the psychic state of the uroboros as one of complete unity between mother and child, for which he used the term *participation mystique.*

26 Neumann, "Meaning of the Earth Archetype", 183.

27 Ibidem, 185.

28 Neumann, "The Psych and the Transformation of the Reality Plans," 9.

29 Neumann, "Meaning of the Earth Archetype", 184–85.

30 Neumann, "The Psych and the Transformation of the Reality Plans", 5.

Neumann differentiated between the baby's infantile experience, and the experience of a unified world by the mature conscious, for which he used the term *unitary reality*, referring to a heightened psychological state in which the boundaries between conscious and unconscious, inner and outer, are blurred.[31]

Returning to the individual's psychology, for the infant, *participation mystique* with the mother belongs to the uroboric stage of the primal relationship, one of Neumann's most important and less recognized contributions to the analytical and relational developmental dialogue. The primal relationship was described by Neumann as taking place during the first year of an individual's human life, in which the positive primal relationship will ensure the healthy development of the psychic structure and authorities. This leads to the conscious development and progression from the uroboros layer to the matriarchate. This time in an individual's life corresponds to the collective time before the nascent consciousness of humankind, which Jung referred to as "archaic man." For the individual's psychology, this phase of primal relationship implies that the baby experiences itself floating in the oceanic water, careless, submerged in the heavenly fulfillment of all its needs: shelter, comfort, nourishment, and refuge. Humanity at this stage was still primitive and fully submerged in nature, a species among all others on earth. Neumann asserted that this is a prehistoric state, what Jean-Jacques Rousseau projected as the "natural state" of the savage in which the desire toward conscious is "unnatural" and specific to the human species.[32] The significant importance Neumann attributed to the uroboric stage of the primal relationship was that the baby is as yet unaware of any differentiation, not between itself and its mother, nor between her and the world. Therefore, the mother represents the world for the baby, and its relationship with her becomes the prototype of its relationship to the world. Hence, a positive primal relationship will culminate in a natural and archetypal progression of the development of psychic structure and thus will enable psychic health. A negative primal relationship, on the other hand, will result in damage to the development of the psychic structure and thus with pathologies.

Neumann theorized that the essence and the consequence of a positive primal relationship is the establishment of an *ego-Self axis*, another concept imprinted by Neumann which became a significant contribution to the relational developmental analytical dialogue. The ego-Self axis is a crucial structural element of psychic health, which is the essence of being oneself in one's own body, and thus it is a prerequisite of successful psychic development and

31 Neumann, "Narcissism, Normal Self-Formation", 83.

32 Neumann, *The Origins and History of Consciousness*, 15–16.

the process of self-formation that are the basis of psychological development.[33] Neumann theorized that at the initial stage of the primal relationship, as the baby has not yet been born psychologically, its relatedness aspect of the Self is externalized to the mother, or rather remains deposited with her, while the baby holds only the bodily aspect of the Self, which Neumann defined as the body-Self, a sensory experience. In the positive primal relationship, as the mother holds the functional aspect of the Self, the relatedness, she also manifests the regulating factor while she compensates negative experiences by soothing, containing, and holding. As consciousness develops, the baby gradually internalizes the Self to reach full integration when the primal relationship finally dissolves at about one year of age. Accordingly, Neumann theorized, when the mother fulfills her archetypal role, the baby is able to develop a positive attitude toward its mother, others, and the world, or to put it another way, a positive primal relationship assures psychic health, manifesting in positive relationships within and without.[34] In the process of growing ego-conscious and the establishment of the ego-Self axis, the ego emerges frequently and in a gradual way, only to dissolve each time back again into the mother-Self. Neumann theorized this rhythmic movement of emergence and dissolving as the matriarchal order. This means that one is loved, accepted, and feels a part of a greater order, that is, the seed of ecological stance. He explained that at its depths, the matriarchal order is the essence of morality, as it is the deepest "order of things."[35] This is significant as here Neumann established a connection between a healthy primal relationship and matriarchal morality, rooted within the maternal Self as the authority. Neumann theorized patriarchal morality as significantly different and rooted in cultural authority. At the same time, with these bursts of ego emergence, the baby's consciousness is getting closer and closer to the point of initial encounter with the opposites, at this point through the negative experience of hunger and discomfort as opposed to the positive overall experience. The ability to perceive opposites, manifestes in the ability to perceive an image, and therefore the mother, who initially was the world, gradually now becomes the Great Mother Earth. If the primal relationship were positive, she will eventually become the Good Mother image, while a negative primal relationship will lead to the establishment of the Terrible Mother image. It is important to note here that Neumann emphasized that disturbances in the primal relationship for which the mother is unable to compensate, and which

33 Neumann uses the term *self-formation* reciprocally with *automorphism*, which is one's tendency to become oneself; "Narcissism, Normal Self-Formation," 88.

34 Neumann, *The Child*, 21.

35 Ibidem, 51–55.

may lead to the creation of the negative image, are not necessarily the mother's fault and may be the outcome of external circumstances which she cannot control, for example, war. I suggest that the circumstances of humankind's relation to Earth throughout the development of the conscious, as described earlier, also manifest such outside circumstances, which are not to be blamed on Mother Earth. This point in Neumann's theory becomes even more relevant and important in the light of André Green's dead mother complex.

Thinking back on humankind and the way Neumann theorized his relationship with Earth, it seems like humanity had a positive primal relationship with Mother Earth. At the uroboric layer of humankind's development, before the separation of the world parents to Sky and Earth, humankind was fully submerged in nature; Earth was both within and without, in a *participation mystique* experience. Nevertheless, the way Western culture's perception of Earth evolved and changed during the development of humankind's conscious, as was analyzed by Neumann, may suggest a disturbance in the primal relationship, along with the possible pathologies that are the consequence.

5 André Green's Dead Mother Complex

André Green was an important figure in the psychoanalytical field, whose theoretical contributions are widely appreciated, mainly that of the dead mother complex. This paper suggests a synthesis between Green's individual complex as described from the psychoanalytical perspective, and Neumann's analytical psychology's archetypal perspective, to indicate the possibility of an ecopsychological collective and cultural complex.

In his pivotal essay, "The Dead Mother Complex," Green defined an inner image of "a mother who remains alive but who is, so to speak, psychically dead in the eyes of the young child in her care."[36] The dead mother complex was recognized by Green as a phenomenon within transference, in which in the midst of the analytical process, once the therapist becomes a love object, the analysand develops a depression which manifests in the transference, at the presence of the love object. Green explained the depression theoretically as a reaction of the reactivation, through the transference, of the dead mother complex. He theorized that the complex was historically created by an emotional withdrawal of the mother, which took place after the initial bond between the mother and her child was positively established. This withdrawal

36 Green, "The Dead Mother," 142.

radically changes the mother imago, which is mutative, and thus what was until then a vivid and vital object becomes empty and deadened.[37] Green theorized that due to outside circumstances that deeply affect the mother's emotional state, she becomes emotionally withdrawn and therefore creates an absence and becomes a *cold core*. Moreover, claimed Green, in addition to the love that was suddenly gone, the baby also loses a sense of meaning, as it "disposes of no explication to account for what has happened."[38] Interestingly, in describing the goodness which was present and which, in an instant, vanished, Green used a metaphor of the collective to demonstrate it: "As with the disappearance of ancient civilization, the cause of which is sought in vain by historians, who make the hypothesis of an earthquake to explain the death and destruction of palace, temple... nothing is left but ruins."[39] Although Green did not hold an archetypal perspective, and I doubt if he read Neumann, in this example he gave to his readers, he created a possible collective and cultural implication to the phenomenon he recognized on the personal level.

In this theoretical point, an important similar element is found in Neumann's and in Green's formulation. Neumann described disturbances in the primal relationship in which the mother is present, and the disturbance is in the way she fails to fulfill her archetypal role as the positive Great Mother. Like Neumann, Green defined the complex created when a child has been taken care of by a depressed, sad, deadened mother who has been absorbed by bereavement. He wrote, "*The essential characteristic of this depression is that it takes place in the presence of the object, which is itself absorbed by a bereavement.* The mother for one reason or another, is depressed."[40] At this point, the argument becomes clear: if indeed humankind had a positive primal relation with the Great Mother Earth, then the way humankind withdrew from her could be seen as an experience of a deprivation of her love, which led to bereavement and a loss of meaning.

6 The Wounds

Both Neumann and Green referred to the pathologies, or wounds, as a consequence of the deprivation of maternal love and care. Green emphasized the personal emotional deprivation leading to a "transference depression," while

37 Ibidem, 149.
38 Ibidem, 150.
39 Ibidem.
40 Ibidem, 149; [italics are original].

Neumann, who held a Jungian archetypal perspective, described the archetypal level of deprivation leading to the incarnation of the negative archetypal image of the Great Mother.[41] Importantly, both Neumann and Green suggested a narcissistic wound, the consequence of which is a loss of meaning.

Green described the experience of the sudden loss of love as a "catastrophe" and as a "narcissistic traumatism" that "constitutes a premature disillusionment ... [and] carries in its wake, beside the loss of love, the loss of meaning, for the baby disposes of no explication to account for what has happened."[42] Green postulated that the loss of meaning is imagined by the child as his fault, linked with his way of being, and in this way Green created a theoretical connection between the sudden loss of love; a premature awakening; and significantly, a loss of meaning with guilt feeling.

Green's formulations are in line with Neumann's, who wrote that if some experience of positive primal relationship did take place, then some ego stability was established, and thus the ability to register experiences already exists. Therefore, if a deprivation from love and care occurs, the negative experience becomes a negative charge, on the young ego, that will lead to "a distressed and negativized ego," which Neumann described as "over-accentuation"and as "awakened too soon and driven to independence ... forced to develop a narcissism that is the expression of an ego reduced to its own resources."[43] The pathological manifestation of such early awakening, theorized Neumann, will be the primary guilt feeling, the conviction that "not to be loved is identical with being abnormal and 'condemned.'"[44] As mentioned before, the sense of being a part of the matriarchate order is the essence of morality, and therefore, being thrown out of this order is experienced as a sentence of the "higher court," which leads to the primary guilt.[45] When Neumann wrote about an ego that was reduced to its own resources, he critically described a damage to the ego-self axis, in which case, the ego lacks the inner maternal element, the inner love and compensation, acceptance, care, and motherly tolerance. Consequently the ego, which was led by the lack of maternal love to rigidity and negativism, is now also led to intolerance toward oneself, and, Neumann theorized, thus the deep sense of inadequacy creates the secondary guilt feeling.

Neumann theorized that with the lack of connection to the Self, the ego that is thrown out of the matriarchal order falls prey to the patriarchate. As

41 Neumann, *The Child*, 8.

42 Green, "The Dead Mother," 150.

43 Neumann, *The Child*, 74, 77–78.

44 Neumann, "Narcissism, Normal Self-Formation", 96.

45 Ibidem.

development proceeds, the transition to the patriarchate layer naturally takes place; then the lack of an inner sense of the matriarchal order of the Self is compensated by the judgment of the patriarchal order, executed by a rigid superego.[46] Neumann suggested some cultural implications of his idea when he explained that in opposition to the Self, whose goal is self-fulfillment and wholeness, the patriarchal superego leads to a split personality.[47] Furthermore, he wrote: "It is a collective authority, introjected only later, whose object is to enforce the demands of the 'father,' of the collective, in opposition to the individual."[48] Neumann goes on to explain that the adaptation to these collectivized demands is possible only by "the violent suppression ... of the individual's own nature ... [A]n adaptation contrary to its nature, and to nature is general ... represents a self-alienation."[49] Once again, Neumann's theory has ecopsychological implications, as he indicates that Western culture's bias toward the patriarchy means, from a depth psychological perspective, alienation of one from oneself.

The relationship of humankind and Earth as the prototype of the relationship of a baby with its mother, in light of the two theorists' formulation, suggests an ecopsychological wounding. Accordingly, in the genesis of humankind, during the nascence of consciousness, man dwelled on the land and experienced *participation mystique* with the world surrounding him. As he progressed, and his consciousness developed, in the natural duration of things, he turned his back on the Earth and was fascinated by the Sky. This process alienated man from the spirit of Earth, and from Sophia, the most differentiated image of the feminine wisdom. This cultural wound is the wound of a child whose love object became bereaved, forming a cold core, a child of Mother Earth who lost meaning.

7 Conclusion

As was described, Neumann's theory is centered on the Feminine, describing extensively the significance of the feminine qualities of comforting, containing, nourishing, and cultivating to the health of human psyche at all time periods. In his pivotal ecopsychological essay, "The Meaning of the Earth Archetype for Modern Times," Neumann described Western man's current

46 Neumann, "The Psych and the Transformation of the Reality Plans", 98–103.
47 Neumann, "Narcissism, Normal Self-Formation", 98.
48 Ibidem, 99.
49 Ibidem.

relation to Earth as one in which a lack of unified worldview leads to a lack of meaning. Nevertheless, Neumann concluded with a very optimistic view when he suggested that unique "great individuals" may lead the transformation.[50] He believed that among the mass collective, there are creative and artistic individuals whose inner femininity in the image of Mother Earth is positive and creative, who develop psychologically to reach the image of Sophia and experience the world through the *unitary reality*, and who will carry humanity on their shoulders and turn the wheel of transformation, which will set free the spirit of the Earth. Maybe Erich Neumann himself was one such "great individual." Neumann, the ecopsychologist, quoted Rilke:[51]

> Earth, isn't this what you want: an invisible
> re-arising in us? Is it not your dream
> to be one day invisible? Earth! invisible!
> What is your urgent command, if not transformation?
> Earth, you darling, I will!

References

Fisher A., *Radical Ecopsychology: Psychology in the Service of Life*, Albany: State University of New York Press, 2002.

Green A., "The Dead Mother", in *On Private Madness*, New York: Routledge, 2018. [Originally published 1986].

Jung, C. G., "A Radio Talk in Munich", in *The Symbolic Life*, v. 18, *The Collected Works*, Princeton, NJ: Princeton University Press, 1976. [Originally published 1930].

Jung C. G., "The Relations between the Ego and the Unconscious", in *Two Essays on Analytical Psychology*, v. 7, *The Collected Works*, Princeton, NJ: Princeton University Press, 1972. [Originally published 1935].

Jung C. G., "The Role of the Unconscious", in *Civilization in Transition*, v. 10, *The Collected Works*, Princeton, NJ: Princeton University Press, 1964. [Originally published 1918].

Jung C. G., "Symbols and the Interpretation of Dreams", In *The Symbolic Life*, v. 18, *The Collected Works*, Princeton, NJ: Princeton University Press, 1976. [Originally published 1961].

50 E. Neumann, "Art and Time", in *Art and the Creative Unconscious* (Princeton, NJ: Princeton University Press, 1959), 100.

51 M. Rilke, *Duino Elegies*, trans. J. B. Leishman and Stephen Spender (New York: W. W. Norton, 1939), quoted in Neumann, "Art and Time", 97.

Neumann E., "Art and Time", In *Art and the Creative Unconscious*, 81–134. Princeton, NJ: Princeton University Press, 1959. [Originally published 1951].

Neumann E., *The Child: Structure and Dynamics of the Nascent Personality*, London: Karnac Books, 1973. [Originally published 1963].

Neumann E., *The Great Mother*, trans. R. Manheim, Princeton, NJ: Princeton University Press, 1991. [Originally published 1955].

Neumann E., "The Meaning of the Earth Archetype for Modern Times", in *The Fear of the Feminine and Other Essays on Feminine Psychology*, 165–226. Princeton, NJ: Princeton University Press, 1994. [Originally published 1953].

Neumann E., "Narcissism, Normal Self-Formation and the Primary Relation to the Mother", *Spring* (1966): 81–106. [Originally published 1955].

Neumann E., *The Origins and History of Consciousness*, trans. R. F. C. Hull. Princeton, NJ: Princeton University Press, 2014. [Originally published 1949].

Neumann E., "The Psych and the Transformation of the Reality Plans", (1952), in *The Essays of Erich Neumann*, v. 3, *The Place of Creation*. Princeton, NJ: Princeton University Press, 1989.

Neumann E., "The Significance of the Genetic Aspect for Analytical Psychology", *Journal of Analytical Psychology* 4, no. 2 (1959): 125–37.

Rilke M., *Duino Elegies*, trans. J. B. Leishman and S. Spender, New York: W. W. Norton, 1939, in: E. Neumann, "Art and Time".

Roszak T., *The Voice of the Earth: An Exploration of Ecopsychology,* Grand Rapids, MI: Phanes Press, 2001. [Originally published 1992].

Sabini M. (ed.), *The Earth Has a Soul: C. G. Jung on Nature, Technology and Modern Life*, Berkeley, CA: North Atlantic Books, 2008.

CHAPTER 15

Wotan and Cocks: Reframing Jungian Sociology for the Early 21st Century

Johann Graaff

Abstract

Jung's well-known Wotan article, first published in 1936 and then again in 1946, identified this Norse god as the key archetypal lodestar for understanding the essence of the German nation. To appreciate just how inappropriate it was sociologically, one needs to place it in its historical context of German cultural revival at the end of the 19th and beginning of the 20th century, with strong political roots. Jung's article is very much a child of the *völkisch* movement of that time. But 21st century symbolic anthropology has produced an attractive alternative model of archetypal Jungian sociology through writers like Clifford Geertz, shorn of Jung's long-term timeframes.

Keywords

Jung, sociology, Wotan, symbolic anthropology, Clifford Geertz, Robert Darnton, German völkisch movement

1 Introduction

This paper starts with a discussion of a famous article by anthropologist Clifford Geertz on the Balinese cockfight. Why bring him into a Jungian conference? Because, as a symbolic anthropologist, working in a hermeneutic mode, he sets a wonderful example of what profound and subtle Jungian sociology should look like.[1] Then I am going to examine Jung's famous and very intricate Wotan article, its logical structure, its rhetorical strategy, and its cultural roots. Thirdly, I will compare these two articles according to where their relative strengths and weaknesses are. I will argue that Geertz and Jung overlap in

1 C. Geertz, "Deep Play: Notes on the Balinese Cockfight", in *Interpretive Social Science*, P. Rabinow & W. Sullivan (eds.), (Berk: University of California Press, 1979a), 181–223.

 | DOI:10.1163/9789004468757_017

their extraordinary cross-disciplinary versatility but that ultimately Jung (and Jungians) have much to learn from symbolic anthropology.

As I have intimated, this paper will have a strong methodological slant. It asks questions about what sociology is, what *Jungian* sociology is, and how one does sociological work with archetypes.

2 Geertz: Deep Play: Notes on the Balinese Cockfight

Geertz's piece opens with an intriguing and amusing story about Geertz and his wife arriving in a small Balinese village in 1958, and, soon after, being caught up in a police raid on a cockfight happening in the central square. We are immediately brought to understand that this is an illegal activity (to which local authorities mostly turn a blind eye, but not this time). More importantly, and this is the ostensible point of the story, Geertz and his wife flee headlong, along with the rest of the village population, before the advancing police. The local Balinese are delighted and gratified by this act of solidarity.

From here, Geertz describes and analyzes a typical cockfight by progressively unveiling deeper and deeper layers of it. Smith would say that the story is captivating precisely because of this detective-story structure.[2]

At the first level, the symbolism of cocks and cockfighting, says Geertz, suffuses Balinese culture. It stands for male sexuality in a range of contexts, myths, and jokes. The word for *cock* in the Balinese language, as in English, also stands for male genitalia. Balinese men spend "an enormous amount of time" attending to their cocks, feeding, grooming, stroking, preparing, inspecting them – "We're all cock crazy" says one man. And Geertz summarizes, "Cocks are symbolic expressions or magnifications of their owner's self, the narcissistic male ego writ out in Aesopian terms."[3]

Secondly, this suffusion and fascination is remarkable given the Balinese disgust at animal behavior of any kind and its association with evil demons. They "treat their large of number dogs not merely callously but with phobic cruelty,"[4] and demons are represented often in animal form. There is a clear and explicit connection between cockfighting and "the Powers of Darkness." The cockfight is a significant form of blood sacrifice to placate demons and

2 P. Smith, "The Balinese Cockfight Decoded: Reflections on Geertz, the Strong Program and Structuralism," *Cultural Sociology*, 2, no. 2 (2008): 169–186.

3 Geertz, *Deep Play*, 189.

4 Ibidem.

"their ravenous, cannibal hunger,"[5] and a cockfight always precedes (now legally) the important public holiday of The Day of Silence. Here is Geertz once again pulling this all together: "In the cockfight, man and beast, good and evil, ego and id, the creative power of aroused masculinity and the destructive power of loosened animality fuse in a bloody drama of hatred, cruelty, violence and death."[6]

Thirdly, there follows a detailed description of the happening of the cockfight, the matching up of the birds to ensure a close fight, the affixing of the spurs (explicitly ritual objects—that may be sharpened only at eclipses and the dark of the moon), the rehabilitation of wounded birds, the role of the umpire in applying detailed and elaborate rules, and the old traditions of the sport. All of this constructs a secure containing framework within which wild animality is let loose. It is, says Geertz, a social entity, a focused gathering rather than a group or a crowd (following Goffman), with fluctuating participants, taking its form from the floor, the cockpit, and the cultural meanings around which it is brought into being.[7]

At the fourth level, the kernel of the cockfight and the crux of Geertz's analysis is the matter of gambling, the fact that money is bet on the outcome of the contest. The central concept of the whole piece, the simple two words of the title, "deep play," comes directly from the world of betting, and indicates the greater import that the fight has, once significant amounts of money are laid. It is important that these heavily betted fights are those in which the cocks are most meticulously matched, where the outcome is most unpredictable. "In deep (contests), where the amounts of money are great, much more is at stake than material gain: namely, esteem, honour, dignity, respect—in a word, though in Bali a profoundly freighted word, status."[8] This is the point at which the social expresses itself most clearly through the cockfight, for it is in the end "a simulation of the social matrix, the involved system of cross-cutting, overlapping, highly corporate groups—villages, kin-groups, irrigations societies, temple congregations, 'castes'—in which its devotees live."[9] It is a display and acknowledgement of the shadow, the other, the foundation on which hierarchy is built, an explicit unveiling of the envy, hatred, and anger which

5 Ibidem.
6 Ibidem, 190.
7 Ibidem, 192.
8 Ibidem, 202.
9 Ibidem, 205.

in Balinese society is concealed behind "a haze of etiquette, a thick cloud of euphemism and ceremony, gesture and allusion."[10]

But ultimately, and finally, the cockfight is symbol, it is metaphor, it is theatre, with all the subtle disturbances (Geertz calls it "disquietfulness") and transformations that these things entail, and as with all great theatre, symbol, and metaphor, it points to the unanswerables of human life—"death, masculinity, rage, pride, loss, beneficence, chance."[11] It is a window on the complexity of "our" subjectivity, but it is also, with all the bodily mimesis that goes with watching a cockfight, a process in which subjectivity is formed.

From a Jungian perspective, the key aspect to notice is how much use Geertz makes of the unconscious, most clearly in his comparison of the conduct of everyday Balinese life enveloped as it is in "a haze of etiquette, a thick cloud of euphemism and ceremony, gesture and allusion," on the one hand, with the explicit aggression and cruelty on display in the cockfight, on the other hand. The cockfight here is an unconscious unveiling of what is consciously suppressed.

3 Jung: Wotan

Let us now turn to Jung's article "Wotan," published in 1936, and again in 1946. Jung's central theme is the chaos that the archetype, Wotan, has been causing since World War I, in politics, religion, and literature, over the landscape of northern and southern Europe.

> And what came after the war was a veritable witches' sabbath. Everywhere fantastic revolutions, violent alterations of the map, reversions in politics to medieval or even antique prototypes, totalitarian states that engulf their neighbours and outdo all previous theocracies in their absolutist claims, persecutions of Christians and Jews, wholesale political murder ….[12]

Wotan, the god, is characterized especially by his furious and wild influence. "He is the god of storm and frenzy, the unleasher of passions and the lust of battle; more over he is a superlative magician and artist who is versed in all

---

10 Ibidem, 216.

11 Ibidem, 213.

12 Carl Jung, "Wotan," in *Civilizations in Transition*, v. 10, (Princeton: Princeton University Press, 1936/1970).

secrets of an occult nature."[13] Jung finds multiple synonyms for frenzy and fury: intoxication, exuberance, Dionysus, unrest and strife, passions, lust of battle, a state of being seized or possessed, *furor teutonicus*, a cyclone, a raving beserker, hurricane, mighty rushing wind, rouser of this tempest, like "a rock crashing down a hill."

But Wotan is particularly central to understanding the German people. Wotan is "a Germanic datum of first importance, the truest expression and unsurpassed personification of a fundamental quality of the Germans."[14] It is particularly German leaders who have been possessed (*Ergriffen*) by the archetype, and they who have spread/infected the rest of the country with their energy.

Examples of this possession are the experiences of *particular individuals* like Nietzsche, the philosopher and poet, writing of the impact of Zarathustra; of Martin Nink who wrote a book exploring the varied character of Wotan; of Jakob Wilhelm Hauer; of writer Bruno Goetz, who foresaw in many ways what was going to happen; and of course Adolf Hitler himself. Then there are examples of *movements* like the German youth who sacrifice sheep for their ceremonies and "wander" over the German landscape, the German faith movement, and the thousands of unemployed who likewise walked great distances through Germany.

In between all of this there is the unfolding detail of Wotan's many-sided character, his long-lasting influence over "more than a thousand years," his superior power over Christianity, and the unpredictable nature of where he will appear in the future. "Things must be concealed in the background which we cannot imagine at present, but we may expect them to appear in the course of the next few years or decades."[15] A great deal of this Wotan article is taken up with explaining and elaborating on the Wotan archetype. It is an article much-quoted by those who wish to explain Jung's notion of the archetype.[16]

4 By Way of Comparison

In the following section, I put Geertz and Jung next to each other as examples of symbolic/archetypal analysis of social and political realities.

13 Ibidem, § 375

14 Ibidem, § 389.

15 Ibidem.

16 J. Jacobi, *Complex, Archetype, Symbol in the Psychology of CG Jung*, (Princeton: Princeton University Press, 1971); A. Samuels, *A Critical Dictionary of Jungian Analysis*, (London: Routledge, 1986).

4.1 *Levels of Empirical Focus*

The immediately striking difference between these writers is the precise and detailed focus of Geertz, and the broader, high level generalizing style of Jung. Geertz, as we have seen, homes in on one particular, and quite old, cultural practice in Bali. For his part, Jung ranges widely across the whole of Europe and Russia, spanning a period of about 50 years, but with references now and again to "more than a thousand years." And this makes one suspicious of Jung, his style easily leads to a criticism of cherry-picking his evidence and ignoring the contrary information.

But let us pursue this issue of empirical focus further for a moment. What does it mean to say that Geertz is more detailed? For his part, Geertz is well-known for his method of "thick description" of the cultural surroundings of his topic.[17] This implies a deep and thorough immersion of the writer in their topic, whether it be a culture, an event, an institution, or a ritual. But it is more than exhaustive detail. Here is Robert Darnton explaining:

> In his view, descriptions thickened when the ethnographer seized on the multiple meanings transmitted through a symbol and followed their interplay with other symbols until a cultural system emerged in view—fuzzy at first, but increasingly clear as the interpretations led round and round a hermeneutic circle... His genius, I believe, consisted in grasping at a thread in such a way as to unravel an entire pattern of culture.[18]

This is Geertz himself explaining:

> Accounts of other people's subjectivities can be built up without recourse to pretensions to more-than-normal capacities for ego-effacement and fellow-feeling ... Understanding the form and pressure of ... natives' inner lives is more like grasping a proverb, catching an allusion, seeing a joke—or, as I have suggested, reading a poem—than it is like achieving communion.[19]

That explanation says much about Darnton's own work because his case of the cat massacre is exactly about a joke that he gradually unravels outwards into

17 C. Geertz, *The Interpretation of Cultures*, (New York, 1973).

18 R. Darnton, "Foreword: Anthropology, History and Clifford Geertz", in C. Geertz (ed.), *The Interpretation of Cultures: Selected Essays*, (New York: Basic Books, 2017).

19 C. Geertz, "From the Native's Point of View: On the Nature of Anthropological Understanding", in P. Rabinow & W. Sullivan (eds.), *Interpretive Social Science*, (Berk: University of California Press, 1979b).

a whole cultural system. It bears emphasizing also that, when Geertz refers to Bali and Indonesia as being well-studied, he is referring to several books that he has written about the area.[20] Geertz knows what he is talking about!

What shall we say, then, about Jung's mobilization of situational surroundings? Jung is striking in his Wotan article by the way he participates in the impact of the archetype. There is a palpable passion in the way Jung writes about this "magnificent" archetype, the way that he shares in the passion of other writers like Hauer and Mink. Jung has been intuitively drawn into the power of the archetype.

At the same time, Jung is nothing if not large with his sweeping references to northern and southern Europe, and Russia. And indicating that there is a single archetype which covers both northern and southern Europe does raise one's eyebrows. Italy and Spain have deep roots in classical Roman and Greek cultures, as well as Islam, which is starkly different from Nordic and Norse northern Europe.

By contrast, Jung is markedly more detailed in his discussion of the different features, and the history, of Wotan. As a general remark about Jungian sociologists, one might say that they are, like Jung, much stronger on the amplification of archetypes than on connecting to the concrete situation on the ground,[21] which is not how Jung and Jungians go about the analysis of individual dreams. It is true too that Jung can write large parts of his book *Symbols of Transformation*, starting from the written text of Mrs. Frank Miller's dream, a woman whom he never met nor knew much about,[22] but in many other cases he is detailed and meticulous in cross-referencing life details and dream symbols. It is a puzzle why he cannot do the same in his sociological and political writing.

4.2 *Talking Durkheim and the Rules of Sociological Method*

Now, one might object that in the Wotan article Jung does have quite fine detail drawn, for example, from the writings of Friedrich Nietzsche, or from his friend Wilhelm Hauer. But we need to be precise here on how Jung is using this material. Is Nietzsche a representative example of German culture? Or is he simply an individual (and quite an exceptional individual at that) who

20 C. Geertz, *Peddlers and Princes: Social Development and Economic Change in two Indonesian towns*, (Chicago: Univeristy of Chicago Press, 1963); *Agricultural Involution: the Process of Ecological Change in Indonesia*, (Chicago: University of Chicago Press, 1964); *The Religion of Java*, (Chicago: University of Chicago Press, 1976); *Negara: the Theatre State in 19th century Bali*, (Princeton: Princeton University Press, 1980).

21 This characteristic of thin empirical detail is very visible in later Jungian writers like Singer, Bernstein, and Thibaudier (Bernstein, 2007; Singer, 2002; Thibaudier, 2007).

22 C. G. Jung, *Symbols of Transformation*, (Princeton: Princeton University Press, 1967).

happens to have had some Wotan-like experiences in his life? I would venture here to say that it is the latter case that Jung intends and that Jung is confusing psychology and sociology.

To understand that statement, we need to do a brief detour through Émile Durkheim, and more specifically his work *The Rules of Sociological Method*.[23] There is no doubt that Jung was not a Durkheimian and knew very little about Durkheim.[24] But Durkheim was here laying down the now widely accepted fundamentals of a sociological approach, against which one can judge how well or badly Jung's sociological attempt is carried out. Durkheim was writing at a time when sociology was in its infancy and needed clear boundaries with other cognate disciplines. The line between psychology and sociology was therefore a key issue.

So what is it that distinguishes sociology from psychology? Durkheim's principle of emergence, well-known today in systems or gestalt theory, is that the whole is greater than the sum of the parts.[25] There is "something else" that appears when a number of people milling around in the town square now join together into a sports crowd or a political rally.

Durkheim's second principle follows from the principle of emergence. Here, Durkheim indicates that social phenomena must be explained by social factors. A social entity is something more than a multiplication of individuals.[26] You cannot use psychological factors to explain social phenomena; society is not the individual writ large.

His example of suicide is a very helpful one.[27] If one wants to understand the behavior of a particular suicidal individual, one asks questions about her/his emotional experience, grief, loss, depression, bleakness, the meaning of life. But these questions do not help us at all in understanding the rate of suicide in a country (i.e., how many people commit suicide each year, or the way this rate changes from one population group to another). In this case, says Durkheim, writing in the 1890s, one looks at sociological factors like location in urban or rural areas, religion, or marital status. As a general rule, rural, Catholic, and

23 É. Durkheim, *The Rules of Sociological Method 8th ed*, trans. S. Solovay & J. Mueller, (Glencoe, Ill.: Free Press, 1895/1964).

24 Jung did know about Lévy-Bruhl, who was a Durkheimian, but in anthropology, not sociology.

25 A. Giddens, *Capitalism and modern social theory*, (London: Cambridge University Press, 1971a).

26 A. Giddens, *Capitalism and modern social theory: an analysis of the writings of Marx, Durkheim and Weber*, (Cambridge: Cambridge University Press, 1971b).

27 É. Durkheim, *Suicide: a study in sociology*, (Glencoe, Illinois: The Free Press, 1897/1951).

married people have significantly lower rates of suicide than urban, Protestant, and single people.[28]

To take a more recent example, we might understand the roots of an individual *Narcissistic Personality Disorder* (NPD) by pointing to their traumatic experiences of early maternal disconnection, as Kohut has indicated.[29] By contrast, in order to understand how millions of people have imbibed values of a *narcissistic culture*, we have to look at very different processes of conformism, socialization, and modeling. These people have not all suffered a deep wound.[30]

To return to Jung's example, then, does he use Nietzsche as an example of an exceptional individual whose individual clinical history might make him vulnerable to possession by the Wotan archetype, the psychological angle, or of one who has just modeled himself on others of his family and proximate social groups who were propagating these values, the sociological angle? Is he Friederich Nietzsche, or is he just another turn-of-the-century German? It seems clear that Jung, contra Durkheim, is using the individual, Nietzsche, to make a sociological point about the national archetype, Wotan.

Now notice what happens, by contrast, when Geertz quotes individual Balinese cockfighters. None of them has a name, and they are always in the plural. "They" say things like "We're all cock crazy." Geertz is clear that he is examining a social institution, not multiple individuals and their personal values. A cockfight is, as I have indicated earlier, "a social entity, a focused gathering rather than a group or a crowd (following Goffman), with fluctuating participants, taking its form from the floor, the cockpit, and the cultural meanings around which it is brought into being."[31] This is the "something else" that emerges when disparate individuals come together in this time and space and "perform" this particular social identity.

4.3 *Influences from the Völkisch Movement*

Pietikainen has suggested that Jung's psychology drew several elements from the principles of the völkisch cultural movement so much in evidence in Germany at the beginning of the 20th century.[32] It is unlikely, in my view, that Jung drew his original inspiration from this movement principally. But it is clear

28 I am, of course, aware that Geertz drew much more in the end from Weber than from Durkheim.

29 H. Kohut, *The Analysis of the Self*, (New York: International Universities Press, 1971).

30 C. Lasch, *The Culture of Narcissism: American Life in an Age of Diminishing Expectations*, (New York: Norton, 1979).

31 Geertz, *Deep Play*.

32 P. Pietikainen, "The Volk and Its Unconscious: Jung, Hauer and the 'German Revolution'", *Journal of Contemporary History*, 35, no. 4, (2000): 523–539.

that, in his Wotan article, Jung has great sympathy for this movement and is himself powerfully animated by the Wotan archetype, which was central to the movement. Jung was, at the time of writing the article, also collaborating with Jakob Wilhelm Hauer, initiator of the deeply völkisch German Faith Movement, in research on Indo-European religions.

A significant area of overlap between Jung and the völkisch movement was the movement's romantic anti-modern stance, its critique of positivist science, urbanization, and industrialization. For his part, Jung spoke often of the Enlightenment as the "Endarkenment," of how "modern man" had lost "his" soul.

This movement drew on writers like Wilhelm Wundt (1832–1920) and Johan Herbart (1776–1841) to speak of the German nation's *Volkseele* (the soul of the nation) and its *Volksgeist* (the spirit of the nation) having a separate and supra-individual existence, the nation being a "unitary factor which functioned like a single individual" and could be explained by the same principles of psychology.[33] These are all ideas that have echoes in Jung's work.

Pietikainen also argues that Jung's ideas on the archetype and the search for a transhistorical essence beyond the reach of socio-economic forces were very close to the ideas of the völkisch movement on the *Urphenomen*. National Socialists, for example, sought to transcend the hollowness of private time (anomie) and provide Germans with a sense of deeply meaningful time. This manipulation of collective mentality was sustained by a careful staging of rituals, which enabled "the ego or 'small' self to give way to a higher, supraindividual Self." This "higher Self" represented a vital link to the organic unity of the Volk, to the imaginative wholeness of Gemeinschaft, which maintained a feeling of collective redemption.[34] In like manner, Jung's psychology is focused on the individual attainment of the "new Wholeness" by transcending the historical and hence profane mode of being and reaching the timeless therapeutic psychomyth. It was close to the biological search of the late 19th century for the "pure" origins of species, before later polluting influences took hold.[35]

5 Problems with "Wotan"

A central problem with Jung's use of the Wotan archetype is the implication that a whole nation can be driven by a single archetype. But note first that

33 Ibidem.
34 Ibidem.
35 Ibidem.

Hitler and the Nazi party rejected significant parts of the völkisch ideology.[36] They were clear that they needed industrial technology to promote their economic development and produce their military hardware. In addition, they were highly critical of the Völkisch movement. Hitler referred to them as "cretins."

> Hitler himself derided "those cretins" who made asses of themselves by worshipping Wotan and Odin and the ancient, but now obsolete, German mythology ... at the same time nazi leaders were well aware that Germany's future as a military power depended on technology, industry and the capitalist-bourgeois social structure.[37]

Furthermore, there is the important statistic that in the 1929 federal election, only 33% of the votes were for the NSDAP, while in the 1933 election they again failed to get a majority, with 43% of the votes. Remember that the 1933 election was accompanied by an extended Nazi campaign of violent intimidation of other parties.[38] In short, one can hardly talk of the whole German nation being possessed by the Wotan archetype or even of Hitler himself being possessed.

The curious thing here is how coy Jung is about this overlap between his own views and the völkisch movement. He never uses the word *völkisch* in his article, but he is himself significantly carried away by the energy of the archetype, and Wilhelm Jakob Hauer was a personal friend at the time. He published this article twice, once in a journal (1936) and once as a book (1946), both times against the strong advice of friends and colleagues. Deirdre Bair says that on both occasions it caused him massive trouble.[39] In a clinical situation, one would say that this looks very much like a complex.

6 Conclusion

So what do we see when we put these articles, one by Clifford Geertz and one by C. G. Jung, alongside each other? In this context, Geertz looks stylish (in a literary sense), intuitive in his analysis of the intra-psychic dimensions of the cockfight, deeply researched, focused, and neat. By contrast, Jung looks

---

36 N. Goodrick-Clarke, *The Occult Roots of Nazism: Secret Aryan Cults and Their Influence on Nazi Ideology*, (New York: New York University Press, 1992).

37 Pietikainen, *The Volk*, 6.

38 R. J. Evans, *The Coming of the Third Reich*, (New York: Penguin Press, 2004).

39 D. Bair, *Jung: a Biography*, (Boston: Little, Brown and Company, 2003).

messy, pursuing too many goals at the same time, like political/sociological analysis, teaching readers about archetypes, and warm appreciation of the Wotan archetype. And his sociology is suspect, mixing social and individual phenomena in the same analysis. His application of the archetype is far too broad, unfocused, lacking in empirical backing. And he flirts with the occult in his quote from Nostradamus as the head quote to his article.

But on the other hand, he poses some interesting methodological questions for us. I have indicated Jung's intuitive absorption of the potency of the archetype. Should we then be judging his writing by somewhat different rules, accepting that he was an unusually intuitive individual and that some seemingly outrageous things he says might be true/valid just because he said them?

Finally, there is Jung's pioneering mode of what Edward Edinger calls "archetypal psycho-history" which became evident in the volume Aion.[40] This is history over thousands of years. Perhaps we should be asking ourselves whether Jung's Wotan analysis has not got one foot in just such "archetypal psycho-history" that Jung feels uncomfortable in limiting himself to smaller units of time. Against this background, of course, reference to Jungian studies in the 21st century indicates not a conventional progression of the social sciences but rather the end of the aeon of Pisces—each aeon seen to be lasting 2,100 years.[41]

References

Bair D., *Jung: a Biography*. Boston: Little, Brown and Company, 2003.

Bernstein J., "Archetypal Reality in Politics." *Spring* 78, Fall 2007: 1–31.

Darnton R., "Foreword: Anthropology, History and Clifford Geertz." In *The Interpretation of Cultures: Selected Essays* edited by Clifford Geertz. New York: Basic Books, 2017.

Durkheim É., *The Rules of Sociological Method 8th ed.* Translated by S. Solovay & J. Mueller. Glencoe, Ill.: Free Press, 1895/1964.

Durkheim É., *Suicide: a study in sociology.* Glencoe, Illinois: The Free Press, 1897/1951.

Edinger E., *The Aion Lectures: Exploring the Self in CG Jung's Aion,* Toronto: Inner City Books, 1996.

40 C. G. Jung, *Aion: Researches into the Phenomenology of the Self,* v. 9(II), (Princeton: Princeton University Press, 1969).

41 E. Edinger, *The Aion Lectures: Exploring the Self in CG Jung's Aion,* (Toronto: Inner City Books, 1996).

Evans R. J., *The Coming of the Third Reich,* New York: Penguin Press, 2004.

Geertz C., *Peddlers and Princes: Social Development and Economic Change in two Indonesian towns*, Chicago: University of Chicago Press, 1963.

Geertz C., *Agricultural Involution: the Process of Ecological Change in Indonesia*, Chicago: University of Chicago Press, 1964.

Geertz C., *The Interpretation of Cultures*, New York, 1973.

Geertz C. *The Religion of Java*, Chicago: University of Chicago Press, 1976.

Geertz C., "Deep Play: Notes on the Balinese Cockfight", in *Interpretive Social Science* eds. P. Rabinow & W. Sullivan, 181–223. Berk: University of California Press, 1979a.

Geertz C., "From the Native's Point of View: On the Nature of Anthropological Understanding", in *Interpretive Social Science* ed. P. Rabinow & W. Sullivan, 181–223. Berk: University of California Press, 1979b.

Geertz C., *Negara: the Theatre State in 19th century Bali*, Princeton: Princeton University Press, 1980.

Giddens A., *Capitalism and modern social theory: an analysis of the writings of Marx, Durkheim and Weber,* Cambridge: Cambridge University Press, 1971.

Giegerich W., "The Provenance of CG Jung's Psychological Findings", in *The Neurosis of Psychology: Primary Papers towards a Critical Psychology Vol. 1*, ed. W. Giegerich, New Orleans: Spring Journal Books, 2005.

Goodrick-Clarke N., *The Occult Roots of Nazism: Secret Aryan Cults and Their Influence on Nazi Ideology*, New York: New York University Press, 1992.

Jacobi J., *Complex, Archetype, Symbol in the Psychology of CG Jung,* Princeton: Princeton University Press, 1971.

Jung C. G., *Civilization in Transition* (*Vol. 10*), Princeton: Princeton University Press, 1936/1970.

Jung C. G., *Symbols of Transformation*, Princeton: Princeton University Press, 1967.

Jung C. G., *Aion: Researches into the Phenomenology of the Self,* v. 9[II]), Princeton: Princeton University Press, 1969.

Jung C. G., *Memories, Dreams, Reflections*, New York: Vintage Books, 1973.

Kohut H., *The Analysis of the Self,* New York: International Universities Press, 1971.

Lasch C., *The Culture of Narcissism: American Life in an Age of Diminishing Expectations,* New York: Norton, 1979.

Pietikainen P., "The Volk and Its Unconscious: Jung, Hauer and the 'German Revolution'", *Journal of Contemporary History,* 35 no. 4 (2000): 523–539.

Samuels, A. *A Critical Dictionary of Jungian Analysis*, London: Routledge, 1986.

Singer T., "The Cultural Complex and Archetypal Defenses of the Collective Spirit: Baby Zeus, Elian Gonzales, Constantine's Sword, and Other Holy Wars", *The San Francisco Jung Institute Library Journal,* 20 no. 4 (2008): 5–28.

Smith P., "The Balinese Cockfight Decoded: Reflections on Geertz, the Strong Program and Structuralism", *Cultural Sociology,* 2 no. 2 (2008): 169–186.

Thibaudier V., "The French and the Revolution Syndrome", *Spring, 78* Fall 2007.

PART 3

Psychological Significance in Social Processes

CHAPTER 16

Thinking of a Social Hierarchy as an Instinctual and Archetypal Phenomenon

Andrew Kuzmicki

Abstract

The paper describes some of the factors that play a role in the process of social hierarchization within a society. I refer here not only to the instinctual and archetypal forces, but also to the less "psychological," more "systemic" factors influencing this process, the factors associated with systems dynamics and describing patterns of self-organizing of those systems seen in a more "natural," biological, or even physical way. In this last point I will refer to an example of the Pareto Law. The intention of the paper is not only to describe the *dynamis* of the hierarchization process, but also to support a postulate of social discussion of the hierarchy pattern chosen by the society.

Keywords

archetype, instinct, social hierarchy, social hierarchization factors, Pareto distribution, inequality

1 Why Talk about the Hierarchization Process in a Society?

When we discuss the phenomenon of a social hierarchy, we analyze it from the perspective either of already having existed within an internally organized social structure or of the processes *instatu nascendi*. The social hierarchy is usually discussed and associated not only with power, social functions, and relationships (see, for example, the work of Max Weber),[1] but also with the concept of inequality; therefore when discussed, it often evokes emotions and resentments. In this paper I would like to focus on the dynamic aspects

1 Cf. Max Weber's theory of the social structure. M. Weber, *Economy and Society: A New Translation*, trans. K. Tribe, (Cambridge, Massachusetts: Harvard University Press, 2019); R. Bendix, *Max Weber: An Intellectual Portrait*, (Berkeley: University of California Press, 1977).

 | DOI:10.1163/9789004468757_018

of an appearing social hierarchy and show some psychological, instinctual, and archetypal origins (perspectives of interpretation) of this process. Doing so will allow us to unleash deeper levels of shaping this process and make us more aware of the factors actively shaping it. My general intention here is not to "fight" against such a phenomenon but rather to confront those aspects of it that in the long term may bring negative consequences to the present and the next generations' lives, such as (a) poverty, (b) not allowing some social groups to realize their basic humanitarian needs, (c) exploiting others, and (d) blocking other peoples' development in the name of particular social groups' interests. I believe that through discussing this social process, we may increase our ability to understand it better and take for consideration supporting different variants and directions the process can take.

2 Images Associated with the Concept of a Social Hierarchy

When we attempt to analyze the social hierarchy, we usually reach for the structures that already exist. We do it to extract a figure from the background. We visualize this in many forms. Below, we can see a few examples of this kind of visualization.

FIGURE 16.1 Ancient Egypt's social structure

For example, the social hierarchy of Egypt (Figure 16.1),[2] starting from the top to the bottom, consisted of Pharaohs, Nobles, Priests, Soldiers, Scribes,

2 Picture used with its author's (Dirk Laukens) permission. https://www.ancient-egypt-online.com/ancient-egypt-social-structure.html.

Merchants, Craftsmen, and Farmers and Slaves. The Pharaoh was at the top of the hierarchy and the farmers and slaves at the bottom. The Pharaohs were believed here to be gods in human form and the ultimate authority in Egypt. It was their duty to make the laws and maintain order in the Kingdom.[3]

Mayan society was divided between nobles, commoners, serfs, and slaves. The social order was maintained by a downward flow of honors, responsibilities, and titles and an upward flow of resources and goods. The upward flow of resources also helped to maintain the functioning and existence of the social hierarchy.[4] Nobles served as rulers, government officials, military leaders, high priests, local administrators, etc. They typically lived in the central areas of Maya cities. Commoners worked as farmers, laborers, and servants.[5]

In medieval feudal social structure in England there were two basic principles to feudalism: Every man had a lord, and every lord had land. The king was connected through this "chain" of people to the lowest man in the country. At each level a man had to promise loyalty and service to his lord. The king was at the top of the social hierarchy. Below the king was a tenant-in-chief—usually a baron (but also other Nobles, for example, Church officials, etc.). Below the barons were the knights. Below the knights were the peasants. The king gave large estates to his main nobles in return for a promise to serve him when necessary. The nobles also had to give the king part of the produce of the land.[6]

3 Innate Tendencies to Create a Social Structure

We've mentioned above that the social hierarchy is usually associated with dimensions like wealth, power, and social functions or relationships; but in the context of the contemporary post-industrial reality and free market of (sometimes very abstract) services, we should also add to those dimensions a factor of a general competence. When we think of the psychological factors influencing people's tendency to take part in this process, we can mention here, among others: the roles of instincts, innate archetypal tendencies, inborn tendencies

3 Cf. https://www.ancient-egypt-online.com/ancient-egypt-social-structure.html; https://www.ancient.eu/article/1123/social-structure-in-ancient-egypt/; https://www.ucl.ac.uk/museums-static/digitalegypt

4 Cf. H. McKillop, *The Ancient Maya*, (Santa Barbara, Denver: ABC-CLIO Inc., 2004); G. Morley Sylvanus, *The Ancient Maya*, (Palo Alto, CA: Stanford University Press, 1946).

5 Cf. L. V. Foster, *Handbook to Life in the Ancient Maya World*, (Facts On File, Inc.; Oxford: Oxford University Press, 2002).

6 Cf. F. Barlow, *The Feudal Kingdom of England 1042–1216*, (London: Routledge, 1999); D. McDowall, *An Illustrated History of Britain*, (Harlow: Pearson Education Limited, 1999).

of organizing complex systems, innate tendencies to develop one's abilities, task-related competences and our ability to imagine the "ideal," most valuable versions of reality that then become the forces pushing us towards the "most desirable" outcomes of our actions.

When it comes to instincts or innate behaviors, we should mention here that they are considered to be an inherent inclination of living organisms towards a particular complex behavior. They are considered to be the innate aspects of human behavior that emerge in us without training or education.[7] In general, we may say that any behavior can be treated as instinctive if it is performed without being based upon prior experience (that is, in the absence of previous learning) and is therefore an expression of innate biological factors. (For example, sea turtles, newly hatched on a beach, will automatically move toward the ocean.)

Instincts are seen here as inborn complex patterns of behavior that exist in most members of the species. The instinct-derived behaviors can be observed when we analyze more complex patterns of reactions and also when we think of the way we value particular, "more desired" versions of outcomes, behaviors, or our path of life. Some instinctive behaviors depend on maturational processes to appear. Instinctive behaviors are neither "genetically determined" nor rigid and unmodifiable. They depend on an internal mechanism that develops as a result of complex gene-environment interactions. We can add here that we should consider the archetypes as having the same immanent nature.

To describe the instinctive behaviors we use the terms "fixed action patterns"[8] or "modal action patterns."Ethology implies that, to denote instinctive behavioral sequences that are relatively invariant within the species and that almost inevitably manifest themselves completely, those action patterns are produced by the innate releasing mechanisms in response to external sensory stimuli known as the sign stimuli or the releasers. They are thought to be "hard-wired" in our brains. Konrad Lorenz, a famous Austrian ethologist who was one the key founders of the *fixed action patterns* concept, identified six characteristics of fixed action patterns. According to him those patterns are: stereotyped, complex, species characteristic, released, triggered, and independent of experience. To demonstrate this phenomenon he famously used a goose imprint on his boots. As a result of it, the goose would follow whoever wore the boots. This experiment demonstrated that the identity of the goose's mother was

---

7 This and the next paragraphs compare with: F. B. Mandal, *Textbook of Animal Behaviour*, (Dehli: PHI Learning; 3 rd edition, 2015); D. McFarland, *Animal Behaviour: Psychobiology, Ethology and Evolution*, (London: Longman; 3rd edition 1999).

8 Cf. J. Alcock, *Animal Behavior*, (Sunderland, Massachusetts: Sinaeur; 10th edition, 2013).

learned, but the goose's behavior (being focused on this external object) was conditioned by the innate instinctive factor.

Some of the theorists tended to use the word *instinct* as referring to the "propensity" for goal-directed combinations of the many innate human abilities that can be loosely and variably linked. In this perspective we can see the instinctual behaviors as showing some sort of plasticity. Some researchers underlined that a behavior might be considered as instinctual when it: is automatic, is irresistible, occurs at some point of development, can be triggered by some events in the environment, occurs in every member of the species, is usually unmodifiable, and when an organism doesn't need training in it but may profit from previous experiencing of it.[9] The source of instinct behaviors is to be seen as a result of the process of excitation occurring in the mind, and the immediate aim of it is to act towards removing this organic or mental stimulus.

Among the simple forms of instincts that have been observed in humans, we can mention, for example: (a) fear of snakes—which was found in six-month-old children, (b) the herd instinct—which was found in human children and in baboon infants, (c) infant cry—which is considered to be an instinctual reaction evoked internally, (d) maternal instinct—manifested particularly in response to the infant cry. Among more subtle, complex forms of instinctive behaviors not only in humans, but also in other animals, we can mention: (a) altruistic behaviors, (b) co-operative, for example, reciprocal behaviors, (c) mating-related behaviors, (d) building-relationships-related behaviors, and so on.[10] In primates the researchers observed the set of behaviors that were

---

9 "Criteria for instinctual behaviour are to (a) be automatic, (b) be irresistible, (c) occur at some point in development, (d) be triggered by some event in the environment, (e) occur in every member of species, (f) be unmodifiable, and (g) govern behaviour for which organism needs no training. Behaviours like hibernation, migration, nest building, mating are instincts. Psycho-analysts refer instinct to human motivational forces. Use of term motivational forces is replaced by instinctual drives. Instincts in humans are seen in instinctive reflexes. Babinski reflex, fanning of toes when foot is stroked is seen in babies and is indicative of development stages. A sense of fairness could be considered instinctual. Innate behaviour may be classified into seven types—irritability, tropism, kinesis, taxis, reflexes, instincts, and motivation. Taxis and kinesis belong to orientation behaviour." – Mandal, *Textbook of Animal Behaviour*.

10 Cf. Alcock, *Animal Behavior*. It's important here to mention that comparing human beings and animals has to be done very carefully and that we can't equate straight away these two realms. We have to approach this task cautiously. Robert A. Hinde writes about it in the book: *Individuals, Relationships and Culture. Links between Ethology and the Social Sciences* (Cambridge: Cambridge University Press, 1987). We can read there the following: "A final issue concerns the difficulty of knowing the level of analysis at which to search for parallels between animals and human species. Thus some have sought for parallels at a global level, comparing for instance the human propensity to seek for exclusive group

directed towards shaping and maintaining the group "social structure."[11] In Frans de Waal's book *Chimpanzee Politics: Power and Sex among Apes* we read: "The human economic system, with its reciprocal transactions and centralisation, is recognizable in the group life of Chimpanzees. They exchange social favors rather than gifts or goods."[12]

Instinctive behavior can be potentially affected or conditioned by hormones. For example, testosterone (main male sex hormone) nudges us to seek status by reducing fear and increasing our tolerance for risk. Testosterone is sometimes even called a status hormone. In men, the level of testosterone varies depending on many factors—for example, it has been observed that the level of testosterone in men may increase significantly in response to a competition or in the case of being susceptible to the smell of an ovulating woman. Research demonstrates that testosterone primes several instinctual sets of reactions, especially related to sexuality and dominance, but can also evoke tendencies to self-affirmation, dominating others, particular ways of responding to violent signals in other men, and with weakening of empathy. Once both primates and people make it to the top of a social hierarchy (in Chimpanzees it refers especially to males, as females are less hierarchically organized),[13] the

---

or individual rights over a particular area with animal territoriality, whilst others work at a lower level of analysis, for instance searching for animal models of the mechanisms of depression. In either case it is important to remember that superficial similarities in behavioural/psychological characteristics do not necessarily imply similar underlying mechanisms or similar functional significance. The converse, of course, is also true. In yet other cases, the problem is to find the right level for making comparisons." – ibidem, p. 9.

11 We need to underline here that we recognize the signs of a social structure among the animals on the basis of their interaction patterns and behaviors. It is we who "perceive" the social structure in the network of the interactions and relationships among the primates. The social structure or the social hierarchy emerges from those observed patterns. Cf. more on that in: McFarland, *Animal Behaviour*, 154f.

12 F. de Waal, *Chimpanzee Politics: Power and Sex among Apes*, (Baltiomore: Johns Hopkins University Press; 25th anniversary edition, 2007), 207.

13 On the subject of similarities between primates and humans cf. V. Morell, *Gorillas have developed humanlike social structure…*, https://www.sciencemag.org/news/2019/07/gorillas-have-developed-humanlike-social-structure-controversial-study-suggests (doi:10.1126/science.aay7809); L. Rodseth et al., "The Human Community as a Primate Society", (*Current Anthropology*, 32 (3), (1991)); C. C. Grueter, B. Chapais, D. Zinner, "Evolution of Multilevel Social Systems in Nonhuman Primates and Humans", *International Journal of Primatology*, 33(5), (2012): 1002–1037; doi: 10.1007/s10764-012-9618-z; F. L. Pryor, "What Does it Mean to be Human? A Comparison of Primate Economies", *Journal of Bioeconomics* 5, (2003): 97–145; doi:10.1023/A:1025866006933. De Waal in his book writes: "As a rule high-ranking males copulate more often than subordinates. This makes the evolution of male ambitions understandable, provided that mating success translates into reproductive success. To my eyes, the most striking result is that there seem to be two

tendency is for them to try to stay on top for as long as possible. Status maintenance involves not only continuing to engage in behaviors that demonstrate value, but also watching for threats that may lower one's status and one's position. Therefore, we can refer to this hormone as a potential factor initiating the process of evoking the social hierarchy within the society through stimulating the dominance-related mechanisms.

Different forms of the dominance hierarchy are found all throughout the animal kingdom. No matter the size or the complexity of the ranking systems in different species (see: "pecking order"), what they all have in common is that the hierarchies typically determine resource allocation, with the animals at the top of the hierarchy getting more and better food than the animals at the bottom. Consequently, the animals at the top of the heap are more likely to survive because they have more access to food and also will be more likely to pass their genome to the next generations.

While we are discussing the primates, it's worth mentioning a few other innate mechanisms that shape our interactions with an environment. A human being is "designed" to be immersed within its environment and constantly deals with sensory input (see: sensory deprivation experiments). Man is "designed" not only to orient himself within this environment, to process information, and recognize known and unknown objects in his surroundings, but also constantly **transgresses** the given situation towards increasing its access to new resources and new possibilities. We can, for example, observe it in toddlers who constantly search for new challenges—trying new ways, challenges, and possibilities. For them, new and unknown often means positive, desired, and exciting stimuli. We may say that we are built to be constantly on a border line between the known and the unknown, not only cognitively, but also in a simple physical way. We can demonstrate this by referring to the territorial behaviors of chimpanzees. Their territories consist of two different areas: the border and the core. A border or peripheral area of a territory is the

---

layers of social organisation. The first layer we see is a clear-cut rank order, at least among the most dominant individuals. Although primatologists spend a lot of energy discussing the value of the "dominance concept," they all know that it is impossible to ignore this hierarchical structure. The debate is not about its existence but about the degree to which knowledge of rank relationships helps to explain social processes. I think that, so long as we concentrate on the formal hierarchy, the explanations will be very poor indeed. We should also look behind it, at the second layer: a network of positions of influence. These positions are much more difficult to define..." – De Waal, *Chimpanzee Politics*, 207. De Waal also mentions in his book that researchers sometimes conceptualize Chimpanzees' social life from the perspective of the web social connections, where some individuals had central and other more peripheral positions in the group – Ibidem.

outside area of the community. Males and sometimes females and juveniles go on a regular basis on "patrols" to ensure other chimpanzees do not enter their territory. When they meet other groups of chimps or unknown "intruders," they attack them if the situation calls for such action. The fights end when the intruders leave or are defeated. After this war between chimpanzees and their enemies, the group either has to run away or wins, gaining new territory, food sources, and so on, potentially also new members of the group—in this case females. The addition of more females leads to more chimpanzees in the community and more genetic diversity. Research shows that besides all of these benefits, when there is more territory, females become bigger and have more births, and the population increases. Even if we treat the above as a metaphor, how well it describes the human existence.

4 More Complex Instinctual Behaviors

We can find more complex forms of innate behaviors or interactions between different living organisms in ecology that have been classified as different forms of a **biological interaction**—mutualism, parasitism, competition are only some of the possible forms of relationships or co-existence of the living organisms. We should also point them out when we try to characterize the shaping, the structurizing factors of the social complex systems.

It is interesting to mention here that a competition from the basic ethological perspective is seen as an essentially harmful form of interaction between organisms, in which both competing organisms can be harmed. This perspective emphasizes and brings an additional light to the topic of the human competitive relationships in the modern world. It can be observed especially when people face the situations with very limited resources. Competition both within and between species is an important topic not only in ecology, especially community ecology, but a particularly well observed and documented factor within a human society. Competition occurs by various mechanisms, which can generally be divided into **direct** and **indirect** competitive behaviors. These apply equally to intraspecific and interspecific dimension.[14]

We can mention here two sub-forms, two types of competition: interference and exploitative competition. During interference competition, organisms interact directly by fighting for resources. Interference competition is the process by which individuals directly compete with one another in pursuit of

14 This and the next paragraphs compare with: C. R. Townsend, *Essentials of Ecology*, (New Jersey: John Wiley & Sons; 2nd Edition, 2002).

resources. It can involve fighting, stealing, or ritualized combat. Direct intra-specific competition also includes claiming a territory, which then excludes other individuals from entering the area. There may not be an actual conflict between competitors, but the individual excluded from the territory suffers due to a reduced access to resources. In contrast, during exploitative competition, organisms interact indirectly by depleting available resources. In this case both groups of organisms suffer and gradually lose in terms of their adaptive power. It's worth underlining that in the interspecific competition, when two species compete for a limited resource, one species can even drive the other species to extinction. If we look at this rule as the potential mechanism affecting human relationships, we can realize how tough and potentially dangerous the social life can be, for example, when one group or a society perceives another as a potential threat to their existence (see: Nazi ideology).

The way in which resources are partitioned within a group also varies and can be shaped by the scramble and contest competition. Scramble competition involves a relatively even distribution of resources among a population as all individuals exploit a common resource pool. In contrast, contest competition is the uneven distribution of resources and occurs when hierarchies in a population influence the amount of resources each individual receives. Organisms at the top of the hierarchy obtain a sufficient quantity of the resources, when individuals at the bottom of the hierarchy don't obtain any.

Contest competition takes place when resources are associated with a territory or hierarchical structure within the population. Sometimes the resources are so prized that even potentially fatal confrontations can occur to acquire them.

Scramble competition involves a more equal distribution of resources than contest competition and occurs when there is a common resource pool that an individual cannot be excluded from. For instance, grazing animals compete more strongly for grass as their population grows, and food becomes a limiting resource. As all individuals compete here for the same quantity of food, each of them receives less and less food, which can gradually lead to unstable dynamics of this population. This equal division of resources can result in population crashes.

In light of the above examples of the intra- and inter-specific patterns of interactions observed in the animal kingdom, we should for the purpose of this paper add here that this instinctual background seems to affect and shape the whole range of our human patterns of behavior, values, and preferences. It happens on a very basic, preconscious, or even unconscious level and shapes not only our interpretations of our or other people's actions and the social reality, but also our choices undertaken in different social situations. In the context of our intensified competitive attitude, we may perceive and value particular actions leading us toward particular places within a social hierarchy. Our tendencies to search for new possibilities, to become the best within particular social groups, or our efforts to discover and acquire new territories or resources, we can consider as coming from those primal, instinctual background or biological adaptive forces.

5 Archetypes and a Social Structure

Remembering the above instinctual domain, I would like to focus now on the context of archetypal influences shaping and driving our psychological experience within a society. We know in the context of Jung's theory that the archetypes are the collectively inherited unconscious imaginary factors that shape our thinking and imagining. They also induce some of the patterns of our behavior. They are present in a human mind *in potential* and shape our actions in unconscious or pre-conscious ways.[15]

FIGURE 16.2 The pyramids of Giza

We observe them in a culture (see Figure 16.2)[16] or our dreams through not only recurring symbols, motifs in literature, motifs in paintings or myths, but also in more contemporary stories observed in the media. They have a trans-cultural character and have been observed independently in various historical or sociological contexts.

15 Cf. C. G. Jung, *The Archetypes and the Collective Unconscious*, in *The Collected Works*, v. 9.1, (London: Routledge; 1991).

16 https://pixabay.com/photos/pyramids-egypt-egyptian-ancient-2371501/ - Pixabay License, free for commercial use, no attribution required.

Jung in one of his papers described them this way:

> My views about the "archaic remnants", which I call "archetypes" or "primordial images"... The term "archetype" is often misunderstood as meaning certain definite mythological images or motifs, but these are nothing more than conscious representations. Such variable representations cannot be inherited. The archetype is a tendency to form such representations of a motif – representations that can vary a great deal in detail without losing their basic pattern.[17]

Each human mind retains these basic unconscious factors shaping our understandings of the human condition and the collective knowledge of our species. As we know Jung locates them within a realm of the collective unconscious. The archetypes are in this perspective innate; collectively universal; and able to shape reoccurring images, symbols, or ideas. They influence not only our thinking, but also interpreting and organizing perceived data. Below we can demonstrate a few examples of the archetypal images related to the mother complex. We can also notice here how those images gradually gain a more abstract, more "archaic" quality and how they transgress towards the Great Mother archetype (see Figures 16.3, 16.4 and 16.5).[18]

Jung analyzed in his papers some of the archetypal images—the wise old man, the child, the mother, the king—that are shaping our unconscious understandings of the human condition and represent the collective knowledge of our species. Other Jungian authors also described other archetypal figures: the innocent, the orphan, the hero, the caregiver, the explorer, the rebel, the lover, the creator, the magician. In that perspective we can say that archetypes not only shape our imagination or understanding of the particular roles within a society, but also are associated with particular key forms of our experience in our life. In the above case the images point at the collectively imagined, experienced mother, which meaning gradually acquires more abstract, symbolic, mythological attributes. We need to remember then, for the purpose of our efforts of better understanding the phenomenon of the social structure and

17 C. G. Jung, *Man And His Symbols*, (New York: Dell Publishing Co., Inc., 1968).

18 On the mother archetype cf. C.G. Jung, *Four Archetypes*, (London: Routledge, 2003); Figure 16.3 https://pixabay.com/photos/people-woman-pregnant-mother-baby-2575991/; Figure 16.4 https://pixabay.com/illustrations/bougereau-william-adolphe-1231632/; Figure 16.5 https://pixabay.com/photos/fantasy-landscape-monument-child-3097474/ - Pixabay License, free for commercial use, no attribution required.
E. Neumann, *The Great Mother: An Analysis of the Archetype*, (Princeton, New Jersey: Princeton University Press, 2015).

FIGURES 16.3–16.5 A variety of depictions of the great mother archetype

hierarchy, that archetypes affect not only "the figures" we find as symbolically meaningful, significant, and important, but also the way we perceive, interpret, and value particular information or ideas. They also fuel our motivations towards particular goals, dreams, or desires. They influence a shared collective social *imaginarium* within any cultural, biological, religious, or mythological context.

6 Static versus Dynamic

Although we usually approach the archetypes through their actualized and to some extent "**static**" structural forms related to a perceived "figure" of meaning, as imaginative structured forms—for example, symbols, archetypal images, and so on, we can also experience them through their more "**dynamic**," processual nature, as a directing factor that shapes and "crystallizes" psychological or behavioural processes, often perceived in a teleological perspective like as described by Jung's process of individuation. We observe in this case an archetype *in statu nascendi*, in the state of "being born," emerging. The archetype reveals here a universal, collective direction of the changes within a system in which a new pattern emerges.

In the second of the abovementioned forms, the archetypal forces especially strongly "merge" with the instinctual reactions or patterns of behavior. Jung visualized the innate relationship between archetypes and instincts as two sides of the same coin or as two ends of the spectrum similar to the spectrum of the electro-magnetic waves from infrared to ultraviolet. We may say that archetypes and instinctive drives mutually arise in our experience and interpenetrate each other. That's why it was important to describe above the examples of the instincts potentially influencing a dynamic of forming of the social hierarchy.

Before we go further, I would also like to differentiate for the purpose of this paper two more potential archetypal factors:

1. the archetypal forms referring to the most primary or basic experiences of human life[19] and
2. the archetypal forms that express or refer to more complex experiences, in this case also more complex social patterns that emerged along the line of the historic progress of the society but potentially haven't been observed in the past (for example, hundreds of thousands of years ago).

Both of those factors can be considered as having internally emergent character. We can try to describe them as not physically existing "at the beginning of time" but then gradually emerging in the evolution of the human species. They have the emergent character similar to a language[20] or the way the birds' singing emerged in the history of living organisms.

When we think of dynamic "processual" forms of the archetypal experiences, we direct our attention towards the most crucial life experiences human beings go through. Jung described some of these kinds of dynamic processes—for example, the process of integrating an individual shadow, or the process of individuation. More contemporary, Christopher Booker in the book: *The Seven Basic Plots: Why We Tell Stories*[21] focused on the basic archetypal patterns underlining the main socially presented stories:

1. Overcoming the Monster (see Figure 16),
2. Rags to Riches,
3. The Quest,

19 Cf. example the book: R. L. Moore, *King Warrior Magician Lover: Rediscovering the Archetypes of the Mature Masculine*, (London: Bravo Ltd.,1992); C. S. Pearson, *Hero Within - Six Archetypes We Live by* (Orphan, Innocent, Magician, Wanderer, Warrior, Altruist), (New York: Harper Elixir, 2016).

20 On the topic of acquiring of language cf. S. Pinker, *The Language Instinct*, (London: Penguin, 2015).

21 Cf. R. L. Moore, *The Archetype of Initiation: Sacred Space, Ritual Process, and Personal Transformation*, (Bloomington: Xlibris, 2001); J. Campbell, *The Hero with a Thousand Faces*, (San Fransisco: New World Library, 2012); C. Booker, *The Seven Basic Plots: Why We Tell Stories*, (London-New York: Continuum, 2005).

4. Voyage and Return,
5. Comedy,
6. Tragedy,
7. Rebirth.

FIGURE 16.6 A depiction of the archetypal defeat of the monster[22]

In comparative mythology, after studying myths around the world, Joseph Campbell extracted from them what he called **a monomyth**, or the hero's journey, that describes a hero who goes on an adventure, and in a decisive crisis wins a victory, and then comes home changed or transformed. We may say in the context of our efforts that the hero journey is a reflection, imprint, or impression of the influence of the innate instinctual and archetypal forces that shaped, in interaction with the natural external environmental circumstances, the emergent forms of the human adventure of life. These forms can be perceived not only as "distilled" or "extracted," but also as emergent forms of general collective or core experiences of human beings. In this case we may talk about "archetypal" in the sense described by Jung as the process of integrating the personal shadow, integrating the opposites, and so on. We talk here about the generalized form being on one hand, potentially present in us, and on the other hand, being a result of the abstraction process referring to billions of individual experiences of our species. Those core experiences have the "semantic power" of being "core," "iconic" experiences similar, for example, to experiences of being born, giving birth, dying, mating, fighting for life,

22 Figure 16.6 https://pixabay.com/illustrations/are-jorge-dragon-tales-stories-1503439/ - Pixabay License, free for commercial use, no attribution required.

and so on. We may say that on this higher level—describing more internally differentiated, culturally conditioned, appearing later in the human history forms—the primary archetypal forces are more "conditioned" by their cultural or sociological context, and I'd like to see the monomyth from this perspective.

7 A Social Hierarchy and the Figure of the King

As we mentioned earlier, the social hierarchy is considered to be a "natural," biologically rooted phenomenon but is also closely related to the concepts of power, competence, wealth, social significance, etc. In a social narration, one of the figures that expresses or personifies this power is a figure of the king (see Figure 16.7).[23] Jung described and analyzed this figure and its archetypal meaning in many papers, especially in the context of his studies on the king's symbolic relevance as an iconic psychological transformation of a psyche—the process of individuation. He saw the king not only as an archetypal form of the human being, but also as the final goal of the individuation process. The king was not only associated with being the highest point of the social structure or with a power, but was also seen as an expression of the idea of the finite destination of the individuation and the individual life.

FIGURE 16.7
The archetypal figure of the King

23 On the figure of king cf. C. G. Jung, *Psychology and Alchemy*, in *The Collected Works*, v. 12, (London: Routledge, 1991); A. Kuzmicki, *Symbolika Jaźni*, (Warsaw: Eneteia, 2008). Figure 16.7 https://pixabay.com/photos/tutankhamun-pharaoh-mask-gold-mask-1038544/ - Pixabay License, free for commercial use, no attribution required.

The king's figure represents the highest point of the social hierarchy. From the book of James Frazer *The Golden Bough*,[24] we know that the figure of the king is not transculturally homogeneous and that in different social contexts, kings—see also: shamans—were associated with different roles, tasks, and qualities, but they always carried on their shoulders the projection or a blue print of their social "uniqueness," super-natural qualities, extraordinary powers, *mana*, and so on. In a social perception and imagination the king or emperor was always someone at the top of the hierarchy, someone special and extraordinary. He was someone being blessed by the superpowers, blessed by the gods—or even being considered as an incarnation of god or the God Himself.

In society we not only imagine and fantasize about this top element of the hierarchy, but also visualize unconsciously, automatically a desired shape of a social structure itself, and we fuel our efforts on the way to the higher steps of the social ladder. On the base we may conclude that dynamic processes involved in shaping a social hierarchy include:

1. instinctual hierarchization of a social group (see also: hierarchization among primates, etc.) and
2. archetypally driven psychological processes—imagining, valuing, motivating (e.g., related to subjectively perceived power or imagination) related to efforts towards taking the higher places within the hierarchy.

After describing the above two dimensions, I'd like to refer at the end to the third group of factors—the laws influencing the structuring process within the complex systems. I mean here the regularities or patterns that can be observed within the complex systems and that seem "to shape" the structure of the systems, in our case also stratifying a society. Below I'd like to focus on one of those patterns or observed regularities—*the Pareto Law* or *Pareto distribution.*

8 Other Natural Hierarchization Factors—Pareto Distribution

The Pareto distribution is named after Italian economist Vilfredo Pareto who noted the 80/20 connection in 1896 (he published it in his first work *Cours d'économie politique*). Pareto showed that approximately 80% of the land in Italy at that time was owned by 20% of the population. He carried out surveys

24 J. G. Frazer, *The Golden Bough A Study in Magic and Religion*, (Oxford: Oxford University Press, 2009).

on a variety of other countries and found out to his surprise that a similar distribution applied.

Many natural phenomena have been shown empirically to exhibit such a distribution. When the probability of measuring a particular value of some quantity varies inversely as a power of that value, the quantity is said to follow a power law, also known variously as Zipf's law or the Pareto distribution. The origin of power-law behavior has been a topic of debate in the scientific community for more than a century. Those forms of distribution appear widely in physics, biology, earth and planetary sciences, economics and finance, computer science, demography, and the social sciences. For instance, the distributions of the sizes of cities, earthquakes, forest fires, solar flares, moon craters, and people's personal fortunes all appear to follow this pattern of regularity.[25] Dynamical systems to some extent seem to "display" this self-organizing feature.

From research we know that the generalized Pareto law, which belongs to the so-called power laws, can give us a valuable point of reference to interpreting and predicting changes within the complex systems—it's a valuable universal approximation of the observed distributions in a population. On the other hand, we have to remember that this law has some limitations and is usually used as one of the applied tools of interpreting data due to, let's say, its "ideal" character. We can usually observe it in its approximate forms when we attempt, on the basis of the empirical data, to generalize the Pareto curve.[26]

This innate feature of the complex systems corresponds directly to the process of social hierarchization, for example, through the wealth status of the members of the society. The other dimension of that process is inequality present within the system. Although the inequality seems to be in-natively associated with the social system, we are still studying and questioning its nature.[27] We can, as an example of these studies, mention here the World Inequality Database project, which is focused on contemporary studies of the inequality

25 Cf. for example: M.E.J. Newman, "Power laws, Pareto distributions and Zipf's law", *Contemporary Physics* 46, (2005): 323–351; B. J. Kim, V. Singh, R. S. Winer, "The Pareto rule for frequently purchased packaged goods: an empirical generalization", in *Marketing Letters* 28, (2017): 491–507, Springer, https://doi.org/10.1007.

26 Cf. C.Stone, D.Trisi, A.Sherman, J.Beltrán, A Guide to Statistics on Historical Trends in Income Inequality (updated on 13.01.2020), The Center on Budget and Policy Priorities, www.cbpp.org.

27 Cf. for example: T. Piketty, *Capital in the Twenty-First Century, Capital in the Twenty-First Century*, Cambridge, Massachusetts: Harvard University Press, 2017.

in the world. One of the results of this project was the *World Inequality Report 2018*.[28] Its authors describe the report in these words:

> The World Inequality Report 2018 relies on a cutting-edge methodology to measure income and wealth inequality in a systematic and transparent manner. By developing this report, the World Inequality Lab seeks to fill a democratic gap and to equip various actors of society with the necessary facts to engage in informed public debates on inequality.
>
> We show that income inequality has increased in nearly all world regions in recent decades, but at different speeds. The fact that inequality levels are so different among countries, even when countries share similar levels of development, highlights the important roles that national policies and institutions play in shaping inequality.
>
> How has inequality evolved in recent decades among global citizens? We provide the first estimates of how the growth in global income since 1980 has been distributed across the totality of the world population. The global top 1% earners has captured twice as much of that growth as the 50% poorest individuals. The bottom 50% has nevertheless enjoyed important growth rates. The global middle class (which contains all of the poorest 90% income groups in the EU and the United States) has been squeezed.

In the context presented above, we may ask again: *Why do we need to talk about the social hierarchy and the hierarchization or stratification process?* I would give here a few answers:

1. First, to make us aware of the patterns and involved factors of this process. In this context, the hierarchization process would be presented as "natural" and unavoidable and supported not only by our instinctual and archetypal tendencies, but also through other internally-associated-with-complex-systems regularities that can be observed in nature—in this case the self-organizing patterns within the highly complex dynamic system.
2. Second, from the Jungian perspective, to open us to the eventual possibility/necessity of choosing particular values shaping the socio-economic reality, knowing that it will affect the structure and internal dynamic within the social structure. From the psychoanalytical perspective, it would mean (a) first, to realize not only the conscious but also

28 *World Inequality Report 2018*. The report 2022 is also available on: https://wir2018.wid.world/.

the unconsciously accepted (as a normative point of reference to our) values—the values that "rule" our automatic, subconscious choices and preferences; and (b) second, to undertake the effort of "choosing" those of them that can hypothetically shape a better future for our society as a whole,[29] the values that can lay the foundation of our collective future with a particular social structure and with its inner, core axiological hierarchy.

On the basic level it can mean to position on the opposite ends of our normative axiological spectrum two visions or postulates:

- The strongest, most intelligent, most resourceful, most powerful (but sometimes also most manipulative, relentless) individuals can flourish. They have the right to have access to the majority of the resources.
- Every human being has the right to a "decent" life and meeting his or her fundamental needs.

From the Jungian perspective, it could practically mean that we would have to make an effort towards increasing (consciously) our ability of "choosing" or "supporting" particular archetypalpower-related forms or images (for example Mahatma Gandhi versus Adolf Hitler) and this way "support" our socially active values. This process would probably need an attitude focused on the ability to regulate our relationship with the innate archetypal or instinctual factors not only with awareness of their potential influence on us, but also with awareness of psychological processes of inflation and alienation mentioned by Jung. One will be able to undertake such efforts only by remembering that:

- we don't personally (consciously, as the conscious subjects) decide if or when archetypes activate themselves in our psyche,
- only "activated" or active archetypes/instincts can be perceived (recognized) as activated, and finally
- only when the archetypes have been activated and have influenced our psychic content, can they be brought to consciousness/attention (by getting into a direct relationship to the "I") and eventually lose their dominating power over our choices (see: inflation).

Only through conscious recognition and discussion of those "natural" forces lying within us and within the society or culture, we can hypothetically consciously/volitively "choose" or shape the future of our society.

When we analyze "positive" or "negative" aspects or consequences of the contemporary observed social hierarchical processes and their inequality, we

---

29 It's important to underline here that we can think of that as a real possibility of our collective choice only if we take for consideration a democratic social system. Only this system seems to give all society members the ability to shape top levels of the social structure.

can see how basic decisive problems are in front of us. I will demonstrate it referring to another statistical measure, the Gini Coefficient.

9 Gini Coefficient

The Gini coefficient measures the inequality among values of a frequency distribution—for example, levels of income. A Gini coefficient of **zero expresses perfect equality**, where all values are the same (e.g., where everyone has the same income). A Gini coefficient of **1 (or 100%) expresses maximal inequality** among values (e.g., for a large number of people, where only one person has all the income or consumption, and all others have none, the Gini coefficient will be very near to one).[30]

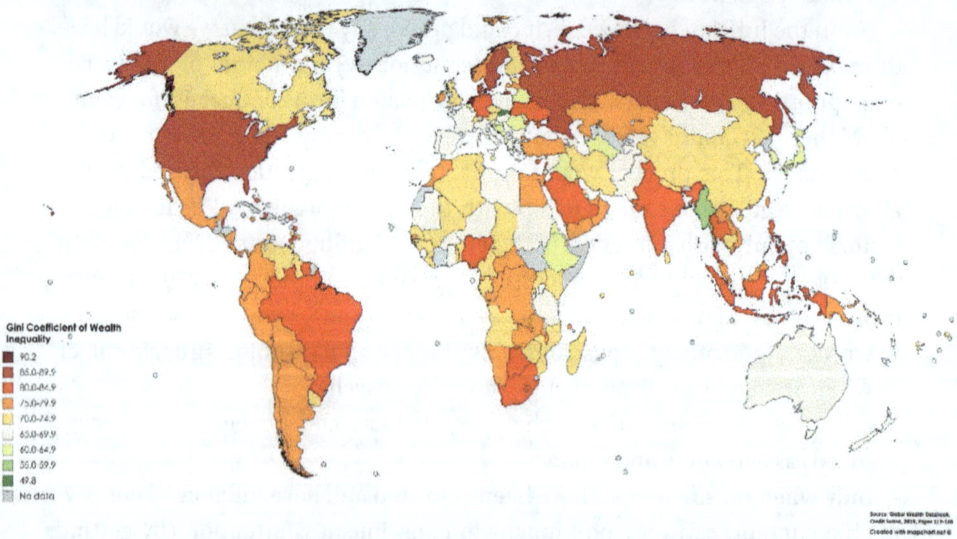

FIGURE 16.8 A map showing Gini coefficients for Wealth within countries for 2019[31]

30 Cf. L. G. Bellù, *Inequality Analysis. The Gini Index*, Agricultural Policy Support Service, Rome: Policy Assistance Division, FAO, 2016 - http://documents.worldbank.org/curated/en/242251476706821424/Poverty-and-shared-prosperity-2016-taking-on-inequality; J. Cuesta; M. Negre et al., *Poverty and shared prosperity 2016: taking on inequality*, World Bank Group, 2016 - http://documents.worldbank.org/curated/en/242251476706821424/Poverty-and-shared-prosperity-2016-taking-on-inequality.

31 A map showing Gini coefficients for Wealth within countries for 2019 based on the report by Credit Suisse, source: DennisWikipediaWiki on Wikipedia, available under CC BY-SA 4.0 (https://creativecommons.org/licenses/by-sa/3.0/legalcode).

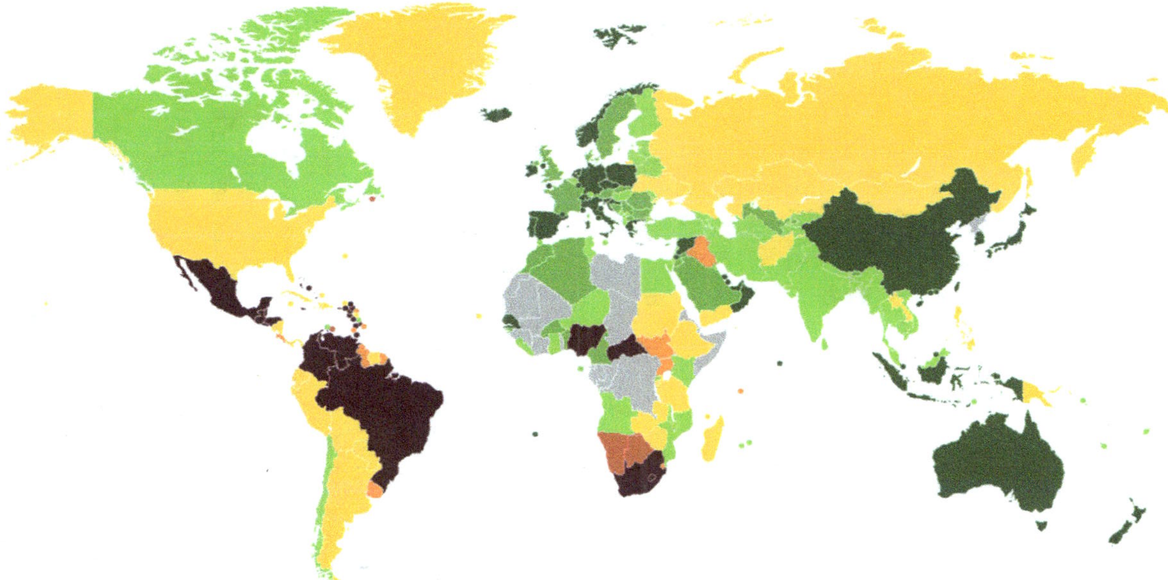

FIGURE 16.9 A map of countries by their most recent available intentional homicide rate (per 100,000 people)[32]

32 Map of countries by their most recent available intentional homicide rate (per 100,000 people), source: Allice Hunter on Wikipedia, available under CC BY-SA 4.0 (https://creativecommons.org/licenses/by-sa/3.0/legalcode).

When we analyze the social structure in the light of the pattern of its inequality, we can see different aspects of their dynamics. For example, some research shows that in the societies with a higher internal inequality are observed higher rates of violence-related acts or crimes.[33]

When we see the world map demonstrating all the countries with different Gini Index values, we can see that lower values of inequality are observed (in general) in the areas of the world with higher poverty rates and lower GDP.

Organizations that monitor the inequality globally—for example, World Inequality Lab or Oxfam International—raise a voice pointing at what they call "the inequality crisis." We can read about it in one of the reports they prepared:

> New estimates show that just eight men own the same wealth as the poorest half of the world. As growth benefits the richest, the rest of society – especially the poorest – suffers. The very design of our economies and the principles of our economics have taken us to this extreme, unsustainable and unjust point. Our economy must stop excessively rewarding those at the top and start working for all people. Accountable and visionary governments, businesses that work in the interests of workers and producers, a valued environment, women's rights and a strong system of fair taxation, are central to this more human economy. [...]It is four years since the World Economic Forum identified rising economic inequality as a major threat to social stability, and three years since the World Bank twinned its goal for ending poverty with the need for shared prosperity. Since then, and despite world leaders signing up to a global goal to reduce inequality, the gap between the rich and the rest has widened. This cannot continue. As President Obama told the UN General Assembly in his departing speech in September 2016: "A world where 1% of humanity controls as much wealth as the bottom 99% will never be stable." Yet the global inequality crisis continues unabated:
>
> – Since 2015, the richest 1% has owned more wealth than the rest of the planet.
> – Eight men now own the same amount of wealth as the poorest half of the world.
> – Over the next 20 years, 500 people will hand over $2.1 trillion to their heirs – a sum larger than the GDP of India, a country of 1.3 billion people.

33 See for example: by J.Hagan, R.Peterson, 1995, *Crime and Inequality*, Stanford University Press; https://www.economist.com/graphic-detail/2018/06/07/the-stark-relationship-between-income-inequality-and-crime; Morgan Kelly; Inequality and Crime. *The Review of Economics and Statistics* 2000; 82 (4): 530–539. doi: https://doi.org/10.1162/003465300559028;

> – The incomes of the poorest 10% of people increased by less than $3 a year between 1988 and 2011, while the incomes of the richest 1% increased 182 times as much.
> – A FTSE-100 CEO earns as much in a year as 10,000 people in working in garment factories in Bangladesh.
> – In the US, new research by economist Thomas Piketty shows that over the last 30 years the growth in the incomes of the bottom 50% has been zero, whereas incomes of the top 1% have grown 300%.
> – In Vietnam, the country's richest man earns more in a day than the poorest person earns in 10 years.
>
> Left unchecked, growing inequality threatens to pull our societies apart. It increases crime and insecurity, and undermines the fight to end poverty. It leaves more people living in fear and fewer in hope.[34]

That's why those organizations call us to address this issue. Some of the proposed solutions are progressive taxation, facilitating access for all citizens to education and well-paying jobs, preventing negative practices of the super-rich and corporations such as using so-called "tax heavens" or reducing wages below the humanitarian minimum. Those organizations are calling us to implement *An Economy for the 99%* (in opposition to what they called the present situation of *economy for the 1%*). When we read about this proposition, it seems to be very important to move towards a new paradigm of looking at the socio-economic reality. To achieve it we have to understand all the factors influencing this aspect of socio-economic life. And one of those factors is our psychological "attraction" to the top elements of a social structure—kings, presidents, CEOs, etc. These figures of the social structure are shining, powerful, fascinating, and attractive, but it looks like the time has come to look at *fascinans* associated with them and choose different values as a core stone of the society, putting in the first place the importance of a good, balanced, and fair life of all members of the society.

It's important to remember the historical evidence of how often elites of the societies abused their power. It can happen again, and some may say, it's happening now. The Financial Times investigative journalist Tom Burgis described one of the examples demonstrating this in his article on the socio-economic reality in DR Congo. He pointed out that the situation there is the combination of staggering wealth, rampant violence, and abject poverty. But he also

34 D. Hardoon, *An economy for the 99%*, 2017, https://www.oxfam.org/en/research/economy-99. Cf. also: L. Chancel, T. Blanchet, R. Clarke et al., *World inequality report*, World Inequality Lab., 2018, https://wir2018.wid.world/.

says that this situation is not coincidence, but part of a pattern causing devastation across Africa. Burgis underlines that the multinational companies hold enormous economic and political power in post-independence African countries. The outcome of it is moving from previous colonial exploitation to modern exploitation.[35] To give another example of this kind of phenomena, I'd like to mention the debt bondage observed in third world countries. Bonded labor in this case involves the exploitive interlinking of credit and labor agreements that devolve into slave-like exploitation due to severe power imbalances between the lender and the borrower.[36]

9.1 *Shall We Then Critically Discuss the Social Structure and the Wealth Distribution?*

In my opinion, it's important to look for new forms of socio-economical systemic regulations to be able to establish a better socio-economical system working for the whole society, not only for 1% of the population, especially knowing humankind's history with slavery or the recent rising power of the international corporations that are able to control or affect even the economies of individual countries or society. To achieve it, we have to re-think the way we perceive or—in the perspective of unconsciousness—we "dream" of the power figures in a society and a normative, axiological system we "visualize," promote, or "desire."

References

Alcock J., *Animal Behavior*, Sunderland, Massachusetts: Sinaeur, 2013.

Alvaredo F., Chancel L., Piketty T. et al., *World inequality report*, World Inequality Lab, 2018 - https://wir2018.wid.world/.

Barlow F., *The Feudal Kingdom of England 1042–1216*, London: Routledge, 1999.

Bellù L.G., *Inequality Analysis. The Gini Index*, Rome: Agricultural Policy Support Service, Policy Assistance Division, FAO, 2006 - http://www.fao.org/policy-support/resources/resources-details/en/c/446282/.

Bendix R., *Max Weber: An Intellectual Portrait*, Berkeley: University of California Press, 1977.

Booker C., *The Seven Basic Plots: Why We Tell Stories*, London & New York: Continuum, 2005.

35 T. Burgis, *The Looting Machine: Warlords, Tycoons, Smugglers and the Systematic Theft of Africa's Wealth*, (New York: Harper Collins, 2016).

36 Cf. https://www.antislavery.org/slavery-today/modern-slavery/.

Burgis T., *The Looting Machine: Warlords, Tycoons, Smugglers and the Systematic Theft of Africa's Wealth*, New York: Harper Collins, 2016.

Cuesta J., Negre M. et al., *Poverty and shared prosperity 2016: talking on ineqality*, World Bank Group, 2016.

Foster, L. V., *Handbook to Life in the Ancient Maya World*, Facts On File, Inc., Oxford: Oxford University Press, 2002.

Frazer J.G., *The Golden Bough A Study in Magic and Religion*, Oxford: Oxford University Press, 2009.

Grueter C. C., Chapais B., Zinner D.,"Evolution of Multilevel Social Systems in Non-human Primates and Humans", *International Journal of Primatology*, 33(5), (2012): 1002–1037; doi: 10.1007/s10764-012-9618-z.

Hagan J., Peterson R., 1995, Crime and Inequality, Stanford University Press.

Hardoon D., *An economy for the 99%* - https://www.oxfam.org/en/research/economy-99, 2017.

Hinde R.A., *Individuals, Relationships and Culture. Links between Ethology and the Social Sciences*, Cambridge: Cambridge University Press, 1987.

Jung C.G., *Man And His Symbols*, New York: Dell Publishing Co., Inc., 1968.

Jung C. G., *The Archetypes and the Collective Unconscious, The Collected Works,* v. 9.1, London: Routledge, 1991.

Jung C. G., *Psychology and Alchemy, The Collected Works,* v. 12, London: Routledge, 1991.

Jung C. G., *Four Archetypes*, London: Routledge, 2003.

Kelly M., *Inequality and Crime*. The Review of Economics and Statistics 2000; 82 (4): 530–539. doi: https://doi.org/10.1162/003465300559028.

Kim B.J., Singh V. & Winer R.S., "The Pareto rule for frequently purchased packaged goods: an empirical generalization", *Mark Lett* 28, (2017): 491–507; https://doi.org/10.1007.

Kuzmicki A., *Symbolika Jaźni*, Warsaw: Eneteia, 2008.

Mandal F.B., *Textbook of Animal Behaviour*, Dehli: PHI Learning, 2015.

McDowall D., *An Illustrated History of Britain*, Harlow: Pearson Education Ltd, 1989.

McFarland D., Animal Behaviour: Psychobiology, Ethology and Evolution, London: Longman, 1999.

McKillop, H., *The Ancient Maya*, Santa Barbara, Denver: ABC-CLIO, Inc., 2004.

Morell V., *Gorillas have developed humanlike social structure…*, source: https://www.sciencemag.org/news/2019/07/gorillas-have-developed-humanlike-social-structure-controversial-study-suggests. doi:10.1126/science.aay7809, 2019.

Morley, S. G., *The Ancient Maya*, Palo Alto: Stanford University Press, 1969.

Moore R.L., *King Warrior Magician Lover: Rediscovering the Archetypes of the Mature Masculine*, London: Bravo Ltd, 1992.

Moore R.L., *The Archetype of Initiation: Sacred Space, Ritual Process, and Personal Transformation*, Bloomington: Xlibris, Corp., 2001.

Neumann E., *The Great Mother: An Analysis of the Archetype*, Princeton, New Jersey: Princeton University Press, 2015.

Newman M. E. J., "Power laws, Pareto distributions and Zipf's law", in: *Contemporary Physics* 46, (2005): 323–351.

Pearson C.S., *Hero Within - Six Archetypes We Live by* (Orphan, Innocent, Magician, Wanderer, Warrior, Altruist), New York: HarperElixir, 2016.

Piketty T., *Capital in the Twenty-First Century, Capital in the Twenty-First Century*, Cambridge, Massachusetts: Harvard University Press, 2017.

Pinker S., *The Language Instinct*, London: Penguin, 1994.

Pryor F.L. (2003), "What Does it Mean to be Human? A Comparison of Primate Economies", *Journal of Bioeconomics* 5, (2003): 97–145; doi:10.1023/A:1025866006933.

Rodseth L. et al., "The Human Community as a Primate Society", *Current Anthropology*, 32 (3), (1991).

Stone C., Trisi D., Sherman A., Beltrán J., *A Guide to Statistics on Historical Trends in Income Inequality* (updated on 13.01.2020), The Center on Budget and Policy Priorities, www.cbpp.org.

Townsend C.W., *Essentials of Ecology*, New Jersey: John Wiley & Sons, 2002.

Weber M., *Economy and Society: A New Translation*, Cambridge, Massachusetts: Harvard University Press, 2019.

CHAPTER 17

Cultural Complex, Death Anxiety, and Individuation during the Times of Populism

A Dialogue between Jungian Psychology and Social Psychology

*Helge Michael Osterhold**

Abstract

A trend towards political polarization and radicalization is observable in many countries across the world. The rise of populist movements and an increasingly heated polarized discourse in the face of mounting environmental and cultural challenges calls for a multifaceted psychological engagement with these phenomena. C.G. Jung's vision of individuation remains crucial for understanding, and possibly mitigating, developments towards radicalization and division within and between cultures. This paper considers classic and contemporary depth psychological ideas regarding individuation, shadow work, and cultural complexes, and applies these ideas to current socio-political developments. To further elucidate, Jungian thought is brought into conversation with the findings of a body of literature within Social Psychology called Terror Management Theory (TMT) that points to unconscious death anxiety as amplifying a sense of separation and otherness, as well as judgment and conflict between individuals and groups. This paper aims to deepen the understanding of current cultural polarization phenomena as well as to explore possibilities for collective healing and growth by synthesizing ideas from Jung and TMT research and to rekindle the fire of individuation as a counter to the trend of polarization, alienation, and conflict.

Keywords

individuation, cultural complex, death anxiety, terror management theory, depth psychology, populism, polarization

* This chapter is an edited version of a paper originally published in the Journal of Analytical Psychology, 2021, 66, 4 - © 2021, The Society of Analytical Psychology.

 | DOI:10.1163/9789004468757_019

1 Introduction

In these times of global uncertainty in relation to growing environmental, social, and cultural challenges, a trend towards populism and polarization can be observed across the world.[1] This paper aims to provide an interdisciplinary psychological perspective to add to the emerging literature on these phenomena. Drawing from two schools of psychology, Jungian psychology and social psychology's Terror Management Theory (TMT), which on the surface may have little in common conceptually and methodologically, this interdisciplinary inquiry hopes to offer integrative and complementary psychological insights about the dynamics of populism and polarization and illustrate possible mitigating directions. In addition, there seems to be an opportunity for mutual enrichment and stimulation between the two respective fields. The following pages will first provide a brief synopsis of the phenomena of rising populism and polarization. Second, a theoretical and research overview illustrates how Jungian depth psychology and TMT conceptualize central factors of *group thinking* and *us versus them dynamics* inherent in both populism and polarization. Finally, this paper will show how both approaches arrive at a common and mutually enriching ground that offers potentially remedial perspectives and insights.

2 Populism and Polarization

Previously more of a marginal phenomenon, populism has enjoyed a steady rise over the past few decades. During the last 20 years, European populist parties have tripled their votes and were elected into 11 national governments, while globally five of the largest seven democracies have elected populist leaders, among them the U.S., India, Brazil, Mexico, and the Philippines.[2] "Populism today is a truly global phenomenon"[3] that was marked by perplexing watershed moments like the election of Donald Trump and Brexit. This development has taken place alongside the continuation of globalization; the 2008

1 P. Lewis, S. Clarke, C. Barr, N. Kommenda, J. Holder, (n.d.), "Revealed: One in four Europeans vote populist", *The Guardian* - https://www.theguardian.com/world/ng-interactive/2018/nov/20/revealed-one-in-four-europeans-vote-populist; C. H. de Vreese, F. Esser, T. Aalberg, C. Reinemann, J. Stanyer, "Populism as an Expression of Political Communication Content and Style: A New Perspective", *The International Journal of Press/Politics,* 2018, 23(4): 423–438.

2 Lewis, Clarke, Barr, Kommenda, Holder, op. cit.

3 de Vreese, Esser, Aalberg, Heinemann, Stanyer, op. cit.

financial crisis and its lasting economic impact; the international migrant flow and refugee crisis; and lastly, the ever-increasing threat of climate change. Emphasizing at times economic, cultural, or class issues, populism's appeal generally seems to rely on economic insecurity as well as on cultural backlash, among other complex factors.[4] Research corroborates that "inequality contributes to individual-level status anxiety, perceptions of unfairness, and elevated intergroup threat, all of which are associated with populist attitudes and/or support for populist candidates".[5]

The definition of the term *populism* has been debated within the social sciences, having been described as an ideology, a movement, a discourse, or a syndrome, and attributed to both left-wing and right-wing politics but seldom claimed by any group or individual.[6] At the same time, there seems to be a general understanding that populism, while not representing one specific, well-founded political or philosophical orientation, typically involves a critical stance towards what is considered "the establishment" and a special regard of the common people. It can thus be defined as a

> thin-centered ideology that considers society to be ultimately separated into two homogeneous and antagonistic camps, 'the pure people' versus 'the corrupt elite,' and which argues that politics should be an expression of the *volonté générale* (general will) of the people.[7]

The brand of populism manifested in the ascent and presidency of Donald Trump is a good example of this. While a member of the wealthy elite himself, Trump succeeded with a the-people-versus-the-elite rhetoric as the core of his political message (i.e. 'draining the swamp'). At the same time, while emphasizing this core tenet, there is little ideological grounding or policy vision for a social justice aim that would be expected from a movement set to better the lives of ordinary people and take power back from the establishment. However, rather than ascribing populism to one party, movement, or entity that supports the will of the people, it needs to be understood "as a political style

4 Ibidem.

5 A. R. Oxendine, "The political psychology of inequality and why it matters for populism", *International Perspectives in Psychology: Research, Practice, Consultation*, 2019, 8(4), 180.

6 C. Mudde, C. R. Kaltwasser, *Populism – A very short introduction*. New York, NY: Oxford University Press, 2017.

7 Ibidem, 5–6.

that is performed, embodied and enacted across a variety of political and cultural contexts" in today's dynamic media and social media environment.[8]

The related phenomenon of political polarization (i.e., a deep ideological division and partisan animosity between opposition groups) can occur alongside populism. As in the ascent of populism, economic inequality has been pointed out as a particular factor that "creates or perpetuates a number of societal challenges, including weakened democracy, sharp political polarization, stunted economic growth, status anxiety, and low levels of trust".[9]

While rising polarization has been observed in countries like Canada, New Zealand, and Switzerland over the past decades, it seems particularly pronounced in the United States,[10] where "partisan animus…has grown dramatically over the past two decades".[11] Along with increasing polarization in recent decades, researchers have observed fundamental social and economic changes, particularly a rise in income inequality.[12]

It has been noted that partisans not only disagree more but also *feel* more negatively about people in the opposing party, and this negativity has become more consistent.[13] Interestingly, negative feelings like fear, anger, and frustration towards members of the opposition are mounting and appear to be equally or more pronounced than the alignment with the positions of one's

8 A critical reflection entailing a nuanced consideration of political, cultural, economic, and environmental and historical circumstances could extrapolate unique features of different regional and national developments of populism; however, such an inquiry is beyond the scope of this paper. Also, this paper takes no position as to whether or not populist movements are ultimately positive or negative as scholars describe them as both a threat and a corrective for democratic politics – B. Moffitt, *The global rise of populism: Performance, political style and representation*, (Stanford, CA: Stanford University Press, 2016), 3; Mudde and Kaltwasser, op. cit.

9 Oxendine, op. cit. 179, citing American Political Science Association Task Force, 2004; Buttrick, Oishi, 2017; Dabla-Norris et al., 2015; McCarty, Poole, Rosenthal, 2006; Muller, Seligson, 1994; Rahn, Rudolph, 2005; Rudolph, Popp, 2010; Rupasingha, Goetz, Freshwater, 2006.

10 L. Boxell, M. Gentzkow, J. M. Shapiro, "Cross-Country Trends in Affective Polarization", *National Bureau of Economic Research Working Paper,* (2020), No. 26669 - https://www.nber.org/papers/w26669.

11 S. Iyengar, M. Krupenkin, "The Strengthening of Partisan Affect", *Advances in Political Psychology*, 39(1), (2018): 201.

12 Polarized America provides in-depth explorations of the relationship between polarization, economic inequality, and immigration among other forces, showing the mutual influence between these factors – N. McCarty, K. T. Poole, H. Rosenthal, *Polarized America: The dance of ideology and unequal riches*, (Cambridge, MA: MIT Press, 2016).

13 Iyengar, Krupenkin, 201.

own political party.[14] In that sense, polarization, besides reflecting a political or cultural reality, may be viewed as a deep, emotional process in which forces related to identity, belonging, and safety supersede cognitive-conscious information gathering and truth finding.[15]

As seems to be the case for polarization, we could conjecture that populism too—with its offering of simple explanations and targeting of identifiable culprits in response to increasingly challenging and complex problems—makes it not only a political option, but also an emotionally appealing route for people under stressful and perturbing societal circumstances.

As political science, economics, and social psychology have studied the dynamics between economic and cultural factors that pressure the psychological drift into populism and polarization, Jungian psychology and Terror Management Theory offer some important contributions to yet deeper psychological undercurrents that may be at play. The propensity to reject, alienate, or scapegoat some identified other, present in both populism and polarization, seems to be particularly suited for this inquiry. The underlying dynamic of us versus them group thinking and the emotional experience of fear, anger, or hatred towards other groups can be explored, not only in the sense of common people versus power structures/establishment, but also in the pure/good people versus other/bad people dynamic that both populist movements and polarization seem to evoke and foster.

3 Individuation and the Problem of Mass Mentality in Jungian Thought

In order to appreciate how Jung's ideas apply to these current socio-cultural developments, it seems necessary to briefly review some basic concepts.

---

14 Pew Research Center, *Partisanship and political animosity in 2016: Highly negative views on the opposing party - and its members*, - https://www.people-press.org/wpcontent/uploads/sites/4/2016/06/06-22-16-Partisanship-and-animosity-release.pdf, (2016): 1.

15 On the contrary, studies showed, for instance, that both liberals and conservatives in the United States display a "similar aversion toward learning about the views of their ideological opponents ... [because they] anticipated that hearing from the other side would induce cognitive dissonance (e.g., require effort, cause frustration) and undermine a sense of shared reality with the person expressing disparate views" – J. Frimer, L. J. Skitka, M. Motyl, "Liberals and conservatives are similarly motivated to avoid exposure to one another's opinions", *Journal of Experimental Social Psychology*, 72, (2017): 2. Due to this underlying "confirmation bias" people expose themselves largely to belief-confirming information, interpret available information in a belief-confirming manner, and remember information that confirms their beliefs – ibidem, 3.

Individuation, the lifelong process of "coming to selfhood," of becoming an "in-dividual," the embracing of one's "innermost, last and incomparable uniqueness"[16] is at the core of Jung's psychology, a leitmotiv around which the different parts of his work cluster and organize. Continuing a long tradition in Western thought of appreciating and emphasizing the coming into being of the unique individual, Jung lays out the psychological trajectory and developmental tasks of this process throughout a human life. Herein, the individuation path begins with development of both the *ego* and the *persona* (i.e., the masks we wear in social contexts), through discovering and manifesting one's unique inclinations and particular style while attempting to fit into family, culture, and society to become an accepted and useful member of the collective. During the second part of life, individuation proper emphasizes the growing awareness and expression of one's deep, innate character against the backdrop of collective expectations; the expansion of ego consciousness occurs by integrating unconscious material and previously exiled or disavowed shadow parts toward an enlarged psychic totality, by "sensing the self".[17] By becoming attuned to the unconscious, working with its contents and integrating the unwanted/foreign opposites within—rather than suppressing them and projecting them onto others—a new extended consciousness arises. And while this progression toward individual authenticity and wholeness is sometimes criticized as a particularly Western and potentially indulgent path of navel-gazing individualism, Jung's vision for individuation, of a self-realized and self-conscious individual, was always embedded in relationality and community.

> This widened consciousness is no longer that touchy, egotistical bundle of personal wishes, fears, hopes, and ambitions that always has to be compensated or corrected by unconscious counter-tendencies; instead, it is a function of relationship to the world of objects, bringing the individual into absolute, binding, and indissoluble communion with the world at large.[18]

16 C. G. Jung, "The relations between the ego and the unconscious", In C. G. Jung, *The Collected Works*, v. 7, trans. R. F. C. Hull, (Princeton, NJ: Princeton University Press, 1966/1928), § 266.

17 Ibidem, § 405.

18 G. Jung, "The relations between the ego and the unconscious", In C. G. Jung, *The Collected Works*, v. 7, trans. R. F. C. Hull, (Princeton, NJ: Princeton University Press, 1966/1928), § 275.

In individuation, Jung deemed the difficult task of differentiation from the collective in relation to conscious and unconscious layers as crucial (regarding both inner and outer manifestations of the collective psyche). He warned that failure in separation would be problematic in two ways. On one side, it would impact the quality of life of the individual whose individuation is stunted so that his true nature remains submerged in a mix of conscious zeitgeist, expectations of the collective culture, and the demands of complexes in the unconscious. On the other side, the life of others will be affected as the un-individuated person "will infallibly try to force the demands of his unconscious upon others, for identity with the collective psyche always brings with it a feeling of universal validity—'godlikeness'—which completely ignores all difference in the personal psyche of his fellows".[19] The quality of an experienced "universal validity" of one's arguments and "godlikeness" of one's convictions Jung describes is currently on vivid display in many polarized political discourses, for example, between liberals and conservatives in the United States, where, as we saw earlier, the political polarization has taken on an increasingly hostile emotionality beyond actual political positions. However, besides this undifferentiated conviction of the validity of one's views and the twin phenomenon of affective aversion, what exactly is being considered bad, threatening, or destructive in members of the "other side," besides being a political opinion, can be looked at more closely through the lens of shadow projection and insufficient individuation. Again, the extreme polarization in the U.S. can serve as an exemplar to illustrate this point as the aggression and oppressive nature in the arguments of the *other side* is often perceived from either side. Democrats may feel fear, frustration, and irritation towards Republicans, seeing them as intolerant, selfish, and lacking compassion. While these qualities may be reflected in actual political positions taken by Republicans, these qualities may also, in a Jungian mirror, appear as shadow projections. A Democrat may be victim to their own shadow in not recognizing how their stance towards Republicans could be a projection of their own intolerance, narcissism, and lack of compassion. And a Republican may feel fearful and spiteful towards Democrats, perceiving their political claims as a threat to their identity and way of life, and judging Democrats as selfish, aggressive, and inconsiderate—all of which again could be seen as shadow projections and reflective of one's own inner stance and behavior (i.e., selfish, aggressive, inconsiderate, etc.). Likewise, judging the "bleeding heart" liberal's consideration of marginalized

19 Jung, op. cit., § 240.

or oppressed groups as overly sympathetic or weak, a Republican may be projecting in defense against the shadow of one's own unexpressed/neglected Christian compassion. By doing the difficult and painful labor of such introspection, one can face and possibly reclaim such shadow aspects of oneself, be humbled by confronting them, less prone to projecting them onto the "other side," and look with less emotional charge and aversion at their positions. Just this element of shadow work alone seems relevant for a possible diffusion of the harsh emotional climate in polarization dynamics.

Besides his concern about the impact of projection and of unfiltered god-like convictions, Jung was generally suspicious of the ethical maturity and intelligent intentionality of mass movements and group thinking. Proclaiming that "the bigger an organization the more unavoidable is its immorality and blind stupidity",[20] Jung saw the individuated individual's creativity and compassion as the ground for positive development of humanity. Moreover, he stated "It is, unfortunately, only too clear that if the individual is not truly regenerated in spirit, society cannot be either, for society is the sum total of individuals in need of redemption".[21] For decades, Jungian thinkers have emphasized how the sum of every individual's expanded consciousness through individuation contributes to the overall consciousness of the collective world.[22]

Jung establishes two interrelated, and in a way, counter-directional movements for true individuation: the distinction and separation from conscious and unconscious collective influences as well as the grounding and expansion of the ego personality into the larger field of the unconscious and the deeper Self. The second point is particularly important, as this transpersonal field is also understood as the spiritual ground of the individual and as the realm in and through which experiences of transcendence are possible. So in a way, individuation leads to further distinction from the collective as well as to a deepened, authentic, and compassionate relationship to collective exterior (society) and collective interior (the archetypal, spiritual realm of possible connection to something transcendent, numinous). Jung cautions that a person without a profound relationship to the unconscious would be vulnerable to collective forces.

> The individual who is not anchored in God [i.e., the Self] can offer no resistance on his own resources to physical and moral blandishments of the world.

---

20 Ibidem.

21 Jung, "The undiscovered self (present and future)", In Jung, *The Collected Works*, v. 10, trans. R. F. C. Hull, (Princeton, NJ: Princeton University Press, 1970a/1957), § 536.

22 E.g. E. Edinger, *The Creation of Consciousness: Jung's Myth for Modern Man,* (Toronto, Canada: Inner City Books, 1984).

> For this he needs the evidence of inner transcendent experience, which alone can protect him from the otherwise inevitable submersion in the mass.[23]

Jung saw a spiritual function and spiritual need as intrinsic to the psyche and their fulfillment as not only necessary to being able to withstand mass thinking and mass behaviors, but also speculated that, conversely, the lack of spiritual fulfillment could be a driving force in impassioned engagement with political and other mass movements, as a quasi-fulfillment of spiritual needs to be connected to something greater.[24] Being related to the deeper psyche "does not mean, of course, that there will not be collisions of opinion and conflicting obligations, or disagreement about the 'right' way"; but rather, in the face of conflict, "one must constantly withdraw and listen to one's inner voice in order to find the individual standpoint that the Self intends one to have".[25]

4 Cultural Unconscious and Cultural Complexes

While Jung was keenly interested in understanding the unique psychological makeup of different cultures, he typically connected conscious expressions of culture directly to the archetypal level of the unconscious, as in his elaboration of the eruption of the "Wotan archetype" attempting to explain the unconscious forces in the German collective psyche leading up to the Second World War.[26] Adding an important distinction to collective aspects of the psyche, Henderson introduced the term "cultural unconscious",[27] designating it to a specific stratum in the unconscious that bridges personal and archetypal realms. Based on this conceptual ground, the idea of cultural complexes has

---

23 Jung, „The undiscovered self", § 511.

24 While this warrants a much larger discussion beyond the scope of this paper, it should be clarified that the religious function of the psyche and spiritual fulfillment, to Jung, are not religious questions in the traditional sense of the word. While experiencing the numinous was ultimately important to Jung, at a base level, being in touch and in relation with the unconscious and doing the inner work of becoming conscious towards one's own wholeness serves this spiritual need within the psyche. Overall, it is evident that individuation is crucial for a mature centeredness and authenticity that rises from being rooted in deeper parts of the psyche and thereby one is less vulnerable and malleable in relation to pressures, expectations, and temptations coming from collective currents.

25 M. L. von Franz, "The process of individuation", In Jung, *Man and his symbols*, (New York, NY: Anchor Press, 1954), 223.

26 Jung, „Wotan", In Jung, *The Collected Works*, v. 10, op. cit., 179–194.

27 J. Henderson, *Cultural attitudes in psychological perspective*, (Toronto, Canada: Inner City Books. 1984).

been developed more recently (e.g., Kimbles,[28] Singer,[29] Singer and Kimbles;[30] Raschke, Singer).[31] Singer and Kimbles explain that, just as personal complexes form out of the personal unconscious and its relation to deeper archetypal layers and are informed by early experiences with parents and caregivers, "cultural complexes can be thought of as arising out of the cultural unconscious"[32] and "are based on repetitive, historical group experiences, which have taken root in the cultural unconscious of the group"[33] and are internalized in the psyche of the individual.

Cultural unconscious and cultural complexes play roles in two directions.[34] On the one hand, the honoring of shared history and value systems, common expectations, and definitions of uniqueness and destiny aids in identity formation and provides a sense of belonging for individuals and groups. On the other hand, cultural complexes reflect and shape attitudes towards other groups, determine fears, animosities, and feelings of superiority or inferiority, to name just a few. Cultural complexes can be constellated around different levels of identity and group formation, from national, racial, ethnic, religious, or gender characteristics, to social identities like sexual orientation, political association, or ability/disability status. Including conscious and unconscious elements, cultural complexes inform a conglomerate of thoughts, emotions, and behaviors that could be referred to as "collective mentality"[35] that should be brought to awareness in the process of individuation, or can otherwise take over the consciousness of an individual or group. Pointing to the powerful influence of cultural complexes in development and activation of us versus them thinking and inter-group conflicts ranging from simple stereotyping to minority oppression and genocidal war, Kimbles concludes that "humans have yet to learn how

---

28 S. Kimbles, "The cultural complex and the myth of invisibility", In *The vision thing: Myth, politics and psyche in the world,* T. Singer (ed.), (New York, NY: Routledge, 2000): 157–169.

29 Singer (ed.), *The vision thing*; Singer (ed.), *Cultural Complexes and the Soul of America: Myth, Psyche, and Politics,* (New York, NY: Routledge, 2020).

30 T. Singer, S. Kimbles (eds.), *The cultural complex: Contemporary Jungian perspectives on psyche and society,* (New York, NY: Routledge, 2004).

31 J. Raschke, T. Singer (eds.), *Europe's many souls: Exploring cultural complexes and identities,* (New Orleans, LA: Spring Journal, Inc, 2016).

32 Singer, Kimbles, *The cultural complex.* 4.

33 Ibidem, 7.

34 Kimbles, „The cultural complex and myth of invisibility".

35 G. Sauer, "About two cultural complexes: The German complex of superiority and the Russian complex of feeling encircled by hungry barbarians", In *Europe's many souls; Exploring cultural complexes and identities,* J. Raschke, T. Singer (eds.), (New Orleans, LA: Springs Journal Inc., 2016), 212.

to deal less destructively with the implications of these powerful intragroup shadow processes".[36]

Cultural complexes are thought of in a similar way to personal complexes rooted in childhood experiences, in that collective historic experiences of a group are stored and interact with the conscious attitude of individuals and groups in similar ways. Hence, similar to the state of being in the grips of a personal complex, under the influence of a cultural complex people "literally cannot see one another for who they really are".[37] Many writers have contributed to this growing field in elucidating how particular cultural complexes in a national or cultural group consciousness can manifest and how shared, often traumatic, histories and experiences shape these inner narratives and their continued expression of shared identity and destiny as well as attitude toward the other (e.g. Singer,[38] Singer and Kimbles,[39] Raschke and Singer,[40] Singer).[41] Returning to the polarized/populist dynamics in the contemporary U.S., for another example, certain cultural complexes related to the Puritan heritage may be at play. The Puritan sensibility to be a "divinely chosen people",[42]

---

36 Kimbles, "The cultural complex and myth of invisibility", 157. To further understand how cultural complexes play into the us versus them dynamics we witness in today's polarized and divisive discourse in many countries, it is helpful to consider the bipolar nature of a complex postulated by Perry and adopted by Kimbles and Singer discussing cultural complexes – J. W. Perry, "Emotions and object relations", *Journal of Analytical Psychology*, 15, (1970): 1–12; Kimbles, Singer, *The cultural complex*. The idea is that, in any complex activation, there is both a *self-referential* and an *other-referential* aspect to the emotion-thought-behavior package that is being activated, which is quite different from the regular consciousness of the individual. On the one side of the bipolar complex is, for example, the person *self-identified* with the victimized child, feeling hurt, wrongly accused, unloved, and so on. On the other side of the complex is the *other-identified* part projected out and onto another person, which, in this case, may be the abusive, bullying father, who is seen as cruel, unjust, dangerous, and so on. Whenever this complex—which is rooted in childhood experiences as well as in archaic archetypal patterns—is activated, the individual would, in a sense, regresses to the old experience of self (as victimized child) and other (as abusive father) and reenact the scenario with people in authority positions in their life.

37 Kimbles, „The cultural complex and myth of invisibility", 167.

38 T. Singer (ed.), *The vision thing: Myth, politics and psyche in the world*, (New York, NY: Routledge, 2000).

39 Singer, Kimbles, *The cultural complex*.

40 Raschke, Singer, *Europe's many souls*.

41 Singer, *Cultural Complexes*.

42 R. Schenk, *American soul: A cultural narrative*, (New Orleans, LA: Springs Journal Inc, 2012), 26.

"sheltered in predestined goodness"[43] and tasked with pursuing the good and rooting out "imperfection rather than seeking the truth"[44] appears to be a psycho-cultural endowment carried forward through the generations, consciously and unconsciously. It is visible not only in American tendencies like exceptionalism, superiority, or domination over what is perceived as other (i.e., unholy, bad, impure, less than, etc.) and found its most cruel historical manifestations in the treatment of indigenous people and people of African descent, but can also be uncovered in many other contexts within the U.S. and abroad. However, the familiar battle of good versus evil and pure versus impure may now too be expressing its feverish conviction in the political arena within groups of shared cultural or ethnic background; now the bad/impure people who must be silenced, shut down, or purged are Trump supporters or the "radical left." Here too, around these deeper tectonic forces of the cultural psychic heritage, introspection and becoming conscious of the oblique dynamics could be a potent remedy for diminishing the emotional intensity and hostile fervor of contemporary us versus them undercurrents. If one can begin to see what is happening in the grip of a cultural complex, the complex may lose its charge in the light of consciousness and bring expanded possibilities for relationship and dialogue to the phenomena around perceived otherness.

5 Terror Management Theory: Death Anxiety and Intergroup Dynamics

The Jungian perspective provides depth and richness, illustrating the psychodynamic shadow projection and cultural complex activation phenomena involved in creation of group mentality and behavior within polarized collective discourses and conflicts. However, its ideas may be further enriched by a conversation with Terror Management Theory and its experimental research.

Inspired by the work of cultural anthropologist Ernest Becker[45] and his conceptualization of the role of mortality awareness in human, culture-based activity, TMT has postulated and supported through hundreds of research studies, how unconscious mortality awareness and death anxiety play an

---

43 S. Carta, "Here's Johnny! American Carnival in modern times", In *Cultural complexes and the soul of America: Myth, psyche and politics*, T. Singer (ed.), (New York, NY: Routledge 2020), 17.

44 B. S. Flowers, "The Purity complex", In *Cultural complexes and the soul of America: Myth, psyche and politics*, T. Singer (ed.), (New York, NY: Routledge, 2020), 39.

45 E. Becker, *The denial of death*, (New York, NY: Free Press, 1973).

important role in in-group/out-group thinking and behavior. In Becker's theory, which draws from a variety of philosophical sources and builds upon the psychoanalytic work of Sigmund Freud[46] and more directly, Otto Rank,[47] the uniquely human juxtaposition of being aware of one's mortality and driven by an instinct for self-preservation creates a fateful inner ecology.

> The idea of death, the fear of it, haunts the human animal like nothing else; it is a mainspring of human activity—activity designed largely to avoid the fatality of death, to overcome it by denying in some way that it is the final destiny for man.[48]

In Becker's framework, to "defend against this potential death anxiety, people must believe that some valued aspect of themselves will continue, either literally or symbolically, after cessation of their biological body".[49] *Literal immortality* is grounded in beliefs in some form of afterlife, which can be found anywhere from traditional/religious belief systems to contemporary afterlife narratives evoked in scientific visions like Cryonics or Singularity. *Symbolic immortality* is found in the reassurance that some valued aspect of oneself (e.g., one's children, but also material, creative, or social achievements) will continue to exist in some form. In this model, literal or symbolic immortality, acting as a cultural buffer against latent death anxiety, consists of two main mechanisms. One is the belief in and commitment to the validity of one's cultural worldview and the values and behaviors associated with that worldview, and another is the belief that one is meeting the standards and expectations of this cultural worldview, which in social psychology is referred to as self-esteem.[50] According to this model "the problem of death resides beneath consciousness and, from there, triggers distal death defenses—the maintenance of worldviews and self-esteem".[51] In other words, cultural belonging serves as an unconscious buffer against the unbearable reality of mortality.[52]

46 S. Freud, *Civilization and its discontents*, trans. J. Riviere, (Mansfield Centre, CT: Martino Publishing, 2016/1930).

47 O. Rank, *Beyond Psychology*, (Mineola, NY: Dover Publications, 2011/1941).

48 Becker, IX.

49 B. L. Burke, A. Martens, E. H. Faucher, "Two decades of terror management theory: A meta-analysis of mortality salience research", *Personality and Social Psychology Review*, 14, (2010), 155.

50 J. Greenberg, T. Pyszczynski, S. Solomon, "The causes and consequences of a need for self-esteem: A terror management theory", In *Public self and private self*, R. F. Baumeister (ed.), (New York, NY: Springer-Verlag, 1986): 189–212.

51 Burke, Martens, Faucher, 156.

52 In addition to this unconscious buffering, death anxiety is also defended against consciously by either relying on and bringing forth afterlife/immortality narratives or by push-

Other social psychologists have attempted to explain why death anxiety/ mortality salience are related to the group association that plays such a vitally important role for human beings, proposing that "the condition of being affiliated with significant others creates a 'haven of safety' in which people can feel secure even in times of severe distress".[53] Overall, these conceptions of group reliance seem to align with cultural complex theory and its emphasis on shared history and trauma as identity-creating forces.

Over the past 30 years, several hundred published TMT studies have focused on how subtly making research subjects aware of their mortality (Mortality Salience or MS) has an impact on their commitment and adherence to their cultural worldview and on their self-esteem.[54]

As a general synopsis, Greenberg and Kosloff concluded that the body of TMT research "shows that when the psychological need to defend one's worldviews is heightened by reminders of death (mortality salience), prejudice, stereotyping, and support for charismatic leaders and aggression against outgroups is increased".[55] Several summaries of TMT research[56] align with this conclusion.

---

ing one's own mortality into a distant future – T. Pyszczynski, J. Greenberg, S. Solomon, "A dual process model of defense against conscious and unconscious death-related thoughts: An extension of terror management theory", *Psychological Review*, 106, (1999): 835–845.

53 Mikulincer, Birnbaum, Woddis, and Nachmias quoted in: D. Niesta, I. Fritsche, E. Jonas, "Mortality salience and its effect on peace processes: A review", *Social Psychology*, 39, (2008), 49, 509.

54 Burke, Martens, Faucher describe the typical experiment set up for these studies. "[P]articipants complete a packet of questionnaires ostensibly for the purpose of assessing personality. However, embedded within this packet, participants are asked to briefly write either about their own death or about a non-death-related (often negative) control topic. Participants then typically complete one or two distraction questionnaires before finally completing a dependent measure that taps their distal death defenses. This delay and distraction between the death prime and the dependent measure is included to allow for death to fade from consciousness…"- Burke, Martens, Faucher, 156.

55 J. Greenberg, S. Kosloff, "Terror management theory: Implications for understanding prejudice, stereo typing, intergroup conflict, and political attitudes", *Social and Personality Psychology Compass*, 5 (2), (2008), 1881.

56 J. Greenberg, S. Solomon, T. Pyszczynski, "Terror management theory of self-esteem and social behavior: Empirical assessments and conceptual refinements", In *Advances in Experimental Social Psychology*, M. P. Zanna (ed.), (New York, NY: Academic Press, 29, 1997): 61–139; T. Pyszczynski, S. Solomon, J. Greenberg, In *The wake of 9/11: The psychology of terror,* (Washington, DC: American Psychological Association, 2003); T. Pyszczynski, S. Solomon, J. Greenberg, "Thirty years of terror management theory: From genesis to revelation", In *Advances in experimental social psychology*, 52, (2015): 1–70; S. Solomon, J. Greenberg, T. Pyszczynski, "The cultural animal: Twenty years of terror management theory and research", In, *Handbook of experimental existential psychology*, J. Greenberg, S. L. Koole, T. Pyszczynski (eds.), (New York, NY: Guilford, 2004): 13–34.

A meta-analysis of 277 published studies[57] found that the mortality salience hypothesis of TMT "is robust and produces moderate to large effects across a wide variety of [mortality salience] manipulations as well as attitudinal, behavioral, and cognitive DVs [dependent variables]".[58] In their review of "Thirty Years of Terror Management Theory," Pyszczynski and colleagues provide some examples from the vast variety of studies up to date, demonstrating how

> mortality salience increases worldview defense in the form of harsher punishment for moral transgressors (e.g., Rosenblatt, Greenberg, Solomon, Pyszczynski, & Lyon, 1989); more positive evaluations of those who praise one's culture and more negative evaluations of those who criticize it (e.g., Greenberg et al., 1990); greater in-group bias (e.g., Castano, Yzerbyt, Paladino, & Sacchi, 2002); less aggression toward those who share one's worldview and more aggression toward those with worldviews different from one's own (e.g., McGregor et al., 1998); greater support for violent solutions to ethnic, religious, and international conflicts (e.g., Hirschberger & Ein-Dor, 2006; Pyszczynski, Abdollahi, Solomon, Greenberg, & Weise, 2006[59]

It could be argued that collective unconscious death anxiety must be on the rise through global and regional developments in regard to a myriad of intensifying threats (whether perceived or actual) to one's culture, religion, country, planet, or way of life. Considering these pressures (from global warming to immigration) adds further appreciation as to how and why populism and polarization may feed into each other and are fed by death anxiety and mortality salience while contributing to activation and reinforcement of latent cultural complexes. With the constant reminders of our mortality, the human penchant for in-group/out-group thoughts, feelings, and behaviors increases, which is used by and further intensified through the us versus them rhetoric in populism and polarization.

6 Possibilities and Directions: A Dialogue between Depth Psychology and Social Psychology

There are several interesting areas of convergence between a depth psychological analysis of the less-individuated person's vulnerability to mass mentality,

---

57 Burke, Martens, Faucher.

58 Ibidem, 187.

59 Pyszczynski, Solomon, Greenberg, "Thirty years of terror", 11.

shadow projection, and cultural complex possession, and TMT's understanding of how unmitigated death anxiety leads to worldview defense. Conversely, shared remedial possibilities emerge out of the dialogue of these two fields that may be worthwhile considering.

Besides demonstrating how unconscious death anxiety increases in-group association as well as judgment and aggression towards out-groups, TMT research also points to possibilities for solutions that are relevant for this conversation. For example, Kesebir[60] (2014) explored whether and how humility could be a remedy. She associates humility with the idea of the "quiet ego" of someone who is "capable of tolerating an honest look at the self and non-defensively accepting weaknesses alongside strengths"[61] and who "tend[s] to be more sensitive and feel more connected to forces larger than themselves, be this force God, humanity, nature, or the cosmos".[62] Kesebir's combination of five studies concluded that humility and an associated quiet ego, characterized by "a willingness to accept the self's limits and its place in the grand scheme of things" can be a mitigating factor that decreases death anxiety and its often-destructive worldview defending consequences.[63]

Obviously, the definitions of what is meant by self and ego differ in the way they are used by social and depth psychologists. However, the meaning of humility and a quiet ego in social psychology is aligned with the Jungian concept of an individuated person—with an advanced level of awareness and acceptance of oneself and of others that is rooted in having done sufficient inner work and experienced a transpersonal (i.e., trans-egoic) psychological reality. Following Kesebir's definitions and findings, it could reasonably be imagined that an individuated person, with a quieter, more humble ego, would also have lower death anxiety and be less vulnerable to destructive in-group/

60 P. Kesebir, "A quiet ego quiets death anxiety: Humility as an existential anxiety buffer", *Journal of Personality and Social Psychology*, 106(4), (2014): 610–623.

61 Ibidem, 611; citing Exline.

62 Ibid.611; citing Worthington.

63 Five studies tested and found support for the hypothesis that a quiet, humble ego buffers death anxiety. The first three studies showed that high self-reported humility and low psychological entitlement were associated with lower death anxiety (Study 2) and lower death anxiety-induced defensiveness—in the form of self-serving moral disengagement (Study 1) or cultural worldview defense (Study 3). It was also established in Study 2 that humility wards off death anxiety above and beyond the potentially related constructs of self-esteem, secure attachment, mindfulness, and general virtuousness. Study 4 provided direct evidence for the existentially soothing role of humility, by documenting that an experimentally induced humility mindset decreases self-reported death anxiety. Finally, Study 5 demonstrated that activating humble self-views can prevent mortality thoughts from draining self control – ibid., 619.

out-group tendencies like shadow projection and constellation of cultural complexes.

Along similar lines, Park and Pyszczynski[64] reviewed several studies that looked into the effects of mindfulness meditation and Buddhist awareness and acceptance practices in relation to the effects of death anxiety and mortality salience. They observed that, across the studies, meditators did not show the increase in worldview defense that non-meditators displayed. While it is important to acknowledge the existence of differences between distinct Buddhist traditions and mindfulness meditation practices, let alone between those approaches and Jungian individuation work, here too seems to be an important common thread: the principle of valuing and practicing awareness and acceptance of one's inner and outer experiences appears to be related to a non-defensive, more relaxed, yet steady inner posture that makes the individual less susceptible to mortality salience and us versus them dynamics.

Other TMT studies have pointed out that self-regulation can be a remedial factor aside from humility, awareness, and acceptance. When a person's "self-regulation can be strengthened in a way to prevent feelings of death from flooding the conscious mind with troublesome thoughts and aversive emotions such as anxiety, they may serve to alleviate resulting detrimental processes of world-view defense ... such as egocentric bias and derogation of outgroup members".[65] Self-regulation too is related to self-awareness and self-acceptance, and while often sought through meditation or other mind-body practices, it can certainly also be an outcome of individuation. As Jung said in speaking about the individuating person who outgrows their troubles, "what on a lower level had led to the wildest conflicts and to panicky outbursts of emotion, from the higher level of personality now looked like a storm in the valley seen from the mountain top".[66]

Besides providing connections to Jungian psychology and possibly an indirect validation for individuation generating a "quiet ego" that is less easily gripped by death anxiety and pulled into unconscious cultural complexes and in-group/out-group dynamics, social psychologists are describing between-group solutions that maybe helpful in conflict processes. Niesta et al. propose that TMT's theoretical approach may provide "a variety of conceivable

64 Y. C. Park, T. Pyszczynski, „Reducing defensive responses to thoughts of death: Meditation, mindfulness, and Buddhism", *Journal of Personality and Social Psychology*, 116(1), (2017): 101–118.

65 Niesta, D., Fritsche, I. & Jonas, E. 'Mortality salience and its effect on peace processes: a review.' Social Psychology, 39, (2008). 55.

66 C. G. Jung, "Commentary on the secret of the golden flower", In C. G. Jung, *The Collected Works*, v. 13, trans. R. F. C. Hull, (Princeton, NJ: Princeton University Press, 1967/1929), § 17.

interventions … that may override genuinely detrimental consequences of MS and help to foster peace processes".[67] In summary, they found that many studies show that, during times of collective crisis (natural disasters, terror attacks, etc.), pro-social behaviors that are based on altruistic values within the cultural worldview (e.g., kindness, compassion, helping those in need) tend to increase. The same is true in mortality salience experiments, however, not surprisingly mainly toward in-group individuals. Nonetheless, reminding people during times of a collective crisis experience of positive, pro-social values within the culture could be helpful in both peace processes and cultural complex work. In addition to examining cultural complexes, attitudes, and mentalities against out-groups, engaging pro-social, altruistic values within one's cultural system (that otherwise may be less accessible and dormant) could be part of a facilitated growth process. Also, by working through personal complexes and cultural complexes as part of individuation work, a common humanity between self and others can be seen and acknowledged, as is an established notion among depth psychologists (e.g., Stein, 2006). Social psychologists are pointing in this direction too, suggesting that "there may be options to reduce negative reactions toward outgroups, if the outgroups are not perceived as threatening the in-group and its worldview or if they are subsumed as subcategories within a common in-group".[68] This is probably a development that can happen under the right conditions and over time organically as, for example, in the European unification process in which certain hostilities and cultural complexes and related fears and judgments have gradually faded and been replaced by a more salient awareness of European identity. However, it seems only too obvious that the individuation process, the coming into relationship with one's deep nature and working through personal and cultural shadow, could accelerate and deepen such possibilities.

Still other TMT studies have shown that boosting self-esteem (i.e., feeling like a worthwhile member of a community) seems to buffer against the worldview-defending effect of mortality salience.[69] Here too, we could point to how individuation may be related to developing the kind of relaxed self-estimation that allows for a more comfortable acceptance of oneself as a member of one's culture or of humanity as a whole.

However, the dynamic between death anxiety, its related effects, and individuation is complex and multi-directional. While individuation could be presumed as having a positive impact on the consequences of death anxiety,

67 Niesta, Fritsche, Jonas, 48.

68 Ibidem, 55.

69 Niesta, Fritsche, Jonas.

conversely death anxiety could also be considered by understanding its impacts on the individuation path: the unconscious fear of death and the need to buffer against its reality through cultural worldview defense and feeling like a valuable member of one's cultural group must exert a formidable influence on the need for *persona* development, as well as group thinking and behavior in conscious (cultural attitudes and opinions) and unconscious (cultural complex) life. Hence, as death anxiety furthers group conformity and development of and adherence to a socially acceptable version of oneself, it conversely leads to greater struggle in individuating from family and culture. When seen through this lens, developing a functioning ego and adaptable persona become more than developmental tasks aimed at finding a sense of belonging and being accepted, and reveal themselves to be an even deeper psychological survival strategy, to ward off the looming threat of mortality. Conversely, the individuation struggle of becoming a distinct and authentic person within and against the backdrop of family and culture expectations, is likely hindered or slowed by our unconscious fear of death and defenses against it, as posited by TMT. Incorporating the effects of death anxiety toward understanding the tension between fitting in/belonging and accepting and living one's true nature, both underlines the difficulty and importance of these archetypal processes and enriches their appreciation within a Jungian context.

7 Conclusion

Considering the evidence, it is apparent that death anxiety is a reality-shaping but probably underappreciated force in psyche and world. Given our daily confrontation with catastrophic news or cataclysmic prognosis of collapsing ecological, cultural, and social structures, death anxiety and mortality salience are possibly at an all-time high level. Jungian psychology and social psychology clearly have much to offer at this challenging moment in history. Several themes related to populism and polarization in the world have been considered, and possible points of mutual validation and enrichment between the two schools were highlighted. A few important points in this discussion seem worth emphasizing:

First, individuation of the personality and the expansion of consciousness through inner work, self-awareness, and being grounded in a deeper, transcendent reality must be seen as a vital task in bringing people together, rather than unconsciously turning against each other, during these challenging times.

Second, the individuated personality as a facilitator of seeing, understanding, and relating to *the other* appears to be supported by the understanding in social psychology of a humble, quiet ego and its potential for lowering death anxiety.

Third, giving more prominence to cultural individuation processes and working through cultural complexes by individuals and groups seem crucial, particularly in light of the findings of TMT research and the detrimental effects of mortality salience on in-group/out-group polarization and conflict. While individuation seems as relevant as ever in mitigating unconscious tendencies that feed into shadow projection and polarization of what is considered *the other*, engaging the cultural unconscious and working through cultural complexes as an additional, actively engaged part of inner work is highly relevant.

And fourth, death anxiety may commonly play an influential role in the individuation journey—from ego and persona development to true individuation. The important issue of our mortality awareness and death anxiety, central in TMT's theory and research, may need further consideration in depth psychology. Death and death anxiety may need added attention—that is, death as an archetypal reality, the confrontation with death as an archetypal challenge, and coming to terms with mortality as a principal task of individuation. It seems particularly significant and necessary to re-emphasize the confrontation with death within individuation, considering both the knowledge about death anxiety and mortality salience provided by TMT and the heightened death anxiety related to apocalyptic scenarios confronting the contemporary collective psyche.

Jungian psychology values dealing with mortality and death but appears to be postponing it to times when death awareness is evoked by being closer to one's own actual death or through other concrete confrontations with death and mortality. While Jung himself had profound experiences/encounters with death and reflected about death throughout his life, he too seemed to conceptually reserve the confrontation with mortality for the second half of life, naturally initiated through one's increased awareness of the finiteness of life, the loss of one's health, the death of a loved one, or later when initiated through the decline of old age.

It appears that, considering the inner and outer contexts portrayed in this paper, facing mortality could potentially have a more prominent position in individuation. Looking at the conceptualization of the individuation path (e.g., von Franz, 1964; Jacobi, 1983; Stein, 2006),coping with one's mortality and eventual death appears somewhat underemphasized, delayed, or left to emerge out of the client's life and dream material in therapy. As being conscious of our mortality is one of the most central realities of being human, shouldn't confronting death be a more central tenant and a core task of the individuation journey? Also, if unattended death anxiety were in fact related to a tighter clinging to persona identity and group conformity (and thereby hinder the individuation process), could engaging mortality and death anxiety earlier, more explicitly ease, accelerate, or enrich the individuation process? We could wonder how contemporary (Western) cultural contexts that are largely death-denying or even death-phobic may be contributing (i.e., in that an actual dialogue about and a confrontation with the reality of death is generally averted, while the culture is at the same time saturated with a surreal but impersonal death obsession in its media and entertainment landscape).

Further research could explore how and where within the analytical field attempts toward privileging confrontation with the death archetype have already been made, how an engaged dialogue about mortality could be facilitated, if and how such facilitated processes would have a measurable effect on death anxiety and its related worldview defending tendencies, or how confronting one's mortality may relate to one's expression of cultural complexes. There may be an opportunity to engage death and mortality differently, earlier, more consciously, more pro-actively, with more directional curiosity as a central task of individuation. Not as yet another attempt of the heroic ego to control what is beyond its reach, but as something to contemplate, to be affected by, to be specifically alert to in engaging with conscious and unconscious psyche; something to inquire into more fully, more methodically.

References

Becker E., *The denial of death*, New York, NY: Free Press, 1973.

Boxell L., Gentzkow M., Shapiro J. M., *Cross-Country Trends in Affective Polarization,* (National Bureau of Economic Research Working Paper No. 26669) - https://www.nber.org/papers/w26669, 2020.

Burke B. L., Martens A., Faucher E. H., "Two decades of terror management theory: A meta-analysis of mortality salience research", *Personality and Social Psychology Review*, 14, (2010): 155–195.

Carta S., "Here's Johnny! American Carnival in modern times", in *Cultural complexes and the soul of America: Myth, psyche and politics*, ed. T. Singer, New York: Routledge, 2020: 13–34.

Edinger E., *The Creation of Consciousness: Jung's Myth for Modern Man,* Toronto, Canada: Inner City Books, 1984.

Ferrer J. N., *Participation and the mystery: Transpersonal essays in psychology, education and religion,* New York, NY: State University of New York Press, 2017.

Flowers B.S., "The Purity complex", in *Cultural complexes and the soul of America: Myth, psyche and politics*, ed. T. Singer, New York, NY: Routledge 2020: 35–43.

Freud S., *Civilization and its discontents*, trans. J. Riviere, Mansfield Centre, CT: Martino Publishing, 2016/1930.

Frimer J., Skitka L.J., Motyl M., "Liberals and conservatives are similarly motivated to avoid exposure to one another's opinions", *Journal of Experimental Social Psychology*, 72, (2017): 1–12.

Greenberg J., Kosloff S., "Terror management theory: Implications for understanding prejudice, stereotyping, intergroup conflict, and political attitudes", *Social and Personality Psychology Compass*, 5 (2), (2008): 1881–1894.

Greenberg J., Pyszczynski T., Solomon S., "The causes and consequences of a need for self-esteem: A terror management theory", In *Public self and private self*, R. F. Baumaister (ed.), New York, NY: Springer-Verlag, 1986: 189–212.

Greenberg J., Solomon S., Pyszczynski T., "Terror management theory of self-esteem and social behavior: Empirical assessments and conceptual refinements", In *Advances in Experimental Social Psychology*, M. P. Zanna (ed.), New York, NY: Academic Press, 1997: 61–139.

Henderson J., *Cultural attitudes in psychological perspective*, Toronto, Canada: Inner City Books, 1984.

Iyengar S., Krupenkin M., "The Strengthening of Partisan Affect", *Advances in Political Psychology*, 39, 1, (2008): 201–218.

Jacobi J., *The way of individuation*, New York, NY: New American Library, 1983.

Jung C. G., "The relations between the ego and the unconscious", In *The Collected Works of C. G. Jung*, v. 7, 2nd ed., trans. R. F. C. Hull, Princeton, NJ: Princeton University Press, 1966/1928: 121–241.

Jung C. G., "Commentary on the secret of the golden flower", In *The Collected Works of C. G. Jung*, v. 13, trans. R. F. C. Hull, Princeton, NJ: Princeton University Press, 1967/1929: 1–56.

Jung C.G., "The undiscovered self (present and future)", In *The Collected Works of C. G. Jung*, v. 10, Princeton, NJ: Princeton University Press, 1970a/1957: 245–305.

Jung C. G., "Wotan", In *The Collected Works of C. G. Jung*, v. 10, 2nd ed., Princeton, NJ: Princeton University Press, 1970b/1936: 179–193.

Kesebir P., "A quiet ego quiets death anxiety: Humility as an existential anxiety buffer", *Journal of Personality and Social Psychology*, 106, 4, (2014): 610–623.

Kimbles S., "The cultural complex and the myth of invisibility", In *The vision thing: Myth, politics and psyche in the world*, T. Singer (ed.), New York, NY: Routledge, 2000: 157–169.

Lewis P., Clarke S., Barr, C., Kommenda N., Holder J. (n.d.), "Revealed: One in four Europeans vote populist", *The Guardian* - https://www.theguardian.com/world/ng-interactive/2018/nov/20/revealed-one-in-four-europeans-vote-populist.

McCarty N., Poole K.T., Rosenthal H., *Polarized America: The dance of ideology and unequal riches*, Cambridge, MA: MIT Press, 2016.

Moffitt B., *The global rise of populism: Performance, political style and representation.* Stanford, CA: Stanford University Press, 2016.

Mudde C., Kaltwasser C.R., *Populism in Europe and the Americas: Threat or Corrective for Democracy?,* New York: Cambridge University Press, 2012.

Mudde C., Kaltwasser C. R., *Populism – A very short introduction.* New York, NY: Oxford University Press, 2017.

Niesta D., Fritsche I., Jonas E., "Mortality salience and its effect on peace processes: A review", *Social Psychology*, 39, (2008): 48–58.

Pew Research Center, "Partisanship and political animosity in 2016: Highly negative views on the opposing party - and its members" - https://www.people-press.org/wpcontent/uploads/sites/4/2016/06/06-22-16-Partisanship-and-animosity-release.pdf, 2016.

Park Y. C., Pyszczynski, T., „Reducing defensive responses to thoughts of death: Meditation, mindfulness, and Buddhism", *Journal of Personality and Social Psychology*, 116(1), (2017): 101–118.

Perry J. W., "Emotions and object relations", *Journal of Analytical Psychology*, 15, (1970): 1–12.

Pyszczynski T., Greenberg J., Solomon S., "A dual process model of defense against conscious and unconscious death-related thoughts: An extension of terror management theory", *Psychological Review*, 106, (1999): 835–845.

Pyszczynski T., Solomon S., Greenberg J., *In the wake of 9/11: The psychology of terror.* Washington, DC: American Psychological Association, 2003.

Pyszczynski T., Solomon S., Greenberg J. L., "Thirty years of terror management theory: From genesis to revelation", In *Advances in experimental social psychology*, Cambridge, MA: Academic Press Inc, 15, (2015): 1–70.

Oxendine A. R., "The political psychology of inequality and why it matters for populism", *International Perspectives in Psychology: Research, Practice, Consultation*, 8, 4 (2015): 179–195.

Rank O., *Beyond Psychology*, Mineola, NY: Dover Publications, 2011/1941.

Raschke J., Singer T. (eds.), *Europe's many souls: Exploring cultural complexes and identities.* New Orleans, LA: Spring Journal, Inc., 2016.

Sauer G., "About two cultural complexes: The German complex of superiority and the Russian complex of feeling encircled by hungry barbarians", In *Europe's many souls; Exploring cultural complexes and identities,* J. Raschke, T. Singer (eds.), New Orleans, LA: Springs Journal Inc., 2016: 211–232.

Schenk R., *American soul: A cultural narrative*, New Orleans, LA: Springs Journal Inc., 2012.

Singer T. (ed.), *The vision thing: Myth, politics and psyche in the world.* New York, NY: Routledge, 2000.

Singer T., Kimbles S. (eds.), *The cultural complex: Contemporary Jungian perspectives on psyche and society*. New York, NY: Routledge, 2004.

Singer T. (ed.), *Cultural Complexes and the Soul of America: Myth, Psyche, and Politics.* New York, NY: Routledge, 2020.

Solomon S., Greenberg J., Pyszczynski T., "The cultural animal: Twenty years of terror management theory and research", In *Handbook of experimental existential psychology*, J. Greenberg, S. L. Koole, T. Pyszczynski (eds.), New York, NY: Guilford, 2004: 13–34.

Stein M., *The principle of individuation: Towards the development of human consciousness,* Asheville, NC: Chiron Publications, 2006.

von Franz M. L., "The process of individuation", In *Man and his symbols,* C. G. Jung, M. L. von Franz (eds.), New York, NY: Anchor Press, 1964: 158–229.

de Vreese C.H., Esser F., Aalberg T., Reinemann C., Stanyer J., "Populism as an Expression of Political Communication Content and Style: A New Perspective", *The International Journal of Press/Politics,* 2018, 23, 4, (2018): 423–438.

CHAPTER 18

Portuguese Sebastianism as an Intersection Field between the Right and Left Political Forces in the Brazilian 2018 Presidential Elections

Gustavo Orlandeli Marques[1]

Abstract

Brazilian culture has its roots in a wide field of foreign cultures, among which Portuguese is one of the most important. This paper will consider, as one significant example of cultural influence from Portugal to Brazil, the mythological sorrow of missing King Sebastian in the 16th century and the popular hope of his return as a messiah who would lead the country to establish its apogee and days of glory. We understand that this historical reference and its collective dynamic can also be found in Brazilian culture. The expectation and hope for a great leader, a wise and strong warrior who would free the country from all of its deficiencies, tend to be a repetitive movement in recent Brazilian history. The 2018 presidential elections, we could suggest, were one more repetition of this cultural psychic movement, in which each of the two exponent candidates seemed to appear as proposals of Sebastianism. Politically divided, the continental country apparently was shaken by the inner forces of its shadow that, in our understanding, passed through this popular Portuguese Sebastian "myth." Considering the strength of this collective experience, as part of an autonomous movement of the Brazilian cultural shadow, we could consider the counterpart of King Sebastian imprinted as an important new element, since both sides of the political force accused the opponent of being both a dangerous trickster and a malefic decoy who would destroy the country. Far from "psychologizing" those events, we understand that analytical psychology offers the possibility to understand them symbolically. In this sense, we add the Jungian symbolic idea of "listening to the dead," rescued by James Hillman and Sonu Shamdasani, in the attempt to find new personal or collective paths of transformation from inside, as it seems that the 2013 Brazilian street protests potentially brought. The explicit political division in Brazil presents a difficult task for its modern history and the development of its cultural identity, so unique for defining its diversity. Recognizing this inner cultural influence of the ancestral Portuguese could

1 Helenice Cristina Azevedo e Silva is the co-author in the historical research of the paper.

 | DOI:10.1163/9789004468757_020

also improve the ties between Brazil and Portugal in a newer form of mutual consideration, as brother countries.

Keywords

Brazilian Sebastianism, Lament of the Dead, cultural myth, Brazilian street protests

1 Introduction

> Kto nie pamieta historii, skazany jest na jej ponowne przeżycie.[2]
>
> GEORGE SANTAYANA, in the Auschwitz Camp

If we could in time and space from modern Brazil to distant 16th century Portugal, perhaps we could do it following some specific cultural lines or paths. In the present paper we hope to be able to invite the reader to do so, searching a specific collective trace we suggest has been mobilized in our country at our present moment. Since January 2019, Brazil has had a new president, who was elected last year by democratic elections, which means that every Brazilian citizen has the right to vote, a true application of British unionist George Howell's famous slogan: "One man, one vote."

As we take a few steps back in time, it is important to mention that the formerly elected Brazilian president Dilma Rousseff was prevented from continuing her term in office by a complex and polemical impeachment process, the second in Brazil's young democracy. She was replaced by her vice-president, Michel Temer. Discussing its details does not meet the objective of the present study. However, the timeline that includes her first election in 2010; the re-election of her predecessor, Luiz Inácio Lula da Silva, the famous "Lula"; and finally, the current President, Jair Messias Bolsonaro, popularly known as "The Myth" by his supporters, is pertinent.

Roussef became the first female Brazilian president after the very popular and apparently successful and prosperous double mandates of the Workers's Party ("Partido dos Trabalhadores" or "PT" in Portuguese), with Luiz Inácio Lula da Silva, in front of the executive power. He left his second mandate with more than 80% of popularity, and the opponent political forces had no chance

2 "Those who do not remember the past are condemned to repeat it".

against his political heir, Dilma Roussef. The Workers's Party was, at the period of Roussef's impeachment, "by far the largest and best-organized left-wing party in the democracy history of Latin America."[3]

After a very unsuccessful first mandate, she won her re-election in 2014 by a very narrow margin. Despite her victory, the country found itself being dragged into a deep political, economic, and social crisis. Her "political capital" was empty. The Brazilian Congress "froze" her government while a deep investigation, made by the Federal Police and the Federal Prosecution, the "Operação Lava Jato" ("Car Wash Operation"), investigated a series of corruption allegations against the Workers's Party and members of the government. According to Kingstone and Power: "In a short period, Brazil had moved from triumphant emerging power to nation divided against itself."[4]

During the 2006 Brazilian presidential election process, when Lula was trying to be re-elected based on his apparent economic and political success, he deliberately used the expression "them against us." What was that? Who were "them," and who were "we"? It was based on a highly populist and left-wing ideology in support of the poor and excluded people of Brazil, especially in the less developed North and Northeast regions of the country, against the wealthier South and Southeast. The idea of "hope" had been deliberately used as propaganda even before this period: the main slogan of Lula's first election being "Hope defeated fear." The Workers's Party had therefore built a very strong and effective "electoral weapon" on feelings of hope and the claims of the poorest classes.

I do remember well during my master's degree years, in the Catholic University of São Paulo (PUC-SP) in Jungian studies, the Brazilian Jungian analyst and professor Dr. Liliana Liviano Wahba's saying something like this in our classes in 2007: "What was started last year with this speech of 'us' and 'them' was a very dangerous and irresponsible act for the Brazilian psyche that we will all probably pay a high price for."

Far from creating a messianic notion of the dear Professor Wahba, the point is that as a Jungian analyst and Brazilian, she was aware of the risks of this kind of collective mobilization. Unfortunately, this mobilization only increased during the years of Roussef's first and second terms. After her impeachment process, Brazil had to face the fact that it had been one of the most incompetent administrations of its history, whose legacy was a political and economic crisis (one of the worst in Brazilian history) and a collective soul divided. From

3 P. R Kingstone, T. J. Power, *Democratic Brazil Divided.* (Pittsburgh: University of Pittsburgh Press, 2017), 23.

4 Ibidem, 3.

one side were the poorest regions, North and Northeast, supported by pro-poor policies but without a full and deeper development of these policies as proposed, and on the other side was the traditional middle class, more concentrated in the South and Southeast regions, which also had good reasons to vote against the Workers's Party.[5] In fact, we are living exactly this very reality in our current time.

During the 2018 elections, the Northeast was the only region where Workers's Party candidate, Fernando Haddad, defeated Bolsonaro. Every state of the region offered the victory to the Workers's Party, even with Operação Lava Jato's effects, the most important being the condemnation to prison of the former president and iconic left-wing leader Lula. Ironically, hope seemed to be defeated by fear this time: even with allthe malefices of the Workers's Party, including the highest levels of corruption discovered and accurate in Brazilian history, the region did opt to maintain Workers's Party policy. We consider ironically because, in Lula's first term election, his slogan was "Hope defeated fear," as mentioned above. He was making reference to a historical resistance from traditional society against the left-wing politics in the country. The fact is:

> In the "hangover" following [Roussef]'s impeachment, Brazil is divided against itself and is currently confronting the deepest political and economic challenges of the New Republic. But it does so drawing on vital sources of strength. The only certainty is that Brazilian democracy will continue to unfold in ways that defy simple categories.[6]

Mentioning "hope," we would like to bring to this reflection an ancient cultural trace that could be connected to our current political and social division, the Portuguese myth of Dom Sebastião (Don Sebastian). In this sense, we hope the myth will be able to help us make the connection between two collective movements in Brazil's recent history: the 2013 country-wide protests and the 2018 election conflicts.

2 Don Sebastian: "O Desejado" ("The Expected One")

History tells us that in the middle of the 16th century, Portugal was under the rule of Don João III. Already of advanced age, he was father to nine male children, of whom all but one — Don João Manuel, who would be heir to the

5 Ibidem.

6 Ibidem, 13.

throne — had died. However, this heir also died before his father, Don João III, generating a great problem for Portugal. His wife was in truth pregnant with the future heir, Don Sebastian, but it was not known at that time whether the child would live or even if it would be a boy.

Don João Manuel's sister, Dona Maria Manuela, married Felipe II of Spain under a marriage contract that declared that if Don João III did not leave an heir, Carlos — the son of this marriage between Maria Manuela and Felipe II of Spain — would inherit the throne. Should this happen, he would be king of Spain and Portugal at the same time, uniting the crowns and creating a single kingdom. In Portugal, however, this idea was universally rejected, since Afonso Henrique had already proclaimed independence, making Portugal totally separate from Castela (Chatelaine). The rejection by the Portuguese of a union of crowns was despite having been considered previously, when at the end of the 15th century Isabel and Fernando of Aragon, Catholic Royals, unified all Spanish kingdoms, Portugal being merely one more territory coveted by the Spanish crown.

Portugal started feeling apprehensive, fearing the birth of a girl, knowing that Don João III was already old and unlikely to have another child, a fact which at that time brought great religious clamor, including an order from a brother of Don João III, who was cardinal at the time, that when Don João Manuel's widow entered into labor, processions and prayers should be organized in an attempt to intercede to God for the child to be born healthy and male. Indeed, as Don Manuel's widow began to feel the first birth pains, Portugal held its collective breath, and joyfully Don Sebastian was born in Lisbon on the 20th day of Januaryin 1554, the "Expected One" because he represented the personification of the collective wish for Portuguese independence.

When Don Sebastian was around three years old, his grandfather died, and Don Sebastian was proclaimed heir to the Portuguese throne. Being still only a child, his grandmother, Dona Catarina — an Austrian noblewoman and the wife of Don João III — ruled provisionally in his place. When she also died, his great uncle, Don Henrique, archbishop of Évora, assumed the role of regent while Don Sebastian was still too young to govern. He eventually took his place on reaching 14 years of age.

During the period when Don Sebastian's great uncle was regent, the church had a great influence, due to the fact that he was archbishop. Don Sebastian trained in close proximity to the Jesuit order, which was founded with the intention of guaranteeing the stability of faith and warding off infidels, and which was very active within Brazil in the process of colonization, Indian catechization, and in maintaining the Christian faith.

Don Sebastian was brought up in this very religious, mystical, and Salvationist environment. This characteristic appeared when he was crowned. When he became king, his rule didn't last, causing significant concern for Portugal's relationship with the southern territories because Portugal had a strong presence of Islamists and Moors and had already disputed some territories in the north of Africa with Turks, in the region of Morocco, after being expelled by the African territory crossing the Strait of Gibraltar. Don Sebastian tried to recover the Portuguese territory, expelling the heretics so that all this land would become Christian. And yet Don Sebastian's crusade spirit led him to ruin because the advance on the Moors took Don Sebastian to the battle of Alcácer-Quibir in 1578. During the fighting Don Sebastian disappeared, never to return. Several stories appeared after he had vanished. A curious fact is that before his death, there had already been mention in the Trovas de Bandarra (a collected work of prophetic ideas) about the coming of an emperor who would save Portugal from its ongoing catastrophes.[7]

There was a general outpouring of hope that the king hadn't died and perhaps would return one day.[8] After his disappearance, one of the potential heirs was none other than Felipe II of Spain, grandson of Don João III. This created a power vacuum because what had been feared had occurred: a Spanish heir by which Portugal would lose its hard-fought independence. In 1580 after the conflict brought by this monarchial substitution, a union between Portugal and Spain was determined, the União Ibérica, that would run from 1580 until 1640, creating a chain effect throughout the Portuguese empire. At this time, the end of the 16th century and the beginning of the 17th century, Brazil was a territory that had been divided by Spain, called the Tratado de Tordesilhas (an imaginary line that separated the land, which to the east belonged to Portugal and to the west belonged to Spain). As the Portuguese and Spanish territories were now under the same king, few worried on which side of the Tratado de Tordesilhas each would be.

The União Ibérica did not mean that the Tratado de Tordesilhas was cancelled, but it no longer made sense. This assured that, in Brazil, for example, the advance of the Bandeirantes, a group of "pathfinders mercenaries," was very important, in historical terms, to the European penetration inside the country. By this time, sugar production was already in decline, and deposits of gold, diamonds, and silver were being prospected, having already been discovered in Spanish America.

The movement bypassed the treaty and began the exploration. In Portugal, the Portuguese were not happy with the idea of being under the same Castellan

7 M. I. P. de Queiroz, *O messianismo no Brasil e no mundo,* (São Paulo: Alfa-Omega, 2003).

8 T. Strobel, *O Sebastianismo: Breve panorama de uma mitogenia nacional,* (Auflage: GRIN Verlag, 2002).

king. Far from being satisfied, the Portuguese, whose whole history was built around autonomy, cried out for its independence once more. The Sebastianist movement was already taking shape when, in 1582, King Felipe I of Portugal ordered the transportation of a body that was believed to be Don Sebastian, burying it in the Monastery of Geronimos in Lisbon, with the intention of ending Sebastianism. The plan didn't work. The Sebastianists continued to believe in and await the return of Don Sebastian. The Spanish King was seen by all as an exploiter. Such was the dissent that during the União Ibérica, four people claiming to be Don Sebastian — some of them very similar in appearance — came forward and demanded that the Spanish should leave. One of best most known among these people was an Italian from Calabria, Marco Calizone who, after being revealed as a fraud, was hanged in the year 1603.[9]

This whole movement and its crusade spirit, based on a messiah, became a part of the Portuguese culture and the Portuguese empire. In Brazil in the 19th century, messianic movements such as the Canudos in Bahia or Contestado in Santa Catarina brought together religious fanaticism and socialist ideals. It was hoped that Don Sebastian would return to Brazil to fight to free the Republic from religious dogma. The essence of this religious mysticism would endure in the imagination, constructing around one individual, the Beloved, a question of national and political identity from which a myth could emerge.[10]

3 Sebastianism in Brazil

Sebastianism originates from the preconceived idea that there is a Messiah who will return as a divine envoy, whose purpose in returning would be to incite great change and whose supporting pillars would bring justice, peace, and happiness. This idea brought an incompatibility with the political situation of the time and an expectation of inexpedient salvation through an illustrious death.

Besselaar describes the concept of Sebastianism in the following way:

> Sebastianism is a type of Messianism. In today's secularized meaning, the word Messianism generally designates the blind faith of the popular masses in a political leader, judged capable of ending current abuses and inaugurating a new era of general well-being. It would be an

9 J. van den Besselaar, *O Sebastianismo - História Sumária. Biblioteca Breve,* (Lisboa: Instituto de Cultura e Língua Portuguesa, 1987), 13.

10 R. Levine, *O Sertão Prometido: o massacre de Canudos,* (São Paulo: Edusp, 1995).

> anachronism if we interpreted the Sebastianism of centuries past in this sense. Without doubt, for Sebastianists, there was no shortage of stubborn faith in the coming of a charismatic emperor, or unshakeable hope in the establishment of a new political and social order. But this faith and hope was, for them, integrated in a distinctly religious view of history.[11] [free translation]

In Brazil this movement has mainly emerged in the Northeast region, presenting its own symbolic characteristics for the popular imagination of the region — explicitly the need for a savior. Two tragic Sebastianist events occurred in Pernambuco: that of Serra do Rodeador, in the municipality of Bonito, between 1819 and 1820, and that of Serra Formosa, in São José do Belmonte, during the period 1836 to 1838.

Sebastianism emerged in the backwoods of Pernambuco as a more aggressive political-religious movement, fanaticism being the most notable characteristic of its leaders. The humble and uneducated people, who had come through great suffering as a consequence of drought and a certain political and social abandonment, were the most affected.

The first occurrence, known as The Tragedy of Rodeador, was led by Silvestre José dos Santos, who founded a camp at a place called Sítio da Pedra, which was destroyed on October 25, 1820, on the order of the governor of Pernambuco, Luiz do Rego. Known as the "massacre of Bonito," the annihilation by government forces left many dead and injured. After the massacre, women and children were imprisoned and sent to Recife.

The second occurrence, The Tragedy of *Pedra Bonita*, took place in Pedra Bonita, located at Serra Formosa, in the municipality of São José do Belmonte, backwoods of Pernambuco. A group of Sebastianist fanatics, led by João Antônio dos Santos, founded a type of kingdom decreeing its own laws and customs, which were at variance with the rest of the country. He preached that the king Don Sebastian had appeared to him and revealed hidden treasure and that the king was about to come back and would turn all his followers into rich, young, beautiful, and healthy people. The large number of poorly educated people who followed the Pedra Bonita fanatics concerned the government, the landowners, and the Catholic Church.

The priest Francisco José Correia de Albuquerque was sent to try to deconstruct this idea. He succeeded in convincing João Antônio dos Santos to stop preaching, but this left his brother-in-law João Ferreira in his place, who

11 J. van den Besselaar, *O Sebastianismo - História Sumária. Biblioteca Breve,* (Lisboa: Instituto de Cultura e Língua Portuguesa, 1987), 13.

became the most fanatical and cruel king of Pedra Bonita. He defended the idea that Don Sebastian would return only if Pedra Bonita were bathed in the blood of people and animals, and he led a massacre of innocent people in May 1838. On May 18th, the camp at Pedra Bonita was destroyed by forces commanded by Major Manoel Pereira da Silva.

The political-religious movement, whose focus was a belief in the coming of a messiah, a redeemer, was also very strong in the backlands of Bahia, with tragic results at the camp of Canudos, led by Antonio Conselheiro during the years 1893 and 1897, resulting in the Canudos War. Documents found at the camp suggest that Conselheiro and his workers believed in the return of Don Sebastian, or at least, used this to ensure the support of their followers. In the case of Canudos, Sebastianism preached the return of Don Sebastian to restore the monarchy and bring down the Republic. In 1897, the camp at Canudos was destroyed by Army troops.

Sebastianism has also contributed to folkloric demonstrations in Brazil. There are records of legends about the return of Don Sebastian, such as the Touro Encantado (Enchanted Bull) and King Sebastian.

On the Island of Lençóis Maranhenses, off the coast of the State of Maranhão, there is a belief that Don Sebastian once lived there, and there remain many legends about him. Numerous inhabitants have reported seeing Don Sebastian travelling around the island accompanied by his cavalry.

With the passage of time, Sebastianism has lost its political-religious strength and gained a literary meaning, at least on the collective conscious.

4 Unmasking Don Sebastian

At the beginning of Homer's *The Odyssey*, in the first book, we find Zeus saying to the gods: "It's disgraceful how these humans blame the gods. They say their tribulations come from us, when they themselves, through their own foolishness, bring hardships which are not decreed by Fate."[12]

Here, as mentioned before, our intention is to localize this autonomous cultural complex acting in the recent Brazilian presidential election and try to catch some dark elements we could find in this process. In this sense what we can see as "hope" seems to be our Achilles's heel to summon up the Sebastianism dynamic, and we can easily find it in Brazilians's collective psyche.

12 Homer, *The Odyssey*, trans. Ian Johnston. (Arlington: Richer Resources Publications, 2006), 09. Available at: https://xet.es/GREEKS/Homer/The%20Odyssey%20Homer.pdf - [Accessed 14 April 2019].

We wrote elsewhere on one of these expressions about the collective mobilization around Ayrton Senna's death.[13] In a period of great difficulties, Senna used to demonstrate great skills and powers raising the Brazilian flag and hymn in foreign lands. It is interesting to point out that his first Formula 1 victory was in the Portugal Grand Prix race on April 21st of 1985, on the same day of Tancredo Neves, the first civil president indirectly elected to lead the new *Magna Carta,* the Constitutional, and the redemocratization of the country. He was also a symbol of hope of a new, democratic, and prosperous country. Another meaningful coincidence around this date is that on April 21st is celebrated the "Tiradentes"[14] holyday, an icon for Brazilians's independence from Portugal. Both collective mobilizations, around Tancredo Neves and Ayrton Senna, are examples of our sorrow fed by our "hope insistence."

Once again, we can appeal to Greek mythology, which suggests to us that hope is one of the worst malefices to humanity; after all, it was inside the box that Pandora opened. Apparently, that was the collective "understanding" that seemed to rise in Brazil in 2013. That event is of central importance to us to try to better understand the Sebastianism matter, since it was a collective awakening with very intense and numerous protests around the country for the first time in decades. Whatwas that?

The movement began around the increasing prices of transport fees and became a fertile field where the public could reclaimother issues like public service provision, corruption, human rights, international sporting events, religious matter, governance, and so on.[15] The unprecedented fact was that different socio-economic classes were reclaiming these issues together, and a sort of "non partidary flag" (nonpartisan flag) was raised. Another very important fact was the awakening of the right-wing views. It is important to say that the concept of "right" became almost a synonym of dictatorship in Brazil after the military governance from 1964 to 1985.

The political, economic, and social (violence) crisis initiated a very strong popular nostalgic speech about the right-wing military dictatorship that Brazil faced from 1964 to 1985. During this period, we suggest that a wide part of the Brazilian collective field was disappointed with the Sebastianism saviors

---

13 G. O. Marques, *Ayrton Senna do Brasil: piloto de uma constelação heróica.* (Monograph), (Bauru: Universidade do Sagrado Coração, 2004).

14 Joaquim José da Silva Xavier, the "Tiradentes", was a dentist, trader, soldier and political activist and member of group that conspired, that became known as "Inconfidência Mineira", against the Portugal Crown and was hanged and quartered by the empire on April 21, 1792.

15 P. R. Kingstone, T. J. Power, *Democratic Brazil Divided,* (Pittsburgh: University of Pittsburgh Press, 2017), 190.

subliminally proposed by the Workers's Party. The corruption and the discovery of the biggest financial robbery of humanity in terms of the amount of money accounted for by the "Car Wash Operation" seemed to be the trigger to a deep explosion. It is important to mention that before Jair Messias Bolsonaro appeared with a possible "incarnation of a new Don Sebastian," as we suggest, the sorrow of military occupation was preparing the collective field of transition. The point here is to emphasize the need for a redeemer in one idea, a group of persons. History shows us how dangerous this kind of condensation of power can be if it is planted as a seed in the germinative soil of a collective deep crisis. This "automatic" dynamic expresses one of the deeper autonomous movements of Brazilian (shadow) soul.

We consider it a matter of great importance to emphasize that the 2013 moment of collective mobilization in Brazil, whichit seems we Brazilians are only in the beginning of in terms of initiating a symbolic dialogue with these massive forces in our shared psychic field, was a massive protest over the country, the largest in a generation in the country.[16] It was an unexpected, spontaneous, and very intensive movement. Inner and foreign researchers are still trying to understand it. It is important to mention some peculiarities of this movement because it seems (a) to bring some light about the Sebastianism dynamic as a counterpart of it (and its passive hope) and (b) to have in its body an unprecedented aspect about social mobilizations.

The spark that detonated the gunpowder keg was the protests to abolish the transport fares in a period of attempts to increase the price of public transports in the cities of Porto Alegre and São Paulo. The movement "Movimento Passe Livre" (Free Pass Movement) was this spark. As with any explosion, Brazil faced a wave of street protests that was latent for decades. For the first time in the history of the country, different sectors of society that had little or nothing in common were together in a spontaneous a way, side by side on the streets, protesting. It started a new format of political contestation in Brazil.[17]

Upper high-class members were protesting for the abolition of transport fees that they did not use, and at the same time the poorest classes were protesting against abusive taxes that they did not pay, and both of them were protesting against high levels of state corruption, lack of investments in infrastructure, healthcare, education, and security. The second unprecedented characteristic of these mobilizations was the initial repugnance of traditional organization groups, political parties, labour unions, social movements,

16 Ibidem.

17 Ibidem.

activists's groups, and so on.[18] We consider these two aspects of this intense spontaneous mobilization of greatest importance to understand ourselves and perhaps to understand different ways to face Don Sebastian and his claims. His claims, symbolically, could be the takeover of our current claims.

Common sense expressions like "O despertar do gigante adormecido" ("The awakening of the sleeping giant") became new slogans that appeared and grew very popular in protesters's mouths like "O gigante despertou" (The giant woke up); "Vem pra rua" ("Come to the Street")[19] instead of the old flags and "war cries" guided by political groups. After the large protests, social media helped to advertise this sort of invitation, and the slogan spread like fire in dry grass. The social media had a very important position in the role.[20]

As in every intense collective mobilization, the protests weren't always and everywhere peaceful. Many of the confrontations and much of the violence originated from both police repression and protesters's aggressions; our kind, happy, and pacific beloved self-promoted image was solved by our violent exposition. A very interesting idea around the matter is proposed by the Discursive Analyst Moraes.[21] After analyzing part of the traditional media vehicle's discourses of June 2013, she argued that they madea departure from a repressive speech of "order," excluding the social movement's claims, to a second one that made efforts to distinguish the social pacific protests from the violent acts. According to the same author, it was a result of "social pressure" and an adaptation of the predominant discursivity to avoid losing its legitimacy. Once more we can emphasize the plurality and diverse forces and their potential of transformation that we faced in the June 2013 protests.

This was a very important mark in our recent history also because, as mentioned before, it started the rise of extreme right movements from the nostalgic speech and the end of Workers' Party hegemony. Together with the combined union action by several distinct sectors of our society, in part touched the opened wound of our division, the Sebastianism seemed to have reappeared after 2013. In this sense we could use Jung's idea about the ancient gods's becoming modern diseases:

---

18 J. Germany, A. W. Pereira, *Understanding contemporary Brazil,* (New York: Routledge Abingdon, 2019).

19 Ibidem.

20 Ibidem.

21 É. de. Moraes, "Brazil 'Redemocratized': a giant that woke up? The media discursivization about June 2013 protests. Revista Mídia e Cotidiano, v. 6, n. 6 (2015): 131–51. Available at: http://periodicos.uff.br/midiaecotidiano/issue/view/563 (Accessed: 14 April 2019).

> We are still as much possessed by autonomous psychic contents as if they were Olympians. Today they are called phobias, obsessions, and so forth; in a word, neurotic symptoms. The gods have become diseases; Zeus no longer rules Olympus but rather the solar plexus, and produces curious specimens for the doctor's consulting room, or disorders the brains of politicians and journalists who unwittingly let loose psychic epidemics on the world.[22]

Unfortunately, it appears that we, symbolically speaking, recognized "the voices of the gods" in 2013 and that we interpreted them again as diseases in the 2014 and 2018 presidential elections. I am indeed quite convinced that it is an ongoing process.

5 Listening for Don Sebastian's Voice

Jair Messias Bolsonaro was a congressman for 26 years in the Brazilian Congress, part of an inexpressive political party with an inexpressive role in legislative power. However, he was more successful in making a political opposition to the Workers's Party than the "official opposition." His strong speeches of force and combat against "communist ideas" and even the homophobic ideas made him a real possibility to run for president. We are convinced that our collective movement at this point was to migrate our Sebastianism hope from the Workers' Party to Bolsonaro, a possible new savior, the fake "O Desejado" ("The Expected one") being unmasked and elected elsewhere at the same time once more. At this time, looking through this Sebastianistic lens, the left-wing political position was the impostor, the conservatism of the so-called traditional values suggested for the right-wing political proposal was the field where we could again plant the seeds of hope. Metaphorically speaking we can say that Don Sebastian couldn't find rest or a proper materiality again.

Departing from the myth in symbolic correspondence with the social and political events, we could also ask in a Jungian symbolic and imaginative way: How long will we wait for Don Sebastian? What does it (he) have to say to us? Hillman and Shamdasani, in their dialogue "Lament of the Dead," remembered that Jung in his *Red Book* and works[23] pointed out that we have the responsi-

22 C. G. Jung, "Alchemical Studies", in *The Collected Works*, ed. G. Adler and R. F. C. Hull, v. 13, (Princeton: Princeton University Press, 1967), § 54.

23 C. G. Jung, "Spirit in man, art, and literature", in *The Collected Works*, ed. G. Adler and R. F. C. Hull, v. 15, (Princeton: Princeton University Press, 1966).

bility for the collective occurrences, the collective context saying that what happens outside us is at some level happening inside of us.

SS: There is a coresponsibility with what is happening into the world. And the problem is how to recognize that.

JH: So that it isn't merely an inner journey.

SS: Paradoxically, it's a journey out. But to go out, he has to go in. There is no direct way to the world without plunging into his solitude. And it's only through that that he reconnects with the living.[24]

They linked this idea of arguing with Jung's expression in the *Red Book* about the lack of connection of modern man with his (our) dead, life, and death. Without the inclusion of the dead in our lives, we won't be able to reach the wholeness, the main task of the individual and collective individuation process.[25]

In this sense Brazilian and Portuguese people could ask themselves, always in symbolic terms, how are they (we) dealing with their (our) dead? How are they (we) dealing with D. Sebastian (inside us)? We are "waiting for him," but when he appears, are we recognizing and accepting him? Are we, as his descendants, prepared to listen to "his claims" instead of being neurotically frozen by our own? How would we and our identities be without this eternal waiting/hope? As the great Sir Paul McCartney sings: "We live in hope of deliverance from the darkness that surrounds us."[26] In simple terms, listening symbolically for Don Sebastian could be understood by us as if we should stop to wait for an external savior.

However, unlike Jung, it seems we are not yet understanding a message that can bring a Beatles's song in through our back window. The fact is that invocated or not he is present, recognized or not he is acting, without body or not he is concretely alive.

Perhaps, we could imagine he is saying, in the first place, that he is not a freer messiah but a regular citizen presently vivid in our choices and acts. During Hillman and Shamdasani's opening dialogue about Jung's *Red Book*,

---

24 J. Hillman, S. Shamdasani, *Lament of the Dead: Psychology after Jung's Red Book*, (New York and London: W. W. Norton & Company, 2013), 25.

25 Ibidem.

26 P. McCartney, *Hope of Deliverance*, Available at: https://www.azlyrics.com/lyrics/paulmccartney/hopeofdeliverance.html (Accessed: 14 April 2019).

the first author affirms, for example, that: "Opening the *Red Book* seems to be opening the mouth of the dead."[27]

And the historicist completed this by saying that a fundamental thing in doing that is: "He [Jung] comes to the realization that unless we come to terms with the dead we simply cannot live, and that our life is dependent on finding answers to their unanswered questions."[28]

Another clue about D. Sebastian's requests, in symbolic terms, could be something close to Jung's dialogue with the Christian order of the Anabaptists that irrupted in his kitchen when they said they were going to the most sacred place to pray.[29] Jung asked if he could go with them, and they said he could not because he had a body. We could ask if the missing body of D. Sebastian is condemning him to an erratic and "eternal" movement wherein he cannot find rest. We've never buried D. Sebastian, and in doing so we are denning his death in the ancestral lands of Africa and making him a prisoner and a being without rest. The paradox around this dynamic is that we are also his prisoners. Shamdasani points out:

> What he [Jung] grapples with is the weight of human history and ancestry. He realizes that he can't move forward without going back, without understanding the implications that the past weighs on him, and this is not purely in a personal sense, which has been the main preoccupation in psychology, but with history as such, and in particular with taking up unfinished business, taking up unanswered questions.[30]

It is widely known in Jungian psychology that the not-yet-integrated contents are the first to repeat themselves. In simple terms, we are able to reach the automatisms of the culture by our individual ones, a path that Hillman proposed equally by Jung when he said:

> Jung tells us how the physician of the culture has to work. He has to go into analysis and go inside himself—not the physician but the patient. If we′re going to restore the culture, we have to go in like a rainmaker[31] and

27 J. Hillman, S. Shamdasani, *Lament of the Dead: Psychology after Jung's Red Book,* (New York and London: W. W. Norton & Company, 2013), 1.

28 Ibidem, 1.

29 C. G. Jung, *The Red Book: Liber Novus*, ed. S. Shamdasani, trans. S. Shamdasani, M. Kyburz, and J. Peck (New York: W. W. Norton & Company Inc., 2009).

30 J. Hillman, S. Shamdasani, *Lament of the Dead: Psychology after Jung's Red Book,* (New York and London: W. W. Norton & Company, 2013), 38.

31 Rainmaker is a reference of Richard Wilhelm's experience in China, when a Rainmaker was requested to help a small village with the problem of an unusual absence of rain.

> put ourselves in order and what a Jungian analyst does. He helps you put yourself in order. Then you can come out and help the culture, and that was used again and again.[32]

In this sense we could argue that the 2013 protest could bring other possibilities of integration; it seems that there we stopped hopingfor an external savior and that we could embrace our darkness, assuming diffuse and polycentric aspects of our demands, of our culture, of our soul. Following closely Jung's idea of the reconnection of inner contents, we could infer that to give voice to Don Sebastian is also to make a more refined relationship with Portugal, which means something like "making peace" with our brother country following one ancestral line that leads to Portugal, and we dare to suggest that together we should make peace with African countries. After all, Don Sebastian disappeared there, and perhaps there he could be buried and finally rest. Following Jung's trail, James Hillman proposes that dealing with the soul, psyche, is dealing with a deepening relation with death and with imagination. The best tip perhaps is the ancient one: bring back the imagination of the collective myth to free Don Sebastian, to free ourselves; then perhaps we can start another alchemical work with more refined basic elements. I again ask James Hillman to help me; he writes:

> We are all in therapy all the time insofar as we are involved with soul-making. The idea here is that if we are each and every one a psychological patient, we are also each and every one a psychotherapist. Analysis goes on in the soul's imagination and not only in the clinic.[33]

We would like to finish by quoting a fragment of a Brazilian song of a rock youth band that emerged from the first youth generation of our capital Brasília in the 1970s and 1980s, called "Capital Inicial", something like "Initial Capital", that says:

> Se um dia eu pudesse ver
> Meu passado inteiro
> E fizesse parar chover

After three days of his arrival the rain did fall; however, once asked by Wilhelm about what he made to bring the rain back, the Rainmaker said that he didn't make anything, just only had meditated to find his own balance with Tao, then naturally the rain came back.

32 Hillman, Shamdasani, *Lament of the Dead*, 146.

33 J. Hillman, *Re-Visioning Psychology*, (New York: Harper, 1992), XVIII.

Nos primeiros erros, ah
Meu corpo viraria sol
Minha mente viraria ar
Mas só chove, chove
Chove, chove…

In a free translation:

If someday I could see
All my past
And could make the rain stop
In the first mistakes, ah
My body would become sun
My mind would become air
But it only rains, rains
Rains, rains…

References

Besselaar J. van den., *O Sebastianismo - História Sumária. Biblioteca Breve,* Lisboa: Instituto de Cultura e Língua Portuguesa, 1987.

Capital Inicial. *Primeiros erros.* Available at: https://www.letras.mus.br/capital-inicial/6791/ - [Accessed: 14 April 2019].

Germany J., Pereira A. W., *Understanding contemporary Brazil,* New York: Routledge Abingdon, 2019.

Hillman J., *Re-Visioning Psychology*, New York: Harper, 1992.

Hillman J., Shamdasani S., *Lament of the Dead: Psychology after Jung's Red Book,* New York and London: W.W. Norton & Company, 2013.

Homer, *The Odyssey*, trans. I. Johnston, Arlington: Richer Resources Publications, 2006. Available at: https://xet.es/GREEKS/Homer/The%20Odyssey%20Homer.pdf (Accessed: 14 April 2019).

Jung C. G., "Spirit in man, art, and literature", In *The Collected Works*, edited by G. Adler and R.F.C. Hull, v. 15. Princeton: Princeton University Press, 1966.

Jung C. G., "Alchemical Studies", In *The Collected Works*, eds. G. Adler and R.F.C. Hull, v. 13. Princeton: Princeton University Press, 1967.

Jung C.G., *The Red Book: Liber Novus,* ed. S. Shamdasani, trans. S. Shamdasani, M. Kyburz, and J. Peck, New York: W.W. Norton & Company Inc., 2009.

Kingstone P. R., *Democratic Brazil Divided,* Pittsburgh: University of Pittsburgh Press, 2017.

Levine R., *O Sertão Prometido: o massacre de Canudos,* São Paulo: Edusp, 1995.

Marques G., O. *Ayrton Senna do Brasil: piloto de uma constelação heróica.* Monograph, Bauru: Universidade do Sagrado Coração, 2004.

McCartney P., *Hope of Deliverance.* Available at: https://www.azlyrics.com/lyrics/paulmccartney/hopeofdeliverance.html - [Accessed: 14 April 2019].

Moraes É. de., "Brazil 'Redemocratized'": a giant that woke up? The media discursivization about June 2013 protests", Revista Mídia e Cotidiano, v. 6, n. 6 (2015): 131–51. Available at: http://periodicos.uff.br/midiaecotidiano/issue/view/563 - [Accessed: 14 April 2019].

Queiroz M. I. P. de., *Messianismo no Brasil e no Mundo,* São Paulo: Alfa-Omega, 2003.

Strobel T., *O Sebastianismo: Breve panorama de uma mitogenia nacional,* Auflage: GRIN Verlag, 2002.

CHAPTER 19

From Compensation to Purpose: A Neo-Jungian Critique of Horkheimer and Marcuse

*Stefano Carpani**

Abstract

In this paper, I look at Horkheimer's view of psychoanalysis and his own sociological reflections on psychoanalysis. Therefore, I look at Horkheimer's view on pleasure, standard of living, religion, and emancipation.

When looking at Marcuse, I underline how close to Freud's dogma the Frankfurters were, and I claim that Marcuse became the keeper of the *dogma* against those who revisited, amplified, or proposed an alternative vision to Freud's. Therefore, I propose that, for Marcuse, psychoanalysis is more a political tool than a cure, the aim of which is to realize socialism.

As an alternative to Horkheimer's and Marcuse's views, I propose Jung's reflection on the religious dimension and the need for "becoming Christ" (instead of *Imitatio Christi*): to become emancipated. Therefore, I introduce my own concept of *ludic life*.

Following this, I propose that the individual might be seen as the outcome of social and psychological roots which are both individual and collective and that, following Jung and contextualizing this in the 21st century, therapy is a creative transformation that enables people to become themselves—clarifying who they are and what they want—while living in a social context that might not be entirely friendly to them; therefore finding one's own purpose (instead of living a life built on never-ending compensations).

* This paper was originally written as a trilogy on Adorno, Horkheimer, and Marcuse, included in my PhD thesis. The first one, titled "From Emancipation to Liberation: A Neo-Jungian Critique of Theodor Adorno" (a), was published on Andrew Samuels's Festschrift (b) which I edited. I am happy to propose here the rest of this trilogy, cropped in one paper only. Cf. (a) - S. Carpani, "From Emancipation to Liberation: A Neo-Jungian Critique of Adorno" in (b) - S. Carpani (ed.), *The Plural Turn: The Development of Jungian and Post-Jungian Studies and the Work of Andrew Samuels,* (London: Routledge, 2020).

 | DOI:10.1163/9789004468757_021

Keywords

Frankfurt School, Adorno, Jung, sociology, psychoanalysis, psychosocial studies, emancipation, liberation, God, religious function

1 Horkheimer and Psychoanalysis: In Search for Happiness and High Standard of Living

In "Die Psychoanalyse aus der Sicht der Soziologie [Psychoanalysis from the perspective of sociology]," in the collection of essays *Gesellschaft im Übergang*,[1] Horkheimer notes that before the advent of psychoanalysis, "knowledge of the human soul was a matter that concerned philosophers and novelists"[2] and credits Freud for developing a theory that "does not study the sensitive facts and physiological relationships by developing tests and experiments, but investigate[s] the human soul and its structure."[3] Horkheimer[4] also underlines that Freud was perfectly conscious that his doctrine was inextricably linked to the exclusiveness of the profession of faith in science, to which Jung and a few others were the exception.[5] He adds that Freud's hope was that science would "obtain a dictatorial preeminence on Men's psychic life."[6]

Horkheimer claims that psychoanalysis must be seen as "an active intellectual force in the transition to a society that is no longer in need of ideology";[7] that is, to a society that is "more collective," "orderly," "planned," and "more just".[8] Simultaneously, for Horkheimer, "the thinking individual, the autono-

1 This essay is not translated into English. I employed the Italian version included – M. Horkheimer, *La Società di Transizione*, (Torino: Einaudi, 1979), 134. I choose this text among other of his essays because it directly examines the relation between sociology and psychoanalysis. This text was presented in 1968 at a conference on this theme and later published as M. Horkheimer, "Die Psychoanalyse aus der Sicht der Soziologie", *Jahrbuch der Psychoanalyse*, V, 1968, 9–19.

2 This and all future quotes from Horkheimer's *Gesellschaft im Übergang* are my translations from the Italian - M. Horkheimer, *La Società*, op. cit., because there is no English translation.

3 Ibidem.

4 Ibid., 132.

5 Hillman underlines that according to Jung, "Psychotherapy, […] was not a science, so there's no point in trying to formulize it or to turn it into a method" – J. Hillman, S. and S. Shamdasani, *Lament of the Dead: Psychology after Jung's Red Book*, (New York - London: W.W. Norton & Company, 2013), 144.

6 Horkheimer, *La Società*, 333 [365].

7 Ibidem, 134.

8 Ibid., 134–135.

mous subject of bourgeois philosophy is actually socially powerless" and "the opposition of individual reason to authority" is what has forced this individual to adapt.[9] But are we sure that ideologies have become obsolete? I propose that it is incorrect to declare the advent of a post-ideological society (as the Frankfurters did) or for that matter, a post-traditional society (as sociologists Beck, Giddens, and Lash did.[10] Jung is helpful here in drawing a parallel between ideologies and myths. In his foreword to *Symbols of Transformation*[11] he wrote:

> It struck me what it means to live with a myth, and what it means to live without one. Myth says a Church Father, is "what is believed always, everywhere, by everybody"; hence the man who thinks he can live without myth, is outside of it, is an exception. He is like one uprooted, having no true link either with the past, or with the ancestral life which continues within him, or yet with contemporary human society. He does not live in a house like other men, does not eat and drink like other men, but lives a life of his own, sunk in a subjective mania of his own devising, which he believes to be the newly discovered truth. This plaything of his reason never grips his vitals. It may occasionally lie heavy on his stomach, for that organ is apt to reject the profit of reason as indigestible. [...] So I suspected that myth had a meaning which I was sure to miss if I lived outside it in the haze of my own speculation. I was driven to ask myself in all seriousness: "what is the myth you are living?"[...]I took it upon myself to get to know "my myth", and I regarded this as the task of tasks.[12]

According to Horkheimer, "Sociological reflections on psychoanalysis begin with the doctor's relationship with those who rely on him" and asks: "Is it possible to think of a more serious way of dealing with the individual and his psychic structure [...]" than psychoanalysis? He adds that we are living "in a world in which individuality is losing ground due to the manifest tendencies of society."[13] It might be questioned why he prioritizes sociological perspectives over psychoanalysis; I propose, instead, that we are dealing with highly relational

9 J. Benjamin, "The End of Internalization: Adorno's Social Psychology", *Thelos*, 1977 (32), 49.

10 U. Beck, A. Giddens, S. Lash, *Reflexive Modernization. Politics, Tradition and Aesthetics in the Modern Social Order*, (Cambridge: Polity Press, 1994).

11 C. G. Jung, C. G., "Symbols of Transformation", in *Collected Works,* v. 5, (Princeton: Princeton University Press, 1956).

12 Ibidem, XXIV.

13 Horkheimer, *La Società*, 131.

and psychosocial facts. Hence, I reiterate here my critique of Adorno[14] and sociology who view psychoanalysis through a sociological lens.

Horkheimer then notes that:

> analysis preserves some decisive moments of what is positive in the bourgeois world, in which the transformation of society is also announced in a way that is no less evident. [...] The specific structures of the patient's thoughts and feelings subsist under fixed categories.[15]

To challenge Horkheimer's idea of fixed categories, I employ German Jungian psychotherapist Günter Langwieler's[16] vision of the analyst's task and his conviction that the "self-critical, non-dogmatic attitude of the therapist" is crucial and means remaining open to "observations during psychotherapy which contradict his theoretical expectations."

Like Adorno, Horkheimer finds pleasure key and believes the supreme goal—"connected with the phase of economic miracle" of the 1960s—is *standard of living*.[17] For him, "the phenomenon of idolatry" connected with the economic miracle of the 1960s, "has rarely been configured in a meaningful way".[18] Horkheimer's focus on the desire for a high standard of living brings us back to Beck and the post-biblical society mentioned earlier. It also brings us—almost 50 years since Horkheimer wrote these words—to recognize that the focus on standard of living (the emancipation of the working class) has been confused with the concept of individualization. Instead, one should speak of a *broken individualization* that prevents individuation and that is equated to "the betrayed promise of freedom and happiness for all."[19] If the supreme aim of the individual[20] is (exclusively) a high standard of living, there is no room for individuation because standard of living hinges on the material rather than the spiritual needs of the individual. Hillman (following Jung) suggested that life should be devoted to a purpose. I therefore propose that individualization breaks when its only purpose is a high "standard of living." In this condition, there is no absolute freedom.

---

14 Carpani, "From Emancipation to Liberation", op. cit.

15 Horkheimer, 131.

16 G. Langwieler, „Jung's Theory of Neurosis between Dissociation and Imagination", *Zeitschrift für Analytische Psychologie*, 2018.

17 Horkheimer, 137.

18 Ibidem.

19 As Giaccardi noted at a conference titled "Social Generativity. What it is and what it is good for" (2018).

20 Born and living in 21st-century advanced industrial or electronic societies.

While one could agree with Horkheimer that, in the 1960s, after years of war, reconstruction, and economic miracle, what mattered most to individuals was standard of living, in today's affluent society, his vision no longer works; namely, standard of living is a process "strongly conditioned by political factors, [...] not to mention material and prestige factors".[21] In my view, the search for a high standard of living that could, from a superficial perspective, be conditioned by Horkheimer's "factors" is linked to Adler's compensation theory—that is, with the compensation of one's own inferiority and the wish to overcome it, to leave a mark, and to gain much more than Andy Warhol's 15 minutes of fame. If this does not happen, as I have underlined somewhere,[22] anomie prevails. Thus, the current advanced electronic society[23] is based, not on the emancipation of the oppressed, but on the wish of the oppressed to compensate their status. Life lived under the spell of compensation—and its constant search for pleasure and high standard of living—is a life at the mercy of illusion, which is constantly renewed in a society based on "never enough." In 21st-century advanced societies, it is this, not religion, that is the prevailing illusion.

Horkheimer underlines that "what subsists, what is worthwhile, what is right determines science; the rest, first and foremost religion, is imagination".[24] Quoting Freud[25]—who believed that religions are a transformation of reality into a mass illusion—he underlines that "if one tries to frame religion in the educational path of humanity, [...] this (religion) finds a confirmation in the neurosis through which every civilized man must pass, in his path from childhood to maturity".[26] To this vision I wish to contrapose Jung's concept of the *religious dimension*, whichalso helps to further clarify my view on Adorno and instincts.[27]

In *Mysterium Coniunctionis*,[28] Jung underlines that "'religion' on the primitive level means the psychic regulatory system that is coordinated with the

---

21 Horkheimer, 137.

22 Carpani, "From Emancipation to Liberation".

23 Marcuse talked about the rise of an "advanced industrial society" in *One Dimensional Man* – H. Marcuse, *One Dimentional Man*, (Boston: Beacon Press, 1964). I propose the rise of an "advanced electronic society" since electronics and electricity shape our daily lives.

24 Horkheimer, 132.

25 Quoted from: S. Freud, *Gesammlte Schriften*, XII, (Wien, 1934), 329; S. Freud, *Introduzione alla Psicoanalisi*, (Torino: Boringhieri, 1969), 562.

26 Horkheimer, 132.

27 Carpani, "From Emancipation to Liberation".

28 Jung, "Mysterium Coniunctionis," *The Collected Works*, v. 14, (Princeton: Princeton University Press, 1977), 603.

dynamism of instincts," and Abt[29] notes that this occurs in a compensatory manner. Jung continues: "On a higher level, this primary interdependence is sometimes lost, and then religion can easily become an antidote to instincts, whereupon the originally compensatory relationship degenerates into conflict, religion petrifies into formalism, and instinct is vitiated." He then adds that "a split of this kind is not due to mere accident, nor is it a meaningless catastrophe. It lies rather in the nature of the evolutionary process itself, in the increasing extension and differentiation of consciousness." Jung concluded that the unconscious (particularly the collective) is intrinsically related to the inborn spiritual attitude of the soul, and that—if this attitude is suppressed *tout court*—neuroses might arise.

It is important to underline that Jung's vision on the spiritual attitude of the soul has little to do with religion as described by Nietzsche, Marx, and Freud. Thus, Jung makes the distinction between "*becoming Christ*" and the "*Imitation* of Christ".[30]

I propose that in Jung's suggestion of "becoming Christ" (which is living one's own life as truly as Christ lived his, therefore going through one's own personal crucifixion)—instead of imitating him (which is a superficial imitation of externals)—lies Jung's central individuation concept to urge people to know and live their own myth, rather than borrowing one. For Jung, the individual must become Christ, not imitate him, to discover who he/she really is. Therefore, genuine individuation is to go through one's own personal crucifixion. This transition is fundamental as it allows the individual to become emancipated. This emancipation is not possible for Freud and the Frankfurters because they are linked to the concept of domination and perpetrator versus victim, to a causal rather than a finalistic approach to life.

Horkheimer[31] described contemporary society (of the 1970s) as that wherein for the bourgeoisie "religion has stiffened to a convention" while "for the workers the Marxian doctrines have been reduced to dull clichés." Thus, he recognized the beginning of a transformation that would later be described in detail

29 T. Abt, *Introduction to Picture Interpretation*, (Zurich: Living Human Heritage Publications, 2005).

30 Jung, "Psychology and Religion: West and East," *The Collected Works*, v. 11, (Princeton: Princeton University Press, 1969), § 522; Jung, "Psychology and Alchemy," *The Collected Works*, v. 12, (Princeton: Princeton University Press, 1957), §§ 7–8.

31 Horkheimer, 137.

by authors including Beck,[32] Bauman[33] and Giddens.[34] Horkheimer's vision is interesting and—to a certain extent—correct within 20th-century rationalistic and enlightened society wherein both the bourgeoisie and working class adhered to what Jung called *imitatio Christi* and where the working class's priority—beyond emancipation—was to live the materialistic pleasures of a bourgeois life. Today, however, in advanced electronic societies, religious and Marxian doctrines (both can be seen as ideologies!) could be considered passé. Both the grandsons of the bourgeoisie and of the working classes now seek fulfillment of their wishes (high standard of living), the pursuit of which is far from religious or Marxist values. Therefore, as I proposed elsewhere (2004), the purpose of millions of people in 21st-century advanced society is to fulfill their "ludic" wishes. To live a *ludic life*.

The *ludic life* is related to Freud's view that a healthy life involves a balance of work and enjoyment and the active pursuit of wish fulfilment. Horkheimer[35] considered the purpose of analytic therapy to comprise "the ability to operate in the existent, in an emotional life" and moreover to be able to react to the world as it is, "without delusions." Thus, Horkheimer[36] emphasizes that Freud's theory is marked by "modern positivistic thinking" and that for Freud "putting the patient in a position to work and enjoy means healing him".[37]

In the 21st century, I propose, the work-play balance is out of sync. Work is seen as an impediment to one's wish to enjoy. This enjoyment, the ludic life (see also Friederichs Shiller's *play drive*, Donald Winnicott's *ludic self* and Soren Kierkegaard's *aesthetic life*) brings to *over-ludism* from an initial state of *no-ludism* (pertinent of the industrial and advanced industrial societies) and consequent *broken-ludism* or *broken individualization*, as I underlined somewhere else.[38] The state of *broken ludism* or *ludism for ludism* is not healthy because, almost like an addiction, it seeks pleasure for pleasure's sake while

32 U. Beck, *Risikogesellschaft – Auf dem Weg in eine andere Moderne*, (Berlin: Suhrkamp Verlag, 1986); U. Beck, E. Beck-Gernsheim, *Individualization: Institutionalized Individualism and its Social and Political Consequences*, (London: Sage, 2002).

33 Z. Bauman, *Liquid Modernity*, (Cambridge: Polity Press, 2000); Bauman, *The Individualized Society*. (Cambridge: Polity Press, 2001).

34 A. Giddens, *The Consequences of Modernity*. Cambridge: Polity Press, 1990); Giddens, *Modernity and Self-identity. Self and Society in the Late Modern Age*. Cambridge: Polity, 1991).

35 Horkheimer, 132.

36 Ibidem, 133.

37 Ibidem.

38 Carpani, "The Consequences of Freedom", in *Jungian Perspectives on Indeterminate States: 'Betwixt and Between' Borders*, eds. E. Brodersen and P. Amezaga, (London: Routledge, 2020).

avoiding responsibilities, and when pleasure is missing, boredom and anomie arise. It is not a healthy life because it doesn't involve a balance of work and enjoyment (focusing exclusively on the active pursuit of wish fulfillment).

The *ludic life* is a way out (compensation) of anomie for those who "fit badly" into the expected social character of a specific society or institution(s) because, as Riesman underlined in *The Lonely Crowd*,[39] those that "fit badly pay a high price in anomie, in contrast to the release of energy provided by congruence of character and task." This is, I believe, where the process of individuation should be insinuated in the 21st century—in the leap/link between "fitting badly" (whether or not one is aware of it), the consequent fall into anomie, and the opportunity to realize that one can shape one's own life independently.

Following Jung, I propose that curing a patient means making him/her aware of his/her neurosis. Thus, the cure is clarification and knowledge,[40] rather than restoration to a position to work and enjoy.

For Freud, to live a life that makes sense is to live a life where work and enjoyment are in balance. Today, however, this balance has been lost. Giegerich[41] recalls Jung's example of a woman who "does not live the life that makes sense [...] because she is nothing. But if she could say, 'I am the daughter of the Moon. Every night I must help the Moon, my Mother, over the horizon'—ha, that is something else! Then she lives, then her life makes sense, and makes sense in all continuity, and for the whole humanity".[42] While, according to Jung, "she would be cured",[43] Giegerich rejects this, claiming that the "pueblo-Indian model" cannot be prescribed to the modern woman because it would involve "an endless, futile search",[44] and thus "Jung's suggestion feeds her neurotic craving, her 'addiction'".[45]

Furthermore, Horkheimer underlines that "it is difficult to establish what enjoyment means," adding that"we can say that it goes from the satisfaction of hunger and sexuality to the aesthetic; it includes all kinds of entertainment, as long as you live it consciously as such".[46] While I agree that enjoyment must be lived consciously, I disagree that it merely involves satisfaction of hunger, sexuality, and aesthetic enjoyment, which I consider materialistic needs. Instead,

---

39 D. Riesman, *The Lonely Crowd*, (New Haven and Lodnon: Yale University Press, 1949).

40 Carpani, „The Consequences of Freedom".

41 W. Giegerich, *The Soul Always Thinks*, (New Orleans: Spring Journal Books, 2010).

42 Jung, "The Symbolic Life," *The Collected Works*, v. 18, (Princeton: Princeton University Press, 1976), § 630.

43 Giegerich, 233.

44 Ibidem, 233.

45 Ibid., 234.

46 Horkheimer, 133.

hunger for knowledge (of oneself and of the "world")—Eros as opposed to Sexuality—will allow one to connect with self, others, and the "world," thus bringing one to a state of appreciation rather than pleasure. Appreciation always links to "the good enough" and the "enough," thus, to limits. A life in balance between conscious and unconscious elements, a life in which unconscious elements are integrated into conscious life, must be the goal. This might lead to comfort, calmness, and reassurance in a world that sociologists and philosophers claim to be out of joint.

In conclusion, I agree with Horkheimer[47] that Freud, like Kant, saw that the transformations that are occurring today in the family structure and inter-sex relations "are pregnant with cultural and psychological consequences." I also agree that "from the genesis of society, religion, fire and many other archaic developments, up to the most recent wars, Freud has contributed to the knowledge of collective psychology".[48] I wonder, however, why the Frankfurters were unable to go beyond Freud and his dogma, keeping in mind that—as Jessica Benjamin[49] underlines—"Fromm's rejection of Freud's patricentric theory" was not accepted by Adorno and that "when Adorno and Horkheimer began to systematically synthesize Freud's theory of society they were already dissatisfied by the efforts of Fromm and Reich to achieve this integration." In fact, both Fromm and Reich, as will be seen in the following section on Marcuse, distanced themselves from Freud's dogma, a sin that Adorno and Horkheimer could not tolerate. They preferred Marcuse, but Marcuse was no psychoanalyst, and like Adorno and Horkheimer, he made the mistake of taking psychoanalysis sociologically.

Therefore, I do not understand how Horkheimer claimed that "psychotherapists and sociologists must work together"[50] when he and Adorno were *ungenerative* in relation to Fromm and Reich. Why has the Frankfurt School failed to integrate sociology and psychoanalysis as equal and mutually influencing disciplines, while imposing a top-down relation of sociology over psychoanalysis (as the title of the essay employed for this paragraph implies) and by imposing a dogmatic Freudian–Marxian conception of society where sociology has supremacy over psychoanalysis and where the voices of the psychoanalysts have been silenced? In contrast to Horkheimer's view that "we cannot establish a priori if we will get precise psychological and sociological knowledge, and of what species," I employ the work of Erich Fromm (1941), Ian Craib (1989), Jessica Benjamin (1988 and 1995), Steven Frosh (2013), Susie

47 Ibidem, 136.
48 Ibidem.
49 Benjamin, 42 – in footnotes.
50 Horkheimer, 138.

Orbach (2014), Andrew Samuels (1989), and Mary Watkins (2003 and 2008) to confirm that sociology and psychoanalysis can merge into one new discipline called psychosocial studies.

2 Marcuse and "Neo-Freudian Revisionism": An Overview

In his essay "Critique of Neo-Freudian Revisionism" (*Eros and Civilization*, 1955/1974),[51] Herbert Marcuse confirms how close to Freud's dogma the Frankfurters were, although Marcuse—instead of following Adorno and Horkheimer in openly criticizing Freud—became the keeper of the *dogma* against those who revisited, amplified, or proposed an alternative vision to Freud's. I have selected this essay as my source of reference because, in it, Marcuse is particularly critical of any non-dogmatic view of psychoanalysis and because his reiteration to stick to Freudian dogma is at its best.

Marcuse[52] reminds us that Freudian "psychoanalysis elucidates the universal in the individual experience" and that it "is consistently oriented on early infancy—the formation of the universal fate of the individual." He claims that the function of psychoanalysis changed in response to the "fundamental social changes that occurred during the first half of the century" as reflected in "the collapse of the liberal era and of its promises, the spreading totalitarian trend and the effort to counteract this trend."[53] According to Marcuse, before World War I, psychoanalysis developed its concepts for "critique of the most highly praised achievement of the modern era: the individual" and "Freud demonstrated that constraint, repression, and renunciation are the stuff from which the 'free personality' is made." In this sense, Marcuse rightly claims that psychoanalysis was radically critical theory.

Marcuse underlines that the subsequent revision to psychoanalysis began when "the psychoanalytic conception of man [...] appeared as 'reactionary'" and when it "seemed to imply that the humanitarian ideals of socialism were humanly unattainable."[54] Here, I would underline the Frankfurters' inability to look beyond Freud to those who developed his theory and as such became his antagonists. For Freud and the Frankfurters, all those who diverged from the original teachings (dogma) were to be called traitors and expelled, as

51 H. Marcuse, *Eros and Civilization*, (Boston: Beacon Press, 1955/1974).

52 Ibidem, 253–254.

53 Ibid., 238.

54 Ibid., 239. I wonder whether Marcuse would include Stalinism within the concept of humanitarian ideals of socialism, but this is a theme for another paper.

happened to Fromm and Reich when they presented their post-Freudian ideas to Adorno and Horkheimer, and to Jung when he published *Symbols of Transformation*. Strangely, something similar also happened to Freud when—returning to Vienna from Paris, after a stint working with Charcot—his report was dismissed by the Austrian Medical Society.[55]

Marcuse criticized Reich's view for neglecting "the historical dynamic of the sex instincts and of their fusion with the destructive impulses" and for rejecting "Freud's hypothesis of the death instinct and the whole depth dimension reviled in Freud's late metapsychology,"[56] as well as for adopting "sexual liberation" as "a panacea for individual and social ills." His main gripe was that Reich minimized the problem of sublimation and reduced freedom to "a mere release of sexuality," in essence, that he distanced himself from certain aspects of Freud's theory that Marcuse considers essential.

For Marcuse, psychoanalysis is more a political tool than a cure, the aim of which is to realize socialism. This clarifies why the Frankfurters were unable to dissociate from Marx and Freud and why these two figures represent the only possible ideology, at a time when the symbolism of the Bible was ceasing to affect people's lives. When examining Jung—described as "right wing" compared to the "left wing" Reich—Marcuse[57] claims that his psychology is "obscurantist pseudo-mythology" but unfortunately says no more. This adds to Walter Benjamin's opinion of Jung (see my paper on Adorno [2020a]). Marcuse attacks what he calls *the Neo-Freudian schools* for wishing to attain what Freud attained, by claiming that "the psyche can [...] be redeemed by idealistic ethics and religion: and the psychoanalytic theory of the mental apparatus can be rewritten as a philosophy of the soul."[58] This is clearly an explicit attack on Jung, but not only on him. Marcuse adds that "the revisionists have discarded those of Freud's psychological tools that are incompatible with the anachronistic revival of philosophical idealism—the very tools with which Freud uncovered the explosive instinctual and social roots of the personality."[59]

Progoff claimed that Jung sees man's social quality as inherent in human nature, and thus "the individual must be understood in terms of the social situation in which he lives".[60] Progoff also claimed that—for Jung—since the

55 S. Zweig, *Freud*, (Rome: Castelvecchi, 2015/1931).

56 Marcuse, 239.

57 Ibidem.

58 Ibid., 240.

59 Ibid.

60 I. Progoff, *Jung's Psychology and its Social Meaning*, (London: Routledge 2013/1955), 167. Progoff also states that Freud's view was that the individual came first and only then society – ibidem, 161.

individual comes before society, it cannot live without society, or indeed culture,[61] and furthermore, Progoff[62] claims that "in understanding the individual as a derivate of society," Jung "is following his more fundamental idea that 'consciousness comes from the unconscious'".[63] In other words, just as psychic contents are brought to consciousness by "clarifying of the ambiguities of the unconscious,""the individual emerges out of society by a process of differentiation and individualization".[64] Here, again, we may claim that the individual (more than the personality as described by Marcuse) is the outcome of social and psychological roots that are individual and collective. It should also be reiterated that, for Jung, *the social* is a mix of traits from a specific society and culture and comprises the cradle within which an individual is born.

Marcuse continues that "the 'center' of revisionism took shape in the cultural and interpersonal schools" where psychoanalysis became an ideology.[65] These schools resurrected the personality "in the face of a reality which has all but eliminated the conditions for the personality and its fulfilment."[66] For Freud, Marcuse underlines "the work of repression in the highest values of Western civilization—which presupposes and perpetuates unfreedom and suffering."[67] Therefore Marcuse adds that "the Neo-Freudian schools promote the very same values as cure against unfreedom and suffering—as the triumph over repression. The intellectual feat is accomplished by expurgating the instinctual dynamic and reducing its part in the mental life." Marcuse—who rejects this approach as a "philosophy of the soul"—claims that the new schools switched their orientation to "secondary factors and relationships [...] to emphasize the influence of the social reality on the formation of the personality." However, he adds—and this is of fundamental importance here—"we believe that the exact opposite happens—that the impact of society on the psyche is weakened."[68]

Jung demonstrated that his therapeutic approach encapsulates a view of society (the collective unconscious) and links it with one's own individual unconscious, with the immediate environment and the environment at large,

---

61 Ibidem, 161.

62 Ibid., 163–164.

63 Ibid., 161.

64 Ibid., 163–164.

65 Marcuse, 240. One could ask whether Freudian psychoanalysis also became an ideology (replacing religion and to the same extent as Marxism) for the Frankfurters, but I will not investigate this here.

66 Ibidem.

67 Ibidem.

68 Ibid.

as well as with one's own purpose and finality (or lack thereof). To contrast Marcuse's view, I provide the following example from Jung's work. Jung writes about a man who contacted him to cure his homosexuality. This man was

> little over twenty, still entirely boyish in appearance. There is even a touch of girlishness in his looks and manner of expression. [...] he is intelligent with pronounced intellectual and aesthetic interests [...] his feelings are tender and soft, given to the enthusiasms typical of puberty, but somehow effeminate. There is no trace of adolescent callowness.[69]

Jung proceeded to frame a diagnosis that "undoubtedly he is too young for his age, a clear case of retarded development." The patient, telling Jung that he wanted to be cured of his homosexuality,[70] added, giving association to his initial dream, "Naturally I remembered yesterday that I was going to you for treatment and was in search for cure".[71] In this regard Jung writes that "the patient merely came to the doctor to be treated for that unpleasant matter, his homosexuality, which is anything but poetical."[72] For Jung, what is unpoetical is to go to a doctor for treatment, not the young man's homosexuality.

This point is also vital in freeing Jung from accusations of homophobia perpetrated by some of his detractors. Here, Jung does not suggest curing the patient of his homosexuality; he wants the patient to develop and mature according to his own nature. In this case, becoming a mature masculine means becoming a human of male sex (and whatever gender), responsible and prepared to cope with society. Prepared does not mean, as Adorno[73] and Marcuse emphasized, repressing instincts in light of sublimation; rather, it means that this man—having clarified his nature, having understood who he is and what he wants—should live his life and fulfill his own purpose in a society that does not accept homosexuality and claims it to be a sickness that needs to be cured. Thus, while the patient knocks at Jung's door to be cured, Jung instead supports the patient to face and clarify his nature and thus to transform into a mature human being. To contrast Marcuse, Jung also helps the patient to examine the impact of his nature (homosexuality) on his psyche and his immediate social context, which has led him to the search for a cure. Jung adds: "The patient had

69 Jung, "Two Essays on Analytical Psychology," in *The Collected Works*, v. 7, (Princeton: Princeton University Press, 1957), 167.

70 Ibidem, 169.

71 Ibid., 168.

72 Jung underlined that certain dreams are poetical, and the one brought by this patient is so.

73 Cf. Carpani, "From Emancipation to Liberation".

of course nothing like an adequate understanding of the treatment to which he was about to submit himself."[74] This is very often the case. Patients enter therapy because of an inner pain, and perhaps they can adduce ideas or reasons, but the real reason is often not apparent to them when they enter the analyst's room for the first time.[75] It is only analysis that will help to clarify why they have come.

For Jung, the initial dream gives the analyst the opportunity to understand his real problem, and in this case, it is not the patient's homosexuality; rather, his lack of separation from his mother and his mother complex have caused his retarded development. In fact, the patient confirms his closeness to his mother, as is the case for many males. Jung adds "By this we are not to understand a particularly good or intense conscious relationship, but something in the nature of a secret, subterranean tie which expresses itself consciously, perhaps, only in the retarded development of character, i.e., in a relative infantilism."[76] It is important to underline here that Jung is not speaking of homosexuality in general; he is speaking about this individual only, who appeared immature to him because he was too close to his mother and/or his mother complex. Jung adds,"The developing personality naturally veers away from such an unconscious infantile bond; for nothing is more obstructive to development than persistence in an unconscious [...] state."[77]

I propose that the link between psyche and the impact of society, and viceversa, is immense. We first recognize that the patient is too close to his mother and therefore is immature and unseparated. This is the psychic aspect. The social impact on the patient is provided by the patient's homosexuality in 20th-century Swiss society where homosexuality was not accepted. Therefore, the patient, who is well enough adapted (perhaps too adapted and therefore one-sided) to the social reality of his time, seeks therapy to be cured of this, instead of being cured of his real problem: his immaturity and the fact that he has not yet been born. Hence, he lives in an embryonic state (unseparated from his mother and the mother complex) and must separate.

Reiterating my view about Adorno,[78] it is not correct to claim that psychoanalysis leads to the annulment of oneself and one's own instincts, to let sublimation prevail, or following Horkheimer, that a high standard of living means

74 Jung, „Two Essays", 170.

75 And if they do, as Jung suggested, they must go through the work of the analysis (instead of the intellectual work of understanding) and have a genuine wish to change their lives.

76 Jung, „Two Essays", 171.

77 Ibidem.

78 Cf. Carpani, "From Emancipation to Liberation".

the satisfaction of hunger, sexuality, and the aesthetic, or following Freud, that to enable the patient to work and enjoy means curing him. In fact, following Jung and contextualizing this in 21st century advanced electronic society, therapy is a creative transformation that enables people to become themselves—clarifying who they are and what they want—while living in a social context that might not be entirely friendly to them.

Furthermore, building on my critique to Adorno[79] and the fact that, according to Jung, "religious symbols have a distinctly 'revelatory' character",[80] the symbolism of the church is important here. According to the Frankfurt School, the church could be regarded as an oppressive institution, as the authority in society where one confesses one's sins and is redeemed from homosexuality. In Jung's terms, "the Church represents a higher spiritual substitute for the purely natural, or 'carnal' tie to the parents."[81] This could lead one to view the church as a place of initiation and Baptism as initiation, perhaps into adulthood. Here, the Church is where one accomplishes the "rite of initiation into manhood".[82] Jung underlines that in ancient Greece, homosexuality and education were synonymous. He also claims that the "homosexuality of adolescence is only a misunderstanding of the otherwise very appropriate need for masculine guidance",[83] a man's effort to balance his unconscious closeness to his mother, and to improve relationships with women from an immature relationship to a mature one. Therefore, Jung underlines—and here again is the link between psyche and society—that "according to the dream, [...] what the initiation of the treatment signifies for the patient is the fulfillment of the true meaning of his homosexuality, that is, his entry into the world of the adult man."[84]

Returning to Marcuse—when he re-examines the revisionists and particularly Fromm—he claims that in "aiming at the reified, readymade form rather than at the origin of the societal institution and relations, [they] fail to comprehend what these institutions and relations have done to the personality that they are supposed to fulfil."[85] Marcuse criticized Fromm for distancing himself from Freud and weakening "the psychoanalytic conception," particularly Freud's theory of sexuality, which he believed would lead to "a weakening of the sociological critique and to a reduction of the social substance of

79 Ibidem.

80 Jung, "The Symbolic Life", 807.

81 Jung, "Two Essays", 172.

82 Ibidem.

83 Ibid., 173.

84 Ibid., 174.

85 Marcuse, 241.

psychoanalysis."[86] Fromm was not the first to do so, however. Before Fromm, Jung and Adler had been ousted by Freud's inner circle. Marcuse accuses Fromm of having distanced himself from another dogma of therapy, namely the fact that "the analyst rejects patricentric-authoritarian taboos and enters into a positive rather than neutral relation with the patient."[87] Marcuse adds that this "new conception" involves an "unconditional affirmation of the patient's claim for happiness".[88] Here, let us pause and comment in depth. First, I propose that therapy is not a static relationship, nor is it a top-down relationship, and it is certainly not neutral. Instead, it is a fluid relational relationship in which each party affects the other.

Therefore, I would ask provocatively: what does Marcuse know about the patient-therapist relationship given that he was not a therapist, did not undergo training analysis himself, and never worked therapeutically with patients? Clearly, he should not discuss theories of which he has no experience and his view of the therapeutic relationship (although he refers to it as a taboo)—which he calls neutral although it is called "abstinent"—is biased by the spirit of his time and his one-sided Freudian approach. It is fundamental not to confuse neutrality with abstinence, and the relational school does so, putting at the centre the analyst and patient as a whole. Otherwise—contrary to Marcuse's view underlined above (and what we saw previously with Adorno)—the dichotomy of dominator/dominated already present in society is replicated in the analytical relationship.

When examining what the therapist is or does, I propose the analogy of a gardener. A gardener is someone who knows nature, who knows when to be neutral (for example, when plants freeze in winter, the gardener does not expect anything from the plant) and when to intervene and be directive (when it is appropriate to cut the old branches and prepare for spring). A gardener also knows when to water and when not. Therefore, the gardener is anything but neutral and accompanies nature towards its purpose (whatever that may be: even accompany nature towards the goal of the owner of the garden, which is usually significantly different from the goal nature would have pursued on her own). Likewise, the analyst is anything but neutral and as a human being himself/herself—despite having undergone training analysis—also has emotions which are fundamental in the analytical relationship.

86 Ibidem, 243.

87 Ibid., 244.

88 Ibid. Fromm (1935), cited in Marcuse.

Therefore, I propose the need for a pluralistic approach that is the opposite of a dogmatic one, as proposed by the Frankfurters (wrapped in Marxian and Freudian ideology and theory).

Secondly, based on my clinical experience, I propose that some patients who enter analysis are seeking happiness. This is also what Adorno proposed, when discussing the emancipation of the working class, or what Horkheimer foresaw when discussing the high standard of life. Therefore, there is a contradictory view within the Frankfurters themselves.

Returning to Fromm and the fact that patients seek happiness—building on the example of the man who sought therapy to cure his homosexuality—it is important to mention that emancipation (and 21st-century individualization) has turned into the false myth of happiness, wherein happiness is seen as the compensation for the current state of anomie, which hinders happiness. Moreover, in 21st-century advanced electronic societies, emancipation equates to the idealization of happiness. Therefore, I propose that some patients enter analysis in a state of anomie and are seeking happiness (to compensate for their dissatisfaction at not yet having reached a high standard of living which equates to emancipation, success, and therefore—as its ultimate goal—happiness). Thanks to therapy, they might be cured of this idealization, namely, of happiness.

Marcuse is wrong in saying that "with these demands, psychoanalysis faces a fateful dilemma," the claim for happiness, that "if truly affirmed, aggravates the conflict with a society which allows only controlled happiness, and the exposure of the moral taboos extends his conflict to an attack on the vital protective layers of society."[89] Happiness and controlled happiness are relative and very personal concepts, and we should be on guard against seeking happiness as a compensation to the lack thereof. Under these circumstances, happiness is not attainable, and people become neurotic.

Marcuse is also wrong that "the affirmative attitude toward the claim for happiness then becomes practicable only if happiness and the 'productive development of the personality' are redefined so that they become compatible with the prevailing values" and are "internalized and idealized." This vision is passé because, despite the need for a "productive development of the personality," I question Marcuse's view that this development is linked to the prevailing values, a criticism I also levelled against Adorno.[90] If analysts follow this path, and claim to "know" what is right or wrong for the patient—hence to make him/her compatible with the prevailing values—the analysis will fail,

89 Marcuse, 244–245.

90 Carpani, "From Emancipation to Liberation".

since the analyst might impose knowledge that goes against the nature of the analysand and, borrowing from the previous example, would acknowledge the right to treat homosexuality so that the patient lives a life "compatible with the prevailing values." This, to me, is controlled happiness, as well as controlled freedom. Absolute happiness, therefore absolute freedom, means enabling the patient to come in contact with and live his/her own nature and to accept it unconditionally and critically. In this way, self-confidence (and a sense of balance) will arise as the consequence of the therapy. Therefore, as underlined when examining Adorno,[91] it is not a matter of internalization; it is a matter of clarification, knowledge, and acceptance of one's own nature.

Marcuse underlines that "this redefinition must in turn entail a weakening of the explosive content of psychoanalytic theory as well as of its explosive social criticism".[92] I propose that it is rather the opposite because when a person clarifies who he/she is and knows what he/she wants and his/her purpose, this person can live life freely and face the life tasks that arise in a more balanced way.

To Marcuse "the revisionists fail to recognize (or fail to draw the consequences from) the actual state of alienation which makes the person into an exchangeable function and the personality into an ideology".[93] However, he fails to recognize that when the Frankfurters investigated the concepts of emancipation, high standard of living, or happiness, they did not realize that they were theorizing people's alienation from their own nature in light of forced emancipation. Therefore, somehow, people must search for their own freedom and happiness. I question this as well as Marcuse's claim that "the revisionists claim that their psychoanalysis is in itself a critique of society."[94] I agree with Clara Thompson's view that psychoanalysis "goes beyond merely enabling man to submit to the restrictions of his society; in so far as it is possible it seeks to free him from its irrational demands and make him more able to develop his potentials and to assume leadership in building a more constructive society".[95]

I also agree with Fromm—cited and criticized by Marcuse[96]—that man's "ability to take himself, his life and happiness seriously [...] rests upon his

91 Ibidem.

92 Marcuse, 245.

93 Ibidem, 254.

94 Ibid., 260.

95 C. Thompson, *Psychoanalysis: Evolution and Development,* (New York: Routledge, 1950/1917), 153.

96 Marcuse, 266.

courage to be himself and to be for himself".[97] This, one could say, is a very Jungian statement which links to another critique levelled at Fromm by Marcuse that "'the psychoanalytic cure of the soul' becomes education in the attainment of a 'religious' attitude."[98] In my opinion, the religious attitude—or religious dimension—as seen previously in relation to Horkheimer, is a fundamental step in the maturational process, without which individuals will have—as their only purpose in life—the attainment and accumulation of capital (of whatever sort) but not cultivating their soul.[99]

In conclusion, I believe that the approach of the Frankfurt school was valid at a time when the Western world was divided into authoritarian and inflexible top-down relationships and into the dichotomy of unpaired categories such as bourgeois versus working class; male versus female; race, gender, and so on. However, in 21st-century advanced electronic societies, the Frankfurters' model of authority/perpetrator versus victim no longer works.

Having briefly illustrated the views of Horkheimer and Marcuse on psychoanalysis, I want to underline that a change of paradigm is needed when examining the formation of narratives of self-identity at the beginning of the 21st century in advanced societies and a new vision is required to contrast that offered by sociology (that the world is out of joint [Beck, 2017]). I propose that Jung and the Post-Jungians as well as psychosocial studies offer such a new paradigm, since, following Jung, "there is no valid recipe for every case."[100]

References

Abt T., *Introduction to Picture Interpretation*, Zurich: Living Human Heritage Publications, 2005.

Bauman Z., *Liquid Modernity*, Cambridge: Polity Press, 2000.

Bauman Z., *The Individualized Society*, Cambridge: Polity Press, 2001.

Beck U., *Risikogesellschaft – Auf dem Weg in eine andere Moderne*, Berlin: Suhrkamp Verlag, 1986.

Beck U., *Risk Society: Towards a New Modernity*, London: Sage, 1992.

97 E. Fromm, *Man for Himself*, (New York: Henry Holt and Company, 1943), 250.

98 Ibidem.

99 L. Zoja, *Coltivare l'Anima*, (Bergamo: Moretti & Vitali, 2013).

100 Translated from Italian - Jung, (2003/2006). *Analisi dei sogni (seminario tenuto nel 1928–1930)*, (Torino: Bollati. Boringhieri 2003/2006). 317. Text originally published in 1984 – Jung, *Dream Analysis*, (Routledge and Kegan Paul: London, 1984).

Beck U., Beck-Gernsheim E., *Individualization: Institutionalized Individualism and its Social and Political Consequences,* London: Sage, 2002.

Beck U., Giddens A., Lash S., *Reflexive Modernization. Politics, Tradition and Aesthetics in the Modern Social Order*, Cambridge: Polity Press, 1994.

Benjamin J., 'The End of Internalization: Adorno's Social Psychology' in *Thelos*, 1977 (32), 42–64.

Benjamin J., *The Bonds of Love*, New York: Pantheon Books, 1988.

Benjamin J., *Like Subjects, Love Objects: Essays on Recognition and Sexual Difference*, New Haven: 1995 in Carpani S., *The Formation of Narratives of Self-identities. A Study of the Turkish Community in Berlin*, Unpublished M.Phil. thesis. University of Cambridge, 2004.

Carpani S., "The Consequences of Freedom" in E. Brodersen and P. Amezaga (eds.), *Jungian Perspectives on Indeterminate States: 'Betwixt and Between' Borders*, London: Routledge 2020.

Carpani S., 'From Emancipation to Liberation: A Neo-Jungian Critique of Adorno', in S. Carpani (ed.), *The Plural Turn: The Development of Jungian and Post-Jungian Studies and the Work of Andrew Samuels,* London: Routledge 2020 (a).

Carpani S., *The Plural Turn: The Development of Jungian and Post-Jungian Studies and the Work of Andrew Samuels*, London: Rourledge 2020 (b).

Craib I., *Psychoanalysis and Social Theory*, Hemel Hempstead: Harvester Wheatsheaf, 1989.

Freud S., *Introduzione alla Psicoanalisi*, Torino: Boringhieri, 1969.

Fromm E., *Zeitschrifht fur Sozialforschung* IV, 1935: 374–375.

Fromm E., *Escape from Freedom,* New York: Holt Paperbacks, 1941.

Fromm E., *Man for Himself,* New York: Henry Holt and Company, 1943.

Frosh S., "Transdisciplinary Tension and Psychosocial Studies", in *Enquire* 2013, 6(1), pp. 1–15.

Giddens A., *The Consequences of Modernity*, Cambridge: Polity Press, 1990.

Giddens A., *Modernity and Self-identity. Self and Society in the Late Modern Age,* Cambridge: Polity, 1991.

Giegerich W., *The Soul Always Thinks*, New Orleans: Spring Journal Books, 2010.

Hillman J., Shamdasani S., *Lament of the Dead: Psychology after Jung's Red Book,* New York - London: W.W. Norton & Company, 2013.

Horkheimer M., "Die Psychoanalyse aus der Sicht der Soziologie", *Jahrbuch der Psychoanalyse*, V, 1968, 9–19.

Horkheimer M., *La Società di Transizione*, Torino: Einaudi, 1979.

Jung C.G. - Except as below, references are to *The Collected Works* (CW) and by volume and paragraph number:

Jung C. G., "Symbols of Transformation," *CW* 5, Princeton: Princeton University Press, 1956.

Jung C. G., "Two Essays on Analytical Psychology," *CW* 7, Princeton: Princeton University Press, 1957.

Jung C. G., "Psychology and Religion: West and East," *CW* 11, Princeton: Princeton University Press, 1969.

Jung C. G., "Psychology and Alchemy," *CW* 12, Princeton: Princeton University Press, 1957.

Jung C. G., "Mysterium Coniunctionis," *CW* 14, Princeton: Princeton University Press, 1977.

Jung C. G., "The Symbolic Life," *CW* 18, Princeton: Princeton University Press, 1976.

Jung C.G., *Analisi dei sogni (seminario tenuto nel 1928–30)*, Torino: Bollati. Boringhieri 2003/2006, (text originally published in 1984. *Dream Analysis*. Routhledge and Kegan Paul: London).

Kierkegaard S., *Either/Or*. London: Penguin, 1992.

Langwieler G., „Jung's Theory of Neurosis between Dissociation and Imagination", in *Zeitschrift für Analytische Psychologie*, 2018.

Marcuse H., *Eros and Civilization*. Boston: Beacon Press, 1974/1955.

Marcuse H., *One Dimentional Man*, Boston: Beacon Press, 1964.

Orbach S., (2014). "Democratizing Psychoanalysis", in *Relational Psychotherapy, Psychoanalysis and Counselling: Appraisals and Reappraisals*, D. Loewenthal and A. Samuels (eds.), New York and London: Routledge, 2014.

Progoff I., *Jung's Psychology and its Social Meaning*, London: Routledge, 2013/1955.

Riesman D., *The Lonely Crowd*, New Haven and Lodnon: Yale University Press, 1949.

Samuels A., *The Plural Psyche*, London: Routledge, 1989.

Schiller F., *Essays*, London: Bloomsbury, 1993.

Thompson C., *Psychoanalysis: Evolution and Development*, New York: Routledge 1950/1917.

Watkins M., "Dialogue, Development, and Liberation", in *Dialogicality in Development*, I. Josephs (ed.), Westport, CT: Greenwood, 2003.

Watkins M. and Shulman H., *Toward Psychologies of Liberation*, New York: Palgrave Macmillan, 2008.

Zoja L., *Coltivare l'Anima*, Bergamo: Moretti & Vitali, 2013.

Zweig S., *Freud*, Roma: Castelvecchi 2015/1931.

CHAPTER 20

Mania of Contemporary Capitalism: A Polish Perspective

Michał Wróblewski

Abstract

For Polish Jungians like Zenon Waldemar Dudek and Tomasz Olchanowski, it is important to understand psychical life in the context of the present culture. Their culture psychology is often critical of modern civilization. Older traditions are replaced by a new economical and technological order, which is supported by neoliberal technology. This new environment favors inflationary patterns, which drive people to negative inflation and many psychical disorders connected with it, for example, manic-depression disorders. Dudek and Olchanowski use arrangements made by theorists of post-modern culture like Zygmunt Bauman, Wojciech Burszta, Steiner Kvale, and Wolfgang Welsch, who also pay attention to the dangers that arise from consumerism and technologies, especially new digital media. Both Polish authors are also critical of academic psychology, giving the impression of being handmaids of neoliberal ideology.

Keywords

culture psychology, negative inflation, capitalism, new media, neoliberal ideology

1 Culture Psychology: A Polish Perspective

There are many authors in Poland who write about Carl Gustav Jung's psychology. One of them is Zenon Waldemar Dudek, who is the author of the first handbook of Jungian psychology written in Polish. For him, Jungian psychology is a base upon which to build integral psychology and culture psychology. Dudek underlines connections between natural archetypes and culture symbols and also draws attention to problems of contemporary civilization. This "sociological turn" is also present in the works of Tomasz Olchanowski, who names contemporary culture as a "maniac culture." For them, living in the present society is not easy because time actually favors negative inflation. Many psychological

 | DOI:10.1163/9789004468757_022

problems, like maniac-depression disorders, borderline personality, and many others, are connected with this kind of inflation. Many non-Polish post-Jungian authors, for example, James Hillman and Arnold Mindell, focus on cultural and social conditions of psychical disorders while developing their own approach to psychotherapy.

I am often reminded, by the title of one of Hillman's books: *We've Had a Hundred Years of Psychotherapy and the World's Getting Worse*, that many human psychological problems have sociological and cultural causes. This is the reason that individual psychotherapy is in many aspects useless and powerless and also produces many illusions. These illusions involve individuals in other psychological problems. Of course in the past, people had psychological problems, but what is also obvious is that the present time is apt to format many other psychological problems. They could be described as new complexes, which are taking their power from the collective unconsciousness archetypes, that is, the assumption of Jungian psycholgy. Dudek and Olchanowski, bringing the psychic condition of the present time closer, show inflationary patterns of contemporary capitalism, which is combined with digital technology (mass media, computers, Internet), and the current worldview, especially neoliberal ideology also supported by academic psychology.

2 Negative Inflation

In Jungian psychology, the conscious ego is confronted with the power of the unconscious, which has two layers. The first layer is individual and contains individual complexes; the second layer is collective and is a source of power for complexes. The power of complexes is taken from collective unconscious archetypes. These archetypes are recognized by cultural symbols, which can identify when we have contact with arts, religion, or dreams. The part of the conscious ego that exists without contact with symbols survives in alienation, which can be positive or negative. The part of the conscious ego that has contact with symbols lives in inflation. Inflation, like alienation, can be positive or negative. Positive inflation gives the conscious ego inspiration and energy, but negative inflation can possess the ego, and this is the reason why it is sometimes hard to estimate when inflation is positive or negative. Dudek compares negative inflation to a ship that cannot come back to port. In negative inflation the ego is dominated by archetypal forces. Another example of the inflation ego is drug addiction, when, after chemical ecstasy, the person who is taking drugs suffers from a hangover.

Cultures and religions have developed many ways to stop negative inflation. Among archaic people there were totemic symbols and taboos. The Ancient

Greeks have a good word for negative inflation; that word was *hubris*, which means a pride that blinds a person and makes it impossible for that person to recognize the situation. This pride drives one to exceed the limits appointed by the gods, who finally take their revenge. There were many Greek heroes who lived in hubris: Agamemnon, Acteon, Ayax, Otus, Icarus, and Ixion. In the East, it is the concept of karma and samsara. In the Zen Buddhist tradition, there are many techniques against inflation: the principium of ignorance and koans. In monotheist religions there are also many ways to stop negative inflation: The Ten Commandments, the concept of sin, even the cruel law of Sharia. There are limits for individuals who want to break social norms. Moreover, it is good to remember that the specific human way of being, based on reflection and consciousness, does not change, and that man and his desire are part of a greater whole, a part of nature. This reflective consciousness often drives people to a tyranny of mind that impairs the life impulse, making human desires unsatiated.

Another kind of negative inflation is quasi-individuation. For Carl Gustav Jung, the aim of individuation was to make a strong connection between the conscious ego and the archetype of Self.

For Olchanowski, many people miss the Self archetype with the complex of the distended ego. This distended ego has more desires and lives in illusion about unlimited possibilities. These illusions are produced by wanton imagination. On one hand, the imagination creates self-illusion; on the other hand, it can give way to liberation from many illusions. The problem is that this solution could give other illusions. In this way, psyche is in the noose of affirmation and negation. Ego, which is introduced into inflation, is alienated from the Self, becoming quasi-Self.[1] Many people confuse regression with progress, fantasies about themselves with self-consciousness. The complex of distended ego is one of many cases of alienation from archetypes, which lead to many ways of negative inflation. These are many compensations, which drive one to many different maniacal behaviors.

For Dudek, many compensations came from the unmet need for security. It is good to remember that the need for security is second—after basic body needs—in Maslow's hierarchy of needs. If the need for security is unmet, it leads to many compensations, like concentration on relationships with other people and ambition (obsession about success). Sometimes we have compensations taken from the body: for example, fitness obsession. Dudek associates compensations not only with a lack of contact with an archetype, especially

1 T. Olchanowski, *Wola i opętanie*, (Warsaw: Eneteia, 2010), 163–174.

the archetype of the Great Mother. Dudek said: "The deficit of a sense of security, shifts consciousness to the past, directs it to immediate attempts to reduce threats and anxiety, and in extreme cases persists in the perception of a constant threat."[2] This deficit leads to many addictions, which are parts of maniac culture, because the pyramid of Maslow's hierarchy of needs loses stability. These two approaches (made by Dudek and Olchanowski) complement each other because Dudek focuses on the fear, but Olchanowski focuses on the desire.

3 Inflationary Patterns of Capitalism

Norwegian psychologist Steiner Kvale distinguishes three places of three major epochs in human history. The first of them is the Church because in the past, people got knowledge from revelation. The Church was the place where society adored and recognized revelations, for example, public reading of the Bible. After the epoch of the Church came time for the Factory, which is the place for production. Humans also produce knowledge, which is made by methodology. Now humanity lives in the epoch of the Market. The shopping center is the best concrete realization of what the Market is. The Market leads to consumption, and consumption drives the Market. Knowledge at present is collected through applications. In the time of the Market, the most important law is the law of maximum desire, which depends on economy growth.[3] The effectiveness of this expulsion requires re-evolution of everything for money. For example, self-realization became another product to buy (it is overcoming the opposition: "To have or to be" – made by Erich Fromm), and the principle of reality is replaced by the principle of efficiency. The contemporary man buys to satisfy psychological needs: security; affiliation; appreciation; and last, but not least, self-realization.

This maniacal vision attracts the fall, which is drowned out with antidepressant drugs. Olchanowski compares contemporary man to "hungry ghosts" from Buddhist iconography. Hungry ghosts want to eat and drink, but they have small mouths, thin necks and big stomachs. The world of hungry ghosts is a world of obsessive thoughts, which are correlated with greed. The nature

---

2 Z. W. Dudek, A. Pankalla, *Psychologia kultury*, (Warsaw: Eneteia, 2008), 291.

3 S. Kvale, "The Church, the Factory, and the Market as Metaphors for Psychology: Scenarios for Psychology in the Postmodern Age", in *Psychology at the Turn of the Millennium, T.2. Social. Social Development and Clinical Perspectives*, C. von Hofsten, L.Bäckman (eds.), (New York: Psychology Press, 2002), 409–436.

of greed is still insatiable; the inner void could not be filled, which does not change the fact that because of greed, people still want more. Greed is also the reason that people do not want to let go of what they have, and also, they do not want to share with others. Moreover, greed is the reason that people cling to things and situations that are not always good for them, and they also have influence on perception of the difference between good and evil, for example, anger or envy. These "bad feelings" give the impression that they are good because people can build their identity on them, obscuring the inner void. This is another metaphor for the consumer human, who has other perceptions of time and space, than the people from the Church and the Factory.

When Olchanowski speaks about the Market, he takes a credit from two post-modern thinkers: Zygmunt Bauman and Wolfgang Welsch. In Bauman's book about consumer life, is introduced a concept of point time. This kind of time is not a cyclic time of traditional societies, which is correlated with the Church; and moreover that kind of time is not a linear time of productive societies, which is correlated with the Factory. Point time has many cracked and broken moments, changes by fleeting impressions and experiences. Points on computer screens vanish, and they blur boundaries between the real and the virtual. There is no road in point time, and there is no place for waiting. Olchanowski said: "Not to wait for anything, never to be bored—it seems not to perceive by senses what is."[4] This need for immediate gratification reduces direct experience. This reduction contains the experience of travel, realized by touristic products; the experience of lecture, realized by operations with Google books; and also the contemplation of nature, which is realized through trips with sophisticated technology (including expensive clothes). That kind of trip, like that kind of traveling and reading, is not adventure, but rather another occasion to meet with an overblown ego.

Moreover, the Market changes human experience of space, which is particularly visible in an anesthetic state of mind. Welsch said: "Anesthetic is a state wherein the ability to feel is overcoming—this ability is a basic condition for esthetic."[5] Living in an anesthetic state depends on an excess of incentives. These incentives lead to consumption, making a state that is near to the trance of indifference. It means that in postmodern culture, the sensations are weakening, but the state of arousal increases, crippling what people refer to as "free will." In point time and the anesthetic space of the Market, the state of arousal increases, leading to desire and mania, which demands immediate

4 T. Olchanowski, *Kultura manii*, 55.

5 W. Welsch, „Estetyka i anestetyka", in *Postmodernizm – antologia przekładów*, ed. R. Nycz, (Cracow: Baran i Suszczyński, 1996), 522.

gratification. After that gratification, the mind makes a rational explanation or thinking a damnation, to improve the mood, by desire for new incentives. This mind becomes a servant of incentives; this mind even becomes a stimulus. These incentives prevent our ability to think and imagine, which can be helpful, but they need a favorable atmosphere to work.

4 From Percept-Culture to Imagopathy

To understand culture psychology, it is helpful to take lessons from the theory of Jungian psychological types. In this theory, there are two kinds of assimilation: rational (connected with thinking and feeling functions) and irrational (connected with perception and intuition functions). For Dudek, in contemporary times is the advantage of irrational assimilation, especially perception. He names contemporary, Western civilization as a Percept-culture—"perceptokultura" in the Polish language. (It is neologism, which combined two words: *perception*[*percepcja*] and culture [*kultura*]). Dudek said:

> Civilization of the contemporary West prefers a perceptual channel of assimilation; the expression of this is a hysterical invasion of sensual impressions, not only in public life (information noise taken from audiovisual media, the Internet, advertisement, and so on), but also in private life (reality shows on television, mobile phones). Similarly, these same people, which are shaped in the spirit of the perceptual, collective conciseness, take for primitive release of intuitive truth: fantastic, religious propositions from Eastern and Western prophets, infantile pseudo-astrological interpretations, mysticizing tarot divination or pseudo-shamanic initiations, which are not analyzed and consistently built into the personality, but threaten like «revelation» from another world; it is like an intuitive reception.[6]

The above theory is compatible with many considerations of Neil Postman, the author of the famous book "Technopolis." Postman said that we live in times when technique dominates culture. This process had begun to happen in the 16th century and had created a contemporary technopolis with present day media: television, computer, smart phone, and so on. In technopolis, the goal of the work is efficiency. Something that cannot be measured does not exist

6 Z. W. Dudek, *Podstawy psychologii Junga*, (Warsaw: Eneteia, 2006), 288.

or has no value. In psychoanalytic terms, the principle of efficiency applicable in technopolis replaces the principle of reality, knowing from Freudian works about maturing of the ego.

Olchanowski also introduces two terms to describe living in times of percept-culture and technopolis: logerea and imagopathy. *Logerea* is a term created by Polish anthropologist Wojciech Burszta. Logerea seems to be a confusion of words and pictures with meta-commentary. These word-pictures make a home in our imaginations.[7] *Imagopathy* is a term that was created during a conservation between Dudek and Olchanowski; it is a state in which virtual reality becomes only reality, which is experienced by a subject and is depreciated to what is beyond a screen. It seems that things that were always real are depreciated into things that are unreal.[8] These terms are useful to understand because in the present time, great cultural change is being done that is created by the Internet. This great cultural change never happened in the past. Olchanowski said:

> This is imagopathy: it is a state in which the most real are pains and pleasures caused by virtual pictures. However, the pleasure does not get as intense as the pain that is experienced through the virtual world, because that pain results from the awareness of self-scrapping. Paradoxically, such a unit alive with illusions, that in an easy way it will fill up, it is enough to buy something, do what makes mediated authority, and even in a moment transform your own ugly body, gaining a beautiful coat of idol.[9]

Marie-Louise von Franz, one of Jung's best students, distinguished five stages of projection assimilation: identifying the image of imagination with reality, distinguishing the image of the imagination from reality, making the assessment, realizing the projection, and searching for the causes of the projection.[10] In comes imagopathy to save the human psyche in the first stage from the above-distinguished stages of projection assimilation. However, there is one important difference: instead of images of the imagination, nowadays people deal with images from various types of screens. This kind of projection can change into introjections. With imagopathy, man projects his own possibilities onto pictures from various screens, then absorbs them back. After that, these possibilities are deformed and standardized. This is the way that the contemporary

7 W. Burszta, *Preteksty*, (Danzig: Katedra, 2015), 134.

8 T. Olchanowski, *Kultura manii*, 191.

9 Ibidem, 194.

10 M-L. von Franz, Psychotherapie, (Cologne: Konigfurt, 2004), 262.

human gains a "happiness" to be an unsatiated consumer and at the same time a consumer product.

5 Academic Psychology as a Handmaid of Neoliberal Ideology

Walter Benjamin compares capitalism to religion. For him, capitalism is specifically a kind of religion that contains a history of Christianity. Capitalism is a religion of pure cult, without dogmas and theology; it is a religion of permanent cult without ordinary days. This pure and permanent cult makes people guilty. Last, but not least, in the capitalism religion, God must be hidden, and we can turn to him only when we feel guilty.[11] Moreover, many people think that without the free market, the world would be lost. It drives everyone to fight with everyone else, including fights between man and nature, which is comparable to the relation between humans's heads and other parts of their bodies. It is paradoxical because the free market is the reason why the world goes to catastrophe, where nature is destroyed. It is a problem with greed, which is often connected with human nature but does not always become an obsession. The above-indicated mechanisms show that the free market is like a vicious circle. Under the guise of a rational *homo oeconomicus*, taken from Adam Smith's conception, is a selfish predator.

The current socio-economic system is suppurated by neoliberal ideology that is sometimes known as turbo-capitalism, which is supported. To quote Burszta, neoliberal ideology is based on narration that is taken from economics. Neoliberal worldview has not only changed but still is changing contemporary thinking about work, relations (with others and nature), community issues, healing (physical and spiritual), education, and creativity based on economical value. For Olchanowski, neoliberal ideology of hungry ghosts creates paranoid people, who very often live in our societies. They have several techniques, which they confirm in their ideology. These techniques are rationalization, intellectualization, identification, fake reaction, cancellation, idealization, separating, creating roles, and armoring feelings. Also correlated with these techniques are acting out and anesthesia with alcohol. All of them indicate shortcomings of Western civilization:a lack of ability to combine discipline and relaxation. Discipline gives birth to tension. Relaxation is easily transformed into destructive rebound.[12]

11 W. Benjamin, „Kapitalizm jako religia", trans. P. Mościcki, *Krytyka Polityczna*, no. 11–12, (2007): 133.

12 T. Olchanowski, *Kultura manii*, 136–137.

Olchanowski also said that in contemporary times, psychology also becomes a handmaid of neoliberal ideology. He thinks particularly about academic psychology, especially about cognitive-behavioral psychology and evolutionary psychology. Both of them are back to positivism, which is a kind of reduction to a structural and mechanical approach in psychology and psychotherapy. This kind of reduction operates on a limited understanding of the psyche and human life, which is compatible with neoliberal ideology and market environment, governed by the principle of efficiency. A genetic vision of human nature changes humans to consumers of drugs—legal narcotic substances. They are kind of doping in the struggle for existence. The academic psychology makes the foundations of many "good life guidebooks," which make happiness dependent on the use of specific instructions. These instructions only make people more efficient employees and more effective consumers. The contemporary human becomes a consumer also when he or she decides on psychotherapy.

In contemporary times, psychotherapy is not taken between the therapist and the patient but between the therapist and the client. In many kinds of psychotherapy, there is a reductive and limited vision of the human, making him a product of an unhappy childhood, unfavorable environment, "bad genes," or mechanisms programmed to strive for pleasure and avoid annoyance. Olchanowski says:

> The adoption of a genetic vision of human nature easily turns an individual into a consumer of far-officials, legal narcotic substances, semi-legal doping agents and teaching courses, on how to get out of the struggle for existence victorious. If not much depends on me, I use techniques that either serve survival or allow me to make the most of the natural resources of my body. If the image of a man, who has a shaped society (specific environment) speaks to us, then we become consumers of ideal educational programs, ranging magic speaks to us, and as parents we often use expensive crèches, kindergartens, schools of various levels and universities, where our child will not come in contact with an unwanted person, who turns her head in his head and draws on the social bottom.[13]

Academics create their psychology as a science, not an art of "cure talk." But in this sense two sides of therapeutic situation are vanished. Therapist is absence for patient, and patient is absence for therapist. Both of them are virtual persons for each other. The therapist, who wants to be a scientist and expert, becomes a caricature of archetypical symbols: the Great Mother and the Old Wise Man.

13 Ibidem, 109.

6 Pessimistic Diagnosis of Our Time

Reading the above-quoted Polish psychologists of culture (Dudek, Olchanowski), it is hard to get the impression that our time is a time of social crisis. Polish psychologists of culture point to two reasons for that crisis. One of them is the contemporary world order of capitalism and is supported by this order neoliberal ideology. There are the roots of inflationary patterns, which lead to negative inflation and the principle of efficiency, which end by different kinds of manic-depressive disorders. The second of them is the latest, digital technology, which transforms not only public life, but also individual perception of reality. The Internet and screens are everywhere, which turn psychical worlds of projection to imagopathy. The principle of efficiency and imagopathy are products of irrational, especially perceptive assimilation—percept-culture. This kind of understanding of the human psyche impacts on practicing psychology and psychotherapy, which often supported an unhealthy social system of contemporary times.

This pessimistic diagnosis of our time is relatively easy to dispose of as morality. Similarly, opinions concern left-wing discourse. Jungian culture psychology often turns back to the ancient ways to stop a human tendency to negative inflation. This is the reason why what many Jungian psychologists, similarly to Carl Gustav Jung, are interested in only reminds us of the truths known to past thinkers, like Buddhist monks and stoic wise men, among others, who to a large extent call for self-working and overcoming passions through spiritual exercises. Jung's merit therefore seems to be to remind people of the truth about the familiar traditions and to recall them in terms that claim the right to call themselves empirical doctrine, which is combined with anthropologic knowledge. This is the essence of Jung's cultural psychology, which not only repeats after Jolanda Jacobi that responsibility lies with the individual, but also increasingly recognizes the fact that the individual not only increases his or her responsibility for himself or herself, but also for the society in which he or she lives.

References

Benjamin W., „Kapitalizm jako religia", In *Krytyka Polityczna*, trans. P. Mościcki, 11–12 (2007).
Burszta W., *Preteksty*, Danzig: Katedra, 2015.
Dudek Z. W., *Podstawy psychologii Junga*, Warsaw: Eneteia, 2006.
Dudek Z. W., Pankalla A., *Psychologia kultury*, Warsaw: Eneteia, 2008.

Franz M.-L. von, *Psychotherapie*, Cologne: Konigfurt, 2004.
Kvale S., "The Church, the Factory, and the Market as Metaphors for Psychology: Scenarios for Psychology in the Postmodern Age", in *Psychology at the Turn of the Millennium. T.2. Social. Social Development and Clinical Perspectives*, New York: Psychology Press, 2002.
Olchanowski T., *Kultura manii*, Warsaw: Eneteia 2016.
Olchanowski T., *Wola i opętanie*, Warsaw: Eneteia, 2010.
Welsch W., „Estetyka i anestetyka", in: *Postmodernizm – antologia przekładów*, ed. R. Nycz, Cracow: Baran i Suszczyński, 1996.

Index

www.ingramcontent.com/pod-product-compliance
Lightning Source LLC
LaVergne TN
LVHW021724021026
849161LV00004BA/678